New 6th Edition

BRITISH RAILWAYS PRE-GROUPING ATLAS & GAZETTEER

Revised & Enlarged

Ian Allan
PUBLISHING

First published 2015

ISBN 978 0 7110 3817 2

Published by Ian Allan Publishing Ltd, Hersham, Surrey, KT12 4RG

Printed in Bulgaria

Visit the Ian Allan Publishing website at www.ianallanpublishing.com

Contents

Introduction 3

Index to map numbers 5

Maps 6

Gazetteer 51

1 List of abbreviations 52

2 Index to Tunnels 54

3 Index to Water troughs 56

4 Index to Summits 57

5 Index to Bridges and Viaducts 57

6 Index of Locations 58

Introduction to the First Edition of *Pre-Grouping Atlas and Gazetteer*

Just 35 years ago many of the separate railway companies operating in Britain as self-contained units were grouped into four major systems by the provisions of the Railways Act 1921, and on the 1st January 1923 these individual units lost their titles in the initials LMSR, LNER and SR, only the GWR keeping its identity although extending its territory by the accretion of the many small railways in Wales. Many of these lines were in fact controlled by the GW somewhat earlier than the date above mentioned. Similarly, the L&YR was amalgamated with the L&NWR in 1921. It can be noted here that in the sheets that follow, all these railways are shown as independent concerns as a matter of interest, but the general picture presented is of the railway system of Britain as it existed in the years prior to 1923.

Taking into account all the minor narrow-gauge lines, the various joint undertakings, committees, etc, there were something like 150 titles extant in the period depicted on these maps and many of these names still live. Through the 25 years of the grouped systems and even now, in Nationalisation days, many of the old names not only are used by members of the railway staffs in day to day working, but such names are currently quoted in official documents, working timetables, etc.

An examination of this Atlas will show that numbers of station names of the 1920s have disappeared, either due to re-naming or to the abandonment of the station through lack of passenger usage. Many branch lines were closed after the amalgamations either to passenger working (a goods and parcel service being maintained) or in their entirety. Since Nationalisation much more has been done in this respect. However, some lines and stations which had in fact been closed by 1922 have been shown in this atlas for the sake of interest and as a record of their existence.

In addition to the inclusion of every railway company at work in the years before 1923, much other matter has been shown. A great many junctions, many still in use as timing points in working timetables, are indicated together with physical features such as the more important viaducts, tunnels, etc, locomotive shed locations and railway workshops. Track water troughs also receive attention and in areas of tourist interest scenic features in the railway vicinity are indicated. It is hoped that such data will add to the interest and usefulness of this volume.

Many towns with complicated railway layouts have been shown as enlarged insets, and in addition areas such as London, South Wales, The West Riding, etc, with ramified railway routes and connecting lines points receive attention in separate sheets. Interpretation of the initials of the various companies will be found in the list of abbreviations shown on pp 52-53.

Both the checking of the sheets which follow and the compilation of the gazetteer have been undertaken by Mr U. A. Vincent and the writer is greatly indebted to him for his valued guidance and interest in unearthing obscure matters of cartographic importance and in generally keeping him 'on the right lines' in the draughting of these maps.

W. Philip Conolly

(1958)

DIAGRAM OF MAPS

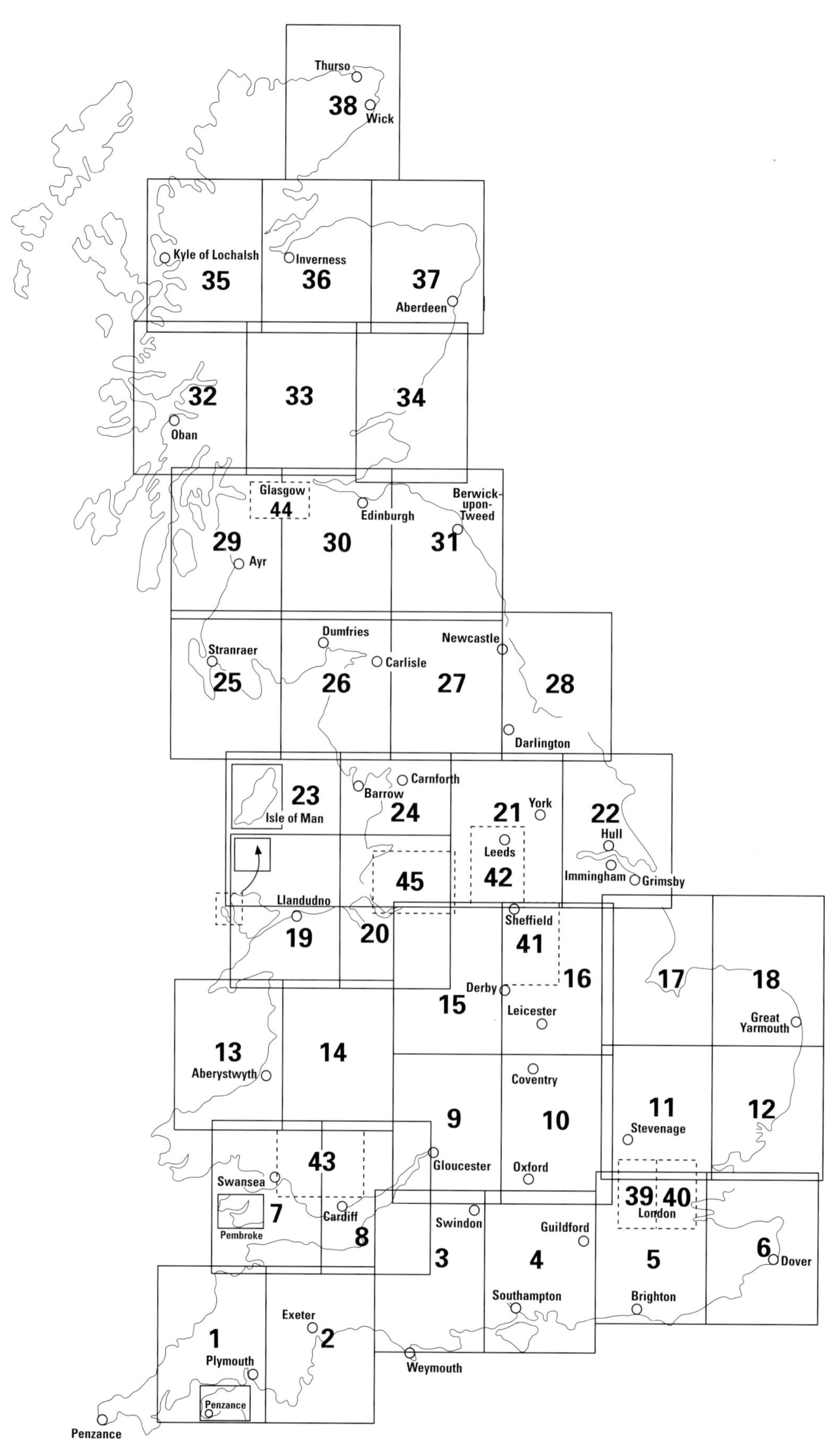

Thurso
38
Wick
Kyle of Lochalsh
35
Inverness
36
37
Aberdeen
32
Oban
33
34
Glasgow
44
Edinburgh
Berwick-upon-Tweed
29
Ayr
30
31
Dumfries
Newcastle
Stranraer
Carlisle
25
26
27
28
Darlington
23
Isle of Man
Carnforth
Barrow
24
21
York
22
Hull
Leeds
42
45
Immingham
Grimsby
Llandudno
19
20
Sheffield
41
16
17
18
Derby
15
Leicester
Great Yarmouth
13
Aberystwyth
14
Coventry
9
10
11
Stevenage
12
43
Gloucester
Oxford
Swansea
7
Pembroke
Cardiff
8
39
40
London
Swindon
Guildford
3
4
5
6
Dover
Southampton
Brighton
Exeter
1
2
Plymouth
Weymouth
Penzance
Penzance

Index to map numbers

1 Cornwall; Devon W. 6
2 Devon 7
3 Somerset; Dorset; Wilts. W. 8
4 Wilts. E.; Hants.; Berks. S.; Sussex W. 9
5 Sussex; Surrey; Kent W.; Greater London; Essex S. 10
6 Sussex E.; Kent E.; Essex E. 11
7 Devon N., South Wales W.; Pembroke 12
8 South Wales E.; Monmouth; Somerset; Gloucester W. 13
9 Hereford; Gloucester; Wilts. N. 14
10 Warwicks.; Northants.; Bucks.; Beds. W.; Oxford; Berks. N. 15
11 Beds. E.; Hunts.; Cambs.; Essex N. 16
12 Norfolk S.; Suffolk; Essex E. 17
13 Pembroke N.; Cardigan; Carmarthen; Birmingham 18
14 Montgomery; Brecknock; Radnor; Hereford W.; Salop W. 19
15 Cheshire; Salop.; Staffs.; Warwicks. N.; Derby W. 20
16 Derby; Notts.; Leics.; Rutland; Lincs. W. 21
17 Lincs. S.; Norfolk W.; Cambs. N. 22
18 Norfolk 23
19 North Wales 24
20 Denbigh; Flint; Cheshire; Lancs.; Salop. N.; Staffs. N. 25
21 Yorks. W. & S. 26
22 Yorks. E.; Lincs. N. 27
23 Isle of Man 28
24 Lancs.; Yorks. N. & W. 29
25 Wigtown; Ayr S.; Kirkcudbright 30
26 Kirkcudbright E.; Dumfries S.; Cumberland 31
27 Northumberland W.; Durham W.; Westmorland 32
28 Northumberland E.; Durham E.; North Yorkshire 33
29 Stirling W.; Dumbarton; Ayr; Glasgow; Clyde Coast 34
30 Stirling E.; Dunfermline; Lanarks. E.; The Lothians; Edinburgh 35
31 Berwick; Northumberland N.; Roxburgh 36
32 Oban, Mallaig & West Highlands 37
33 Kinross, Perth & Central Highlands 38
34 Aberdeen S.; Kincardine; Angus; Dundee; Fife 39
35 Ross & Cromarty 40
36 Inverness; Nairn; Moray; Banff W. 41
37 Banff E.; Aberdeenshire 42
38 Caithness 43

Enlargements

39 London – West Side 44
40 London – East Side 45
41 Nottingham-Sheffield Area 46
42 Leeds-Sheffield-West Riding Area 47
43 South Wales 48
44 Glasgow Area 49
45 Liverpool-Manchester Area 50

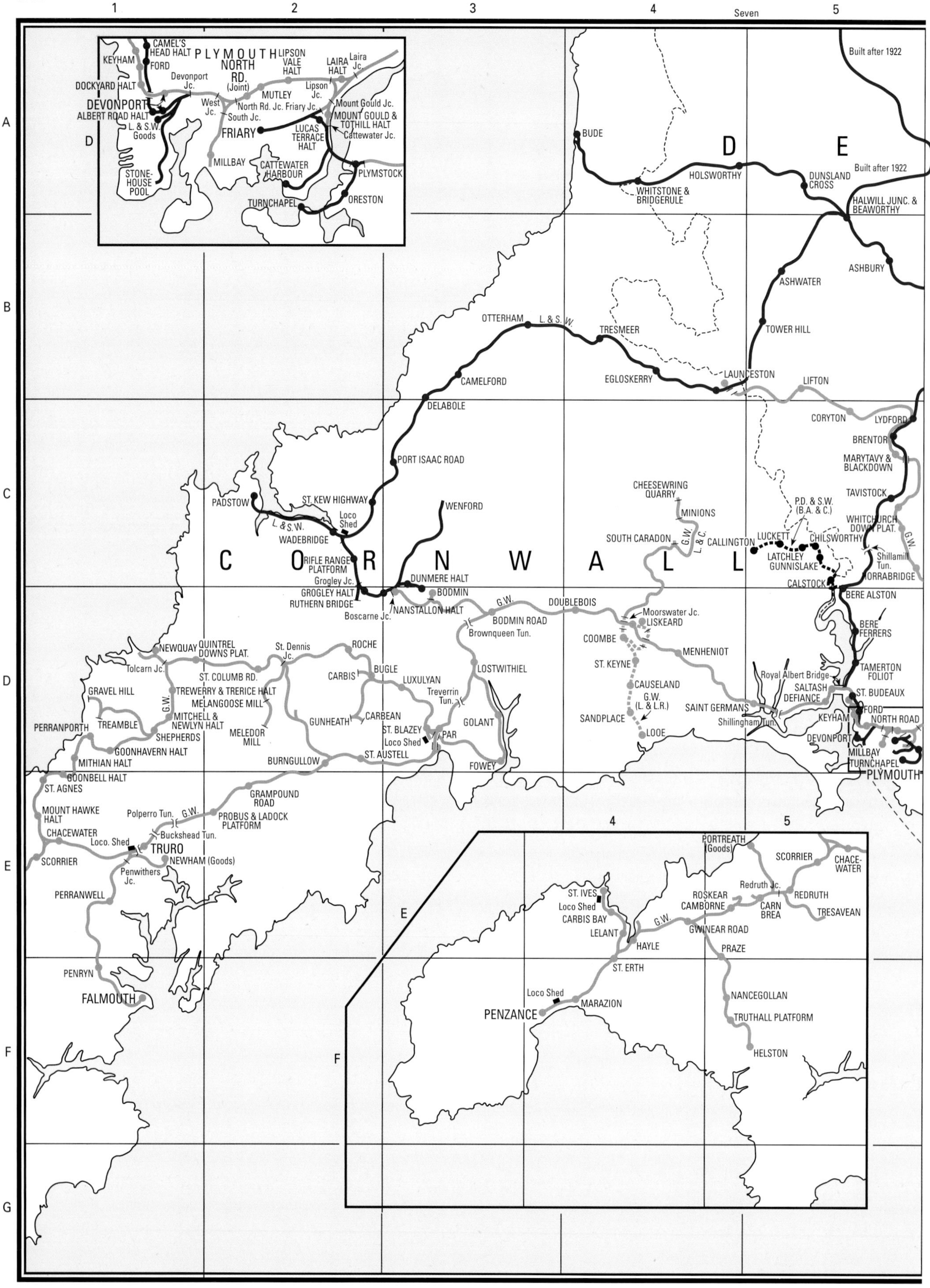

PLYMOUTH NORTH RD. (Joint)
FRIARY
DEVONPORT
CORNWALL
BUDE
HOLSWORTHY
LAUNCESTON
PADSTOW
WADEBRIDGE
BODMIN
NEWQUAY
TRURO
FALMOUTH
ST. AUSTELL
LISKEARD
LOOE
FOWEY
PENZANCE
ST. IVES
HELSTON
PLYMOUTH
Built after 1922

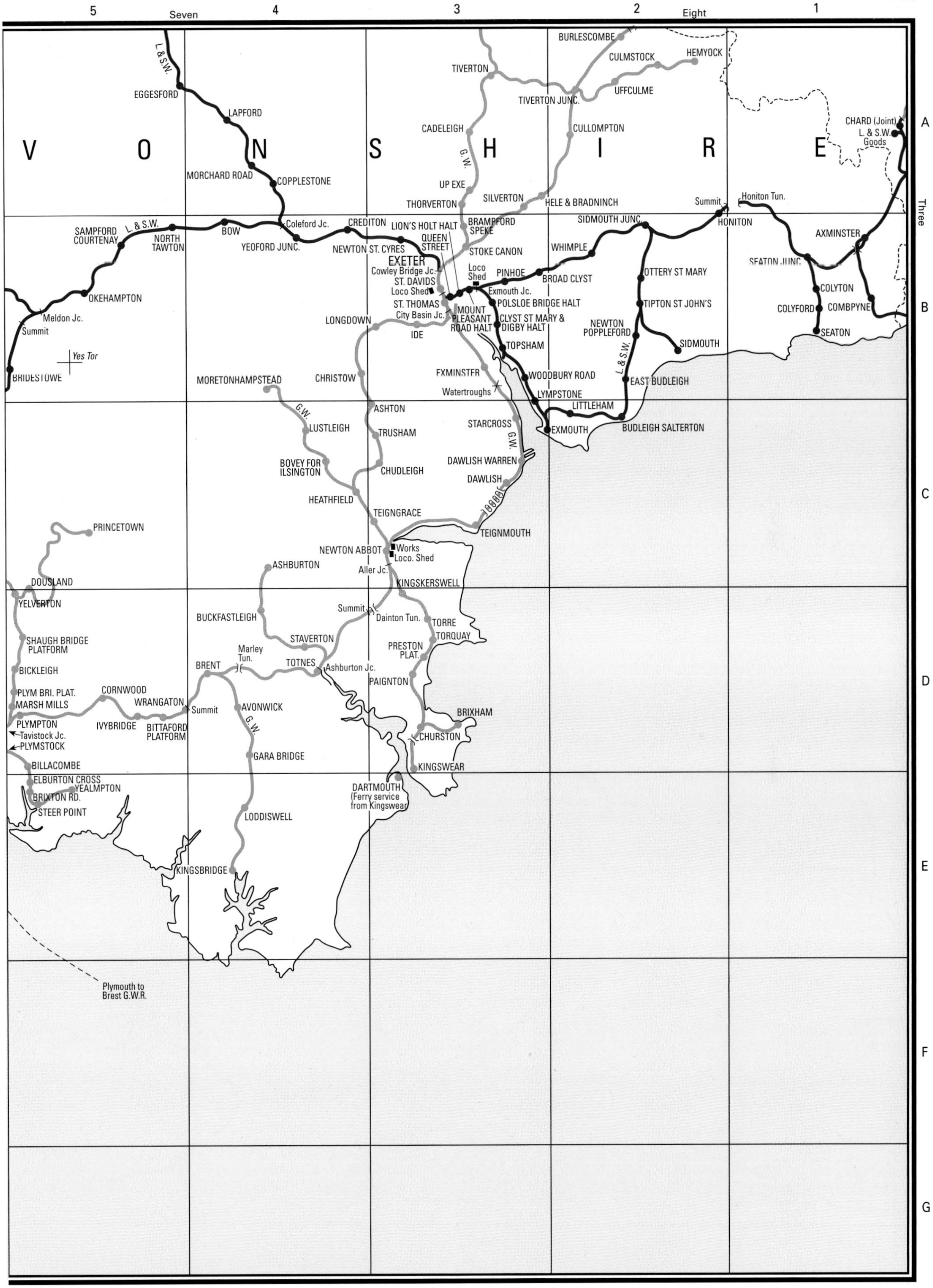

5 Seven 4 3 2 Eight 1

V O N S H I R E

L.& S.W.
EGGESFORD
LAPFORD
MORCHARD ROAD
COPPLESTONE
BURLESCOMBE
CULMSTOCK
HEMYOCK
TIVERTON
UFFCULME
TIVERTON JUNC.
CULLOMPTON
CADELEIGH
G.W.
UP EXE
THORVERTON
SILVERTON
HELE & BRADNINCH
CHARD (Joint)
L.& S.W.
Goods
Summit
Honiton Tun.
HONITON
SIDMOUTH JUNC.
AXMINSTER
SAMPFORD COURTENAY
L.& S.W.
BOW
NORTH TAWTON
Coleford Jc.
YEOFORD JUNC.
CREDITON
NEWTON ST. CYRES
LION'S HOLT HALT
QUEEN STREET
BRAMPFORD SPEKE
STOKE CANON
WHIMPLE
EXETER
Cowley Bridge Jc.
ST. DAVIDS
Loco Shed
Loco Shed
PINHOE
BROAD CLYST
Exmouth Jc.
OTTERY ST MARY
SEATON JUNC.
COLYTON
OKEHAMPTON
ST. THOMAS
City Basin Jc.
MOUNT PLEASANT ROAD HALT
POLSLOE BRIDGE HALT
CLYST ST MARY & DIGBY HALT
TIPTON ST JOHN'S
COLYFORD
COMBPYNE
Meldon Jc.
Summit
LONGDOWN
IDE
NEWTON POPPLEFORD
TOPSHAM
SIDMOUTH
SEATON
Yes Tor
L.& S.W.
BRIDESTOWE
MORETONHAMPSTEAD
CHRISTOW
EXMINSTER
Watertroughs
WOODBURY ROAD
LYMPSTONE
EAST BUDLEIGH
G.W.
ASHTON
LITTLEHAM
LUSTLEIGH
TRUSHAM
STARCROSS
EXMOUTH
BUDLEIGH SALTERTON
G.W.
DAWLISH WARREN
BOVEY FOR ILSINGTON
CHUDLEIGH
DAWLISH
HEATHFIELD
TEIGNGRACE
PRINCETOWN
TEIGNMOUTH
NEWTON ABBOT
Works
Loco. Shed
ASHBURTON
Aller Jc.
DOUSLAND
KINGSKERSWELL
YELVERTON
Summit
Dainton Tun.
BUCKFASTLEIGH
TORRE
TORQUAY
SHAUGH BRIDGE PLATFORM
STAVERTON
PRESTON PLAT.
Marley Tun.
BICKLEIGH
BRENT
TOTNES
Ashburton Jc.
PAIGNTON
PLYM BRI. PLAT.
CORNWOOD
MARSH MILLS
WRANGATON
Summit
AVONWICK
BRIXHAM
PLYMPTON
IVYBRIDGE
BITTAFORD PLATFORM
G.W.
CHURSTON
Tavistock Jc.
PLYMSTOCK
GARA BRIDGE
KINGSWEAR
BILLACOMBE
ELBURTON CROSS
YEALMPTON
DARTMOUTH (Ferry service from Kingswear)
BRIXTON RD.
STEER POINT
LODDISWELL
KINGSBRIDGE
Plymouth to Brest G.W.R.

A
Three
B
C
D
E
F
G

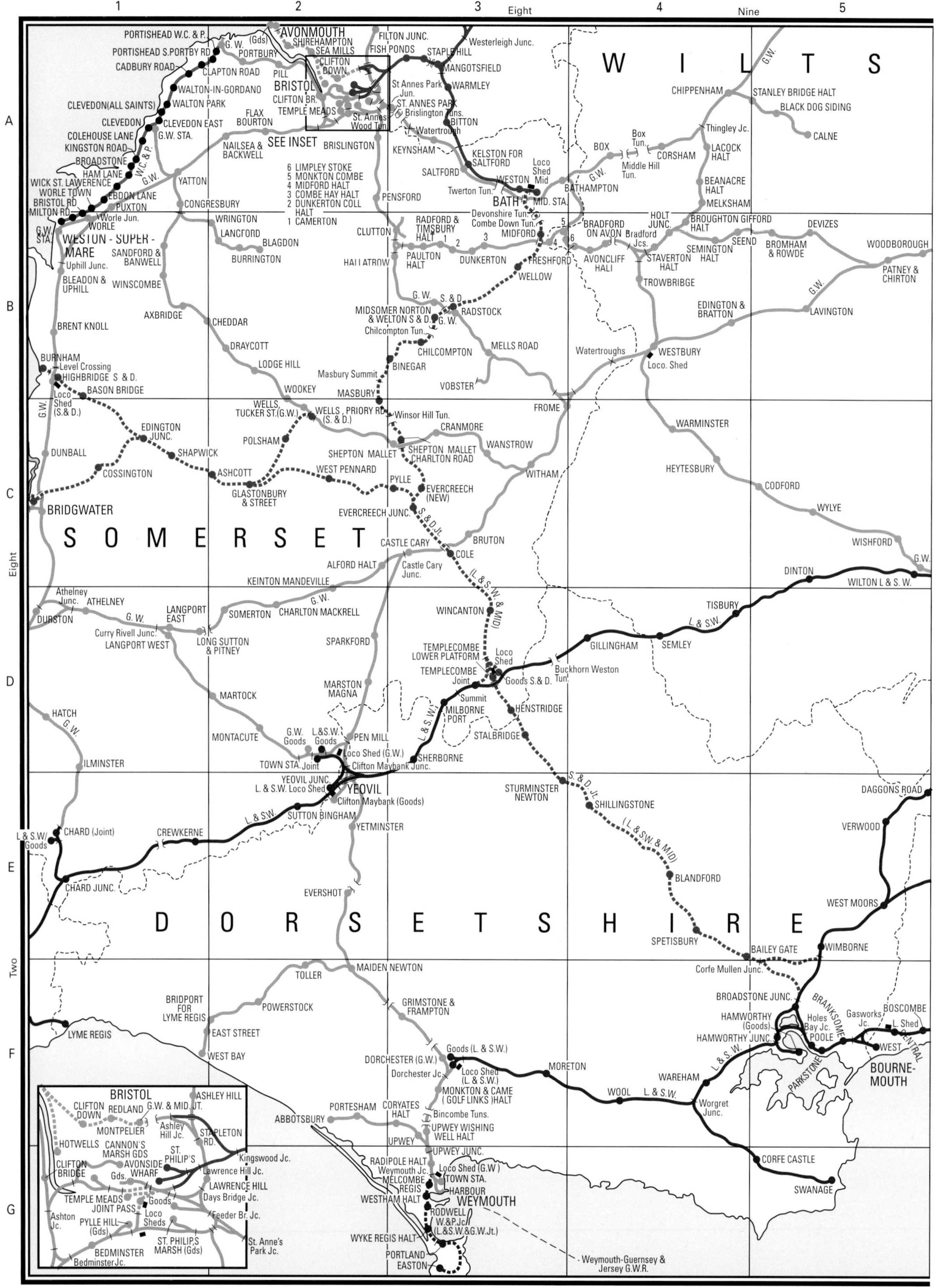
1
2
3
Eight
4
Nine
5
A
B
C
D
E
F
G
Eight
Two
WILTS
SOMERSET
DORSETSHIRE
PORTISHEAD W.C. & P.
PORTISHEAD S.PORTBY RD
CADBURY ROAD
G. W.
(Gds)
PORTBURY
AVONMOUTH
SHIREHAMPTON
SEA MILLS
CLIFTON DOWN
FILTON JUNC.
FISH PONDS
STAPLE HILL
Westerleigh Junc.
MANGOTSFIELD
CLAPTON ROAD
PILL
BRISTOL
CLIFTON BR.
TEMPLE MEADS
St. Annes Wood Tun.
St Annes Park Jun.
ST. ANNES PARK
Brislington Tuns.
WARMLEY
BITTON
Watertrough
WALTON-IN-GORDANO
WALTON PARK
CLEVEDON(ALL SAINTS)
CLEVEDON
CLEVEDON EAST
G.W. STA.
FLAX BOURTON
COLEHOUSE LANE
KINGSTON ROAD
BROADSTONE
HAM LANE
WICK ST. LAWRENCE
WORLE TOWN
BRISTOL RD
MILTON RD
W.C. & P.
NAILSEA & BACKWELL
SEE INSET
BRISLINGTON
KEYNSHAM
KELSTON FOR SALTFORD
SALTFORD
Loco Shed
WESTON
Mid
Twerton Tun.
BATH
MID. STA.
BATHAMPTON
BOX
Box Tun.
Middle Hill Tun.
CORSHAM
Thingley Jc.
CHIPPENHAM
STANLEY BRIDGE HALT
BLACK DOG SIDING
CALNE
LACOCK HALT
BEANACRE HALT
MELKSHAM
YATTON
EBDON LANE
PUXTON
CONGRESBURY
6 LIMPLEY STOKE
5 MONKTON COMBE
4 MIDFORD HALT
3 COMBE HAY HALT
2 DUNKERTON COLL HALT
1 CAMERTON
PENSFORD
Devonshire Tun.
Combe Down Tun.
MIDFORD
Worle Jun.
WORLE
G.W. STA.
WESTON - SUPER - MARE
Uphill Junc.
WRINGTON
LANGFORD
BLAGDON
BURRINGTON
SANDFORD & BANWELL
CLUTTON
HALLATROW
RADFORD & TIMSBURY HALT
PAULTON HALT
DUNKERTON
FRESHFORD
WELLOW
BRADFORD ON AVON
Bradford Jcs.
AVONCLIFF HALT
HOLT JUNC.
STAVERTON HALT
TROWBRIBGE
BROUGHTON GIFFORD HALT
SEMINGTON HALT
SEEND
BROMHAM & ROWDE
DEVIZES
WOODBOROUGH
PATNEY & CHIRTON
BLEADON & UPHILL
WINSCOMBE
AXBRIDGE
CHEDDAR
G. W.
S. & D.
RADSTOCK
MIDSOMER NORTON & WELTON S & D.
Chilcompton Tun.
EDINGTON & BRATTON
LAVINGTON
BRENT KNOLL
DRAYCOTT
CHILCOMPTON
MELLS ROAD
Watertroughs
WESTBURY
Loco. Shed
BURNHAM
Level Crossing
HIGHBRIDGE S & D.
BASON BRIDGE
Loco Shed (S.& D.)
LODGE HILL
BINEGAR
Masbury Summit
MASBURY
WOOKEY
VOBSTER
FROME
WELLS, TUCKER ST.(G.W.)
WELLS, PRIORY RD (S. & D.)
Winsor Hill Tun.
CRANMORE
WANSTROW
WARMINSTER
EDINGTON JUNC.
POLSHAM
SHAPWICK
SHEPTON MALLET
SHEPTON MALLET CHARLTON ROAD
DUNBALL
HEYTESBURY
COSSINGTON
ASHCOTT
WEST PENNARD
WITHAM
CODFORD
GLASTONBURY & STREET
PYLLE
EVERCREECH (NEW)
BRIDGWATER
EVERCREECH JUNC.
S. & D. Jt.
WYLYE
CASTLE CARY
BRUTON
WISHFORD
COLE
ALFORD HALT
Castle Cary Junc.
(L. & S.W. & MID)
DINTON
WILTON L & S. W.
KEINTON MANDEVILLE
Athelney Junc.
ATHELNEY
DURSTON
G. W.
LANGPORT EAST
SOMERTON
CHARLTON MACKRELL
WINCANTON
TISBURY
L & S.W.
Curry Rivell Junc.
LANGPORT WEST
LONG SUTTON & PITNEY
SPARKFORD
GILLINGHAM
SEMLEY
TEMPLECOMBE LOWER PLATFORM
TEMPLECOMBE Joint
Loco Shed
Goods S.& D.
Buckhorn Weston Tun.
MARSTON MAGNA
MARTOCK
Summit
MILBORNE PORT
HENSTRIDGE
HATCH
STALBRIDGE
MONTACUTE
G.W. Goods
L&S.W. Goods
PEN MILL
Loco Shed (G.W.)
SHERBORNE
ILMINSTER
TOWN STA. Joint
Clifton Maybank Junc.
YEOVIL JUNC.
L. & S.W. Loco Shed
YEOVIL
Clifton Maybank (Goods)
STURMINSTER NEWTON
SHILLINGSTONE
DAGGONS ROAD
SUTTON BINGHAM
YETMINSTER
L & S.W.
CHARD (Joint)
L & S.W. Goods
CREWKERNE
VERWOOD
(L & S.W. & MID)
CHARD JUNC.
EVERSHOT
BLANDFORD
WEST MOORS
SPETISBURY
BAILEY GATE
WIMBORNE
Corfe Mullen Junc.
MAIDEN NEWTON
TOLLER
BROADSTONE JUNC.
BRANKSOME
BOSCOMBE
BRIDPORT FOR LYME REGIS
POWERSTOCK
GRIMSTONE & FRAMPTON
HAMWORTHY (Goods)
Holes Bay Jc.
Gasworks Jc.
L. Shed
HAMWORTHY JUNC.
POOLE
WEST
CENTRAL
LYME REGIS
EAST STREET
WEST BAY
Goods (L. & S.W.)
DORCHESTER (G.W.)
Dorchester Jc.
Loco Shed (L. & S.W.)
MORETON
WAREHAM
PARKSTONE
BOURNEMOUTH
WOOL
Worgret Junc.
MONKTON & CAME (GOLF LINKS) HALT
PORTESHAM
CORYATES HALT
ABBOTSBURY
Bincombe Tuns.
UPWEY WISHING WELL HALT
UPWEY
UPWEY JUNC.
RADIPOLE HALT
Weymouth Jc.
Loco Shed (G.W)
MELCOMBE REGIS
TOWN STA.
HARBOUR
WEYMOUTH
WESTHAM HALT
RODWELL
W.&P.Jc.
(L.&S.W.&G.W.Jt.)
WYKE REGIS HALT
PORTLAND
EASTON
Weymouth-Guernsey & Jersey G.W.R.
CORFE CASTLE
SWANAGE
BRISTOL
ASHLEY HILL
CLIFTON DOWN
REDLAND
G.W. & MID. JT.
MONTPELIER
Ashley Hill Jc.
STAPLETON RD.
HOTWELLS
CANNON'S MARSH GDS
ST. PHILIP'S
CLIFTON BRIDGE
AVONSIDE WHARF
Gds.
Kingswood Jc.
Lawrence Hill Jc.
LAWRENCE HILL
TEMPLE MEADS JOINT PASS.
Goods
Days Bridge Jc.
Ashton Jc.
PYLLE HILL (Gds)
Loco Sheds
Feeder Br. Jc.
BEDMINSTER
Bedminster Jc.
ST. PHILIPS MARSH (Gds)
St. Anne's Park Jc.

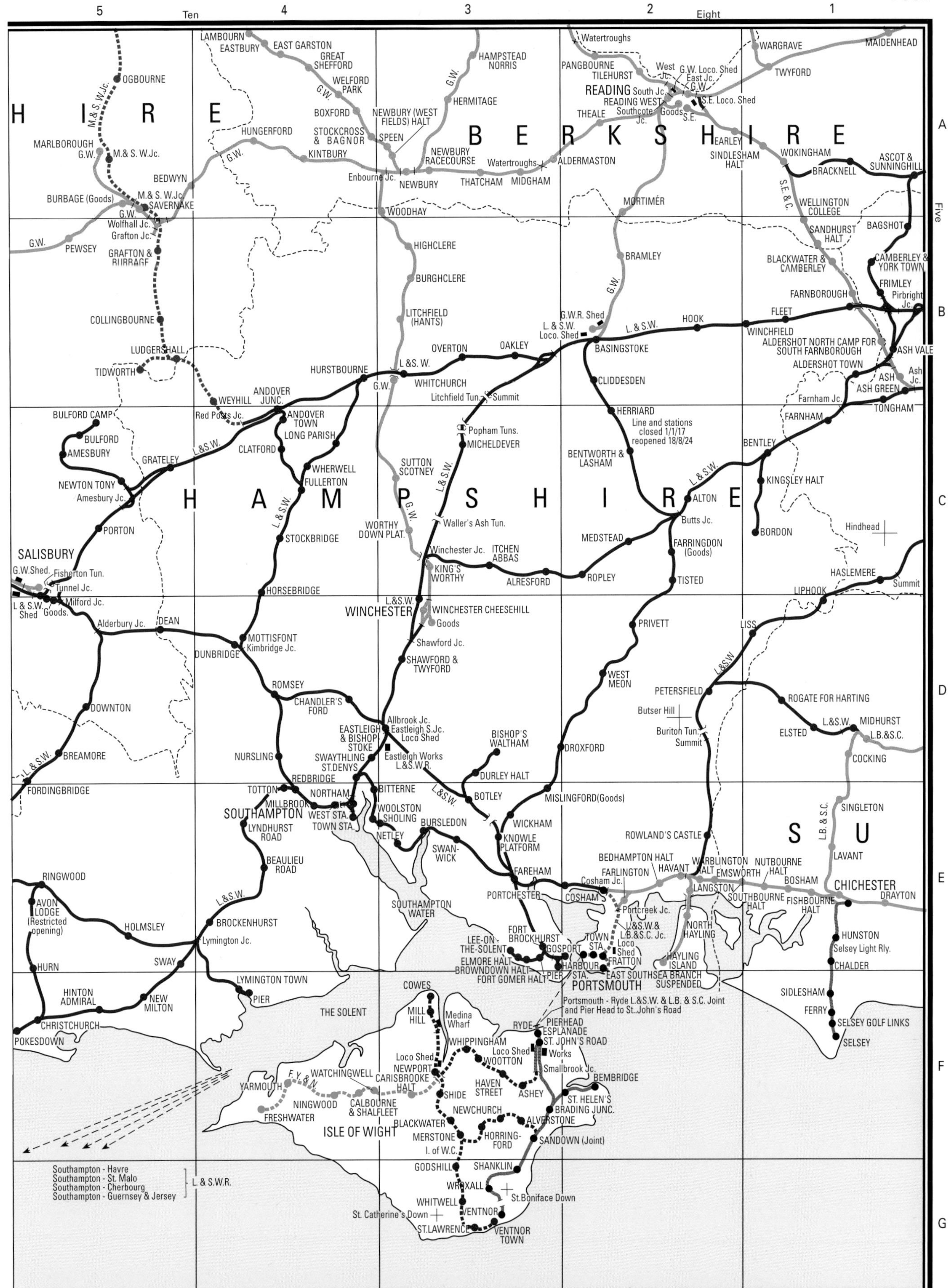

5
Ten
4
3
2
Eight
1
A
B
C
D
E
F
G
Five
BERKSHIRE
HAMPSHIRE
HIRE
SU
READING
WINCHESTER
SOUTHAMPTON
PORTSMOUTH
SALISBURY
CHICHESTER
ISLE OF WIGHT
THE SOLENT
SOUTHAMPTON WATER
Line and stations closed 1/1/17 reopened 18/8/24
Portsmouth - Ryde L.&S.W. & L.B. & S.C. Joint and Pier Head to St.John's Road
Southampton - Havre
Southampton - St. Malo
Southampton - Cherbourg
Southampton - Guernsey & Jersey
L. & S.W.R.

1 2 3 4 5

A B C D E F G

Eleven

Four

(SEE SHEETS THIRTY NINE & FORTY)

SURREY

SUSSEX

8 NEW SOUTHGATE
9 ALEXANDRA PALACE
10 BOWES PARK
11 WINCHMORE HILL
12 GRANGE PARK
13 SILVER STREET
14 WHITE HART LANE

1 CARSHALTON
2 HACKBRIDGE
3 BEDDINGTON LANE
4 WEST CROYDON
5 WADDON
6 WALLINGTON
7 BEECHES HALT (later CARSHALTON BEECHES)

1 HOLLAND ROAD HALT
2 DYKE JUNC. HALT
3 FISHERGATE HALT
4 BUNGALOW TOWN HALT
5 HAM BRIDGE HALT

Newhaven-Dieppe L.B. & S.C.

5
4
3
Twelve
2
1
A
B
C
D
E
F
G
G.E.
WOODHAM FERRERS
FAMBRIDGE
ALTHORNE
BURNHAM ON CROUCH
WICKFORD
BATTLESBRIDGE
G.E.
HOCKLEY
ROCHFORD
RAYLEIGH
MID. L.T. & S.
PITSEA
SOUTHEND - ON - SEA FOR WESTCLIFF & THORPE BAY
PRITTLEWELL
L. Shed
BENFLEET
LEIGH - ON SEA
THORPE BAY
Independent Light Railway
WESTCLIFF-ON-SEA
SOUTHEND-ON- SEA
SHOEBURYNESS
CORYTON
Canvey Island
CORRINGHAM
THAMESHAVEN
URALITE HALT
HIGH HALSTOW HALT
CLIFFE
MIDDLE STOKE HALT
CRAIN CROSSING HALT
PORT VICTORIA
DOCKYARD
SHEERNESS- ON-SEA
SHEERNESS EAST
Hoo Jc.
HIGHAM
SHARNAL ST.
BELUNCLE HALT
PIER
QUEENBOROUGH
EAST MINSTER-ON-SEA
Rochester Br. Jc.
ROCHESTER BRI.
MINSTER-ON-SEA
EASTCHURCH
STROOD
Fort Pitt Tun.
L. Shed
BRAMBLEDOWN HALT
HARTY RD. HALT
LEYSDOWN
GILLINGHAM
CUXTON
Gillingham Tun.
RAINHAM
King's Ferry Bri.
ROCHESTER
Chatham Tun.
CHATHAM
NEWINGTON
HALLING
West Jc.
East Jc.
SITTINGBOURNE
TEYNHAM
SNODLAND
AYLESFORD
EAST MALLING HALT
Preston Hall Tuns.
EAST
BARMING
BARRACKS
WEST
TESTON CROSSING HALT
TOVIL
EAST FARLEIGH
MAIDSTONE
WATERINGBURY
BEARSTED & THURNHAM
HOLLINGBOURNE
HARRIETSHAM
LENHAM
CHARING
HOTHFIELD
WHITSTABLE HARB.
WHITSTABLE TOWN & TANKERTON
TANKERTON HALT
SOUTH STR.HALT
GRAVENEY (Goods)
FAVERSHAM
Loco. Shed
Faversham Jc.
BLEAN & TYLER HILL HALT
STURRY
SELLING
Selling Tun.
WEST
CANTERBURY
EAST
SOUTH
CHARTHAM
CHILHAM
WYE
HERNE BAY
S.E. & C.
WESTGATE-ON-SEA
SANDS
MARGATE
EAST
WEST
BIRCHINGTON-ON-SEA
BROADSTAIRS
EBBSFLEET & CLIFFSEND HALT
Minster East Jc.
Minster West Jc.
RAMSGATE TOWN
HARB.
MINSTER
Minster 'B' Jc.
GROVE FERRY
CHISLET COLLIERY HALT
RICHBOROUGH PORT (goods)
EBBSFLEET & CLIFFSEND HALT
ASH TOWN
STAPLE
SANDWICH
ROMAN ROAD
WOODNESBOROUGH
BEKESBOURNE
WINGHAM COLLIERY
EASTRY
EASTRY SOUTH opened 1927
BRIDGE
ADISHAM
DEAL
KNOWLTON
ELVINGTON
BISHOPSBOURNE
SNOWDOWN & NONINGTON HALT
EYTHORNE
WALMER
BARHAM
East Kent Light R.
SHEPHERDS WELL
Lydden Tun.
STONEHALL + LYDDEN HALT
MARTIN HILL
ELHAM
KEARSNEY
Buckland Jc.
Charlton Tun.
Guston Tun.
Priory Tun.
PRIORY
Harb.Tun.
MARDEN
STAPLEHURST
S.E. & C.
HEADCORN
PLUCKLEY
LYMINGE
Abbotscliff Tun.
HARBOUR
Archcliffe Jc.
DOVER
MARINE
Dover to Calais. S.E. & C.
HORSMONDEN
FRITTENDEN ROAD
Loco Shed
Ashford Works
ASHFORD
CHERITON HALT
Saltwood Tun.
Martello Tun.
Loco Shed
CENT.
TOWN
Shakespeare Tun.
JUNC. STA.
FOLKESTONE
HARB.
BIDDENDEN
SMEETH
Sandling Tun.
SANDLING JUNC.
WESTENHANGER
GOUDHURST
HIGH HALDEN ROAD
SANDGATE
SHORNCLIFFE CAMP
HYTHE
Folkestone to Boulogne. S.E.&
CRANBROOK
TENTERDEN ST. MICHEALS
HAM STREET & ORLESTONE
TENTERDEN TOWN
HAWKHURST
ROLVENDEN
Kent & East Sussex Light Railway
APPLEDORE
WITTERSHAM ROAD
ETCHINGHAM
NORTHIAM
SALEHURST HALT
BODIAM
JUNCTION ROAD
BROOKLAND
ROBERTSBRIDGE
S.E.& C.
NEW ROMNEY & LITTLESTONE-ON- SEA.
RYE
Tramway
LYDD
Mountfield Tun.
WINCHELSEA
RYE HARBOUR
CAMBER SANDS
SNAILHAM HALT
DOLEHAM HALT
DUNGENESS
BATTLE
THREE OAKS & GUESTLING HALT
CROWHURST
Bopeep Tunnel
Ore Tun.
ORE
COODEN BEACH HALT
WEST ST. LEONARDS
Loco Shed
Mount Pleasant Tun.
SIDLEY
HASTINGS
BEXHILL
ST. LEONARDS (WEST MARINA)
Hastings Tun.
ST. LEONARDS (WARRIOR SQUARE)
Bopeep Jc.
BEXHILL
WEST BEXHILL HALT

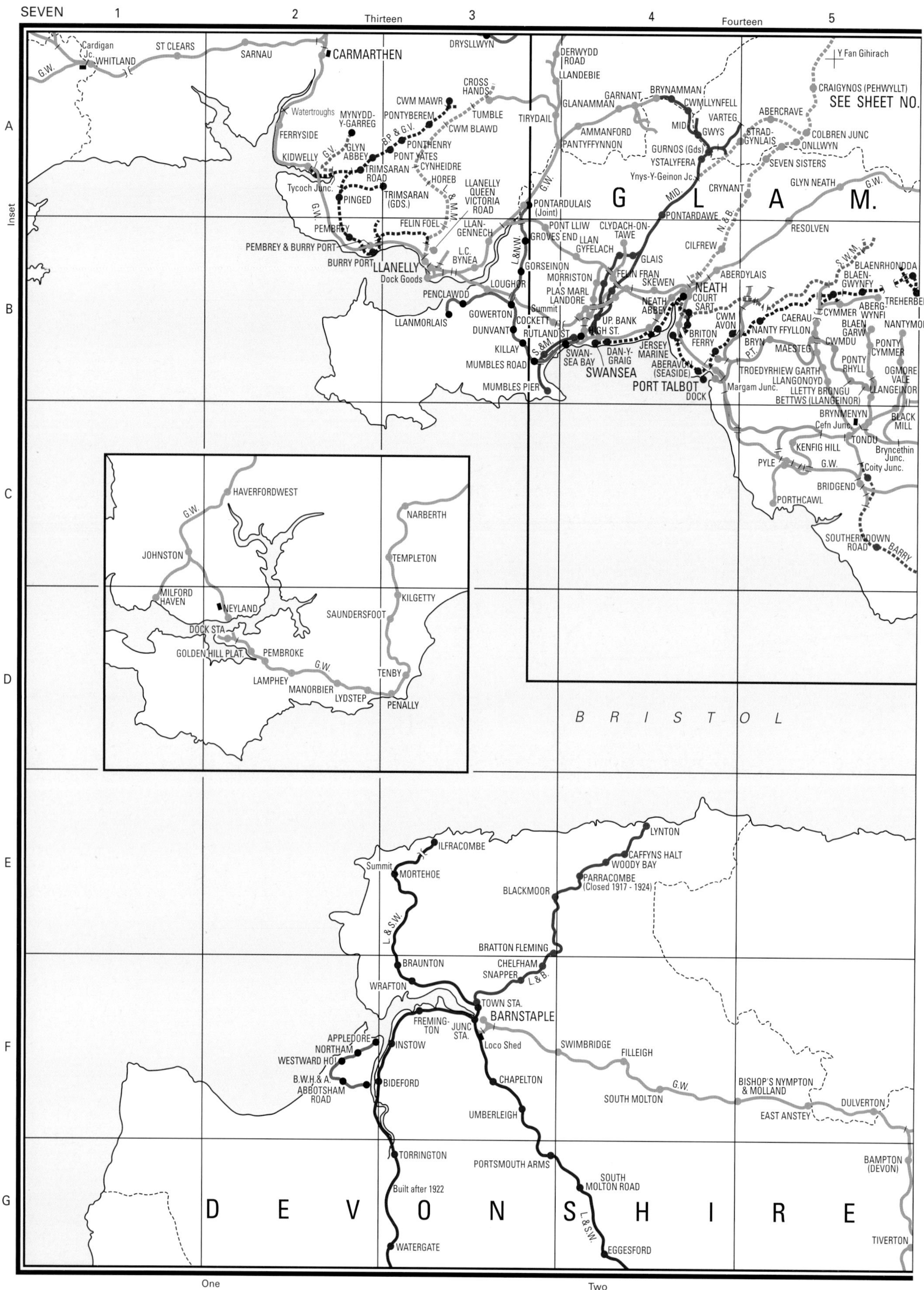

SEVEN
1
2
Thirteen
3
4
Fourteen
5
A
B
C
D
E
F
G
Inset
Cardigan Jc.
WHITLAND
G.W.
ST CLEARS
SARNAU
CARMARTHEN
DRYSLLWYN
DERWYDD ROAD
LLANDEBIE
Y Fan Gihirach
CRAIGYNOS (PEHWYLLT)
SEE SHEET NO.
CROSS HANDS
CWM MAWR
TUMBLE
Watertroughs
MYNYDD-Y-GARREG
PONTYBEREM
CWM BLAWD
TIRYDAIL
GARNANT
GLANAMMAN
BRYNAMMAN
CWMLLYNFELL
ABERCRAVE
FERRYSIDE
GLYN ABBEY
B.P. & G.V.
PONTHENRY
AMMANFORD
MID.
GWYS
VARTEG
STRAD-GYNLAIS
COLBREN JUNC
ONLLWYN
KIDWELLY
G.V.
PONT YATES
PANTYFFYNNON
GURNOS (Gds)
YSTALYFERA
SEVEN SISTERS
TRIMSARAN ROAD
CYNHEIDRE
Tycoch Junc.
HOREB
L. & M.M.
Ynys-Y-Geinon Jc.
GLYN NEATH
G.W.
LLANELLY QUEEN VICTORIA ROAD
CRYNANT
PINGED
TRIMSARAN (GDS.)
PONTARDULAIS (Joint)
G L A M.
MID.
N. & B.
PONTARDAWE
PEMBREY
FELIN FOEL
LLAN-GENNECH
PONT LLIW
CLYDACH-ON-TAWE
RESOLVEN
PEMBREY & BURRY PORT
GROVES END
LLAN GYFELACH
CILFREW
L.C. BYNEA
L.&N.W.
BURRY PORT
LLANELLY
GLAIS
Dock Goods
GORSEINON
MORRISTON
FELIN FRAN
SKEWEN
ABERDYLAIS
S.W.M.
BLAENRHONDDA
BLAEN-GWYNFY
LOUGHOR
NEATH
PENCLAWDD
PLAS MARL
LANDORE
NEATH ABBEY
COURT SART
TREHERBERT
ABERG-WYNFI
Summit
GOWERTON
COCKETT
CYMMER
CAERAU
LLANMORLAIS
UP. BANK
CWM AVON
BLAEN GARW
NANTYMOEL
RUTLAND ST.
HIGH ST.
BRITON FERRY
NANTY FFYLLON
DUNVANT
BRYN
MAESTEG
CWMDU
PONTY CYMMER
S.& M.
JERSEY MARINE
P.T.
KILLAY
SWAN-SEA BAY
DAN-Y-GRAIG
ABERAVON (SEASIDE)
PONTY RHYLL
OGMORE VALE
MUMBLES ROAD
SWANSEA
TROEDYRHIEW GARTH
LLANGONOYD
PORT TALBOT
Margam Junc.
LLETTY BRONGU
LLANGEINOR
MUMBLES PIER
DOCK
BETTWS (LLANGEINOR)
BRYNMENYN
Cefn Junc.
BLACK MILL
TONDU
KENFIG HILL
Bryncethin Junc.
PYLE
G.W.
Coity Junc.
BRIDGEND
PORTHCAWL
SOUTHERNDOWN ROAD
BARRY
HAVERFORDWEST
G.W.
NARBERTH
JOHNSTON
TEMPLETON
MILFORD HAVEN
KILGETTY
NEYLAND
SAUNDERSFOOT
DOCK STA.
GOLDEN HILL PLAT.
PEMBROKE
G.W.
TENBY
LAMPHEY
MANORBIER
LYDSTEP
PENALLY
B R I S T O L
LYNTON
ILFRACOMBE
CAFFYNS HALT
WOODY BAY
Summit
MORTEHOE
PARRACOMBE (Closed 1917 - 1924)
BLACKMOOR
L. & S.W.
BRATTON FLEMING
BRAUNTON
CHELFHAM
SNAPPER
L. & B.
WRAFTON
TOWN STA.
BARNSTAPLE
FREMINGTON
JUNC STA.
APPLEDORE
NORTHAM
INSTOW
Loco Shed
SWIMBRIDGE
FILLEIGH
WESTWARD HO!
CHAPELTON
B.W.H.& A.
ABBOTSHAM ROAD
BIDEFORD
G.W.
BISHOP'S NYMPTON & MOLLAND
SOUTH MOLTON
DULVERTON
UMBERLEIGH
EAST ANSTEY
TORRINGTON
PORTSMOUTH ARMS
BAMPTON (DEVON)
SOUTH MOLTON ROAD
Built after 1922
D E V O N S H I R E
L.& S.W.
WATERGATE
EGGESFORD
TIVERTON
One
Two

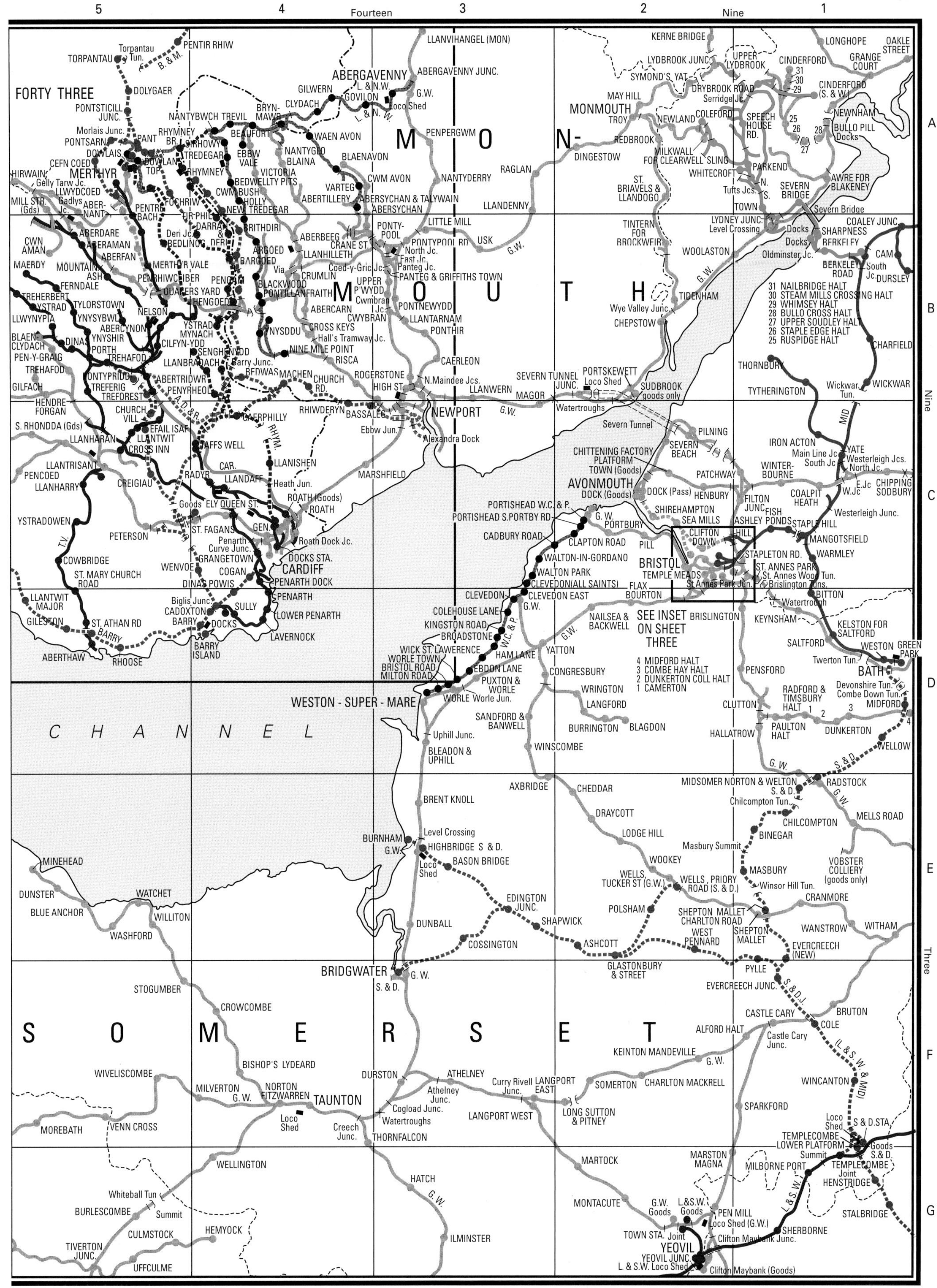
5
4
Fourteen
3
2
Nine
1
A
B
C
D
E
F
G
Nine
Three
Two
Three
FORTY THREE
M O N -
M O U T H
C H A N N E L
S O M E R S E T
TORPANTAU
Torpantau Tun.
PENTIR RHIW
B. & M.
DOLYGAER
PONTSTICILL JUNC.
Morlais Junc.
PONTSARN
PANT
DOWLAIS
CEFN COED
MERTHYR
HIRWAIN
Gelly Tarw Jc.
LLWYDCOED
MILL STR. (Gds)
Gadlys Jc.
ABER-NANT
ABERDARE
ABERAMAN
CWN AMAN
ABERFAN
MAERDY
MOUNTAIN ASH
FERNDALE
TREHERBERT
YSTRAD
TYLORSTOWN
LLWYNYPIA
YNYSYBWL
ABERCYNON
BLAEN-CLYDACH
DINAS
YNYSHIR
PORTH
PEN-Y-GRAIG
TREHAFOD
GILFACH
PONTYPRIDD
TREFERIG
TREFOREST
HENDRE-FORGAN
S. RHONDDA (Gds)
LLANHARAN
CHURCH VILL
EFAIL ISAF
LLANTWIT
CROSS INN
LLANTRISANT
PENCOED
LLANHARRY
CREIGIAU
YSTRADOWEN
PETERSON
COWBRIDGE
ST. MARY CHURCH ROAD
LLANTWIT MAJOR
GILESTON
ST. ATHAN RD
BARRY
ABERTHAW
RHOOSE
NANTYBWCH
TREVIL
RHYMNEY BR.
SIRHOWY
TREDEGAR
RHYMNEY
DOWLAIS TOP
PENTRE BACH
FOCHRIW
TIR-PHIL
DARRAN & DERI
Deri Jc.
BEDLINOG
MERTHYR VALE
PENRHIWCEIBER
QUAKERS YARD
PENGAM
HENGOED
NELSON
YSTRAD MYNACH
CILFYN-YDD
SENGHENYDD
LLANBRADACH
Barry Junc.
ABERTRIDWR
PENYRHEOL
BEDWAS
MACHEN
CAERPHILLY
A. D. & R.
RHYM.
TAFFS WELL
RADYR
LLANDAFF
CAR.
LLANISHEN
Heath Jun.
Goods
ELY
QUEEN ST.
ST. FAGANS
GEN.
ROATH (Goods)
ROATH
Roath Dock Jc.
Penarth Curve Junc.
GRANGETOWN
DOCKS STA.
CARDIFF
WENVOE
COGAN
PENARTH DOCK
DINAS POWIS
PENARTH
Biglis Junc.
CADOXTON
SULLY
LOWER PENARTH
BARRY
DOCKS
BARRY ISLAND
LAVERNOCK
BRYN-MAWR
CLYDACH
GILWERN
GOVILON
L. & N.W.
ABERGAVENNY
ABERGAVENNY JUNC.
G.W.
Loco Shed
LLANVIHANGEL (MON)
BEAUFORT
EBBW VALE
NANTYGLO
BLAINA
WAEN AVON
BLAENAVON
VICTORIA
BEDWELLTY PITS
CWM BUSH
HOLLY
NEW TREDEGAR
CWM AVON
VARTEG
ABERTILLERY
ABERSYCHAN & TALYWAIN
ABERSYCHAN
PENPERGWM
NANTYDERRY
BRITHDIRI
ABERBEEG
ARGOED
BARGOED
LLANHILLETH
CRANE ST.
PONTY-POOL
PONTYPOOL RD
North Jc.
East Jc.
Panteg Jc.
PANTEG & GRIFFITHS TOWN
Coed-y-Gric Jc.
CRUMLIN
BLACKWOOD
PONTLLANFRAITH
Via
UPPER P'WYDD
Cwmbran Jc.
ABERCARN
CWMBRAN
CROSS KEYS
Hall's Tramway Jc.
NYSDDU
NINE MILE POINT
RISCA
PONTNEWYDD
LLANTARNAM
PONTHIR
CAERLEON
CHURCH RD.
ROGERSTONE
HIGH ST.
N. Maindee Jcs.
RHIWDERYN
BASSALEG
Ebbw Jun.
NEWPORT
Alexandra Dock
MARSHFIELD
LITTLE MILL
USK
LLANDENNY
RAGLAN
G.W.
LLANWERN
MAGOR
SEVERN TUNNEL JUNC.
PORTSKEWETT
Loco Shed
SUDBROOK goods only
Watertroughs
Severn Tunnel
DINGESTOW
MONMOUTH
TROY
MAY HILL
REDBROOK
KERNE BRIDGE
LYDBROOK JUNC.
UPPER LYDBROOK
SYMOND'S YAT
DRYBROOK ROAD
Serridge Jc.
NEWLAND
COLEFORD
SPEECH HOUSE RD.
MILKWALL
FOR CLEARWELL
SLING
WHITECROFT
PARKEND
N.
S.
Tufts Jcs.
ST. BRIAVELS & LLANDOGO
TOWN
LYDNEY JUNC.
Level Crossing
SEVERN BRIDGE
Severn Bridge
TINTERN
FOR BROCKWEIR
WOOLASTON
TIDENHAM
Wye Valley Junc.
CHEPSTOW
CINDERFORD
31
30
29
CINDERFORD (S. & W.)
LONGHOPE
GRANGE COURT
OAKLE STREET
25
26
27
28
NEWNHAM
BULLO PILL Docks
AWRE FOR BLAKENEY
COALEY JUNC.
Docks
SHARPNESS
BERKELEY
Oldminster Jc.
BERKELEY ROAD
South Jc.
CAM
DURSLEY
31 NAILBRIDGE HALT
30 STEAM MILLS CROSSING HALT
29 WHIMSEY HALT
28 BULLO CROSS HALT
27 UPPER SOULDEY HALT
26 STAPLE EDGE HALT
25 RUSPIDGE HALT
CHARFIELD
THORNBURY
TYTHERINGTON
Wickwar Tun.
WICKWAR
MID
PILNING
SEVERN BEACH
IRON ACTON
Main Line Jc.
South Jc.
YATE
Westerleigh Jcs.
North Jc.
CHITTENING FACTORY PLATFORM
TOWN (Goods)
AVONMOUTH
DOCK (Goods)
DOCK (Pass)
HENBURY
PATCHWAY
WINTER-BOURNE
E.Jc
W.Jc
CHIPPING SODBURY
COALPIT HEATH
Westerleigh Junc.
FILTON JUNC
SHIREHAMPTON
SEA MILLS
FISH PONDS
ASHLEY HILL
STAPLE HILL
MANGOTSFIELD
WARMLEY
PORTISHEAD W.C. & P.
PORTISHEAD S.PORTBY RD.
G.W. PORTBURY
CADBURY ROAD
CLAPTON ROAD
PILL
CLIFTON DOWN
BRISTOL
STAPLETON RD.
ST. ANNES PARK
St. Annes Wood Tun.
Brislington Tuns.
TEMPLE MEADS
St Annes Park Jun.
WALTON-IN-GORDANO
WALTON PARK
CLEVEDON (ALL SAINTS)
CLEVEDON
CLEVEDON EAST
G.W.
FLAX BOURTON
BITTON
Watertrough
COLEHOUSE LANE
KINGSTON ROAD
BROADSTONE
W.C. & P.
NAILSEA & BACKWELL
SEE INSET ON SHEET THREE
BRISLINGTON
KEYNSHAM
KELSTON FOR SALTFORD
SALTFORD
WESTON
GREEN PARK
Twerton Tun.
BATH
WICK ST. LAWRENCE
WORLE TOWN
BRISTOL ROAD
MILTON ROAD
HAM LANE
EBDON LANE
PUXTON & WORLE
YATTON
CONGRESBURY
4 MIDFORD HALT
3 COMBE HAY HALT
2 DUNKERTON COLL HALT
1 CAMERTON
PENSFORD
Devonshire Tun.
Combe Down Tun.
MIDFORD
WESTON - SUPER - MARE
WORLE
Worle Jun.
WRINGTON
LANGFORD
SANDFORD & BANWELL
BURRINGTON
BLAGDON
CLUTTON
RADFORD & TIMSBURY HALT
1
2
3
PAULTON HALT
DUNKERTON
HALLATROW
Uphill Junc.
BLEADON & UPHILL
WINSCOMBE
WELLOW
G.W.
S. & D.
AXBRIDGE
CHEDDAR
MIDSOMER NORTON & WELTON
S. & D.
Chilcompton Tun.
RADSTOCK
MELLS ROAD
CHILCOMPTON
BINEGAR
Masbury Summit
MASBURY
BRENT KNOLL
DRAYCOTT
LODGE HILL
Level Crossing
BURNHAM
G.W.
HIGHBRIDGE S & D.
Loco Shed
BASON BRIDGE
WOOKEY
WELLS TUCKER ST (G.W.)
WELLS, PRIORY ROAD (S. & D.)
Winsor Hill Tun.
VOBSTER COLLIERY (goods only)
CRANMORE
EDINGTON JUNC.
POLSHAM
SHEPTON MALLET CHARLTON ROAD
SHAPWICK
DUNBALL
ASHCOTT
WEST PENNARD
SHEPTON MALLET
WANSTROW
WITHAM
COSSINGTON
EVERCREECH (NEW)
GLASTONBURY & STREET
PYLLE
EVERCREECH JUNC.
S. & D. J.
BRIDGWATER
G.W.
S. & D.
MINEHEAD
DUNSTER
BLUE ANCHOR
WATCHET
WILLITON
WASHFORD
STOGUMBER
CROWCOMBE
CASTLE CARY
Castle Cary Junc.
BRUTON
COLE
ALFORD HALT
(L. & S. W. & MID)
KEINTON MANDEVILLE
G.W.
BISHOP'S LYDEARD
WIVELISCOMBE
MILVERTON
G.W.
NORTON FITZWARREN
TAUNTON
DURSTON
ATHELNEY
Athelney Junc.
Cogload Junc.
Watertroughs
Curry Rivell Junc.
LANGPORT EAST
SOMERTON
CHARLTON MACKRELL
WINCANTON
LANGPORT WEST
LONG SUTTON & PITNEY
SPARKFORD
Loco Shed
S & D.STA.
MOREBATH
VENN CROSS
Creech Junc.
THORNFALCON
TEMPLECOMBE LOWER PLATFORM
Goods S. & D.
Summit
TEMPLECOMBE Joint
WELLINGTON
MARTOCK
MARSTON MAGNA
MILBORNE PORT
HENSTRIDGE
HATCH
G.W.
Whiteball Tun.
BURLESCOMBE
Summit
MONTACUTE
G.W. Goods
L.&S.W. Goods
PEN MILL
Loco Shed (G.W.)
L. & S. W.
STALBRIDGE
CULMSTOCK
HEMYOCK
SHERBORNE
TIVERTON JUNC.
ILMINSTER
TOWN STA. Joint
Clifton Maybank Junc.
YEOVIL
YEOVIL JUNC.
L. & S.W. Loco Shed
Clifton Maybank (Goods)
UFFCULME

1 2 3 Fifteen 4 SOMERSET RD 5

A B C D E F G

Fourteen

Eight

STOTTESDON
HIGHLEY
PRESCOTT SIDING
C.M. & D.P.
DETTON ROAD SIDING
ARLEY
CLEOBURY TOWN STA
CLEOBURY MORTIMER
WYRE FOREST
NEEN SOLLARS
NEWNHAM BRIDGE
G.W.
Titterstone Clee
ONIBURY
BROMFIELD
Watertroughs
BITTERLEY
MIDDLETON
CLEE HILL
LUDLOW
TENBURY WELLS
WOOFERTON
EASTON COURT
STOURBRIDGE TOWN
LYE
STOURBRIDGE JC.
HAGLEY
CHURCHILL & BLAKEDOWN
KIDDERMINSTER
RIFLE RANGE HALT
BEWDLEY
FOLEY PARK HALT
STOURPORT
HARTLEBURY
G.W.
HALESOWEN
HARBORNE
HUNNINGTON
SELLY OAK
KING'S NORTON
RUBERY
NORTHFIELD
Northfield Jc.
MOSELEY
KING'S HEATH
HAZELWELL
LIFFORD
ACOCKS GREEN
OLTON
HALL GREEN
YARDLEY WOOD PLATFORM
SOLIHULL
MID. HAMPTON-IN-ARDEN
L & N.W.
BERKSWELL
SHIRLEY
WIDNEY MANOR
GRIMES HILL & WYTHALL HALT
Summit
EARLSWOOD LAKES
KNOWLE & DORRIDGE
WOOD END PLATFORM
DANZEY FOR TANWORTH
LAPWORTH
Watertroughs
Summit
BARNT GREEN
BLACKWELL
ALVECHURCH
Lickey Incline
BROMSGROVE
Loco Shed
REDDITCH
WORCESTER
Pass
Stoke Works Jc.
STOKE WORKS (Goods)
DROITWICH
DROITWICH ROAD (Goods)
MID.
FERNHILL HEATH
DUNHAMPSTEAD (Goods)
Tunnel Jc.
Loco Shed
Rainbow Hill Jc.
HENWICK
WORCESTER
Works
SHRUB HILL
G.W.&M. Joint
SPETCHLEY (Goods)
FOREGATE ST.
MID Goods
NORTON JC.
STUDLEY & ASTWOOD BANK
COUGHTON
ALCESTER
WIXFORD
BROOM JUNCTION
SALFORD PRIORS
HENLEY-IN-ARDEN
Goods
N. Jc.
HATTON
S.Jc.
CLAVERDON
WOOTTON WAWEN PLAT.
N.Jc.
BEARLEY
E.Jc.
W.Jc.
WAR
GREAT ALNE
WILMCOTE
Goods
STRATFORD-ON-AVON
Loco Shed
BINTON
BIDFORD-ON-AVON
MILCOTE
G.W.
LEOMINSTER
BERRINGTON & EYE
S. & H.-G.W. & L.N.W.J.
FENCOTE
STEENS BRIDGE
ROWDEN MILL
BROMYARD
KNIGHTWICK
LEIGH COURT
SUCKLEY
Leominster Jc.
BRANSFORD RD.
FORD BRIDGE
Dinmore Tun.
DINMORE
HEREFORD
MORETON-ON-LUGG
Brecon Curve Jc.
Barrs Ct.Jc. N.
Shelwick Jc.
CREDENHILL
WITHINGTON
MOORFIELDS (Gds)
BARTON (Gds)
Loco Shed
BARRS COURT
Barrs Ct.Jc. S
HEREFORD
Rotherwas Jc.
Red Hill Jc.
L & N.W.
HOLME LACY
STOKE EDITH
ASHPERTON
G.W.
COLWALL
G.W.
LEDBURY
MALVERN LINK
GREAT MALVERN
Malvern Jc.
MALVERN WELLS
MID
UPTON-ON-SEVERN
RIPPLE
Abbotswood Jc.
STOULTON
PERSHORE
WADBOROUGH
DEFFORD
ECKINGTON
BREDON
FLADBURY
HARVINGTON
EVESHAM
G.W.
MID.
LITTLETON & BADSEY
BENGEWORTH
HONEYBOURNE
HINTON
WESTON-SUB-EDGE
ASHTON-UNDER-HILL
BEACKFORD
BEACKFORD
LONG MARSTON
Campden Tun.
SHIPSTON-ON-STOUR
LONGDON ROAD
WILLERSLEY HALT
CAMPDEN
BROADWAY
LAVERTON HALT
BLOCKLEY
STRETTON-ON-FOSSE
TRAM INN
BALLINGHAM
FAWLEY
G.W.
DYMOCK
NEWENT
G.W.
TEWKESBURY
Level Crossing
ASHCHURCH
GRETTON HALT
Greet Tun.
TODDINGTON
WINCHCOMBE
GOTHERINGTON
CLEEVE
BISHOP'S CLEEVE
CHELTENHAM RACECOURSE
Hunting Butts Tun.
ST. JAMES'S
MALVERN ROAD
LANSDOWN
Honeybourne Line Jc.
Banbury Line Jc.
CHELTENHAM
CHURCHDOWN
CHELTENHAM S. & LECKHAMPTON
ANDOVERSFORD
NOTGROVE
Hatherley Curve Jc.
MORETON-IN-MARSH
Summit
G.W.
ADLESTROP
STOW-ON-THE-WOLD
KINGHAM
BOURTON-ON-THE-WATER
ROSS-ON-WYE
MITCHELDEAN ROAD
BARBER'S BRIDGE
LONGHOPE
KERNE BRIDGE
OAKLE STREET
Over Jc.
G.W.
MID.
LYDBROOK JUNC.
UPPER LYDBROOK
CINDERFORD
GRANGE COURT
Docks
Engine Shed Jc.
Level Crossing
MID.
GLOUCESTER
Tuffley Jc.
CHARLTON KINGS
ANDOVERSFORD & DOWDESWELL
WITHINGTON
GLOUCESTER
SYMOND'S YAT
DRYBROOK ROAD
Serridge Jc.
S.V.W.
31
30
29
CINDERFORD (S. & W.)
NEWNHAM
MAY HILL
MONMOUTH
TROY
COLEFORD FOR STAUNTON
SPEECH HOUSE RD.
25
26
27
28
BULLO PILL
Docks
NEWLAND
REDBROOK
DINGESTOW
MILKWALL FOR CLEARWELL SLING
PARKEND
WHITECROFT
Tufts Jcs.
N.
S.
ST. BRIAVELS & LLANDOGO
SEVERN BRIDGE
AWRE FOR BLAKENEY
HARESFIELD
Standish Jc.
CHEDWORTH
FOSS CROSS
MID. & S.W.
1 STONEHOUSE
2 EBLEY CROSSING HALT
3 DOWNFIELD CROSSING HALT
4 STROUD (G. W.)
5 RYEFORD
6 DUDBRIDGE
7 BOWBRIDGE CROSSING HALT
8 HAM MILL CROSSING HALT
9 BRIMSCOMBE BRIDGE HALT
10 BRIMSCOMBE
11 ST. MARY'S CROSSING HALT
12 CHALFORD
13 STROUD (MID.)
TOWN
Level Crossing
LYDNEY JUN.
Docks
Severn Bridge
STONEHOUSE Viaduct
FROCESTER
COALEY JUNC.
SHARPNESS
Docks
BERKELEY
Oldminster Jc.
1 2 3 4 5 6 13 7 G.W. 8 9 10 11 12
CAM
DURSLEY
WOODCHESTER
NAILSWORTH
Sapperton Tun.
Summit
CIRENCESTER
KELMSCOTT & LANGFORD
FAIRFORD
LECHLADE
G.W.
CERNEY & ASHTON KEYNES
TINTERN FOR BROCKWEIR
WOOLASTON
G.W.
TIDENHAM
BERKELEY ROAD
South Jc.
MID.
CHEPSTOW
Wye Valley Junc.
CHARFIELD
31 NAILBRIDGE HALT
30 STEAM MILLS CROSSING HALT
29 WHIMSEY HALT
28 BULLO CROSS HALT
27 UPPER SOUDLEY HALT
26 STAPLE EDGE HALT
25 RUSPIDGE HALT
RODMARTON PLAT.
CULKERTON
TETBURY
KEMBLE JUNC.
CRICKLADE
HANNINGTON
HIGHWORTH
THORNBURY
TYTHERINGTON
WICKWAR
Wickwar Tun.
STANTON
BLUNSDON
MINETY & ASHTON KEYNES
PURTON
STRATTON
SHRIVENHAM
SEVERN TUNNEL JC.
Loco Shed
PORTSKEWETT
SUDBROOK goods only
MALMESBURY
Severn Tunnel
PILNING
CHITTENING FACTORY PLATFORM
SEVERN BEACH
TOWN (Goods)
IRON ACTON
MID
YATE
Main Line Jc.
South Jc.
Westerleigh Jcs.
North Jc.
Sodbury Tun.
Alderton Tun.
LITTLE SOMERFORD
BRINKWORTH
HULLAVINGTON
GREAT SOMERFORD
Works
Junc.
Highworth Jc.
SWINDON
TOWN STA.
Rushey Platt Jc.
RUSHEY PLATT (Goods)
CHISELDON
AVONMOUTH
DOCK (Goods)
DOCK (Pass)
PATCHWAY
WINTER-BOURNE
E.Jc
W.Jc.
CHIPPING SODBURY
BADMINTON
WOOTTON BASSETT
DAUNTSEY
PORTISHEAD
HENBURY
FILTON JUNC.
COAL PIT HEATH
W.C.& P.
G.W.
SHIREHAMPTON
PORTBURY
SEA MILLS
ASHLEY HILL
FISH PONDS
STAPLE HILL
Westerleigh Junc.
PILL
CLIFTON DOWN
MANGOTSFIELD
CLAPTON RD
WILTSHIRE
G.W.

Eight Three

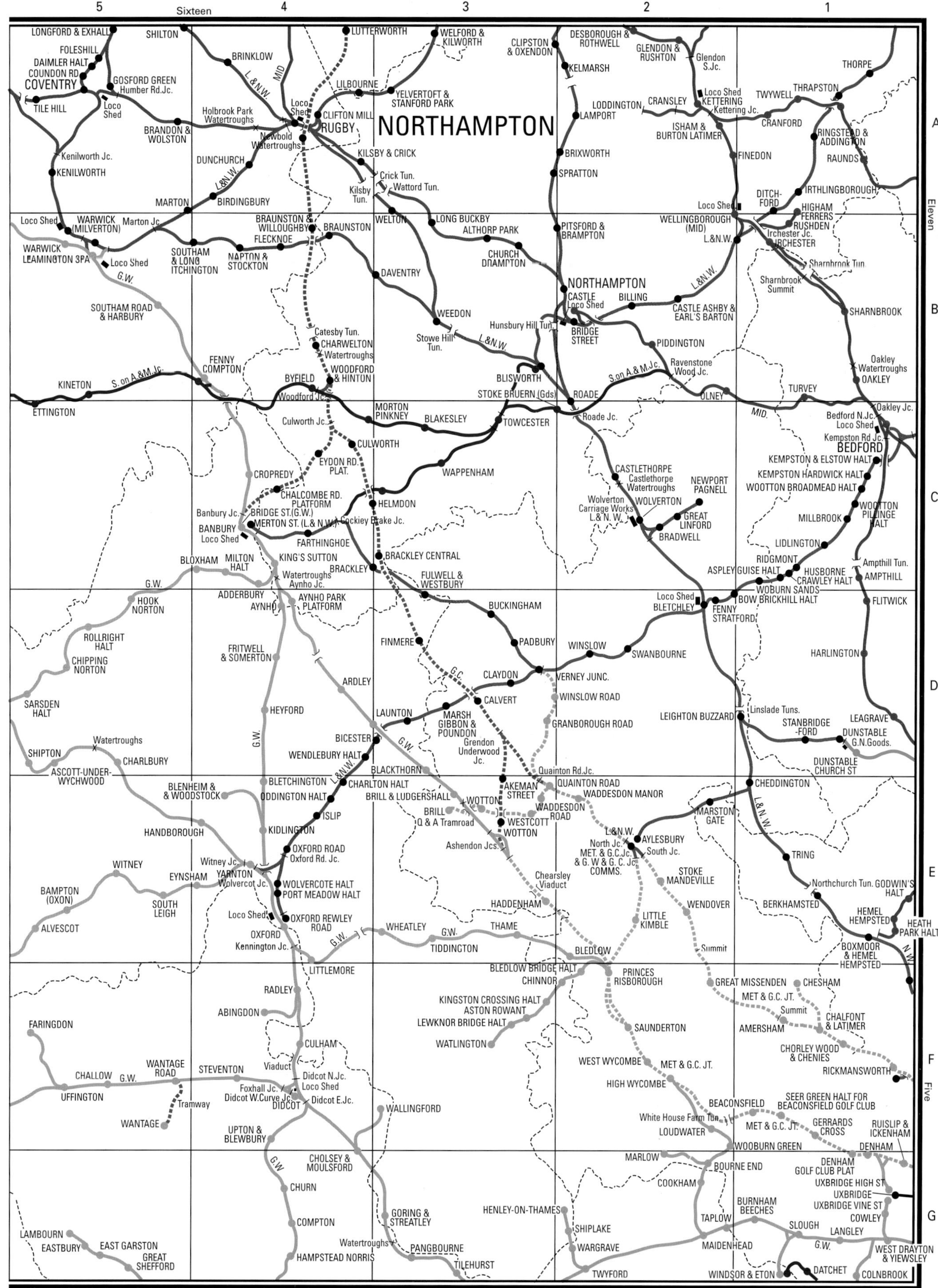
5
Sixteen
4
3
2
1
LONGFORD & EXHALL
SHILTON
LUTTERWORTH
WELFORD & KILWORTH
CLIPSTON & OXENDON
DESBOROUGH & ROTHWELL
GLENDON & RUSHTON
Glendon S.Jc.
THORPE
FOLESHILL
DAIMLER HALT
COUNDON RD
COVENTRY
GOSFORD GREEN
Humber Rd.Jc.
BRINKLOW
L.&N.W.
MID
KELMARSH
TILE HILL
Loco Shed
Holbrook Park Watertroughs
LILBOURNE
YELVERTOFT & STANFORD PARK
Loco Shed
KETTERING
Kettering Jc.
TWYWELL
THRAPSTON
LODDINGTON
CRANSLEY
LAMPORT
CLIFTON MILL
RUGBY
NORTHAMPTON
BRANDON & WOLSTON
Newbold Watertroughs
ISHAM & BURTON LATIMER
CRANFORD
RINGSTEAD & ADDINGTON
A
Kenilworth Jc.
DUNCHURCH
KILSBY & CRICK
BRIXWORTH
FINEDON
RAUNDS
KENILWORTH
Crick Tun.
Wattord Tun.
Kilsby Tun.
SPRATTON
DITCH-FORD
IRTHLINGBOROUGH
MARTON
BIRDINGBURY
Loco Shed
HIGHAM FERRERS
RUSHDEN
Loco Shed
WARWICK (MILVERTON)
Marton Jc.
BRAUNSTON & WILLOUGHBY
BRAUNSTON
WELTON
LONG BUCKBY
ALTHORP PARK
PITSFORD & BRAMPTON
WELLINGBOROUGH (MID)
L.&N.W.
Irchester Jc.
IRCHESTER
Eleven
WARWICK
LEAMINGTON SPA
Loco Shed
SOUTHAM & LONG ITCHINGTON
NAPTON & STOCKTON
FLECKNOE
CHURCH BRAMPTON
Sharnbrook Tun.
G.W.
DAVENTRY
NORTHAMPTON
CASTLE
Loco Shed
BILLING
Sharnbrook Summit
SOUTHAM ROAD & HARBURY
WEEDON
Hunsbury Hill Tun.
BRIDGE STREET
CASTLE ASHBY & EARL'S BARTON
SHARNBROOK
B
Catesby Tun.
CHARWELTON
Watertroughs
Stowe Hill Tun.
PIDDINGTON
FENNY COMPTON
WOODFORD & HINTON
Ravenstone Wood Jc.
Oakley Watertroughs
OAKLEY
KINETON
S. on A.&M.Jc.
BYFIELD
BLISWORTH
S.on A.&M.Jc.
STOKE BRUERN (Gds)
ROADE
TURVEY
Woodford Jc.
OLNEY
MID.
Oakley Jc.
ETTINGTON
MORTON PINKNEY
BLAKESLEY
Roade Jc.
Bedford N.Jc.
Loco Shed
Culworth Jc.
TOWCESTER
Kempston Rd Jc.
BEDFORD
CULWORTH
EYDON RD. PLAT.
KEMPSTON & ELSTOW HALT
CASTLETHORPE
Castlethorpe Watertroughs
CROPREDY
WAPPENHAM
KEMPSTON HARDWICK HALT
NEWPORT PAGNELL
WOOTTON BROADMEAD HALT
CHALCOMBE RD. PLATFORM
HELMDON
Wolverton Carriage Works
L.& N. W.
WOLVERTON
C
WOOTTON PILLINGE HALT
Banbury Jc.
BRIDGE ST.(G.W.)
MERTON ST. (L.& N.W.)
Cockley Brake Jc.
GREAT LINFORD
MILLBROOK
BANBURY
Loco Shed
FARTHINGHOE
BRADWELL
LIDLINGTON
BRACKLEY CENTRAL
RIDGMONT
BLOXHAM
MILTON HALT
KING'S SUTTON
BRACKLEY
ASPLEY GUISE HALT
HUSBORNE CRAWLEY HALT
Ampthill Tun.
AMPTHILL
Watertroughs
Aynho Jc.
FULWELL & WESTBURY
G.W.
WOBURN SANDS
HOOK NORTON
ADDERBURY
AYNHO PARK PLATFORM
AYNHO
Loco Shed
BLETCHLEY
FENNY STRATFORD
BOW BRICKHILL HALT
FLITWICK
BUCKINGHAM
ROLLRIGHT HALT
FRITWELL & SOMERTON
FINMERE
PADBURY
WINSLOW
SWANBOURNE
CHIPPING NORTON
HARLINGTON
G.C.
CLAYDON
VERNEY JUNC.
ARDLEY
D
SARSDEN HALT
WINSLOW ROAD
CALVERT
HEYFORD
LAUNTON
MARSH GIBBON & POUNDON
LEIGHTON BUZZARD
Linslade Tuns.
LEAGRAVE
GRANBOROUGH ROAD
STANBRIDGE -FORD
DUNSTABLE G.N.Goods.
Grendon Underwood Jc.
Watertroughs
BICESTER
G.W.
SHIPTON
CHARLBURY
WENDLEBURY HALT
DUNSTABLE CHURCH ST
ASCOTT-UNDER-WYCHWOOD
Quainton Rd.Jc.
BLACKTHORN
AKEMAN STREET
QUAINTON ROAD
CHEDDINGTON
BLENHEIM & WOODSTOCK
BLETCHINGTON
CHARLTON HALT
L.&N.W.
ODDINGTON HALT
WADDESDON MANOR
BRILL & LUDGERSHALL
WOTTON
MARSTON GATE
ISLIP
BRILL
WADDESDON ROAD
HANDBOROUGH
O & A Tramroad
WESTCOTT
WOTTON
L.&N.W.
AYLESBURY
KIDLINGTON
Ashendon Jcs.
North Jc.
MET. & G.C.Jc.
South Jc.
G. W & G. C. Jc.
COMMS.
TRING
WITNEY
OXFORD ROAD
Oxford Rd. Jc.
Witney Jc.
EYNSHAM
YARNTON
Wolvercot Jc.
STOKE MANDEVILLE
E
WOLVERCOTE HALT
Chearsley Viaduct
BAMPTON (OXON)
PORT MEADOW HALT
Northchurch Tun.
GODWIN'S HALT
SOUTH LEIGH
HADDENHAM
WENDOVER
BERKHAMSTED
Loco Shed
OXFORD REWLEY ROAD
LITTLE KIMBLE
HEMEL HEMPSTED
HEATH PARK HALT
ALVESCOT
OXFORD
WHEATLEY
THAME
G.W.
Kennington Jc.
TIDDINGTON
BLEDLOW
Summit
BOXMOOR & HEMEL HEMPSTED
LITTLEMORE
BLEDLOW BRIDGE HALT
CHINNOR
PRINCES RISBOROUGH
GREAT MISSENDEN
CHESHAM
RADLEY
MET & G.C. JT.
KINGSTON CROSSING HALT
ASTON ROWANT
Summit
ABINGDON
CHALFONT & LATIMER
FARINGDON
LEWKNOR BRIDGE HALT
SAUNDERTON
AMERSHAM
WATLINGTON
CULHAM
CHORLEY WOOD & CHENIES
F
WANTAGE ROAD
STEVENTON
Viaduct
WEST WYCOMBE
MET & G.C. JT.
RICKMANSWORTH
CHALLOW
G.W.
Didcot N.Jc.
Foxhall Jc.
Loco Shed
UFFINGTON
Didcot W.Curve Jc.
DIDCOT
Didcot E.Jc.
HIGH WYCOMBE
Five
Tramway
WALLINGFORD
BEACONSFIELD
SEER GREEN HALT FOR BEACONSFIELD GOLF CLUB
WANTAGE
White House Farm Tun.
MET & G.C. JT.
GERRARDS CROSS
RUISLIP & ICKENHAM
UPTON & BLEWBURY
LOUDWATER
WOOBURN GREEN
DENHAM
CHOLSEY & MOULSFORD
MARLOW
BOURNE END
DENHAM GOLF CLUB PLAT
G.W.
CHURN
COOKHAM
UXBRIDGE HIGH ST
UXBRIDGE
UXBRIDGE VINE ST
GORING & STREATLEY
HENLEY-ON-THAMES
BURNHAM BEECHES
G
COMPTON
SHIPLAKE
TAPLOW
COWLEY
SLOUGH
LAMBOURN
Watertroughs
LANGLEY
EASTBURY
EAST GARSTON
PANGBOURNE
WARGRAVE
MAIDENHEAD
G.W.
WEST DRAYTON & YIEWSLEY
GREAT SHEFFORD
HAMPSTEAD NORRIS
TILEHURST
TWYFORD
WINDSOR & ETON
DATCHET
COLNBROOK
Four

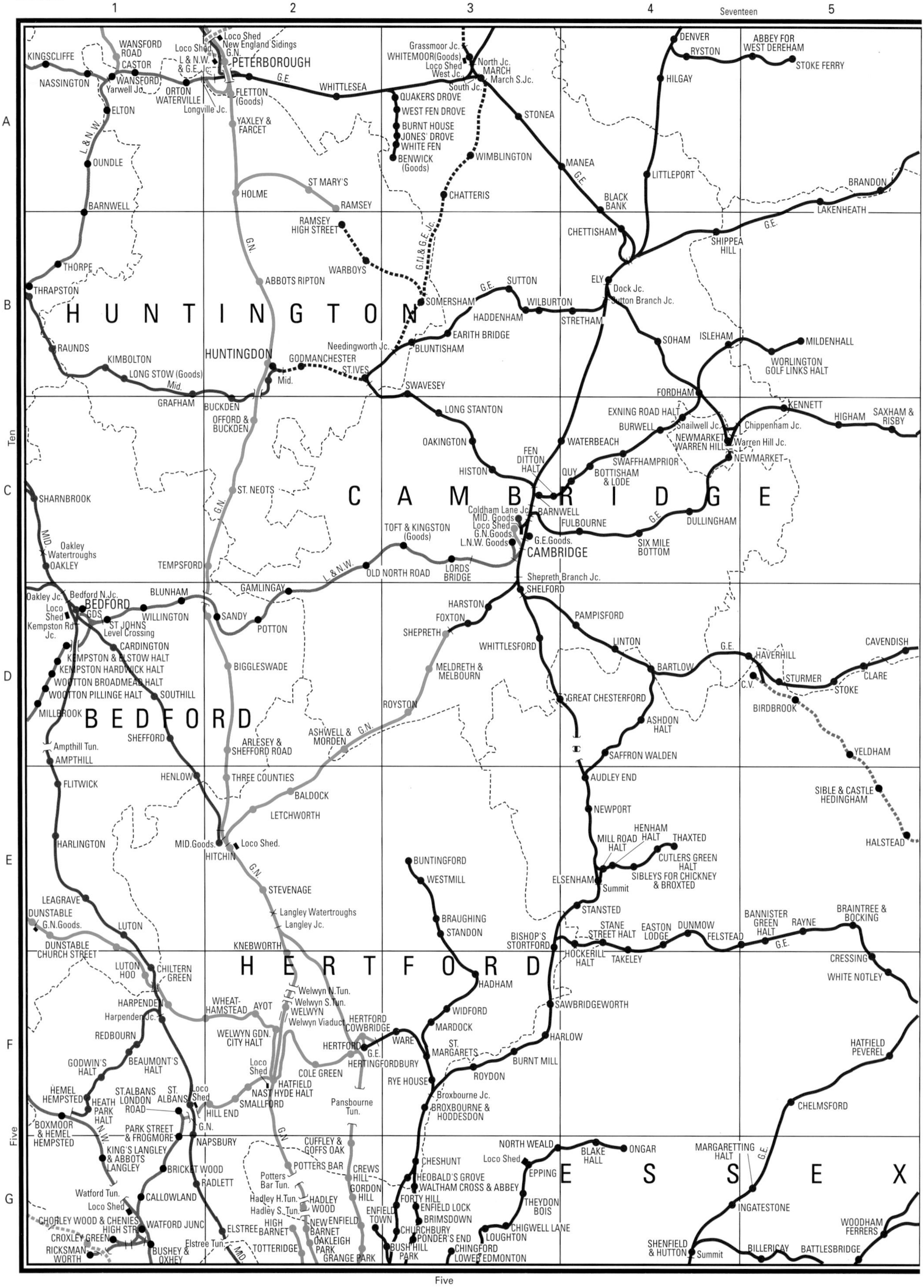

1 2 3 4 Seventeen 5

A

KINGSCLIFFE
WANSFORD ROAD
CASTOR
WANSFORD
Yarwell Jc.
NASSINGTON
ELTON
L. & N.W.
OUNDLE
BARNWELL
Loco Shed
New England Sidings
Loco Shed
L. & N.W. & G.E. Jc.
G.N.
PETERBOROUGH
ORTON WATERVILLE
Longville Jc.
FLETTON (Goods)
YAXLEY & FARCET
G.E.
HOLME
ST MARY'S
RAMSEY
WHITTLESEA
Grassmoor Jc.
WHITEMOOR (Goods)
Loco Shed
West Jc.
North Jc.
MARCH
March S.Jc.
South Jc.
QUAKERS DROVE
WEST FEN DROVE
BURNT HOUSE
JONES' DROVE
WHITE FEN
BENWICK (Goods)
WIMBLINGTON
CHATTERIS
STONEA
MANEA
G.E.
BLACK BANK
DENVER
RYSTON
ABBEY FOR WEST DEREHAM
STOKE FERRY
HILGAY
LITTLEPORT
BRANDON
LAKENHEATH

B

THORPE
THRAPSTON
H U N T I N G T O N
RAUNDS
KIMBOLTON
LONG STOW (Goods)
Mid.
GRAFHAM
RAMSEY HIGH STREET
WARBOYS
G.N.
ABBOTS RIPTON
G.N.& G.E. Jc.
SOMERSHAM
HUNTINGDON
Mid.
GODMANCHESTER
Needingworth Jc.
ST. IVES
BLUNTISHAM
EARITH BRIDGE
G.E.
SUTTON
HADDENHAM
WILBURTON
STRETHAM
CHETTISHAM
ELY
Dock Jc.
Sutton Branch Jc.
SHIPPEA HILL
G.E.
SOHAM
ISLEHAM
MILDENHALL
WORLINGTON GOLF LINKS HALT
SWAVESEY
FORDHAM

Ten

C

BUCKDEN
OFFORD & BUCKDEN
LONG STANTON
OAKINGTON
HISTON
FEN DITTON HALT
WATERBEACH
EXNING ROAD HALT
BURWELL
Snailwell Jc.
NEWMARKET WARREN HILL
KENNETT
Chippenham Jc.
Warren Hill Jc.
HIGHAM
SAXHAM & RISBY
SWAFFHAMPRIOR
QUY
BOTTISHAM & LODE
NEWMARKET
SHARNBROOK
MID.
Oakley Watertroughs
OAKLEY
G.N.
ST. NEOTS
C A M B R I D G E
Coldham Lane Jc.
MID. Goods
Loco Shed
G.N.Goods
L.N.W. Goods
BARNWELL
G.E.Goods.
CAMBRIDGE
FULBOURNE
G.E.
DULLINGHAM
SIX MILE BOTTOM
TOFT & KINGSTON (Goods)
TEMPSFORD
L. & N.W.
OLD NORTH ROAD
LORDS BRIDGE
Shepreth Branch Jc.

D

Oakley Jc.
Bedford N.Jc.
BEDFORD
Loco Shed
GDS
Kempston Rd Jc.
ST JOHNS
Level Crossing
BLUNHAM
WILLINGTON
CARDINGTON
KEMPSTON & ELSTOW HALT
KEMPSTON HARDWICK HALT
WOOTTON BROADMEAD HALT
WOOTTON PILLINGE HALT
SOUTHILL
MILLBROOK
B E D F O R D
SHEFFORD
GAMLINGAY
SANDY
POTTON
BIGGLESWADE
ARLESEY & SHEFFORD ROAD
HARSTON
FOXTON
SHEPRETH
SHELFORD
PAMPISFORD
WHITTLESFORD
LINTON
MELDRETH & MELBOURN
ROYSTON
ASHWELL & MORDEN
G.N.
GREAT CHESTERFORD
BARTLOW
G.E.
HAVERHILL
CAVENDISH
C.V.
STURMER
CLARE
STOKE
BIRDBROOK
ASHDON HALT
Ampthill Tun.
AMPTHILL
SAFFRON WALDEN
YELDHAM

E

FLITWICK
HENLOW
THREE COUNTIES
BALDOCK
LETCHWORTH
AUDLEY END
NEWPORT
SIBLE & CASTLE HEDINGHAM
HARLINGTON
MID.Goods
Loco Shed.
HITCHIN
G.N.
BUNTINGFORD
WESTMILL
MILL ROAD HALT
HENHAM HALT
THAXTED
CUTLERS GREEN HALT
SIBLEYS FOR CHICKNEY & BROXTED
ELSENHAM
Summit
HALSTEAD
LEAGRAVE
DUNSTABLE
G.N.Goods.
LUTON
STEVENAGE
Langley Watertroughs
Langley Jc.
STANSTED
BRAUGHING
STANDON
BISHOP'S STORTFORD
STANE STREET HALT
EASTON LODGE
DUNMOW
FELSTEAD
BANNISTER GREEN HALT
RAYNE
BRAINTREE & BOCKING
G.E.
DUNSTABLE CHURCH STREET
KNEBWORTH
HOCKERILL HALT
TAKELEY
CRESSING
WHITE NOTLEY

F

LUTON HOO
CHILTERN GREEN
H E R T F O R D
HADHAM
HARPENDEN
Harpenden Jc.
WHEAT-HAMSTEAD
AYOT
Welwyn N.Tun.
Welwyn S.Tun.
WELWYN
Welwyn Viaduct
SAWBRIDGEWORTH
WIDFORD
MARDOCK
REDBOURN
WELWYN GDN. CITY HALT
HERTFORD COWBRIDGE
HERTFORD
G.E.
HERTINGFORDBURY
WARE
ST. MARGARETS
HARLOW
BURNT MILL
HATFIELD PEVEREL
GODWIN'S HALT
BEAUMONT'S HALT
Loco Shed
COLE GREEN
RYE HOUSE
ROYDON
HEMEL HEMPSTED
HEATH PARK HALT
ST.ALBANS LONDON ROAD
ST. ALBANS
Loco Shed
HATFIELD
NAST HYDE HALT
SMALLFORD
HILL END
Broxbourne Jc.
BROXBOURNE & HODDESDON
CHELMSFORD
Pansbourne Tun.
BOXMOOR & HEMEL HEMPSTED
L.N.W.
PARK STREET & FROGMORE
G.N.
NAPSBURY

Five

G

KING'S LANGLEY & ABBOTS LANGLEY
BRICKET WOOD
RADLETT
G.N.
POTTERS BAR
CUFFLEY & GOFFS OAK
CREWS HILL
GORDON HILL
CHESHUNT
NORTH WEALD
BLAKE HALL
ONGAR
Loco Shed
EPPING
E S S E X
MARGARETTING HALT
G.E.
THEOBALD'S GROVE
WALTHAM CROSS & ABBEY
Watford Tun.
Loco Shed
CALLOWLAND
Potters Bar Tun.
Hadley H.Tun.
Hadley S.Tun.
HADLEY WOOD
FORTY HILL
ENFIELD LOCK
BRIMSDOWN
THEYDON BOIS
INGATESTONE
CHORLEY WOOD & CHENIES
HIGH STREET
WATFORD JUNC
ELSTREE
HIGH BARNET
NEW BARNET
ENFIELD
ENFIELD TOWN
CHURCHBURY
PONDER'S END
CHIGWELL LANE
LOUGHTON
WOODHAM FERRERS
CROXLEY GREEN
RICKSMANWORTH
BUSHEY & OXHEY
Elstree Tun.
MID.
TOTTERIDGE
OAKLEIGH PARK
GRANGE PARK
BUSH HILL PARK
CHINGFORD
LOWER EDMONTON
SHENFIELD & HUTTON
Summit
BILLERICAY
BATTLESBRIDGE

Five

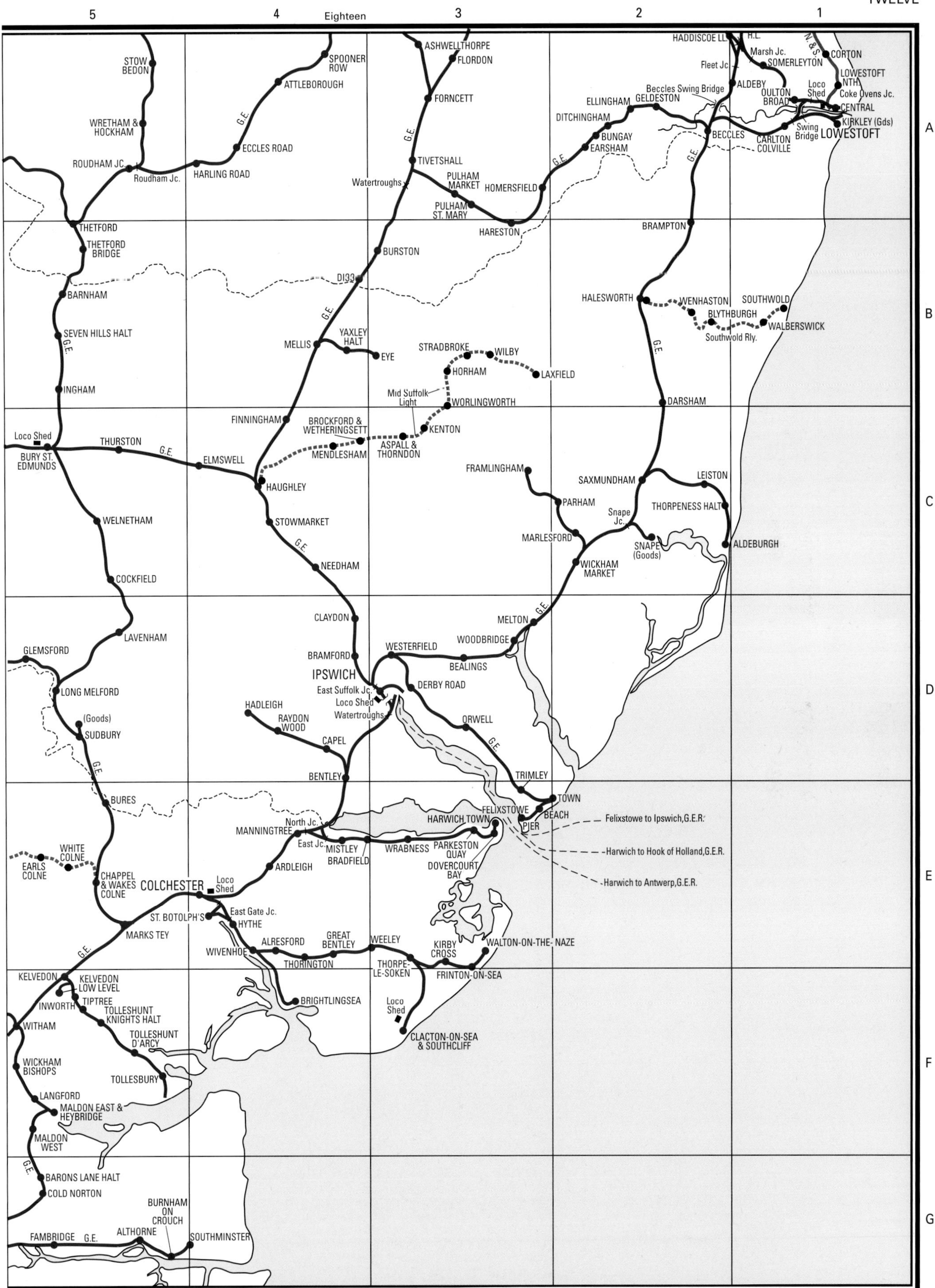
5
4
Eighteen
3
2
1
A
B
C
D
E
F
G
Six
STOW BEDON
WRETHAM & HOCKHAM
ROUDHAM JC.
Roudham Jc.
THETFORD
THETFORD BRIDGE
BARNHAM
SEVEN HILLS HALT
INGHAM
Loco Shed
BURY ST. EDMUNDS
THURSTON
ELMSWELL
SPOONER ROW
ATTLEBOROUGH
ECCLES ROAD
HARLING ROAD
ASHWELLTHORPE
FLORDON
FORNCETT
TIVETSHALL
Watertroughs
PULHAM MARKET
PULHAM ST. MARY
HOMERSFIELD
HARESTON
BURSTON
DISS
MELLIS
YAXLEY HALT
EYE
STRADBROKE
WILBY
HORHAM
LAXFIELD
Mid Suffolk Light
WORLINGWORTH
KENTON
FINNINGHAM
BROCKFORD & WETHERINGSETT
MENDLESHAM
ASPALL & THORNDON
HAUGHLEY
STOWMARKET
NEEDHAM
CLAYDON
BRAMFORD
IPSWICH
East Suffolk Jc.
Loco Shed
Watertroughs
WESTERFIELD
DERBY ROAD
BEALINGS
WOODBRIDGE
MELTON
ORWELL
TRIMLEY
TOWN
BEACH
FELIXSTOWE
PIER
HADLEIGH
RAYDON WOOD
CAPEL
BENTLEY
WELNETHAM
COCKFIELD
LAVENHAM
GLEMSFORD
LONG MELFORD
(Goods)
SUDBURY
BURES
WHITE COLNE
EARLS COLNE
CHAPPEL & WAKES COLNE
COLCHESTER
Loco Shed
MARKS TEY
ST. BOTOLPH'S
East Gate Jc.
HYTHE
ARDLEIGH
MANNINGTREE
North Jc.
East Jc.
MISTLEY
BRADFIELD
WRABNESS
PARKESTON QUAY
HARWICH TOWN
DOVERCOURT BAY
Felixstowe to Ipswich,G.E.R.
Harwich to Hook of Holland,G.E.R.
Harwich to Antwerp,G.E.R.
WIVENHOE
ALRESFORD
GREAT BENTLEY
WEELEY
THORINGTON
BRIGHTLINGSEA
THORPE-LE-SOKEN
KIRBY CROSS
WALTON-ON-THE-NAZE
FRINTON-ON-SEA
Loco Shed
CLACTON-ON-SEA & SOUTHCLIFF
KELVEDON
KELVEDON LOW LEVEL
INWORTH
TIPTREE
TOLLESHUNT KNIGHTS HALT
TOLLESHUNT D'ARCY
TOLLESBURY
WITHAM
WICKHAM BISHOPS
LANGFORD
MALDON EAST & HEYBRIDGE
MALDON WEST
BARONS LANE HALT
COLD NORTON
BURNHAM ON CROUCH
SOUTHMINSTER
ALTHORNE
FAMBRIDGE
G.E.
HADDISCOE LL
H.L.
N.&S.
Marsh Jc.
SOMERLEYTON
CORTON
Fleet Jc.
ALDEBY
LOWESTOFT NTH.
Coke Ovens Jc.
Loco Shed
OULTON BROAD
CENTRAL
KIRKLEY (Gds)
Swing Bridge
LOWESTOFT
CARLTON COLVILLE
Beccles Swing Bridge
ELLINGHAM
GELDESTON
DITCHINGHAM
BUNGAY
EARSHAM
BECCLES
BRAMPTON
HALESWORTH
WENHASTON
SOUTHWOLD
BLYTHBURGH
WALBERSWICK
Southwold Rly.
DARSHAM
FRAMLINGHAM
SAXMUNDHAM
LEISTON
PARHAM
THORPENESS HALT
Snape Jc.
SNAPE (Goods)
ALDEBURGH
MARLESFORD
WICKHAM MARKET

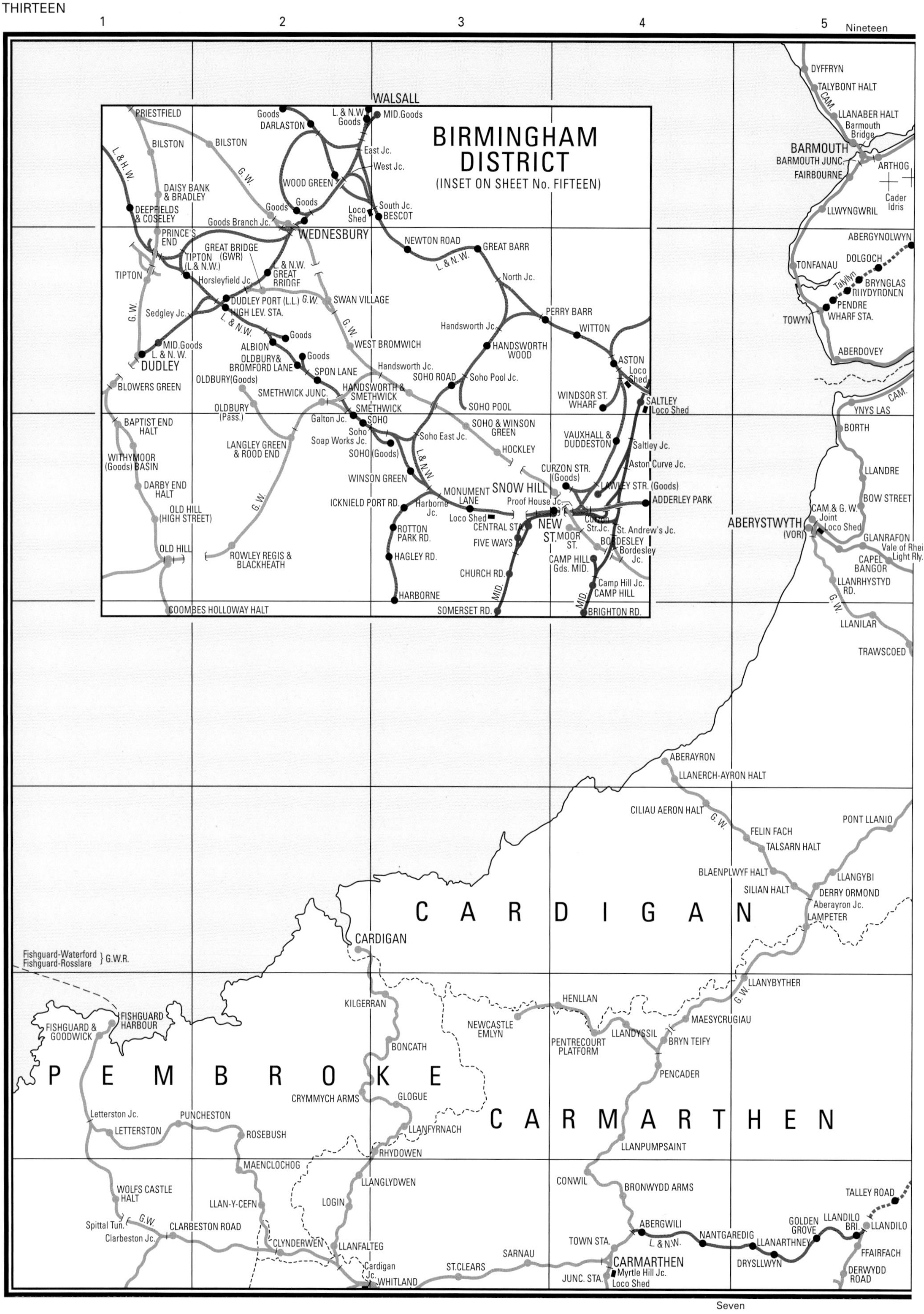

1 2 3 4 5 Nineteen

A B C D E F G

BIRMINGHAM DISTRICT

(INSET ON SHEET No. FIFTEEN)

WALSALL
MID.Goods
L. & N.W. Goods
PRIESTFIELD
Goods
DARLASTON
East Jc.
West Jc.
BILSTON
BILSTON
L.& N.W.
G.W.
WOOD GREEN
DAISY BANK & BRADLEY
DEEPFIELDS & COSELEY
Goods
Goods
Loco Shed
South Jc.
BESCOT
Goods Branch Jc.
WEDNESBURY
PRINCE'S END
NEWTON ROAD
GREAT BARR
L.& N.W.
GREAT BRIDGE (GWR)
TIPTON (L.& N.W.)
L. & N.W. GREAT BRIDGE
TIPTON
Horsleyfield Jc.
North Jc.
DUDLEY PORT (L.L.)
G.W.
SWAN VILLAGE
HIGH LEV. STA.
PERRY BARR
G.W.
Sedgley Jc.
L.& N.W.
Goods
G.W.
WITTON
Handsworth Jc.
MID.Goods
L. & N. W.
DUDLEY
ALBION
WEST BROMWICH
HANDSWORTH WOOD
ASTON
Goods
OLDBURY& BROMFORD LANE
SPON LANE
Handsworth Jc.
Loco Shed
BLOWERS GREEN
OLDBURY(Goods)
SOHO ROAD
Soho Pool Jc.
SMETHWICK JUNC.
HANDSWORTH & SMETHWICK
WINDSOR ST. WHARF
SALTLEY
Loco Shed
OLDBURY (Pass.)
SMETHWICK
SOHO POOL
BAPTIST END HALT
Galton Jc.
SOHO
SOHO & WINSON GREEN
WITHYMOOR (Goods) BASIN
LANGLEY GREEN & ROOD END
Soho Soap Works Jc.
Soho East Jc.
VAUXHALL & DUDDESTON
Saltley Jc.
SOHO (Goods)
HOCKLEY
L.& N.W.
Aston Curve Jc.
DARBY END HALT
WINSON GREEN
CURZON STR. (Goods)
LAWLEY STR. (Goods)
OLD HILL (HIGH STREET)
G.W.
ICKNIELD PORT RD.
MONUMENT LANE
SNOW HILL
ADDERLEY PARK
Harborne Jc.
Proof House Jc.
Loco Shed
CENTRAL STA.
NEW ST.
Curzon Str.Jc.
St. Andrew's Jc.
ROTTON PARK RD.
FIVE WAYS
MOOR ST.
BORDESLEY
OLD HILL
ROWLEY REGIS & BLACKHEATH
HAGLEY RD.
Bordesley Jc.
CAMP HILL Gds. MID.
CHURCH RD.
Camp Hill Jc.
CAMP HILL
MID.
HARBORNE
MID.
COOMBES HOLLOWAY HALT
SOMERSET RD.
BRIGHTON RD.

DYFFRYN
TALYBONT HALT
CAM.
LLANABER HALT
Barmouth Bridge
BARMOUTH
BARMOUTH JUNC.
ARTHOG
FAIRBOURNE
Cader Idris
LLWYNGWRIL
ABERGYNOLWYN
DOLGOCH
TONFANAU
Talyllyn
BRYNGLAS
RHYDYRONEN
PENDRE
TOWYN
WHARF STA.
ABERDOVEY
CAM.
YNYS LAS
BORTH
LLANDRE
BOW STREET
CAM.& G. W. Joint Loco Shed
ABERYSTWYTH (VOR)
GLANRAFON
Vale of Rheidol Light Rly.
CAPEL BANGOR
LLANRHYSTYD RD.
G.W.
LLANILAR
TRAWSCOED

ABERAYRON
LLANERCH-AYRON HALT
CILIAU AERON HALT
G.W.
PONT LLANIO
FELIN FACH
TALSARN HALT
BLAENPLWYF HALT
LLANGYBI
SILIAN HALT
DERRY ORMOND
Aberayron Jc.
LAMPETER

C A R D I G A N

CARDIGAN
Fishguard-Waterford
Fishguard-Rosslare } G.W.R.
LLANYBYTHER
G.W.
KILGERRAN
HENLLAN
FISHGUARD HARBOUR
FISHGUARD & GOODWICK
NEWCASTLE EMLYN
MAESYCRUGIAU
LLANDYSSIL
PENTRECOURT PLATFORM
BRYN TEIFY
BONCATH

P E M B R O K E

PENCADER
CRYMMYCH ARMS
GLOGUE
Letterston Jc.
PUNCHESTON

C A R M A R T H E N

LETTERSTON
LLANFYRNACH
ROSEBUSH
LLANPUMPSAINT
RHYDOWEN
MAENCLOCHOG
LLANGLYDWEN
CONWIL
BRONWYDD ARMS
WOLFS CASTLE HALT
TALLEY ROAD
LLAN-Y-CEFN
LOGIN
G.W.
Spittal Tun.
CLARBESTON ROAD
Clarbeston Jc.
ABERGWILI
GOLDEN GROVE
LLANDILO BRI.
LLANDILO
NANTGAREDIG
CLYNDERWEN
LLANFALTEG
TOWN STA.
L.& N.W.
LLANARTHNEY
SARNAU
CARMARTHEN
DRYSLLWYN
FFAIRFACH
Cardigan Jc.
ST.CLEARS
Myrtle Hill Jc.
DERWYDD ROAD
WHITLAND
JUNC. STA.
Loco Shed

Seven

5
Nineteen
4
3
2
Twenty
1
MONTGOMERY
RADNOR
HEREFORD
BRECKNOCK
1 LLANRHAIADR MOCHNANT
2 PENTREFELIN
3 LLANGEDWYN
4 LLANSILIN ROAD
5 GLANYRAFON
6 LLANYBLODWELL
7 BLODWELL JC.
8 PORTHYWAEN
9 PANT
MACHYNLLETH
LLANIDLOES
CRAVEN ARMS & STOKESAY
BRECON
A
B
C
D
E
F
G
Fifteen
Nine
Seven
Eight

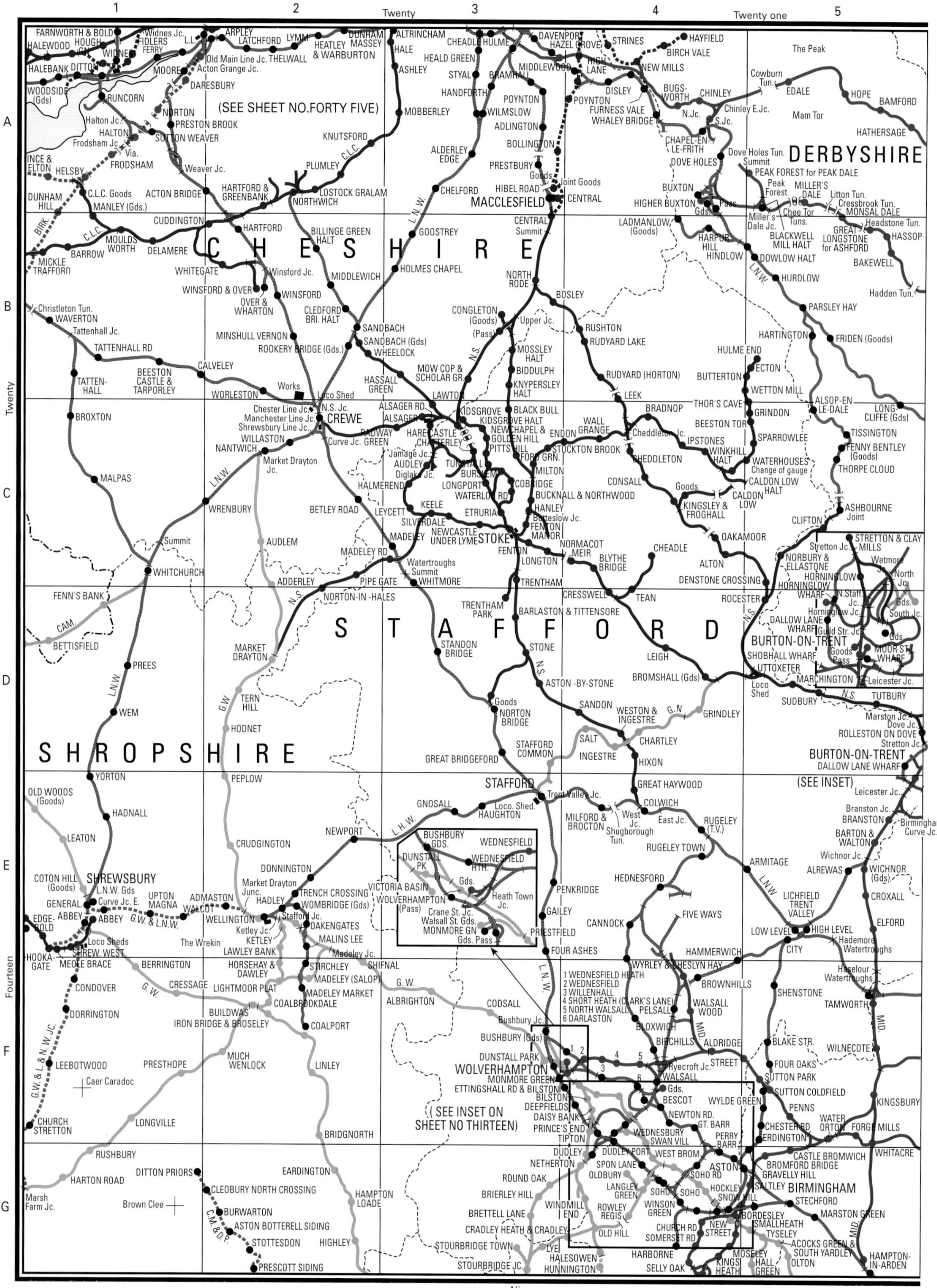
1
2
3
4
5
Twenty
Twenty one
A
B
C
D
E
F
G
Twenty
Fourteen
Nine
CHESHIRE
STAFFORD
SHROPSHIRE
DERBYSHIRE
(SEE SHEET NO.FORTY FIVE)
FARNWORTH & BOLD
HALEWOOD
HOUGH GN.
Widnes Jc.
FIDLERS FERRY
WIDNES
L.L.
ARPLEY
LATCHFORD
LYMM
DUNHAM MASSEY
HEATLEY & WARBURTON
Old Main Line Jc.
THELWALL
Acton Grange Jc.
HALEBANK
DITTON
MOORE
DARESBURY
WOODSIDE (Gds)
RUNCORN
NORTON
PRESTON BROOK
SUTTON WEAVER
Halton Jc.
HALTON
Frodsham Jc.
Via.
FRODSHAM
Weaver Jc.
INCE & ELTON
HELSBY
DUNHAM HILL
C.L.C. Goods
MANLEY (Gds.)
ACTON BRIDGE
HARTFORD & GREENBANK
NORTHWICH
LOSTOCK GRALAM
PLUMLEY
KNUTSFORD
C.L.C.
CUDDINGTON
HARTFORD
MOULDSWORTH
BARROW
DELAMERE
MICKLE TRAFFORD
BIRK.
WHITEGATE
Winsford Jc.
WINSFORD & OVER
OVER & WHARTON
WINSFORD
MIDDLEWICH
BILLINGE GREEN HALT
CLEDFORD BRI. HALT
Christleton Tun.
WAVERTON
Tattenhall Jc.
TATTENHALL RD
MINSHULL VERNON
ROOKERY BRIDGE (Gds.)
SANDBACH
SANDBACH (Gds)
WHEELOCK
TATTEN-HALL
BEESTON CASTLE & TARPORLEY
CALVELEY
WORLESTON
Works
Loco Shed
Chester Line Jc.
Manchester Line Jc.
Shrewsbury Line Jc.
N.S. Jc.
CREWE
Curve Jc.
WILLASTON
NANTWICH
Market Drayton Jc.
BROXTON
MALPAS
WRENBURY
L.N.W.
Summit
WHITCHURCH
AUDLEM
ADDERLEY
FENN'S BANK
CAM.
BETTISFIELD
PREES
WEM
YORTON
HADNALL
OLD WOODS (Goods)
LEATON
ALTRINCHAM
HALE
ASHLEY
MOBBERLEY
CHEADLE HULME
HEALD GREEN
STYAL
HANDFORTH
BRAMHALL
POYNTON
WILMSLOW
ADLINGTON
ALDERLEY EDGE
CHELFORD
L.N.W.
GOOSTREY
HOLMES CHAPEL
PRESTBURY
BOLLINGTON
Goods
Joint Goods
HIBEL ROAD
MACCLESFIELD
CENTRAL
CENTRAL Summit
NORTH RODE
BOSLEY
CONGLETON (Goods)
(Pass)
Upper Jc.
N.S.
MOSSLEY HALT
BIDDULPH
KNYPERSLEY HALT
BLACK BULL
RUSHTON
RUDYARD LAKE
RUDYARD (HORTON)
LEEK
MOW COP & SCHOLAR GR.
HASSALL GREEN
LAWTON
ALSAGER RD.
ALSAGER
RADWAY GREEN
HARECASTLE
CHATTERLEY
KIDSGROVE
KIDSGROVE HALT
NEWCHAPEL & GOLDEN HILL
PITTS HILL
FORD GRN.
ENDON
WALL GRANGE
STOCKTON BROOK
Jamage Jc.
AUDLEY
Diglake Jc.
TUNSTALL
BURSLEM
LONGPORT
WATERLOO RD
COBRIDGE
MILTON
HALMEREND
BETLEY ROAD
LEYCETT
KEELE
ETRURIA
BUCKNALL & NORTHWOOD
HANLEY
Botteslow Jc.
SILVERDALE
NEWCASTLE UNDER LYME
STOKE
FENTON MANOR
FENTON
MADELEY
MADELEY RD
NORMACOT
MEIR
LONGTON
Watertroughs Summit
WHITMORE
PIPE GATE
NORTON-IN-HALES
N.S.
TRENTHAM
TRENTHAM PARK
BARLASTON & TITTENSORE
STANDON BRIDGE
MARKET DRAYTON
STONE
N.S.
ASTON-BY-STONE
Goods
NORTH BRIDGE
G.W.
TERN HILL
HODNET
PEPLOW
CRUDGINGTON
STAFFORD COMMON
GREAT BRIDGEFORD
STAFFORD
Trent Valley Jc.
Loco. Shed.
HAUGHTON
GNOSALL
L.N.W.
NEWPORT
DAVENPORT
HAZEL GROVE
HIGH LANE
MIDDLEWOOD
STRINES
HAYFIELD
BIRCH VALE
NEW MILLS
DISLEY
POYNTON
FURNESS VALE
WHALEY BRIDGE
BUGSWORTH
CHINLEY
Chinley E.Jc.
N.Jc.
S.Jc.
CHAPEL-EN-LE-FRITH
DOVE HOLES
Dove Holes Tun.
Summit
Cowburn Tun.
EDALE
HOPE
BAMFORD
The Peak
Mam Tor
HATHERSAGE
PEAK FOREST for PEAK DALE
Peak Forest
MILLER'S DALE
Litton Tun.
Cressbrook Tun.
MONSAL DALE
Headstone Tun.
HASSOP
BUXTON
HIGHER BUXTON
Gds
Pass
Miller's Dale Jc.
Chee Tor Tuns.
LADMANLOW (Goods)
HARPUR HILL
HINDLOW
BLACKWELL MILL HALT
GREAT LONGSTONE for ASHFORD
BAKEWELL
DOWLOW HALT
L.N.W.
HURDLOW
Hadden Tun.
PARSLEY HAY
HARTINGTON
FRIDEN (Goods)
HULME END
ECTON
BUTTERTON
WETTON MILL
THOR'S CAVE
GRINDON
BEESTON TOR
SPARROWLEE
ALSOP-EN-LE-DALE
LONG CLIFFE (Gds)
TISSINGTON
FENNY BENTLEY (Goods)
THORPE CLOUD
BRADNOP
Cheddleton Jc.
IPSTONES
WINKHILL HALT
WATERHOUSES
Change of gauge
CALDON LOW
CALDON LOW HALT
CHEDDLETON
CONSALL
Goods
KINGSLEY & FROGHALL
OAKAMOOR
ASHBOURNE Joint
CLIFTON
CHEADLE
ALTON
BLYTHE BRIDGE
DENSTONE CROSSING
ROCESTER
CRESSWELL
TEAN
LEIGH
BROMSHALL (Gds)
UTTOXETER
Loco Shed
MARCHINGTON
SUDBURY
N.S.
TUTBURY
Marston Jc.
Dove Jc.
ROLLESTON ON DOVE
Stretton Jc.
BURTON-ON-TRENT
DALLOW LANE WHARF
(SEE INSET)
Leicester Jc.
Branston Jc.
BRANSTON
BARTON & WALTON
Birmingham Curve Jc.
Wichnor Jc.
WICHNOR (Gds)
ALREWAS
ARMITAGE
CROXALL
L.N.W.
LICHFIELD TRENT VALLEY
ELFORD
LOW LEVEL
HIGH LEVEL
CITY
Hademore Watertroughs
Haselour Watertroughs
SHENSTONE
TAMWORTH
MID.
STRETTON & CLAY MILLS
Stretton Jc.
NORBURY & ELLASTONE
Wetmore
HORNINGLOW
North Jc.
HORNINGLOW WHARF
N.Staff. Jc.
Gds.
South Jc.
Horninglow Jc.
DALLOW LANE WHARF
Guild Str. Jc.
BURTON-ON-TRENT
Gds
SHOBHALL WHARF
Goods
Pass
MOOR ST. WHARF
Leicester Jc.
SANDON
WESTON & INGESTRE
G.N.
GRINDLEY
SALT
CHARTLEY
INGESTRE
HIXON
GREAT HAYWOOD
COLWICH
West Jc.
East Jc.
Shugborough Tun.
MILFORD & BROCTON
RUGELEY (T.V.)
RUGELEY TOWN
HEDNESFORD
PENKRIDGE
GAILEY
CANNOCK
FIVE WAYS
PRIESTFIELD
FOUR ASHES
HAMMERWICH
WYRLEY & CHESLYN HAY
BROWNHILLS
L.N.W.
1 WEDNESFIELD HEATH
2 WEDNESFIELD
3 WILLENHALL
4 SHORT HEATH (CLARK'S LANE)
5 NORTH WALSALL
6 DARLASTON
PELSALL
WALSALL WOOD
BLOXWICH
BIRCHILLS
ALDRIDGE
MID.
BLAKE STR.
WILNECOTE
FOUR OAKS
STREET
Ryecroft Jc.
WALSALL
SUTTON PARK
SUTTON COLDFIELD
KINGSBURY
Gds.
BESCOT
WYLDE GREEN
PENNS
NEWTON RD.
GT. BARR
WATER ORTON
FORGE MILLS
CHESTER RD
ERDINGTON
WEDNESBURY
SWAN VILL
PERRY BARR
WHITACRE
CASTLE BROMWICH
BROMFORD BRIDGE
GRAVELLY HILL
ASTON
SOHO RD
SALTLEY
BIRMINGHAM
STECHFORD
MARSTON GREEN
BUSHBURY GDS.
WEDNESFIELD
DUNSTALL PK
WEDNESFIELD HTH.
Gds.
VICTORIA BASIN
WOLVERHAMPTON (Pass)
Heath Town Jc.
Crane St. Jc.
Walsall St. Gds.
MONMORE GN
Gds. Pass
COTON HILL (Goods)
SHREWSBURY
L.N.W. Gds
Curve Jc. E.
GENERAL
ABBEY
UPTON MAGNA
ADMASTON
WALCOT
G.W. & L.N.W.
EDGE-BOLD
Loco Sheds
SHREW. WEST
HOOKA-GATE
MEOLE BRACE
CONDOVER
DORRINGTON
LEEBOTWOOD
Caer Caradoc
CHURCH STRETTON
G.W. & L. & N. W. JC.
BERRINGTON
G.W.
CRESSAGE
The Wrekin
DONNINGTON
Market Drayton Junc.
HADLEY
TRENCH CROSSING
WOMBRIDGE (Gds)
WELLINGTON
Stafford Jc.
Ketley Jc.
OAKENGATES
KETLEY
MALINS LEE
LAWLEY BANK
Madeley Jc.
HORSEHAY & DAWLEY
STIRCHLEY
SHIFNAL
LIGHTMOOR PLAT
MADELEY (SALOP)
MADELEY MARKET
G. W.
ALBRIGHTON
COALBROOKDALE
BUILDWAS
IRON BRIDGE & BROSELEY
COALPORT
CODSALL
Bushbury Jc.
BUSHBURY (Gds)
DUNSTALL PARK
WOLVERHAMPTON
MONMORE GREEN
ETTINGSHALL RD & BILSTON
BILSTON
DEEPFIELDS
DAISY BANK
PRINCE'S END
TIPTON
(SEE INSET ON SHEET NO THIRTEEN)
PRESTHOPE
MUCH WENLOCK
LINLEY
LONGVILLE
BRIDGNORTH
RUSHBURY
HARTON ROAD
DITTON PRIORS
EARDINGTON
Marsh Farm Jc.
Brown Clee
CLEOBURY NORTH CROSSING
BURWARTON
C.M.&D.P.
ASTON BOTTERELL SIDING
STOTTESDON
HIGHLEY
HAMPTON LOADE
PRESCOTT SIDING
DUDLEY
DUDLEY PORT
NETHERTON
SPON LANE
WEST BROM
OLDBURY
ROUND OAK
LANGLEY GREEN
SOHO
SOHO
HOCKLEY
SNOW HILL
BRIERLEY HILL
WINDMILL END
ROWLEY REGIS
WINSON GREEN
BORDESLEY
BRETTELL LANE
CRADLEY HEATH & CRADLEY
OLD HILL
CHURCH RD
SOMERSET RD
NEW STREET
SMALLHEATH
TYSELEY
ACOCKS GREEN & SOUTH YARDLEY
OLTON
HAMPTON-IN-ARDEN
STOURBRIDGE TOWN
LYE
HALESOWEN
HARBORNE
MOSELEY
KINGS HEATH
HALL GREEN
STOURBRIDGE JC.
HUNNINGTON
SELLY OAK

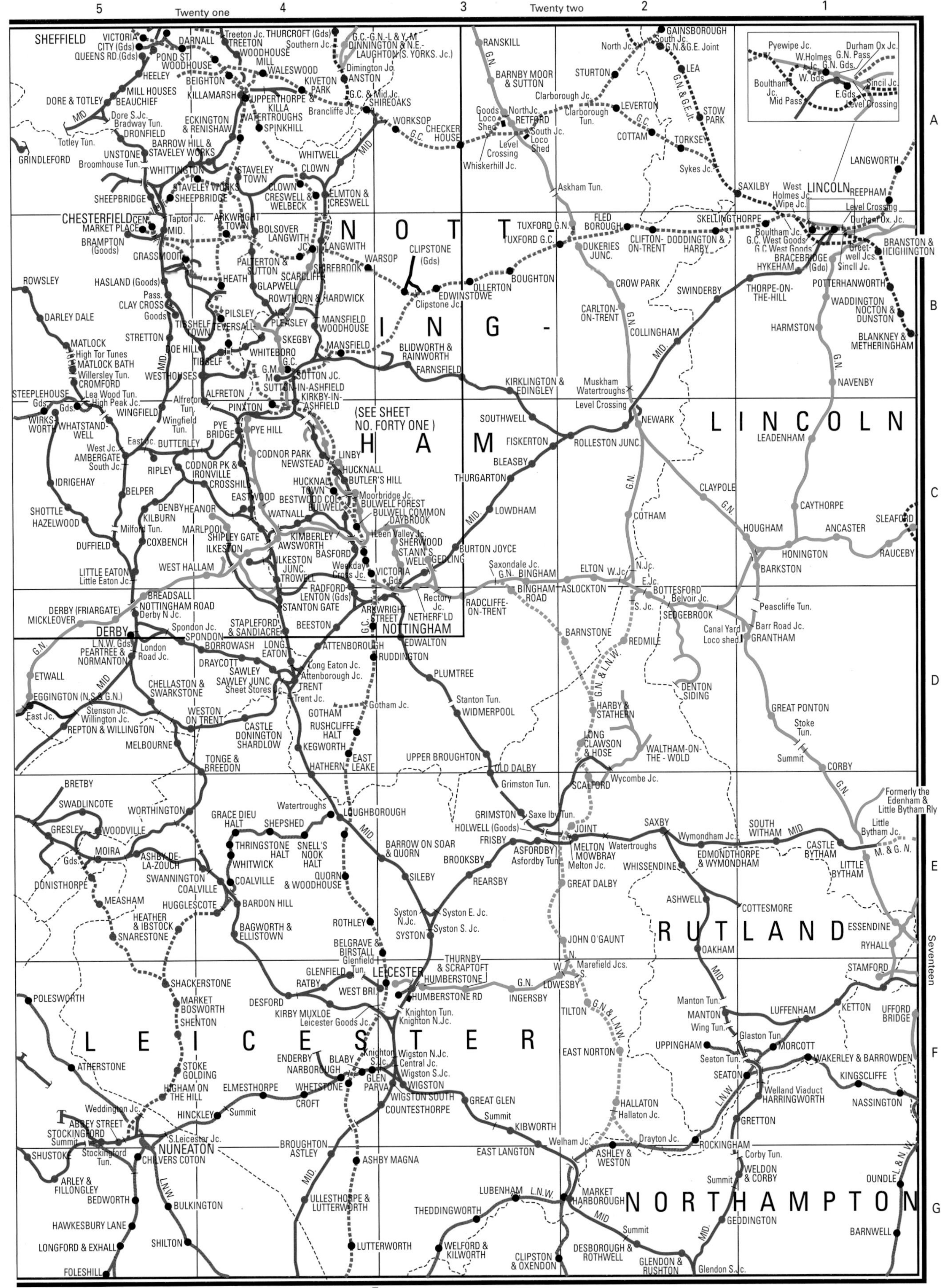
5
Twenty one
4
3
Twenty two
2
1
A
B
C
D
E
F
G
Seventeen
Ten
SHEFFIELD
VICTORIA
CITY (Gds)
QUEENS RD.(Gds)
DARNALL
POND ST
WOODHOUSE
Treeton Jc.
THURCROFT (Gds)
TREETON
WOODHOUSE MILL
Southern Jc.
G.C.-G.N.-L & Y.-M.
DINNINGTON & N.E.-
LAUGHTON (S. YORKS. Jc.)
Dimington Jc.
ANSTON
HEELEY
BEIGHTON
WALESWOOD
KIVETON PARK
G.C. & Mid.Jc.
SHIREOAKS
Brancliffe Jc.
MILL HOUSES
BEAUCHIEF
DORE & TOTLEY
KILLAMARSH
UPPERTHORPE & KILLA
WATERTROUGHS
SPINKHILL
Dore S.Jc.
Bradway Tun.
DRONFIELD
ECKINGTON & RENISHAW
MID
Totley Tun.
BARROW HILL & STAVELEY WORKS
UNSTONE
Broomhouse Tun.
GRINDLEFORD
WHITTINGTON
STAVELEY TOWN
WHITWELL
CLOWN
CRESWELL & WELBECK
ELMTON & CRESWELL
WORKSOP
G.C.
CHECKER HOUSE
STAVELEY WORKS
SHEEPBRIDGE
CHESTERFIELD
CEN
MARKET PLACE
MID.
Tapton Jc.
ARKWRIGHT TOWN
BOLSOVER
LANGWITH Jc.
LANGWITH
BRAMPTON (Goods)
GRASSMOOR
PALTERTON & SUTTON
SCARCLIFFE
SHIREBROOK
WARSOP
CLIPSTONE (Gds)
Clipstone Jc.
EDWINSTOWE
OLLERTON
BOUGHTON
HEATH
GLAPWELL
ROWTHORN & HARDWICK
HASLAND (Goods)
Pass.
CLAY CROSS
Goods
PILSLEY
TEVERSALL
TIBSHELF TOWN
PLEASLEY
MANSFIELD WOODHOUSE
SKEGBY
MANSFIELD
BLIDWORTH & RAINWORTH
FARNSFIELD
ROWSLEY
DARLEY DALE
STRETTON
DOE HILL
WHITEBORO
G.C.
G.N.
M.
TIBSELF
WESTHOUSES
SUTTON JC.
SUTTON-IN-ASHFIELD
KIRKBY-IN-ASHFIELD
MATLOCK
High Tor Tunes
MATLOCK BATH
Willersley Tun.
CROMFORD
Lea Wood Tun.
High Peak Jc.
STEEPLEHOUSE Gds.
Gds.
WIRKSWORTH
WHATSTANDWELL
WINGFIELD
Alfreton Tun.
ALFRETON
Wingfield Tun.
PINXTON
PYE BRIDGE
PYE HILL
East Jc.
BUTTERLEY
West Jc.
AMBERGATE
South Jc.
RIPLEY
CODNOR PK & IRONVILLE
CROSSHILL
CODNOR PARK
NEWSTEAD
LINBY
HUCKNALL
BUTLER'S HILL
HUCKNALL TOWN
BESTWOOD COL.
BULWELL
Moorbridge Jc.
BULWELL FOREST
BULWELL COMMON
DAYBROOK
IDRIGEHAY
BELPER
DENBY
HEANOR
EASTWOOD
WATNALL
KILBURN
Milford Tun.
SHOTTLE
HAZELWOOD
DUFFIELD
COXBENCH
MARLPOOL
SHIPLEY GATE
ILKESTON
AWSWORTH
KIMBERLEY
BASFORD
Leen Valley Jc.
SHERWOOD
ST.ANN'S WELL
GEDLING
ILKESTON JUNC.
TROWELL
Weekday Cross Jc.
VICTORIA Gds
LITTLE EATON
Little Eaton Jc.
WEST HALLAM
RADFORD
LENTON (Gds)
BREADSALL
NOTTINGHAM ROAD
Derby N Jc.
DERBY (FRIARGATE)
MICKLEOVER
DERBY
Spondon Jc.
SPONDON
STAPLEFORD & SANDIACRE
STANTON GATE
BEESTON
ARKWRIGHT STREET
NOTTINGHAM
NETHERF'LD
Rectory Jc.
RADCLIFFE-ON-TRENT
Saxondale Jc.
G.N.
BINGHAM
BINGHAM ROAD
ELTON
W.Jc.
N.Jc.
E.Jc.
ASLOCKTON
BOTTESFORD
Belvoir Jc.
S. Jc.
SEDGEBROOK
Canal Yard
Loco shed
Barr Road Jc.
GRANTHAM
Peascliffe Tun.
L.N.W. Gds
PEARTREE & NORMANTON
London Road Jc.
BORROWASH
LONG EATON
ATTENBOROUGH
EDWALTON
RUDDINGTON
PLUMTREE
DRAYCOTT
SAWLEY
SAWLEY JUNC.
Sheet Stores Jc.
Long Eaton Jc.
Attenborough Jc.
TRENT
Trent Jc.
ETWALL
CHELLASTON & SWARKSTONE
EGGINGTON (N.S. & G.N.)
East Jc.
Stenson Jc.
Willington Jc.
REPTON & WILLINGTON
WESTON ON TRENT
CASTLE DONINGTON SHARDLOW
GOTHAM
Gotham Jc.
RUSHCLIFFE HALT
KEGWORTH
EAST LEAKE
HATHERN
Stanton Tun.
WIDMERPOOL
UPPER BROUGHTON
OLD DALBY
Grimston Tun.
BARNSTONE
REDMILE
G.N. & L.N.W.
HARBY & STATHERN
LONG CLAWSON & HOSE
WALTHAM-ON-THE-WOLD
DENTON SIDING
MELBOURNE
TONGE & BREEDON
BRETBY
SWADLINCOTE
GRESLEY
WOODVILLE
WORTHINGTON
GRACE DIEU HALT
SHEPSHED
Watertroughs
LOUGHBOROUGH
MOIRA
Gds.
ASHBY-DE-LA-ZOUCH
THRINGSTONE HALT
SNELL'S NOOK HALT
WHITWICK
COALVILLE
SWANNINGTON
DONISTHORPE
MEASHAM
HUGGLESCOTE
BARDON HILL
HEATHER & IBSTOCK
SNARESTONE
BAGWORTH & ELLISTOWN
QUORN & WOODHOUSE
BARROW ON SOAR & QUORN
SILEBY
ROTHLEY
BELGRAVE & BIRSTALL
BROOKSBY
REARSBY
Syston N.Jc.
SYSTON
Syston E. Jc.
Syston S. Jc.
GRIMSTON
Saxe Iby Tun.
HOLWELL (Goods)
FRISBY
ASFORDBY
Asfordby Tun.
JOINT
MELTON MOWBRAY
Watertroughs
Melton Jc.
GREAT DALBY
SCALFORD
Wycombe Jc.
SAXBY
Wymondham Jc.
WHISSENDINE
EDMONDTHORPE & WYMONDHAM
SOUTH WITHAM
ASHWELL
COTTESMORE
OAKHAM
JOHN O'GAUNT
SHACKERSTONE
MARKET BOSWORTH
SHENTON
DESFORD
GLENFIELD
Glenfield Tun.
RATBY
LEICESTER
WEST BRI.
THURNBY & SCRAPTOFT
HUMBERSTONE
HUMBERSTONE RD
G.N.
INGERSBY
LOWESBY
Marefield Jcs.
N.
W.
S.
KIRBY MUXLOE
Leicester Goods Jc.
Knighton Tun.
Knighton N.Jc.
TILTON
EAST NORTON
POLESWORTH
ATHERSTONE
STOKE GOLDING
HIGHAM ON THE HILL
ELMESTHORPE
ENDERBY
NARBOROUGH
BLABY
Knighton S.Jc.
Wigston N.Jc.
Central Jc.
Wigston S.Jc.
GLEN PARVA
WIGSTON
WIGSTON SOUTH
WHETSTONE
CROFT
COUNTESTHORPE
GREAT GLEN
HALLATON
Hallaton Jc.
Weddington Jc.
ABBEY STREET
HINCKLEY
Summit
STOCKINGFORD
S.Leicester Jc.
NUNEATON
CHILVERS COTON
Stockingford Tun.
SHUSTOKE
ARLEY & FILLONGLEY
BEDWORTH
BULKINGTON
HAWKESBURY LANE
LONGFORD & EXHALL
SHILTON
FOLESHILL
L.N.W.
BROUGHTON ASTLEY
ASHBY MAGNA
ULLESTHORPE & LUTTERWORTH
LUTTERWORTH
KIBWORTH
Welham Jc.
EAST LANGTON
ASHLEY & WESTON
Drayton Jc.
THEDDINGWORTH
LUBENHAM
WELFORD & KILWORTH
CLIPSTON & OXENDON
MARKET HARBOROUGH
DESBOROUGH & ROTHWELL
GLENDON & RUSHTON
Glendon S.Jc.
ROCKINGHAM
Corby Tun.
WELDON & CORBY
GEDDINGTON
OUNDLE
BARNWELL
L.& N.W.
RANSKILL
BARNBY MOOR & SUTTON
Goods
Loco
Shed
North Jc.
RETFORD
South Jc.
Loco Shed
Level Crossing
Whiskerhill Jc.
Askham Tun.
Clarborough Jc.
Clarborough Tun.
STURTON
GAINSBOROUGH
South Jc.
North Jc.
G.N.&G.E. Joint
LEA
G.N. & G.E.Jt.
LEVERTON
STOW PARK
COTTAM
TORKSEY
Sykes Jc.
SAXILBY
West Holmes Jc.
Wipe Jc.
LINCOLN
REEPHAM
LANGWORTH
Level Crossing
Durham Ox. Jc.
SKELLINGTHORPE
Boultham Jc.
G.C. West Goods
BRANSTON & HEIGHINGTON
BRACEBRIDGE (Gds)
Greetwell Jcs.
Sincil Jc.
HYKEHAM
POTTERHANWORTH
THORPE-ON-THE-HILL
WADDINGTON
NOCTON & DUNSTON
HARMSTON
BLANKNEY & METHERINGHAM
NAVENBY
TUXFORD G.N.
TUXFORD G.C.
FLEDBOROUGH
DUKERIES JUNC.
CLIFTON-ON-TRENT
DODDINGTON & HARBY
CROW PARK
SWINDERBY
CARLTON-ON-TRENT
COLLINGHAM
KIRKLINGTON & EDINGLEY
Muskham Watertroughs
Level Crossing
NEWARK
SOUTHWELL
FISKERTON
ROLLESTON JUNC.
BLEASBY
THURGARTON
LOWDHAM
BURTON JOYCE
COTHAM
CLAYPOLE
CAYTHORPE
HOUGHAM
ANCASTER
SLEAFORD
HONINGTON
RAUCEBY
BARKSTON
LEADENHAM
GREAT PONTON
Stoke Tun.
Summit
CORBY
Formerly the Edenham & Little Bytham Rly
Little Bytham Jc.
M. & G. N.
CASTLE BYTHAM
LITTLE BYTHAM
ESSENDINE
RYHALL
STAMFORD
KETTON
UFFORD BRIDGE
LUFFENHAM
Manton Tun.
MANTON
Wing Tun.
Glaston Tun.
MORCOTT
UPPINGHAM
Seaton Tun.
SEATON
WAKERLEY & BARROWDEN
KINGSCLIFFE
Welland Viaduct
HARRINGWORTH
NASSINGTON
GRETTON
Pyewipe Jc.
Durham Ox Jc.
W.Holmes Jc.
G.N. Pass
G.N. Gds.
W. Gds.
Boultham Jc.
Mid Pass
E.Gds.
Sincil Jc.
Level Crossing
(SEE SHEET NO. FORTY ONE)
N O T T I N G - H A M
L I N C O L N
R U T L A N D
L E I C E S T E R
N O R T H A M P T O N

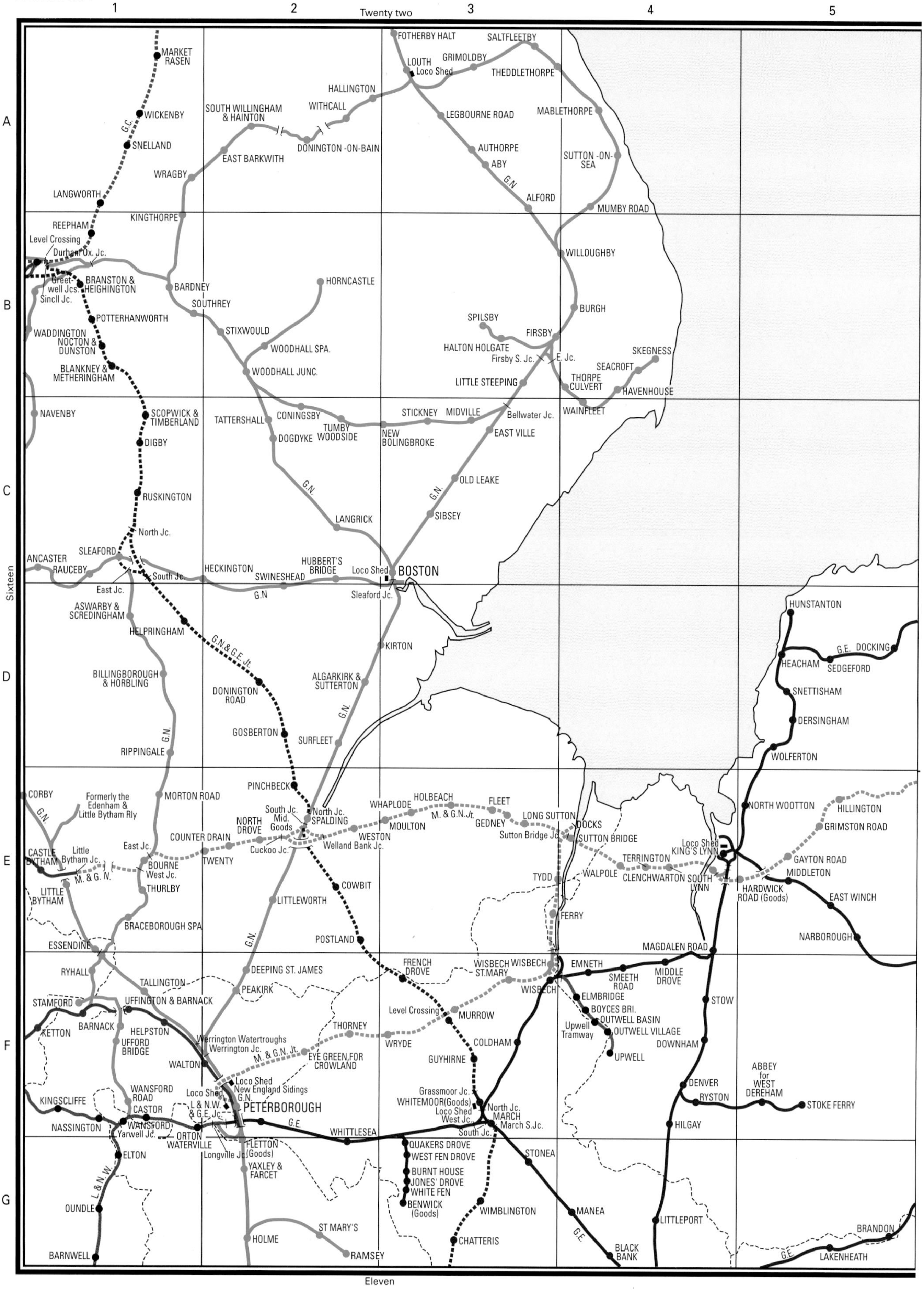

1 2 Twenty two 3 4 5

A B C D E F G

Sixteen

FOTHERBY HALT
SALTFLEETBY
MARKET RASEN
LOUTH
Loco Shed
GRIMOLDBY
THEDDLETHORPE
HALLINGTON
WITHCALL
SOUTH WILLINGHAM & HAINTON
WICKENBY
G.C.
LEGBOURNE ROAD
MABLETHORPE
DONINGTON -ON-BAIN
SNELLAND
EAST BARKWITH
AUTHORPE
ABY
SUTTON -ON-SEA
WRAGBY
G.N.
LANGWORTH
ALFORD
MUMBY ROAD
KINGTHORPE
REEPHAM
Level Crossing
Durham Ox. Jc.
WILLOUGHBY
Greetwell Jcs.
BRANSTON & HEIGHINGTON
BARDNEY
HORNCASTLE
Sincil Jc.
SOUTHREY
BURGH
POTTERHANWORTH
SPILSBY
WADDINGTON
STIXWOULD
FIRSBY
NOCTON & DUNSTON
WOODHALL SPA.
HALTON HOLGATE
SKEGNESS
Firsby S. Jc.
E. Jc.
BLANKNEY & METHERINGHAM
WOODHALL JUNC.
SEACROFT
LITTLE STEEPING
THORPE CULVERT
HAVENHOUSE
NAVENBY
SCOPWICK & TIMBERLAND
TATTERSHALL
CONINGSBY
STICKNEY
MIDVILLE
WAINFLEET
Bellwater Jc.
TUMBY WOODSIDE
DIGBY
DOGDYKE
NEW BOLINGBROKE
EAST VILLE
G.N.
OLD LEAKE
RUSKINGTON
G.N.
SIBSEY
LANGRICK
North Jc.
SLEAFORD
ANCASTER
RAUCEBY
HECKINGTON
HUBBERT'S BRIDGE
Loco Shed
BOSTON
South Jc.
SWINESHEAD
East Jc.
G.N
Sleaford Jc.
ASWARBY & SCREDINGHAM
HUNSTANTON
HELPRINGHAM
G.N.& G.E. Jt.
KIRTON
G.E. DOCKING
HEACHAM
SEDGEFORD
BILLINGBOROUGH & HORBLING
ALGARKIRK & SUTTERTON
DONINGTON ROAD
SNETTISHAM
G.N.
DERSINGHAM
GOSBERTON
SURFLEET
G.N.
RIPPINGALE
WOLFERTON
PINCHBECK
CORBY
Formerly the Edenham & Little Bytham Rly
MORTON ROAD
HOLBEACH
FLEET
NORTH WOOTTON
HILLINGTON
WHAPLODE
G.N.
South Jc.
North Jc.
M. & G.N. Jt.
LONG SUTTON
Mid.
SPALDING
NORTH DROVE
Goods
MOULTON
GEDNEY
DOCKS
GRIMSTON ROAD
COUNTER DRAIN
WESTON
Sutton Bridge Jc.
SUTTON BRIDGE
Loco Shed
East Jc.
Cuckoo Jc.
Welland Bank Jc.
KING'S LYNN
CASTLE BYTHAM
Little Bytham Jc.
TERRINGTON
GAYTON ROAD
BOURNE
TWENTY
M. & G. N.
West Jc.
TYDD
WALPOLE
CLENCHWARTON
SOUTH LYNN
MIDDLETON
LITTLE BYTHAM
THURLBY
COWBIT
HARDWICK ROAD (Goods)
EAST WINCH
LITTLEWORTH
FERRY
BRACEBOROUGH SPA
NARBOROUGH
POSTLAND
ESSENDINE
G.N.
MAGDALEN ROAD
FRENCH DROVE
WISBECH ST.MARY
WISBECH
EMNETH
RYHALL
DEEPING ST. JAMES
SMEETH ROAD
MIDDLE DROVE
TALLINGTON
PEAKIRK
WISBECH
ELMBRIDGE
STAMFORD
UFFINGTON & BARNACK
Level Crossing
STOW
BOYCES BRI.
MURROW
Upwell Tramway
OUTWELL BASIN
THORNEY
KETTON
BARNACK
HELPSTON
OUTWELL VILLAGE
Werrington Watertroughs
WRYDE
COLDHAM
DOWNHAM
UFFORD BRIDGE
Werrington Jc.
M. & G.N. Jt.
UPWELL
EYE GREEN FOR CROWLAND
WALTON
GUYHIRNE
ABBEY for WEST DEREHAM
Loco Shed
New England Sidings
DENVER
WANSFORD ROAD
G.N.
Grassmoor Jc.
Loco Shed
RYSTON
KINGSCLIFFE
L & N.W. & G.E. Jc.
PETERBOROUGH
WHITEMOOR(Goods)
Loco Shed
West Jc.
North Jc.
MARCH
STOKE FERRY
CASTOR
G.E.
NASSINGTON
WANSFORD
March S.Jc.
HILGAY
Yarwell Jc.
ORTON WATERVILLE
WHITTLESEA
South Jc.
FLETTON (Goods)
QUAKERS DROVE
STONEA
ELTON
Longville Jc.
WEST FEN DROVE
YAXLEY & FARCET
BURNT HOUSE
L.& N.W.
JONES' DROVE
WHITE FEN
BENWICK (Goods)
OUNDLE
WIMBLINGTON
MANEA
G.E.
LITTLEPORT
HOLME
ST MARY'S
BRANDON
CHATTERIS
BLACK BANK
BARNWELL
RAMSEY
G.E.
LAKENHEATH

Eleven

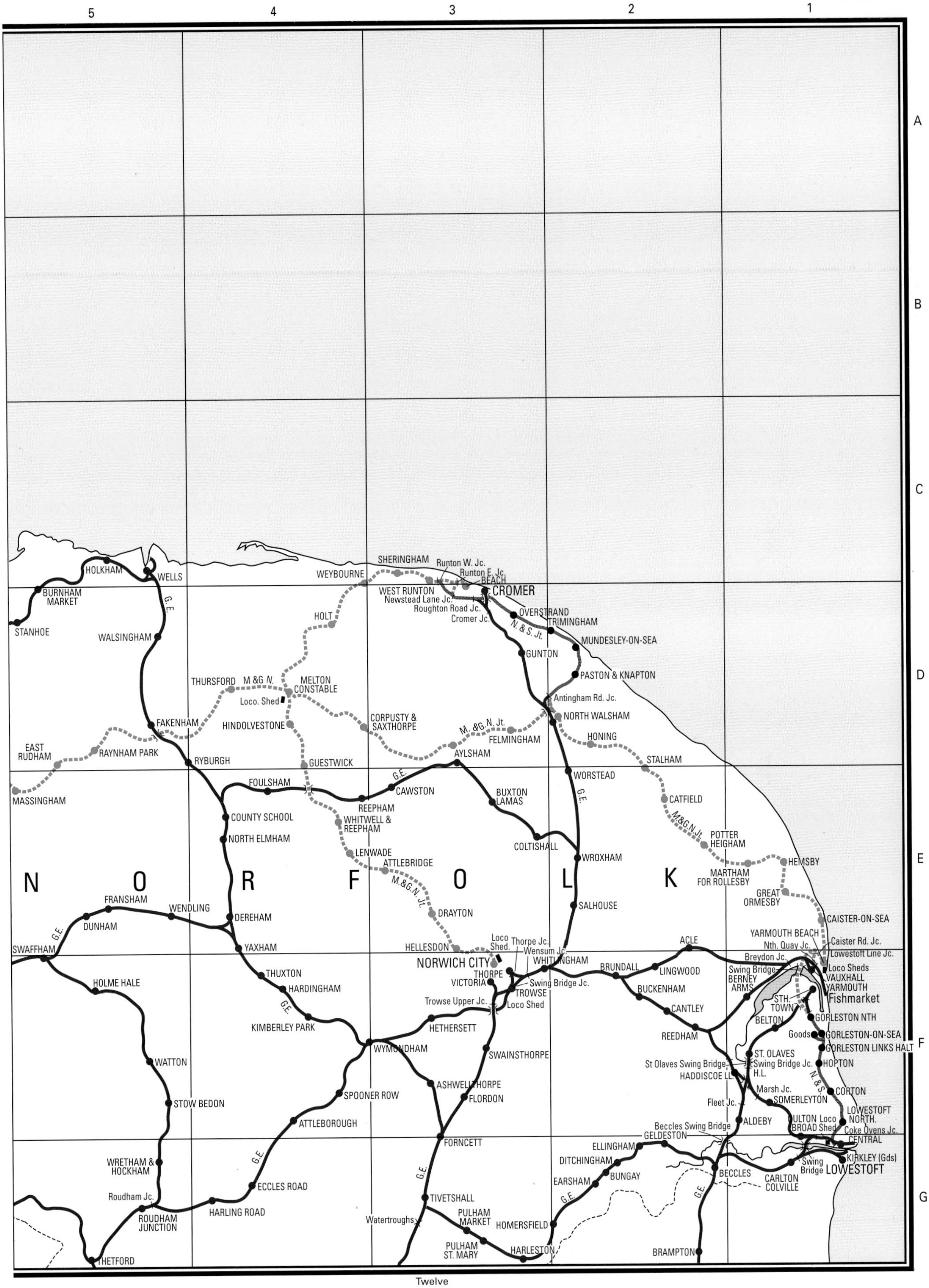

5 4 3 2 1

A

B

C

D

E

F

G

HOLKHAM
WELLS
BURNHAM MARKET
STANHOE
G.E.
WALSINGHAM
SHERINGHAM
Runton W. Jc.
Runton E. Jc.
BEACH
CROMER
WEYBOURNE
WEST RUNTON
Newstead Lane Jc.
Roughton Road Jc.
Cromer Jc.
OVERSTRAND
TRIMINGHAM
N. & S. Jt.
MUNDESLEY-ON-SEA
GUNTON
PASTON & KNAPTON
HOLT
THURSFORD
M &G N.
MELTON CONSTABLE
Loco. Shed
Antingham Rd. Jc.
NORTH WALSHAM
FAKENHAM
HINDOLVESTONE
CORPUSTY & SAXTHORPE
M. &G. N. Jt.
FELMINGHAM
HONING
EAST RUDHAM
RAYNHAM PARK
RYBURGH
GUESTWICK
AYLSHAM
STALHAM
MASSINGHAM
FOULSHAM
G.E.
CAWSTON
BUXTON LAMAS
WORSTEAD
CATFIELD
COUNTY SCHOOL
REEPHAM
WHITWELL & REEPHAM
G.E.
NORTH ELMHAM
M.&G.N. Jt.
POTTER HEIGHAM
COLTISHALL
LENWADE
WROXHAM
HEMSBY
ATTLEBRIDGE
MARTHAM FOR ROLLESBY
N O R F O L K
M.&G.N. Jt.
GREAT ORMESBY
FRANSHAM
WENDLING
SALHOUSE
DUNHAM
DEREHAM
DRAYTON
CAISTER-ON-SEA
G.E.
Loco Shed.
Thorpe Jc.
YARMOUTH BEACH
SWAFFHAM
YAXHAM
HELLESDON
Wensum Jc.
ACLE
Nth. Quay Jc.
Caister Rd. Jc.
Lowestoft Line Jc.
NORWICH CITY
WHITLINGHAM
Breydon Jc.
THORPE
BRUNDALL
LINGWOOD
Swing Bridge
Loco Sheds
THUXTON
VICTORIA
Swing Bridge Jc.
BERNEY ARMS
VAUXHALL
YARMOUTH
HOLME HALE
HARDINGHAM
TROWSE
BUCKENHAM
Fishmarket
Trowse Upper Jc.
Loco Shed
STH. TOWN
G.E.
CANTLEY
GORLESTON NTH
BELTON
KIMBERLEY PARK
HETHERSETT
REEDHAM
Goods
GORLESTON-ON-SEA
WYMONDHAM
GORLESTON LINKS HALT
WATTON
SWAINSTHORPE
ST. OLAVES
St Olaves Swing Bridge
Swing Bridge Jc.
HOPTON
H.L.
HADDISCOE LL.
N. & S.
ASHWELLTHORPE
Marsh Jc.
STOW BEDON
SPOONER ROW
FLORDON
SOMERLEYTON
CORTON
Fleet Jc.
LOWESTOFT NORTH.
ATTLEBOROUGH
ALDEBY
ULTON BROAD
Loco Shed
Beccles Swing Bridge
Coke Ovens Jc.
FORNCETT
GELDESTON
CENTRAL
ELLINGHAM
KIRKLEY (Gds)
WRETHAM & HOCKHAM
G.E.
DITCHINGHAM
Swing Bridge
LOWESTOFT
BECCLES
BUNGAY
CARLTON COLVILLE
ECCLES ROAD
G.E.
EARSHAM
G.E.
Roudham Jc.
TIVETSHALL
G.E.
ROUDHAM JUNCTION
HARLING ROAD
PULHAM MARKET
Watertroughs
HOMERSFIELD
PULHAM ST. MARY
HARLESTON
BRAMPTON
THETFORD

Twelve

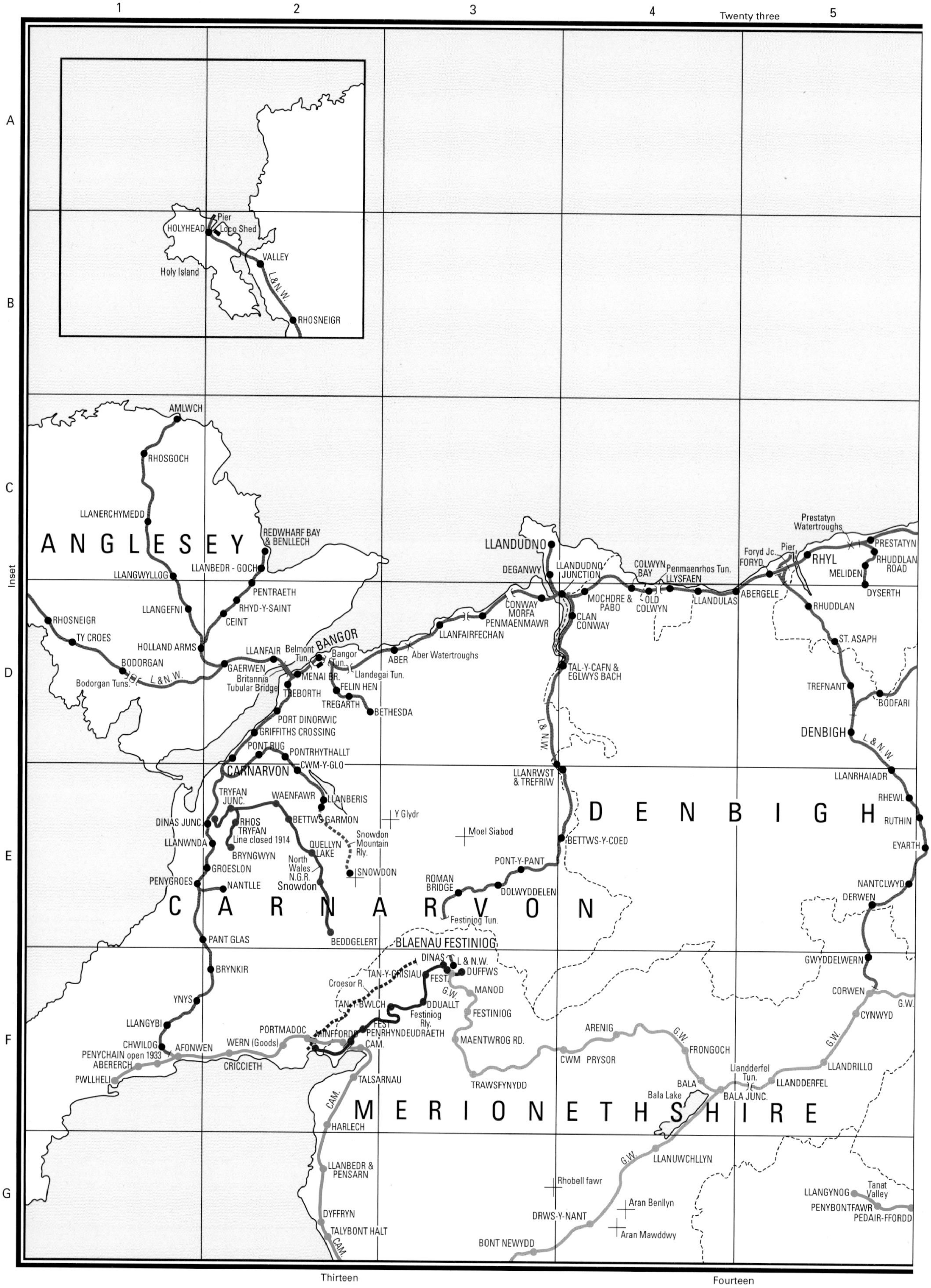

1 2 3 4 Twenty three 5

A
B
C
D
E
F
G

Inset

Pier
Loco Shed
HOLYHEAD
VALLEY
Holy Island
L.&N.W.
RHOSNEIGR

AMLWCH
RHOSGOCH
LLANERCHYMEDD
ANGLESEY
REDWHARF BAY & BENLLECH
LLANBEDR - GOCH
LLANGWYLLOG
PENTRAETH
LLANGEFNI
RHYD-Y-SAINT
CEINT
RHOSNEIGR
TY CROES
HOLLAND ARMS
BODORGAN
Bodorgan Tuns.
L.&N.W.
GAERWEN
LLANFAIR
Belmont Tun.
BANGOR
Bangor Tun.
Llandegai Tun.
Britannia Tubular Bridge
MENAI BR.
TREBORTH
FELIN HEN
TREGARTH
BETHESDA
ABER
Aber Watertroughs
LLANFAIRFECHAN
PENMAENMAWR
CONWAY MORFA
PORT DINORWIC
GRIFFITHS CROSSING
PONT RUG
PONTRHYTHALLT
CARNARVON
CWM-Y-GLO
TRYFAN JUNC.
WAENFAWR
LLANBERIS
DINAS JUNC.
RHOS TRYFAN
Line closed 1914
BETTWS GARMON
Y Glydr
LLANWNDA
BRYNGWYNN
QUELLYN LAKE
Snowdon Mountain Rly.
North Wales N.G.R.
SNOWDON
Moel Siabod
GROESLON
PENYGROES
NANTLLE
Snowdon
CARNARVON
PANT GLAS
BEDDGELERT
BRYNKIR
YNYS
LLANGYBI
CHWILOG
PENYCHAIN open 1933
ABERERCH
PWLLHELI
AFONWEN
WERN (Goods)
CRICCIETH
PORTMADOC
MINFFORDD
FEST.
PENRHYNDEUDRAETH
CAM.
Croesor R.
TAN-Y-GRISIAU
TAN-Y-BWLCH
DDUALLT
Festiniog Rly.
BLAENAU FESTINIOG
DINAS
L & N.W.
DUFFWS
FEST.
G.W.
MANOD
FESTINIOG
MAENTWROG RD.
TRAWSFYNYDD
TALSARNAU
CAM.
HARLECH
LLANBEDR & PENSARN
DYFFRYN
TALYBONT HALT
CAM.

LLANDUDNO
DEGANWY
LLANDUDNO JUNCTION
CONWAY
CLAN CONWAY
MOCHDRE & PABO
COLWYN BAY
OLD COLWYN
Penmaenrhos Tun.
LLYSFAEN
LLANDULAS
ABERGELE
Foryd Jc.
FORYD
Pier
RHYL
Prestatyn Watertroughs
PRESTATYN
RHUDDLAN ROAD
MELIDEN
DYSERTH
RHUDDLAN
ST. ASAPH
TREFNANT
BODFARI
DENBIGH
L.&N.W.
LLANRHAIADR
RHEWL
RUTHIN
EYARTH
NANTCLWYD
DERWEN
GWYDDELWERN
CORWEN
G.W.
CYNWYD
G.W.
LLANDRILLO
TAL-Y-CAFN & EGLWYS BACH
L.&N.W.
LLANRWST & TREFRIW
DENBIGH
BETTWS-Y-COED
PONT-Y-PANT
ROMAN BRIDGE
DOLWYDDELEN
Festiniog Tun.
ARENIG
G.W.
FRONGOCH
CWM PRYSOR
Llandderfel Tun.
LLANDDERFEL
BALA
Bala Lake
BALA JUNC.
MERIONETHSHIRE
G.W.
LLANUWCHLLYN
Rhobell fawr
Aran Benllyn
Aran Mawddwy
DRWS-Y-NANT
BONT NEWYDD
LLANGYNOG
Tanat Valley
PENYBONTFAWR
PEDAIR-FFORDD

Thirteen
Fourteen

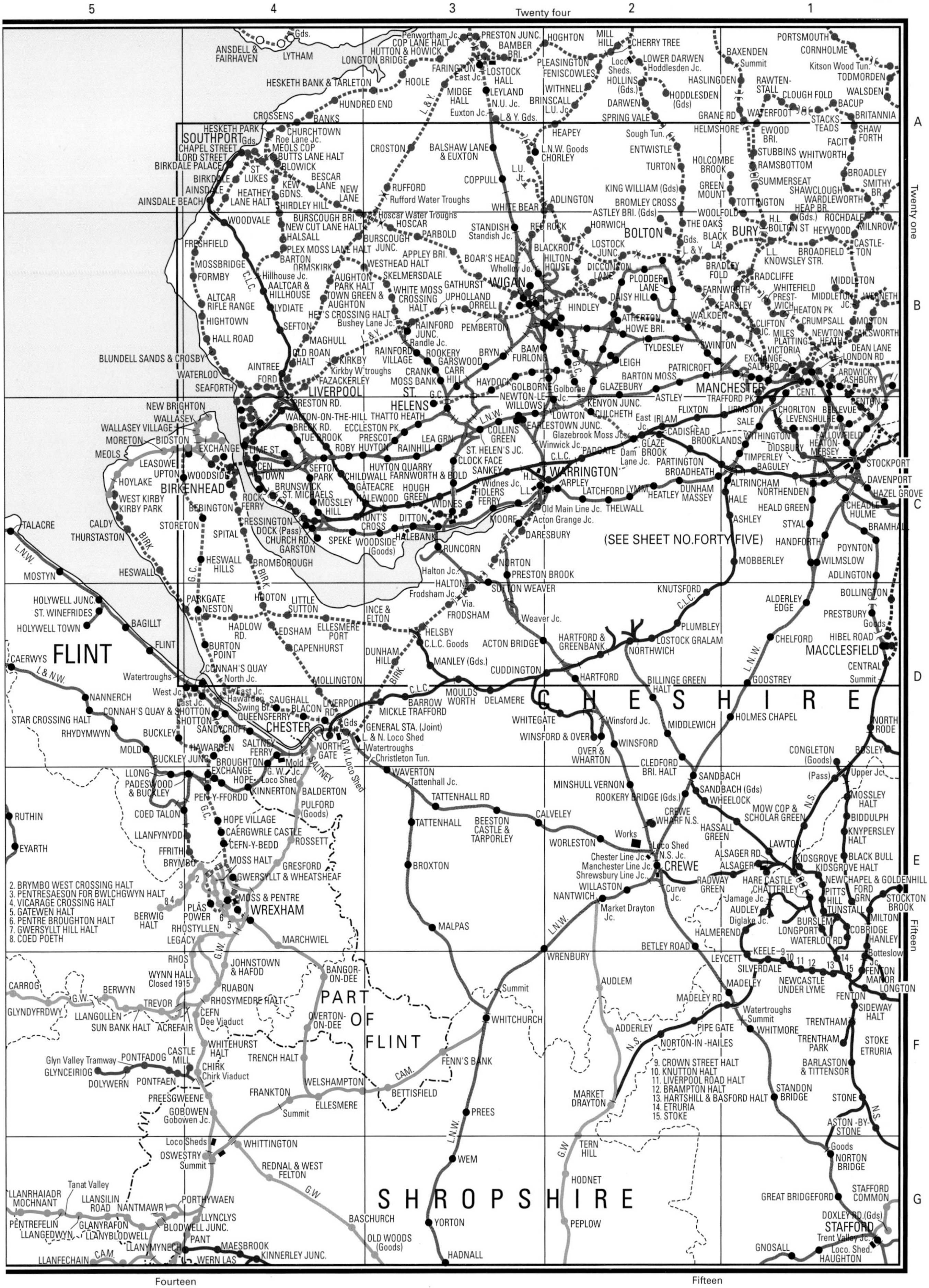

5 4 3 Twenty four 2 1

ANSDELL & FAIRHAVEN
LYTHAM
Gds.
Penwortham Jc.
COP LANE HALT
PRESTON JUNC.
BAMBER BRI.
HUTTON & HOWICK
LONGTON BRIDGE
FARINGTON
East Jc.
LOSTOCK HALL
HOGHTON
MILL HILL
CHERRY TREE
LOWER DARWEN
Hoddlesden Jc.
PLEASINGTON
FENISCOWLES
Loco Sheds.
HESKETH BANK & TARLETON
HOOLE
MIDGE HALL
LEYLAND
N.U. Jc.
Euxton Jc.
L.& Y. Gds.
WITHNELL
BRINSCALL
L.U. Jc.
HOLLINS (Gds.)
DARWEN
SPRING VALE
HODDLESDEN (Gds)
HUNDRED END
CROSSENS
BANKS
BAXENDEN
Summit
HASLINGDEN
RAWTENSTALL
CLOUGH FOLD
GRANE RD
WATERFOOT
PORTSMOUTH
CORNHOLME
Kitson Wood Tun.
TODMORDEN
WALSDEN
BACUP
STACKSTEADS
BRITANNIA
HESKETH PARK
SOUTHPORT Gds
CHAPEL STREET
LORD STREET
BIRKDALE PALACE
CHURCHTOWN
Roe Lane Jc.
MEOLS COP
BUTTS LANE HALT
BLOWICK
ST LUKES
KEW GDNS.
BESCAR LANE
NEW LANE
BIRKDALE
AINSDALE
AINSDALE BEACH
HEATHEY LANE HALT
SHIRDLEY HILL
CROSTON
BALSHAW LANE & EUXTON
RUFFORD
Rufford Water Troughs
COPPULL
HEAPEY
L.N.W. Goods CHORLEY
L.U. Jt.
ADLINGTON
WHITE BEAR
Sough Tun.
ENTWISTLE
TURTON
KING WILLIAM (Gds)
BROMLEY CROSS
HELMSHORE
HOLCOMBE BROOK
GREEN MOUNT
EWOOD BRI.
STUBBINS
WHITWORTH
RAMSBOTTOM
SUMMERSEAT
TOTTINGTON
SHAW FORTH
FACIT
BROADLEY
SHAWCLOUGH
SMITHY BR.
WARDLEWORTH
HEAP BR.
ROCHDALE
MILNROW
WOODVALE
BURSCOUGH BRI.
NEW CUT LANE HALT
HALSALL
Hoscar Water Troughs
HOSCAR
PARBOLD
BURSCOUGH JUNC.
PLEX MOSS LANE HALT
BARTON
ORMSKIRK
APPLEY BRI.
STANDISH
Standish Jc.
RED ROCK
BOAR'S HEAD
Whelley Jc.
ASTLEY BRI. (Gds)
HORWICH
BOLTON
LOSTOCK JUNC.
BLACKROD
HILTON HOUSE
WOOLFOLD
THE OAKS
Gds.
BLACK LA.
L.& Y.
BURY
H.L.
(Gds.)
BOLTON ST
HEYWOOD
L.L.
KNOWSLEY STR.
BROADFIELD
CASTLETON
FRESHFIELD
MOSSBRIDGE
FORMBY
C.L.C.
Hillhouse Jc.
AALTCAR & HILLHOUSE
ALTCAR RIFLE RANGE
HIGHTOWN
HALL ROAD
BLUNDELL SANDS & CROSBY
WATERLOO
SEAFORTH
WESTHEAD HALT
AUGHTON PARK HALT
SKELMERSDALE
TOWN GREEN & AUGHTON
LYDIATE
HEY'S CROSSING HALT
Bushey Lane Jc.
SEFTON
MAGHULL
OLD ROAN HALT
AINTREE
FORD
WHITE MOSS CROSSING HALT
GATHURST
UPHOLLAND
ORRELL
WIGAN
PEMBERTON
RAINFORD JUNC.
Randle Jc.
KIRKBY
Kirkby W'troughs
FAZACKERLEY
LIVERPOOL
RAINFORD VILLAGE
CRANK
ROOKERY
GARSWOOD
CARR HILL
MOSS BANK
BRYN
BAM FURLONG
HINDLEY
DICCONSON LANE
DAISY HILL
PLODDER LANE
BRADLEY FOLD
FARNWORTH
KEARSLEY
WALKDEN
ATHERTON
HOWE BRI.
TYLDESLEY
LEIGH
G.C.
SWINTON
RADCLIFFE
WHITEFIELD
PRESTWICH
HEATON PK
CLIFTON JC.
CRUMPSALL
MILES PLATTING
NEWTON HEATH
VICTORIA
EXCHANGE
SALFORD
MIDDLETON
MIDDLETON JC.
IVERNETH
MOSTON
FAILSWORTH
DEAN LANE
LONDON RD
ARDWICK
ASHBURY
CENT.
GORTON
PATRICROFT
BARTON MOSS
MANCHESTER
TRAFFORD PK
ST. HELENS
G.C.
HAYDOCK
GOLBORNE
Golborne Jc.
NEWTON-LE-WILLOWS
KENYON JUNC.
GLAZEBURY
ASTLEY
NEW BRIGHTON
WALLASEY
WALLASEY VILLAGE
MORETON
BIDSTON
MEOLS
EXCHANGE
LEASOWE
UPTON
HOYLAKE
WOODSIDE
BIRKENHEAD
WEST KIRBY
KIRBY PARK
BEBINGTON
ROCK FERRY
LIME ST.
CEN TOWN
BRUNSWICK
ST. MICHAELS
EDGE HILL
PRESTON RD.
WALTON-ON-THE-HILL
BRECK RD.
TUE BROOK
THATTO HEATH
ECCLESTON PK.
PRESCOT
ROBY
HUYTON
RAINHILL
LEA GRN
SEFTON PARK
CHILDWALL
HUYTON QUARRY
FARNWORTH & BOLD
GATEACRE
HALEWOOD
HOUGH GREEN
MOSSLEY HILL
CRESSINGTON
DOCK (Pass)
CHURCH RD.
GARSTON
HUNT'S CROSS
DITTON
SPEKE
WOODSIDE (Goods)
HALEBANK
WIDNES
L.N.W.
COLLINS GREEN
ST. HELEN'S JC.
CLOCK FACE
SANKEY
Widnes Jc.
FIDLERS FERRY
LOWTON
CULCHETH
EARLESTOWN JUNC.
Glazebrook Moss Jc.
Winwick Jc.
C.L.C.
PADGATE
WARRINGTON
H.L.
ARPLEY
L.L.
Old Main Line Jc.
Acton Grange Jc.
LATCHFORD
LYMM
THELWALL
HEATLEY
East Jc.
IRLAM
Dam Lane Jc.
GLAZEBROOK
PARTINGTON
BROADHEATH
CADISHEAD
FLIXTON
URMSTON
BROOKLANDS
SALE
DUNHAM MASSEY
ALTRINCHAM
TIMPERLEY
BAGULEY
NORTHENDEN
HALE
ASHLEY
HEALD GREEN
STYAL
HANDFORTH
WITHINGTON
DIDSBURY
CHORLTON
LEVENSHULME
BELLEVUE
FALLOWFIELD
HEATON MERSEY
STOCKPORT
DAVENPORT
HAZEL GROVE
CHEADLE HULME
BRAMHALL
POYNTON
WILMSLOW
ADLINGTON
MOBBERLEY
TALACRE
CALDY
THURSTASTON
BIRK.
STORETON
SPITAL
MOORE
DARESBURY

(SEE SHEET NO. FORTY FIVE)

L.N.W.
MOSTYN
HESWALL
HESWALL HILLS
BROMBOROUGH
G.C.
BIRK.
RUNCORN
Halton Jc.
HALTON
Frodsham Jc.
Via.
FRODSHAM
NORTON
PRESTON BROOK
SUTTON WEAVER
Weaver Jc.
HOLYWELL JUNC.
ST. WINEFRIDES
HOLYWELL TOWN
BAGILLT
PARKGATE
NESTON
HOOTON
LITTLE SUTTON
INCE & ELTON
HADLOW RD.
LEDSHAM
ELLESMERE PORT
CAPENHURST
HELSBY
C.L.C. Goods
ACTON BRIDGE
KNUTSFORD
ALDERLEY EDGE
PRESTBURY
BOLLINGTON
Goods
HIBEL ROAD
MACCLESFIELD
CENTRAL
Summit
FLINT
BURTON POINT
CAERWYS
L & N.W.
Watertroughs
CONNAH'S QUAY
North Jc.
DUNHAM HILL
MANLEY (Gds.)
CUDDINGTON
HARTFORD & GREENBANK
NORTHWICH
PLUMBLEY
LOSTOCK GRALAM
C.L.C.
CHELFORD
L.N.W.
NANNERCH
West Jc.
East Jc.
Hawarden Swing Br.
STAR CROSSING HALT
CONNAH'S QUAY & SHOTTON
SHOTTON
QUEENSFERRY
SANDYCROFT
SAUGHALL
BLACON
MOLLINGTON
LIVERPOOL RD
CHESTER
Gds
HARTFORD
BILLINGE GREEN HALT
GOOSTREY
MOULDSWORTH
BARROW
MICKLE TRAFFORD
DELAMERE
C H E S H I R E
RHYDYMWYN
BUCKLEY
MOLD
HAWARDEN
SALTNEY FERRY
NORTH GATE
GENERAL STA. (Joint)
L. & N. Loco Shed
Watertroughs
Christleton Tun.
G.W. Loco Shed
SALTNEY
WHITEGATE
Winsford Jc.
WINSFORD & OVER
OVER & WHARTON
WINSFORD
MIDDLEWICH
HOLMES CHAPEL
NORTH RODE
CONGLETON (Goods)
(Pass)
BOSLEY
BUCKLEY JUNC.
BROUGHTON
LLONG
PADESWOOD & BUCKLEY
EXCHANGE
HOPE
Mold Jc.
G.W.
Loco Shed
KINNERTON
BALDERTON
PEN-Y-FFORDD
WAVERTON
Tattenhall Jc.
TATTENHALL RD
CLEDFORD BRI. HALT
MINSHULL VERNON
ROOKERY BRIDGE (Gds.)
SANDBACH
SANDBACH (Gds)
WHEELOCK
MOW COP & SCHOLAR GREEN
Upper Jc.
N.S.
MOSSLEY HALT
BIDDULPH
RUTHIN
COED TALON
G.C.
HOPE VILLAGE
PULFORD (Goods)
TATTENHALL
BEESTON CASTLE & TARPORLEY
CALVELEY
CREWE WHARF N.S.
HASSALL GREEN
KNYPERSLEY HALT
LLANFYNYDD
CAERGWRLE CASTLE
CEFN-Y-BEDD
ROSSETT
EYARTH
FFRITH
BRYMBO
MOSS HALT
GRESFORD
GWERSYLLT & WHEATSHEAF
WORLESTON
Works
Loco Shed
N.S. Jc.
Chester Line Jc.
Manchester Line Jc.
Shrewsbury Line Jc.
CREWE
ALSAGER RD
ALSAGER
LAWTON
KIDSGROVE
BLACK BULL
KIDSGROVE HALT
BROXTON
2. BRYMBO WEST CROSSING HALT
3. PENTRESAESON FOR BWLCHGWYN HALT
4. VICARAGE CROSSING HALT
5. GATEWEN HALT
6. PENTRE BROUGHTON HALT
7. GWERSYLLT HILL HALT
8. COED POETH
MOSS & PENTRE
WREXHAM
PLAS POWER
BERWIG HALT
RHOSTYLLEN
LEGACY
WILLASTON
NANTWICH
Curve Jc.
Market Drayton Jc.
RADWAY GREEN
HARE CASTLE
CHATTERLEY
Jamage Jc.
AUDLEY
Diglake Jc.
NEWCHAPEL & GOLDENHILL
PITTS HILL
FORD GRN
TUNSTALL
STOCKTON BROOK
BURSLEM
MILTON
LONGPORT
COBRIDGE
WATERLOO RD
HANLEY
MALPAS
L.N.W.
HALMEREND
BETLEY ROAD
LEYCETT
KEELE
SILVERDALE
Botteslow Jc.
NEWCASTLE UNDER LYME
FENTON MANOR
LONGTON
FENTON
MARCHWIEL
G.W.
RHOS
JOHNSTOWN & HAFOD
WYNN HALL Closed 1915
RUABON
BANGOR-ON-DEE
CARROG
BERWYN
G.W.
TREVOR
RHOSYMEDRE HALT
GLYNDYFRDWY
LLANGOLLEN
SUN BANK HALT
ACREFAIR
CEFN
Dee Viaduct
OVERTON-ON-DEE
PART OF FLINT
WRENBURY
AUDLEM
Summit
WHITCHURCH
MADELEY
MADELEY RD
Watertroughs
Summit
WHITMORE
SIDEWAY HALT
TRENTHAM
TRENTHAM PARK
STOKE
ETRURIA
ADDERLEY
PIPE GATE
N.S.
NORTON-IN-HAILES
Glyn Valley Tramway
GLYNCEIRIOG
PONTFADOG
CASTLE MILL
WHITEHURST HALT
TRENCH HALT
CHIRK
Chirk Viaduct
DOLYWERN
PONTFAEN
FENN'S BANK
CAM.
9. CROWN STREET HALT
10. KNUTTON HALT
11. LIVERPOOL ROAD HALT
12. BRAMPTON HALT
13. HARTSHILL & BASFORD HALT
14. ETRURIA
15. STOKE
BARLASTON & TITTENSOR
WELSHAMPTON
BETTISFIELD
FRANKTON
ELLESMERE
Summit
PREESGWEENE
GOBOWEN
Gobowen Jc.
PREES
MARKET DRAYTON
STANDON BRIDGE
STONE
N.S.
ASTON-BY-STONE
Goods
NORTON BRIDGE
Loco Sheds
OSWESTRY
Summit
WHITTINGTON
REDNAL & WEST FELTON
L.N.W.
WEM
G.W.
TERN HILL
HODNET
Tanat Valley
LLANRHAIADR MOCHNANT
LLANSILIN ROAD
NANTMAWR
PORTHYWAEN
G.W.
S H R O P S H I R E
GREAT BRIDGEFORD
STAFFORD COMMON
PENTREFELIN
GLANYRAFON
LLANGEDWYN
LLANYBLODWELL
LLYNCLYS
BLODWELL JUNC.
PANT
LLANYMYNECH
BASCHURCH
OLD WOODS (Goods)
YORTON
PEPLOW
DOXLEY RD.(Gds)
STAFFORD
Trent Valley Jc.
Loco. Shed.
GNOSALL
HAUGHTON
LLANFECHAIN
CAM.
WERN LAS
MAESBROOK
KINNERLEY JUNC.
HADNALL

A B C D E F G
Twenty one
Fifteen

Fourteen
Fifteen

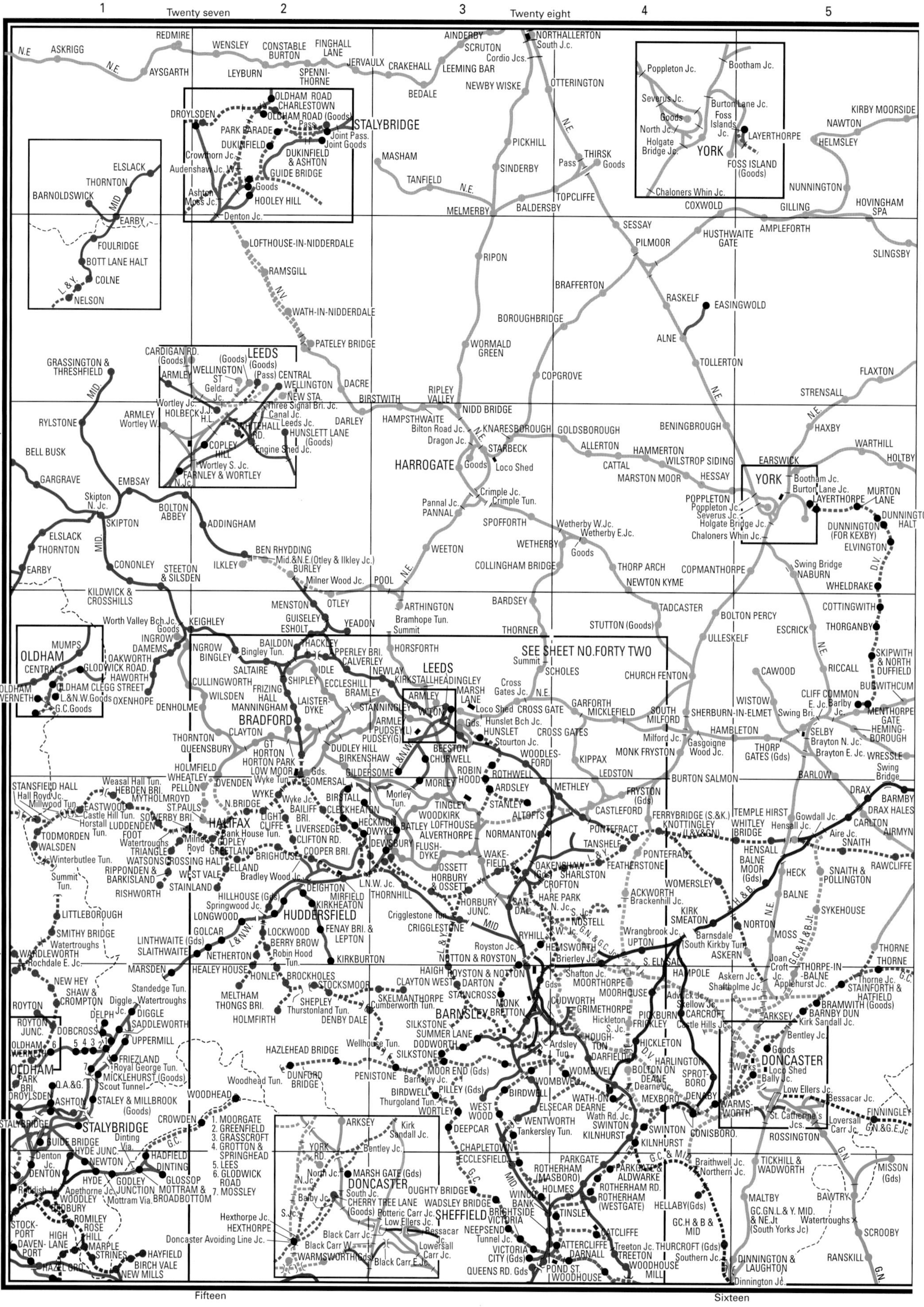

1 Twenty seven 2 3 Twenty eight 4 5

A B C D E F G

Twenty four
Inset
Twenty
Fifteen
Sixteen

REDMIRE
ASKRIGG
N.E.
AYSGARTH
WENSLEY
CONSTABLE BURTON
FINGHALL LANE
LEYBURN
SPENNITHORNE
JERVAULX
CRAKEHALL
BEDALE
AINDERBY
SCRUTON
NORTHALLERTON South J.c.
Cordio Jcs.
LEEMING BAR
NEWBY WISKE
OTTERINGTON
Poppleton Jc.
Bootham Jc.
Severus Jc.
Burton Lane Jc.
Goods
Foss Islands Jc.
North Jc.
Holgate Bridge Jc.
YORK
LAYERTHORPE
FOSS ISLAND (Goods)
Chaloners Whin Jc.
KIRBY MOORSIDE
NAWTON
HELMSLEY
NUNNINGTON
HOVINGHAM SPA
GILLING
COXWOLD
DROYLSDEN
OLDHAM ROAD
CHARLESTOWN
OLDHAM ROAD (Goods)
Pass
STALYBRIDGE
Joint Pass.
Joint Goods
PARK PARADE
DUKINFIELD
DUKINFIELD & ASHTON
GUIDE BRIDGE
Crowthorn Jc.
Audenshaw Jc.
Ashton Moss Jc.
Goods
HOOLEY HILL
Denton Jc.
MASHAM
PICKHILL
SINDERBY
THIRSK
Pass
Goods
TANFIELD
MELMERBY
BALDERSBY
TOPCLIFFE
ELSLACK
THORNTON
BARNOLDSWICK
MID.
EARBY
FOULRIDGE
BOTT LANE HALT
COLNE
L. & Y.
NELSON
LOFTHOUSE-IN-NIDDERDALE
RAMSGILL
N.V.
WATH-IN-NIDDERDALE
PATELEY BRIDGE
SESSAY
PILMOOR
HUSTHWAITE GATE
AMPLEFORTH
SLINGSBY
RIPON
BRAFFERTON
RASKELF
EASINGWOLD
BOROUGHBRIDGE
ALNE
TOLLERTON
WORMALD GREEN
COPGROVE
FLAXTON
STRENSALL
HAXBY
WARTHILL
HOLTBY
GRASSINGTON & THRESHFIELD
CARDIGAN RD. (Goods)
LEEDS
ARMLEY
WELLINGTON ST
(Goods)
(Goods)
(Pass) CENTRAL
WELLINGTON
Geldard Jc.
NEW STA.
Wortley Jc.
Three Signal Bri. Jc.
Canal Jc.
HOLBECK J.L. H.L.
WHITEHALL RD.
Leeds Jc.
HUNSLETT LANE (Goods)
COPLEY HILL
Engine Shed Jc.
Wortley S. Jc.
FARNLEY & WORTLEY
N. Jc.
DACRE
BIRSTWITH
RIPLEY VALLEY
NIDD BRIDGE
RYLSTONE
ARMLEY
Wortley W.
DARLEY
HAMPSTHWAITE
Bilton Road Jc.
Dragon Jc.
KNARESBOROUGH
GOLDSBOROUGH
ALLERTON
HAMMERTON
BENINGBROUGH
BELL BUSK
HARROGATE
Goods
STARBECK
Loco Shed
CATTAL
WILSTROP SIDING
MARSTON MOOR
HESSAY
EARSWICK
GARGRAVE
EMBSAY
Skipton N. Jc.
SKIPTON
BOLTON ABBEY
ADDINGHAM
Crimple Jc.
Crimple Tun.
Pannal Jc.
PANNAL
SPOFFORTH
Wetherby W. Jc.
Wetherby E. Jc.
WETHERBY
Goods
YORK
Bootham Jc.
Burton Lane Jc.
POPPLETON
Poppleton Jc.
Severus Jc.
Holgate Bridge Jc.
Chaloners Whin Jc.
LAYERTHORPE
MURTON LANE
DUNNINGTON HALT
DUNNINGTON (FOR KEXBY)
ELVINGTON
D.V.
ELSLACK
THORNTON
EARBY
CONONLEY
STEETON & SILSDEN
ILKLEY
BEN RHYDDING
Mid. & N.E. (Otley & Ilkley Jc.)
BURLEY
Milner Wood Jc.
POOL
WEETON
COLLINGHAM BRIDGE
THORP ARCH
COPMANTHORPE
Swing Bridge
NABURN
NEWTON KYME
WHELDRAKE
KILDWICK & CROSSHILLS
MENSTON
OTLEY
ARTHINGTON
Bramhope Tun.
Summit
BARDSEY
TADCASTER
BOLTON PERCY
COTTINGWITH
Worth Valley Bch. Jc.
Goods
KEIGHLEY
INGROW
DAMEMS
OAKWORTH
HAWORTH
OXENHOPE
GUISELEY
ESHOLT
YEADON
HORSFORTH
THORNER
STUTTON (Goods)
ULLESKELF
ESCRICK
THORGANBY
MUMPS
OLDHAM
CENTRAL
GLODWICK ROAD
OLDHAM CLEGG STREET
L.&N.W. Goods
G.C. Goods
OLDHAM WERNETH
INGROW
BINGLEY
Bingley Tun.
BAILDON
THACKLEY
APPERLEY BRI.
CALVERLEY
SEE SHEET NO. FORTY TWO
Summit
SCHOLES
CAWOOD
RICCALL
SKIPWITH & NORTH DUFFIELD
SALTAIRE
IDLE
NEWLAY
LEEDS
KIRKSTALL
HEADINGLEY
CHURCH FENTON
BUBWITH
CULLINGWORTH
FRIZING HALL
SHIPLEY
ECCLESHILL
BRAMLEY
ARMLEY
MARSH LANE
Cross Gates Jc.
N.E.
WISTOW
CLIFF COMMON
E. Jc.
Barlby Jc.
MENTHORPE GATE
DENHOLME
WILSDEN
MANNINGHAM
LAISTER-DYKE
STANNINGLEY
W'TON
Loco Shed
CROSS GATE
GARFORTH
MICKLEFIELD
SOUTH MILFORD
SHERBURN-IN-ELMET
Swing Bri.
HEMINGBOROUGH
BRADFORD
CLAYTON
ARMLEY
PUDSEY (L)
PUDSEY (G)
Gds.
Hunslet Bch Jc.
HUNSLET
Stourton Jc.
CROSS GATES
HAMBLETON
SELBY
Milford Jc.
Gasgoigne Wood Jc.
THORP GATES (Gds)
Brayton N. Jc.
Brayton E. Jc.
WRESSLE
THORNTON
QUEENSBURY
GT HORTON
HORTON PARK
DUDLEY HILL
BIRKENSHAW
BEESTON
CHURWELL
WOODLESFORD
KIPPAX
MONK FRYSTON
HOLMFIELD
WHEATLEY
LOW MOOR
Gds.
GILDERSOME
ROBIN HOOD
ROTHWELL
LEDSTON
BURTON SALMON
BARLOW
Swing Bridge
STANSFIELD HALL
Hall Royd Jc.
Millwood Tun.
Weasal Hall Tun.
HEBDEN BRI.
MYTHOLMROYD
ST. PAULS
OVENDEN
Wyke Tun.
GOMERSAL
MORLEY
ARDSLEY
METHLEY
FRYSTON (Gds)
DRAX
BARMBY
DRAX HALES
EASTWOOD
Castle Hill Tun.
Horsfall Tun.
LUDDENDEN FOOT
SOWERBY BRI.
HALIFAX
N. BRIDGE
WYKE
Wyke Jc.
BAILIFF BRI.
LIGHTCLIFFE
BIRSTALL
CLECKHEATON
Morley Tun.
TINGLEY
WOODKIRK
STANLEY
ALTOFTS
CASTLEFORD
FERRYBRIDGE (S.&K.)
KNOTTINGLEY
(L&Y&GN)
TEMPLE HIRST
WHITLEY BRIDGE
Gowdall Jc.
Hensall Jc.
CARLTON
AIRMYN
TODMORDEN
WALSDEN
Watertroughs
Bank House Tun.
COPLEY
Milner Royd
TRIANGLE
GREETLAND
LIVERSEDGE
CLIFTON RD.
COOPER BRI.
HECKMONDWYKE
BATLEY
LOFTHOUSE
ALVERTHORPE
NORMANTON
PONTEFRACT
TANSHELF
L.&Y.
PONTEFRACT
HENSALL
Aire Jc.
SNAITH
Winterbutlee Tun.
WATSONS CROSSING HALT
BRIGHOUSE
DEWSBURY
FLUSHDYKE
WAKEFIELD
OAKENSHAW
(Gds)
FEATHERSTONE
BALNE MOOR (Gds)
HECK
SNAITH & POLLINGTON
RAWCLIFFE
Summit Tun.
RIPPONDEN & BARKISLAND
WEST VALE
ELLAND
Bradley Wood Jc.
OSSETT
HORBURY & OSSETT
SHARLSTON
CROFTON
WOMERSLEY
RISHWORTH
STAINLAND
DEIGHTON
L.N.W. Jc.
MIRFIELD
THORNHILL
HARE PARK
ACKWORTH
Brackenhill Jc.
BALNE
SYKEHOUSE
HILLHOUSE (Gds)
Springwood Jc.
KIRKHEATON
HORBURY JUNC.
SANDAL
N. Jc.
S. Jc.
NOSTELL
KIRK SMEATON
N.E.
LITTLEBOROUGH
LONGWOOD
HUDDERSFIELD
Crigglestone Tun.
CRIGGLESTONE
MID
W. Jc.
G.N. & G.C. Jc.
Wrangbrook Jc.
NORTON
MOSS
SMITHY BRIDGE
Watertroughs
GOLCAR
L&N.W.
LOCKWOOD
FENAY BRI. & LEPTON
RYHILL
UPTON
Barnsdale (South Kirkby Tun)
G.C.H.&B.Jc.
WARDLEWORTH
Rochdale E. Jc.
LINTHWAITE (Gds)
SLAITHWAITE
NETHERTON
BERRY BROW
Robin Hood Tun.
KIRKBURTON
Royston Jc.
HEMSWORTH
Brierley Jc.
S. ELMSALL
ASKERN
THORNE
Joan Croft Jc.
THORNE
THORPE-IN-BALNE
MARSDEN
HEALEY HOUSE
HONLEY
BROCKHOLES
NOTTON & ROYSTON
HAIGH
ROYSTON & NOTTON
Shafton Jc.
HAMPOLE
Askern Jc.
Thorne Jc.
G.C.
NEW HEY
SHAW & CROMPTON
Standedge Tun.
Diggle Jc.
Watertroughs
STOCKSMOOR
CLAYTON WEST
DARTON
Gds
MOORTHORPE
Shaftholme Jc.
Applehurst Jc.
STAINFORTH & HATFIELD
ROYTON
DELPH
DIGGLE
MELTHAM
THONGS BRI.
SKELMANTHORPE
Cumberworth Tun.
STAINCROSS
MONK BRETTON
MOORHOUSE
Adwick Jc.
Skellow Jc.
BRAMWITH (Goods)
BARNBY DUN
ROYTON JUNC.
DOBCROSS
SADDLEWORTH
SHEPLEY
Thurstonland Tun.
HOLMFIRTH
DENBY DALE
SILKSTONE
BARNSLEY
CUDWORTH
GRIMETHORPE
Hickleton S. Jc.
PICKBURN
CARCROFT
FRICKLEY
Castle Hills Jc.
ARKSEY
Kirk Sandall Jc.
OLDHAM WERNETH
6 5 4 3 2 1
UPPERMILL
SUMMER LANE
Wellhouse Tun.
DODWORTH
Ardsley Tun.
HOUGHTON
HICKLETON
D.V.
Bentley Jc.
Goods
DONCASTER
FRIEZLAND
Royal George Tun.
MICKLEHURST (Goods)
HAZLEHEAD BRIDGE
SILKSTONE
MOOR END (Gds)
DARFIELD
HARLINGTON
BOLTON ON DEARNE
SPROTBORO
Works
Loco Shed
Bally Jc.
OLDHAM
PARK BRI.
O.A.&G.
Scout Tunnel
Woodhead Tun.
DUNFORD BRIDGE
PENISTONE
Barnsley Jc.
WOMBWELL
Dearne Jc.
DROYLSDEN
ASHTON
STALEY & MILLBROOK (Goods)
WOODHEAD
BIRDWELL
PILLEY (Gds)
WOMBWELL
WATH-ON-DEARNE
MEXBORO
DENABY
WARMSWORTH
Low Ellers Jc.
Bessacar Jc.
Thurgoland Tun.
WORTLEY
WEST WOOD
ELSECAR
Wath Rd. Jc.
FINNINGLEY
STALYBRIDGE
CROWDEN
1. MOORGATE
2. GREENFIELD
3. GRASSCROFT
4. GROTTON & SPRINGHEAD
5. LEES
6. GLODWICK ROAD
7. MOSSLEY
ARKSEY
Kirk Sandall Jc.
DEEPCAR
WENTWORTH
Tankersley Tun.
SWINTON
KILNHURST
SWINTON
CONISBORO
St. Catherine's Jcs.
Loversall Carr Jc.
GN.&G.E.Jc.
ROSSINGTON
GUIDE BRIDGE
HYDE JUNC.
Dinting Via.
YORK RD.
Bentley Jc.
CHAPLETOWN
KILNHURST
Denton Jc.
DENTON
NEWTON
HADFIELD
DINTING
N. Jc.
North Jc.
MARSH GATE (Gds)
ECCLESFIELD
G.C.
PARKGATE
ROTHERHAM (MASBORO)
PARKGATE & ALDWARKE
G.C. & MID
Braithwell Jc.
Northern Jc.
TICKHILL & WADWORTH
G.N.
MISSON (Gds)
HYDE
GODLEY JUNCTION
GLOSSOP
MOTTRAM & BROADBOTTOM
DONCASTER
South Jc.
OUGHTY BRIDGE
Reddish Jc.
Apethorne Jc.
WOODLEY
Mottram Via.
Balby Jc.
CHERRY TREE LANE
(Goods)
WADSLEY BRIDGE
MID.
HOLMES
WINCOBANK
ROTHERHAM RD.
ROTHERHAM (WESTGATE)
HELLABY (Gds)
MALTBY
BAWTRY
BREDBURY
STOCKPORT
ROMILEY
Hexthorpe Jc.
HEXTHORPE
S. Jc.
Potteric Carr Jc.
Low Ellers Jc.
SHEFFIELD
BRIGHTSIDE
VICTORIA
TINSLEY
GC.H & B & MID
GC.GN.L.& Y. MID. & NE.Jt (South Yorks Jc)
Watertroughs
SCROOBY
HIGH LANE
ROSE HILL
Black Carr Jc.
Bessacar Jc.
NEEPSEND
Tunnel Jc.
CATCLIFFE
THURCROFT (Gds)
DAVEN-PORT
MARPLE
Doncaster Avoiding Line Jc.
Black Carr W.
Lowersall Carr Jc.
VICTORIA CITY (Gds)
ATTERCLIFFE
DARNALL
Treeton Jc.
TREETON
Southern Jc.
RANSKILL
STRINES
HAYFIELD
WARMSWORTH (Gds)
Black Carr E. Jc.
WOODHOUSE MILL
DINNINGTON & LAUGHTON
G.N.
HAZEL GRO.
BIRCH VALE
NEW MILLS
QUEENS RD. Gds
POND ST.
WOODHOUSE
Dinnington Jc.

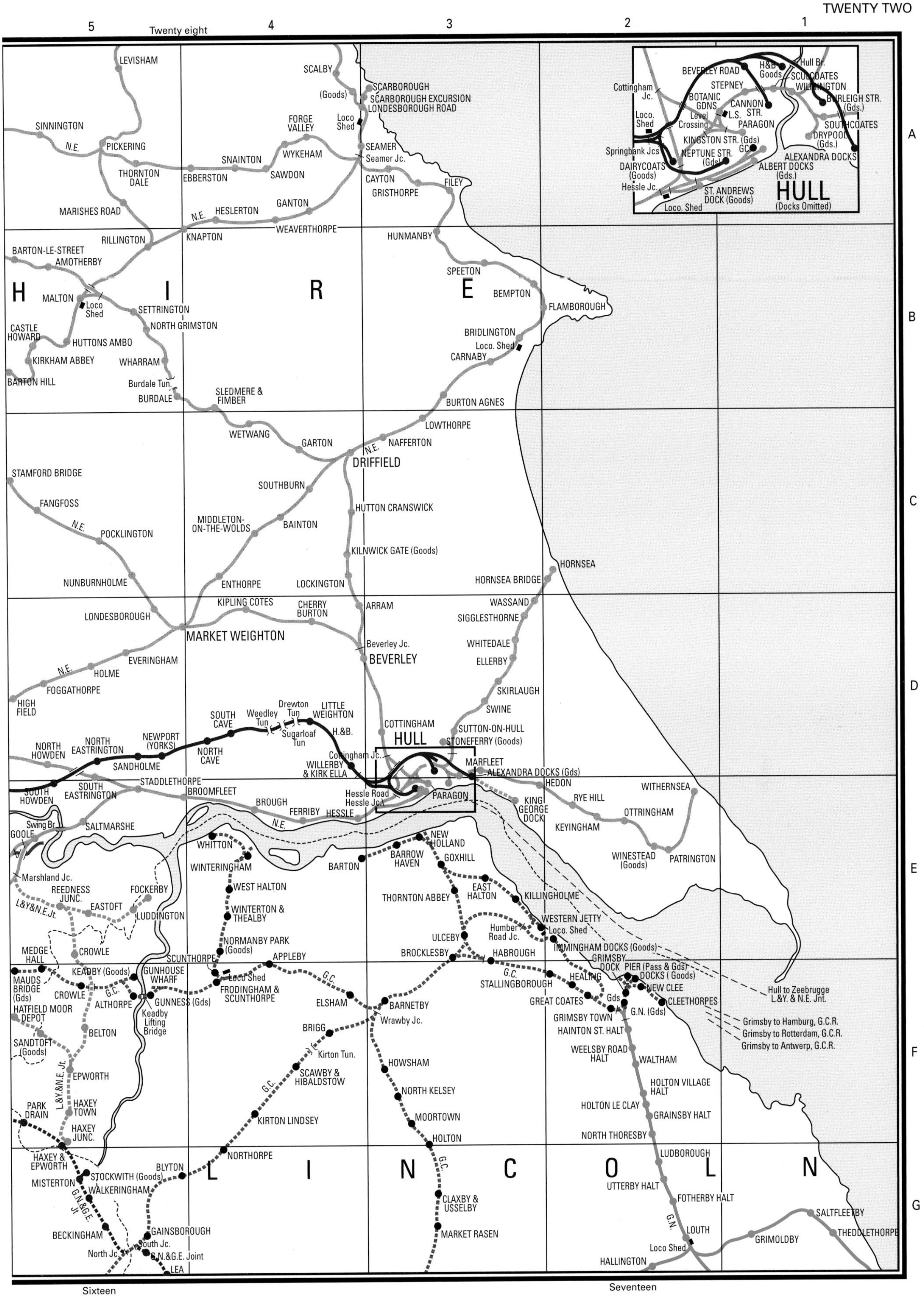

5 Twenty eight 4 3 2 1

LEVISHAM
SCALBY
SCARBOROUGH
(Goods)
SCARBOROUGH EXCURSION
LONDESBOROUGH ROAD
Loco Shed
FORGE VALLEY
SINNINGTON
N.E.
PICKERING
SEAMER
Seamer Jc.
WYKEHAM
SNAINTON
THORNTON DALE
EBBERSTON
SAWDON
CAYTON
FILEY
GRISTHORPE
GANTON
MARISHES ROAD
N.E.
HESLERTON
RILLINGTON
KNAPTON
WEAVERTHORPE
HUNMANBY
BARTON-LE-STREET
AMOTHERBY
SPEETON
H I R E
MALTON
Loco Shed
BEMPTON
FLAMBOROUGH
SETTRINGTON
NORTH GRIMSTON
CASTLE HOWARD
HUTTONS AMBO
BRIDLINGTON
Loco. Shed
KIRKHAM ABBEY
WHARRAM
CARNABY
BARTON HILL
Burdale Tun.
BURDALE
SLEDMERE & FIMBER
BURTON AGNES
LOWTHORPE
WETWANG
GARTON
N.E.
NAFFERTON
DRIFFIELD
STAMFORD BRIDGE
SOUTHBURN
FANGFOSS
HUTTON CRANSWICK
N.E.
POCKLINGTON
MIDDLETON-ON-THE-WOLDS
BAINTON
KILNWICK GATE (Goods)
HORNSEA
NUNBURNHOLME
ENTHORPE
LOCKINGTON
HORNSEA BRIDGE
KIPLING COTES
CHERRY BURTON
ARRAM
WASSAND
LONDESBOROUGH
SIGGLESTHORNE
MARKET WEIGHTON
Beverley Jc.
BEVERLEY
WHITEDALE
EVERINGHAM
ELLERBY
N.E.
HOLME
FOGGATHORPE
SKIRLAUGH
HIGH FIELD
SWINE
Drewton Tun
LITTLE WEIGHTON
SOUTH CAVE
Weedley Tun
Sugarloaf Tun
H.&B.
COTTINGHAM
SUTTON-ON-HULL
HULL
STONEFERRY (Goods)
NORTH HOWDEN
NORTH EASTRINGTON
NEWPORT (YORKS)
NORTH CAVE
SANDHOLME
Cottingham Jc.
WILLERBY & KIRK ELLA
MARFLEET
ALEXANDRA DOCKS (Gds)
STADDLETHORPE
HEDON
SOUTH HOWDEN
SOUTH EASTRINGTON
BROOMFLEET
Hessle Road
Hessle Jc.
PARAGON
RYE HILL
WITHERNSEA
BROUGH
FERRIBY
HESSLE
KING GEORGE DOCK
OTTRINGHAM
N.E.
Swing Br.
GOOLE
SALTMARSHE
KEYINGHAM
WHITTON
NEW HOLLAND
BARROW HAVEN
WINTERINGHAM
BARTON
GOXHILL
WINESTEAD (Goods)
PATRINGTON
Marshland Jc.
REEDNESS JUNC.
FOCKERBY
WEST HALTON
EAST HALTON
L&Y&N.E.Jt.
EASTOFT
THORNTON ABBEY
KILLINGHOLME
LUDDINGTON
WINTERTON & THEALBY
WESTERN JETTY
Loco. Shed
Humber Road Jc.
ULCEBY
NORMANBY PARK (Goods)
IMMINGHAM DOCKS (Goods)
MEDGE HALL
CROWLE
SCUNTHORPE
BROCKLESBY
HABROUGH
APPLEBY
GRIMSBY DOCK
PIER (Pass & Gds)
DOCKS (Goods)
KEADBY (Goods)
GUNHOUSE WHARF
Loco Shed
G.C.
G.C.
STALLINGBOROUGH
HEALING
NEW CLEE
MAUDS BRIDGE (Gds)
CROWLE
FRODINGHAM & SCUNTHORPE
Hull to Zeebrugge L.&Y. & N.E. Jnt.
ALTHORPE
GUNNESS (Gds)
ELSHAM
BARNETBY
GREAT COATES
Gds
CLEETHORPES
HATFIELD MOOR DEPOT
Keadby Lifting Bridge
Wrawby Jc.
GRIMSBY TOWN
G.N. (Gds)
Grimsby to Hamburg, G.C.R.
BELTON
BRIGG
HAINTON ST. HALT
Grimsby to Rotterdam, G.C.R.
Grimsby to Antwerp, G.C.R.
SANDTOFT (Goods)
Kirton Tun.
WEELSBY ROAD HALT
WALTHAM
EPWORTH
SCAWBY & HIBALDSTOW
HOWSHAM
L.&Y.&N.E. Jt.
G.C.
NORTH KELSEY
HOLTON VILLAGE HALT
PARK DRAIN
HAXEY TOWN
HOLTON LE CLAY
GRAINSBY HALT
KIRTON LINDSEY
MOORTOWN
HAXEY JUNC.
HOLTON
NORTH THORESBY
HAXEY & EPWORTH
NORTHORPE
G.C.
LUDBOROUGH
BLYTON
L I N C O L N
STOCKWITH (Goods)
MISTERTON
WALKERINGHAM
UTTERBY HALT
G.N.&G.E. Jt.
CLAXBY & USSELBY
FOTHERBY HALT
SALTFLEETBY
BECKINGHAM
GAINSBOROUGH
MARKET RASEN
G.N.
LOUTH
THEDDLETHORPE
GRIMOLDBY
South Jc.
North Jc.
G.N.&G.E. Joint
Loco Shed
HALLINGTON
LEA

BEVERLEY ROAD
H&B Goods
Hull Br.
SCULCOATES
Cottingham Jc.
STEPNEY
WILMINGTON
BOTANIC GDNS
CANNON STR.
BURLEIGH STR. (Gds.)
Loco. Shed
Level Crossing
L.S.
PARAGON
SOUTHCOATES
DRYPOOL (Gds.)
KINGSTON STR. (Gds)
Springbank Jcs
NEPTUNE STR. (Gds)
GC
ALEXANDRA DOCKS
DAIRYCOATS (Goods)
ALBERT DOCKS (Gds.)
Hessle Jc.
ST. ANDREWS DOCK (Goods)
HULL
(Docks Omitted)
Loco. Shed

A B C D E F G

Sixteen Seventeen

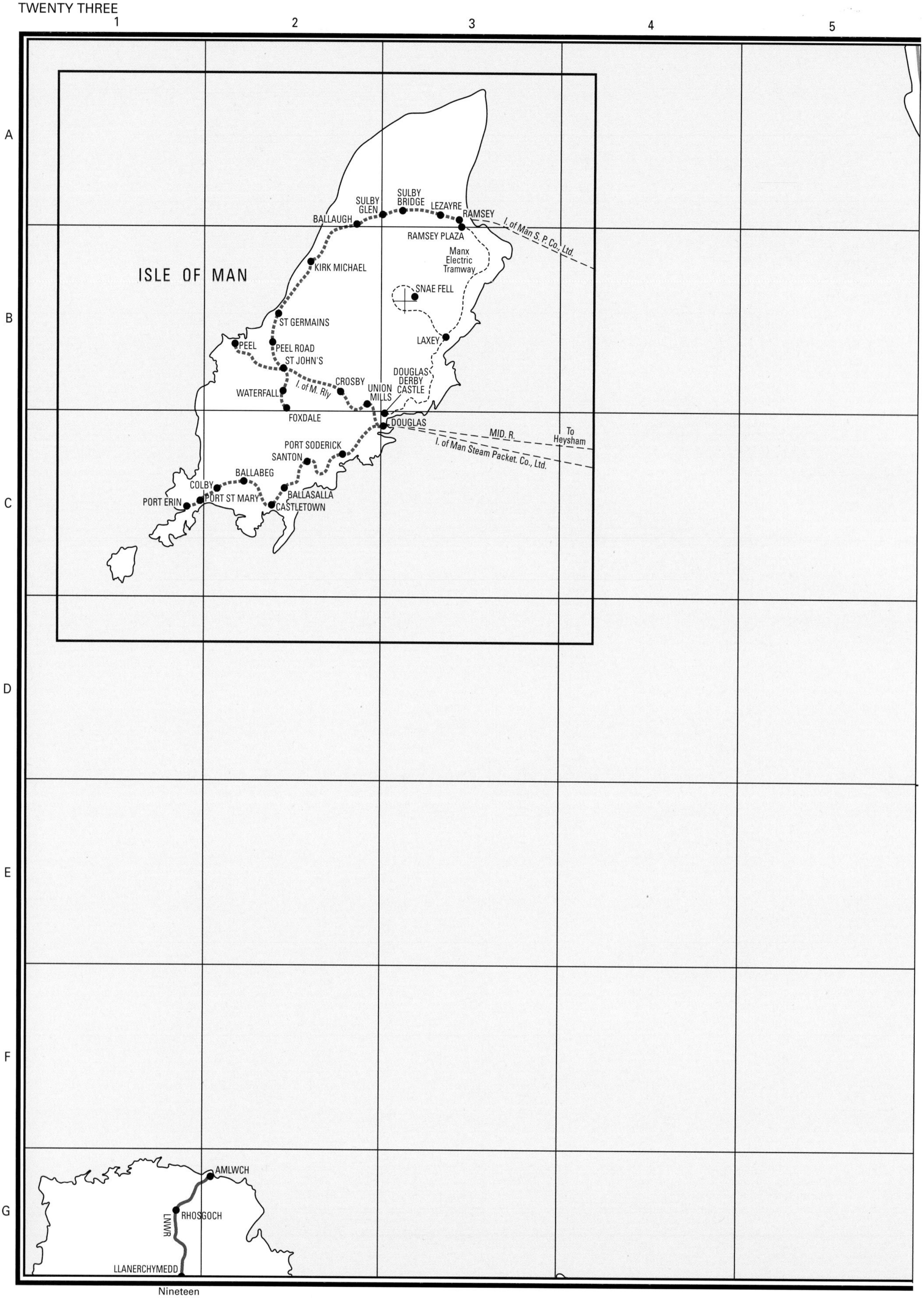

1 2 3 4 5

A B C D E F G

ISLE OF MAN

SULBY GLEN
SULBY BRIDGE
LEZAYRE
RAMSEY
BALLAUGH
RAMSEY PLAZA
I. of Man S. P. Co., Ltd.
Manx Electric Tramway
KIRK MICHAEL
SNAE FELL
ST GERMAINS
LAXEY
PEEL
PEEL ROAD
ST JOHN'S
DOUGLAS DERBY CASTLE
CROSBY
I. of M. Rly
UNION MILLS
WATERFALL
FOXDALE
DOUGLAS
MID. R.
To Heysham
I. of Man Steam Packet. Co., Ltd.
PORT SODERICK
SANTON
BALLABEG
COLBY
BALLASALLA
PORT ERIN
PORT ST MARY
CASTLETOWN

AMLWCH
RHOSGOCH
LNWR
LLANERCHYMEDD
Nineteen

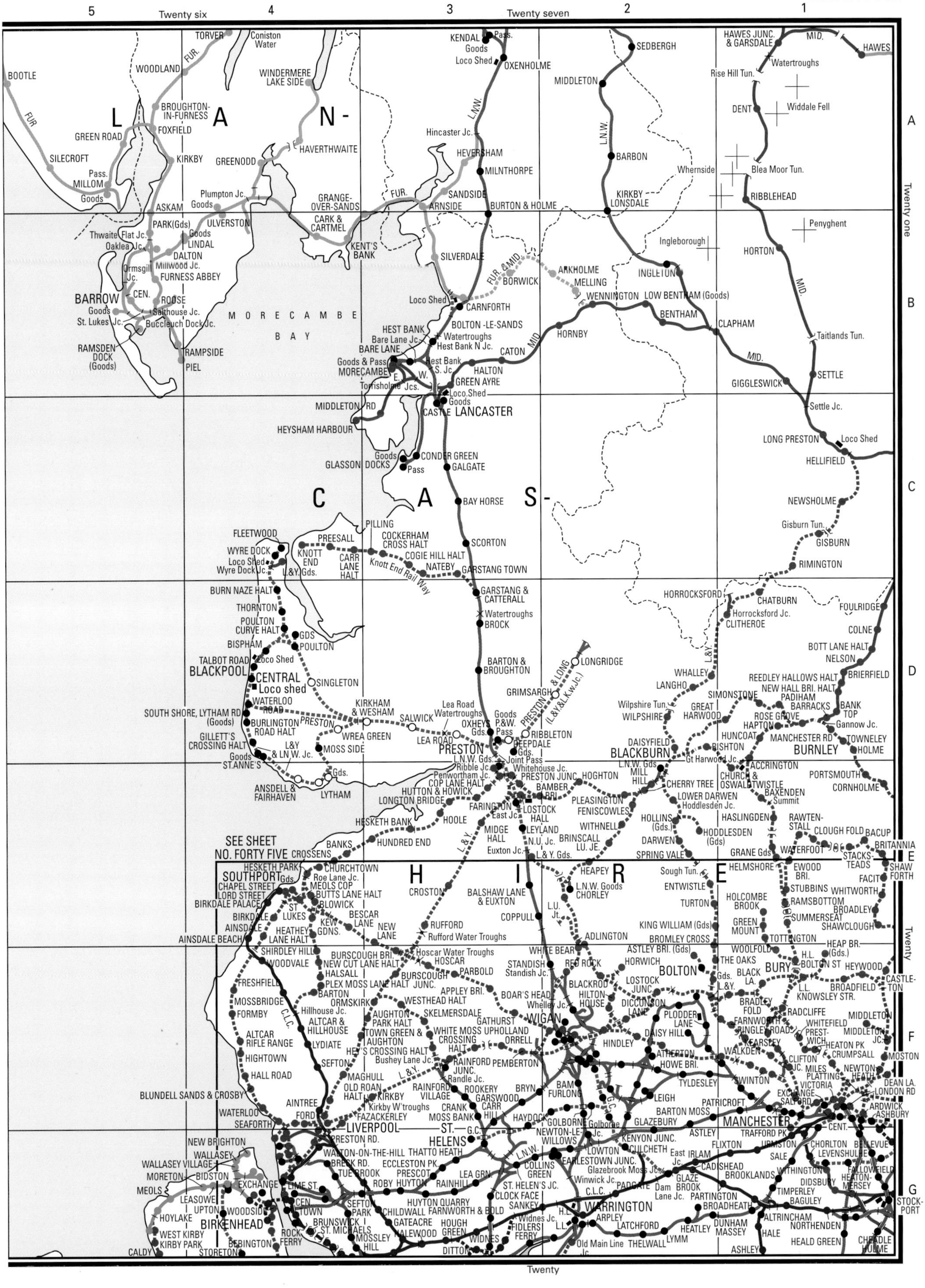

Twenty six
Twenty seven
Twenty one
Twenty
LANCASHIRE
MORECAMBE BAY
TORVER
Coniston Water
BOOTLE
WOODLAND
WINDERMERE LAKE SIDE
KENDAL
OXENHOLME
SEDBERGH
HAWES JUNC. & GARSDALE
HAWES
MIDDLETON
DENT
BROUGHTON-IN-FURNESS
FOXFIELD
GREEN ROAD
SILECROFT
MILLOM
KIRKBY
GREENODD
HAVERTHWAITE
Hincaster Jc.
HEVERSHAM
MILNTHORPE
BARBON
RIBBLEHEAD
ASKAM
ULVERSTON
GRANGE-OVER-SANDS
ARNSIDE
SANDSIDE
BURTON & HOLME
KIRKBY LONSDALE
CARK & CARTMEL
KENT'S BANK
SILVERDALE
BORWICK
ARKHOLME
MELLING
INGLETON
HORTON
DALTON
LINDAL
FURNESS ABBEY
BARROW
ROOSE
RAMPSIDE
PIEL
CARNFORTH
WENNINGTON
LOW BENTHAM (Goods)
BENTHAM
CLAPHAM
BOLTON-LE-SANDS
HEST BANK
BARE LANE
MORECAMBE
HORNBY
CATON
HALTON
GREEN AYRE
SETTLE
GIGGLESWICK
LANCASTER
MIDDLETON RD
HEYSHAM HARBOUR
LONG PRESTON
HELLIFIELD
CONDER GREEN
GALGATE
GLASSON DOCKS
BAY HORSE
NEWSHOLME
GISBURN
SCORTON
PILLING
FLEETWOOD
PREESALL
COCKERHAM CROSS HALT
COGIE HILL HALT
NATEBY
GARSTANG TOWN
RIMINGTON
GARSTANG & CATTERALL
CHATBURN
CLITHEROE
BROCK
BLACKPOOL
POULTON
LONGRIDGE
WHALLEY
BARTON & BROUGHTON
PRESTON
BLACKBURN
BURNLEY
COLNE
NELSON
BRIERFIELD
ACCRINGTON
LYTHAM
ST. ANNE'S
KIRKHAM & WESHAM
LEYLAND
DARWEN
CHORLEY
SOUTHPORT
BOLTON
BURY
WIGAN
ORMSKIRK
MANCHESTER
LIVERPOOL
ST. HELENS
WARRINGTON
BIRKENHEAD
STOCKPORT
SEE SHEET NO. FORTY FIVE

1 2 3 Twenty nine 4 5

A B C D E F G

Tunnel
PINMORE
PINWHERRY
A Y R
BARRHILL
Summit
K I R K C U D
Larne & Stranraer Steamship Company
To Larne
G. & S.W.
GLENWHILLY
W I G T O W N
LOCH SKERROW
Cairnsmore
NEWTON STEWART
PALNURE
GATEHOUSE OF FLEET
Summit
Loch Ryan
NEW LUCE
PORTPATRICK & WIGTOWNSHIRE JOINT
Harbour
Loco Shed
STRANRAER
CASTLE KENNEDY
KIRKCOWAN
CREETOWN
DUNRAGIT
Challoch Jc
GLENLUCE
WIGTON
PORTPATRICK
COLFIN
KIRKINNER
WHAUPHILL
SORBIE
MILLISLE
GARLIESTON
WHITHORN
ISLE OF MAN
SULBY GLEN
LEZAYRE
BALLAUGH
SULBY BRIDGE
RAMSEY
RAMSEY PLAZA
I. of M.
KIRK MICHAEL

Twenty three (inset)

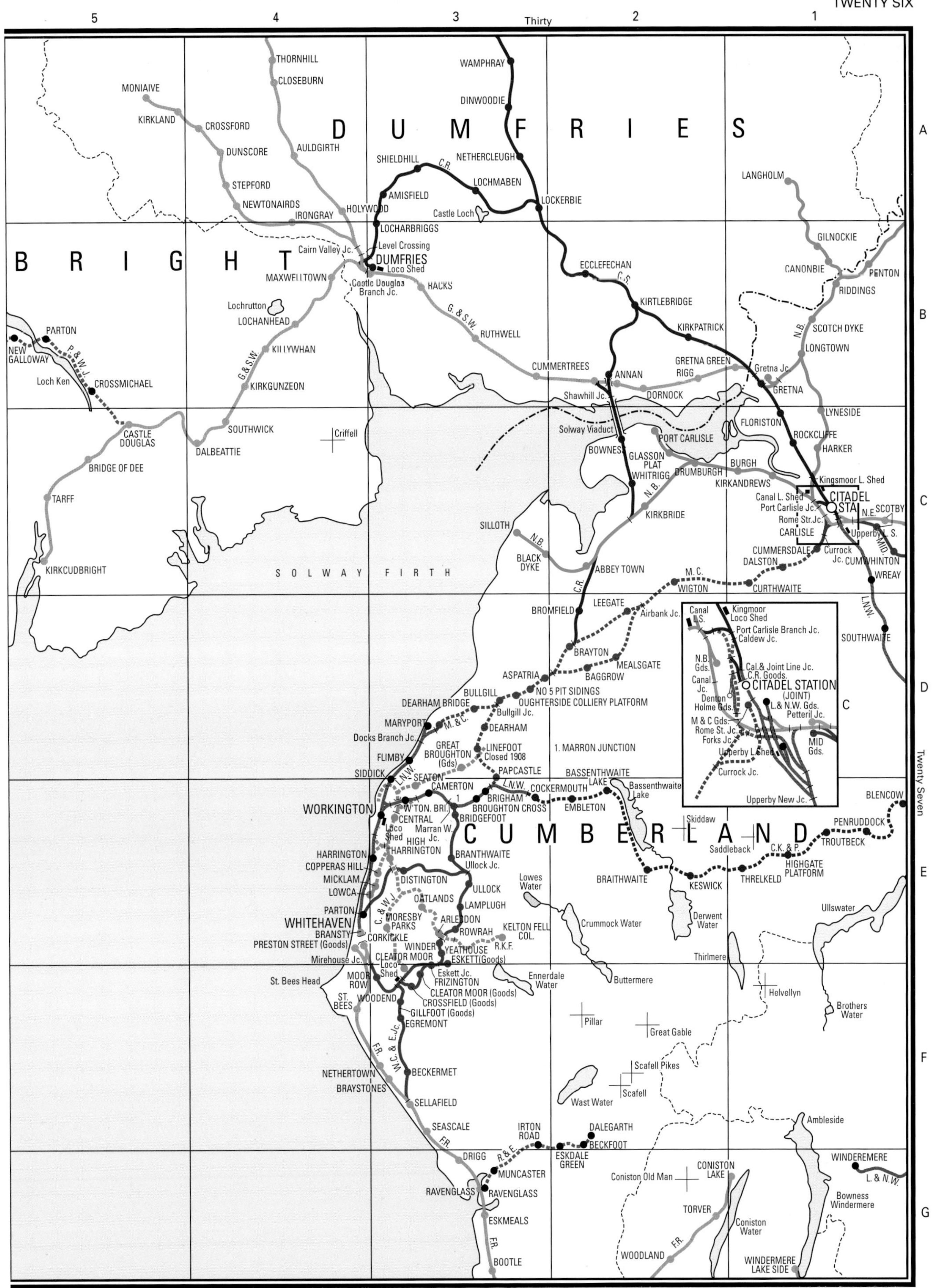
5
4
3
Thirty
2
1
DUMFRIES
BRIGHT
CUMBERLAND
SOLWAY FIRTH
A
B
C
D
E
F
G
Twenty Seven
Twenty four
THORNHILL
CLOSEBURN
MONIAIVE
KIRKLAND
CROSSFORD
DUNSCORE
AULDGIRTH
STEPFORD
NEWTONAIRDS
IRONGRAY
HOLYWOOD
WAMPHRAY
DINWOODIE
SHIELDHILL
C.R.
NETHERCLEUGH
LOCHMABEN
AMISFIELD
Castle Loch
LOCKERBIE
LOCHARBRIGGS
Level Crossing
Cairn Valley Jc.
DUMFRIES
Loco Shed
MAXWELLTOWN
Castle Douglas Branch Jc.
HACKS
Lochrutton
LOCHANHEAD
G. & S.W.
RUTHWELL
KILLYWHAN
KIRKGUNZEON
SOUTHWICK
DALBEATTIE
Criffell
PARTON
NEW GALLOWAY
P. & W.J.
Loch Ken
CROSSMICHAEL
CASTLE DOUGLAS
BRIDGE OF DEE
TARFF
KIRKCUDBRIGHT
ECCLEFECHAN
C.S.
KIRKTLEBRIDGE
KIRKPATRICK
GRETNA GREEN
RIGG
CUMMERTREES
ANNAN
Shawhill Jc.
DORNOCK
Solway Viaduct
BOWNESS
GLASSON
PLAT
WHITRIGG
PORT CARLISLE
DRUMBURGH
BURGH
KIRKANDREWS
N.B.
KIRKBRIDE
SILLOTH
BLACK DYKE
ABBEY TOWN
LANGHOLM
GILNOCKIE
CANONBIE
PENTON
RIDDINGS
SCOTCH DYKE
LONGTOWN
Gretna Jc.
GRETNA
LYNESIDE
FLORISTON
ROCKCLIFFE
HARKER
Kingsmoor L. Shed
CITADEL STA.
Canal L. Shed
Port Carlisle Jc.
Rome Str.Jc.
CARLISLE
N.E.
SCOTBY
Upperby L. S.
CUMMERSDALE
Currock Jc.
DALSTON
CUMWHINTON
MID.
WREAY
M. C.
WIGTON
CURTHWAITE
L.N.W.
SOUTHWAITE
BROMFIELD
LEEGATE
Airbank Jc.
BRAYTON
MEALSGATE
BAGGROW
ASPATRIA
BULLGILL
NO 5 PIT SIDINGS
OUGHTERSIDE COLLIERY PLATFORM
DEARHAM BRIDGE
Bullgill Jc.
MARYPORT
M. & C.
DEARHAM
Docks Branch Jc.
FLIMBY
GREAT BROUGHTON (Gds)
LINEFOOT Closed 1908
1. MARRON JUNCTION
SIDDICK
PAPCASTLE
BASSENTHWAITE LAKE
SEATON
CAMERTON
COCKERMOUTH
Bassenthwaite Lake
WORKINGTON
W'TON. BRI.
BRIGHAM
BROUGHTON CROSS
EMBLETON
CENTRAL
BRIDGEFOOT
Loco Shed
Marron W. Jc.
HIGH HARRINGTON
Skiddaw
Saddleback
C.K. & P.
PENRUDDOCK
TROUTBECK
BLENCOW
HARRINGTON
COPPERAS HILL
BRANTHWAITE
Ullock Jc.
HIGHGATE PLATFORM
THRELKELD
KESWICK
BRAITHWAITE
MICKLAM
LOWCA
DISTINGTON
ULLOCK
Lowes Water
OATLANDS
LAMPLUGH
PARTON
WHITEHAVEN
C. & W.J.
MORESBY PARKS
ARLECDON
Crummock Water
Derwent Water
Ullswater
BRANSTY
CORKICKLE
ROWRAH
KELTON FELL COL.
PRESTON STREET (Goods)
WINDER
YEATHOUSE
R.K.F.
Mirehouse Jc.
CLEATOR MOOR
ESKETT(Goods)
Thirlmere
St. Bees Head
MOOR ROW
Loco Shed
Eskett Jc.
FRIZINGTON
Ennerdale Water
Buttermere
CLEATOR MOOR (Goods)
ST. BEES
WOODEND
CROSSFIELD (Goods)
GILLFOOT (Goods)
EGREMONT
Helvellyn
Brothers Water
Pillar
Great Gable
W.C. & E.Jc.
F.R.
NETHERTOWN
BECKERMET
Scafell Pikes
BRAYSTONES
Scafell
Wast Water
SELLAFIELD
SEASCALE
IRTON ROAD
DALEGARTH
BECKFOOT
ESKDALE GREEN
Ambleside
DRIGG
R. & E.
MUNCASTER
WINDEREMERE
L. & N.W.
CONISTON LAKE
Coniston Old Man
RAVENGLASS
Bowness Windermere
TORVER
Coniston Water
ESKMEALS
WOODLAND
WINDERMERE LAKE SIDE
BOOTLE
Canal L.S.
Kingmoor Loco Shed
Port Carlisle Branch Jc.
Caldew Jc.
N.B. Gds.
Cal.& Joint Line Jc.
C.R. Goods.
Canal Jc.
CITADEL STATION (JOINT)
Denton Holme Gds.
L.& N.W. Gds.
Petteril Jc.
M & C Gds.
Rome St. Jc.
Forks Jc.
MID Gds.
Upperby L. Shed
Currock Jc.
Upperby New Jc.

1 2 Thirty one 3 4 5

A B C D E F G

RICCARTON JUNCTION
SAUGHTREE
DEADWATER
N.B.
STEELE ROAD
KIELDER
PLASHETTS
N. B.
FALSTONE
THORNEYBURN
TARSET
NEWCASTLETON
KERSHOPE FOOT
BELLINGHAM
REEDSMOUTH
WOODBURN
N. B.
KNOWESGATE
FONTBURN
EWESLEY
LONG WITTON
SCOTSGAP
MIDDLETON
ANGERTON
MELDON
WIDDRINGTON
LONGHURST
ASHINGTON
PEGSWOOD
NORTH SEATON
MORPETH
HEPSCOTT
N.E.
CHOPPINGTON
BEDLINGTON
STANNINGTON
BEBSIDE
PLESSEY
CRAMLINGTON

N O R T H U M B E R L A N D

WARK
N.B.
BARRASFORD
CHOLLERTON
HUMSHAUGH
FOURSTONES
WALL
HEXHAM
N.E.
HAYDON BRIDGE
BARDON MILL
GILSLAND
GREENHEAD
HALTWHISTLE
Haltwhistle Tunnel
PLENMELLER PARK
FEATHERSTONE PARK
COANWOOD
LAMBLEY
BURNSTONES
SLAGGYFORD
ALSTON
LOW ROW
NAWORTH
BRAMPTON TOWN
BRAMPTON JUNC.
HOW MILL
HEADS NOOK
WETHERAL
COTEHILL
ELRINGTON
LANGLEY
STAWARD
ALLENDALE
CORBRIDGE
Corbridge Tun.
RIDING MILL
STOCKSFIELD
PRUDHOE
WYLAM
RYTON
PONTELAND
N.E.
DARRAS HALL
CALLERTON
ANNITSFORD
KILLINGWORTH
FOREST HALL
KENTON
COXLODGE
BENTON
LEMINGTON
WEST GOSFORTH
NEWBURN
SOUTH GOSFORD
HEDDON-ON-THE-WALL
NORTH WYLAM
W. JESMOND
JESMOND
SCOTSWOOD
CENTRAL
BLAYDON
SWALWELL
BENSHAM
NEWCASTLE
LOW FELL
ROWLANDS GILL
LAMESLEY
HIGH WESTWOOD
LINTZ GREEN
BIRTLEY
EBCHESTER
SHIELD ROW
BEAMISH
PELTON
SHOTLEY BRIDGE
LEADGATE
W. STANLEY (Gds.)
BLACKHILL
CHESTER LE STREET
CONSETT
KNITSLEY
ANNFIELD PLAIN
ROWLEY
PLAWSWORTH
ARMATHWAITE
Armathwaite Tun.
Baron Wood Tuns.
LAZONBY & KIRKOSWALD
Lazonby Tun.
CALTHWAITE
PLUMPTON
MID.
LITTLE SALKELD
LANGWATHBY
WASKERLEY (Goods)
BURN HILL
LANCHESTER
WITTON GILBERT
DURHAM
ALDIN GRANGE FOR BEARPARK
PARKHEAD (Goods)
USHAW MOOR
Reilly Mill Jc.
WATERHOUSES
BRANDON
TOW LAW
WEARHEAD
EASTGATE
STANHOPE
ST. JOHN'S CHAPEL
WESTGATE-IN-WEARDALE
FROSTERLEY
BRANCEPETH
WOLSINGHAM
N.E.
CROXDALE
HARPERLEY
CROOK
WILLINGTON
SPENNYMOOR

D U R H A M

BEECHBURN
HUNWICK
BYERS GREEN
Twenty six
Loco Shed
PENRITH
Waste Bank Tun.
Culgaith Tun.
CULGAITH
NEW BIGGIN
Red Hills Jc.
Eamont Bri. Jc.
Eden Valley Jc.
CLIFTON
TEMPLE SOWERBY
KIRKBY THORE
CLIBURN
LONG MARTON
CLIFTON & LOWTHER
WITTON-LE-WEAR
WEAR VALLEY JUNC.
ETHERLEY
BISHOP AUCKLAND
COUNDON
EVENWOOD
BUTTERKNOWLE
COCKFIELD
WEST AUCKLAND
Loco Shed
SHILDON
MIDDLETON-IN-TEESDALE
MICKLETON
HEIGHINGTON
APPLEBY
ROMALDKIRK

W E S T M O R L A N D

ORMSIDE
N.E.
WARCOP
COTHERSTONE
LARTINGTON
BARNARD CASTLE
BROOMIELAW
N. E.
WINSTON
GAINFORD
Forcett Jc.
Merrybent Jc.
PIERCEBRIDGE
Helm Tun.
SHAP
MUSGRAVE
BOWES
N.E.
Stainmore Summit
BARRAS
Shap Summit
L.N.W.
CROSBY GARRETT
SMARDALE
Loco Shed
Belah Viaduct
FORCETT DEPOT
BARTON (Goods)
KIRKBY STEPHEN & RAVENSTONEDALE
KIRKBY STEPHEN
GAISGILL
RAVENSTONEDALE
Birkett Tun.
Loco Shed
TEBAY
Dillicar Watertroughs
Wild Boar Fell
High Seat
MOULTON
SCORTON
RICHMOND
CATTERICK BRIDGE
Blease Fell
STAVELEY
LOW GILL
Great Shunner Fell
BURNSIDE
GRAYRIGG
Aisgill Summit
Pass
Baugh Fell
Shotlock Tun.
Moorcock Tun.
KENDAL Gds.
SEDBERGH
HAWES JUNC. & GARSDALE
Watertroughs
MID.
Mossdale Head Tun.
Loco Shed
OXENHOLME
HAWES
N.E
ASKRIGG
Rise Hill Tun.
MIDDLETON

Y O R K

REDMIRE
AYSGARTH
WENSLEY
LEYBURN
SPENNITHORNE
CONSTABLE BURTON
FINGHALL LANE
JERVAULX
CRAKEHALL
BEDALE

Twenty four
Twenty one

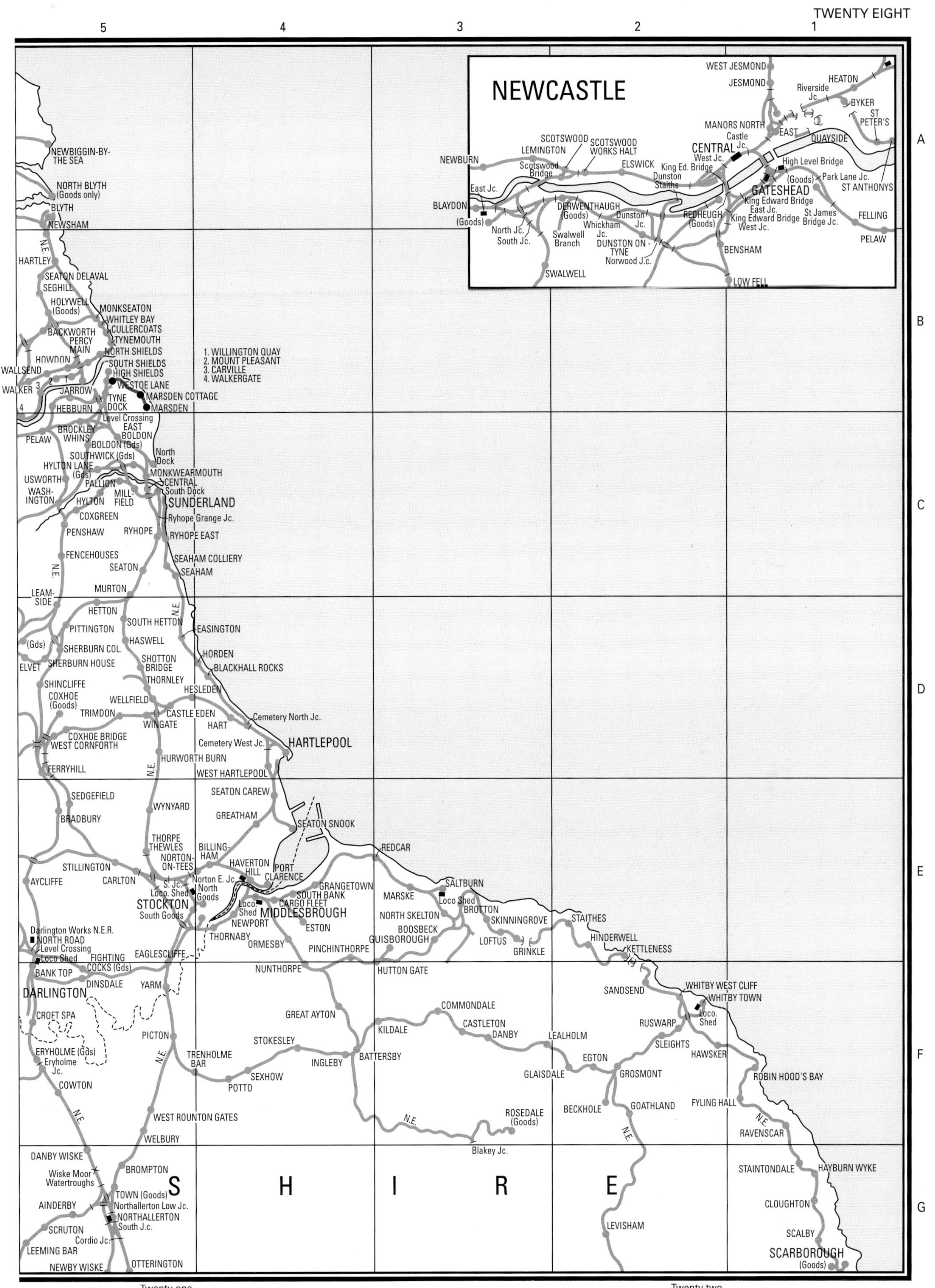
5
4
3
2
1
A
B
C
D
E
F
G
NEWCASTLE
WEST JESMOND
JESMOND
HEATON
Riverside Jc.
BYKER
ST PETER'S
MANORS NORTH
EAST
QUAYSIDE
CENTRAL
Castle Jc.
West Jc.
High Level Bridge
SCOTSWOOD
SCOTSWOOD WORKS HALT
LEMINGTON
NEWBURN
Scotswood Bridge
ELSWICK
King Ed. Bridge
Dunston Staiths
GATESHEAD
(Goods)
Park Lane Jc.
ST ANTHONYS
East Jc.
BLAYDON
DERWENTHAUGH (Goods)
Dunston Jc.
Whickham Jc.
REDHEUGH (Goods)
King Edward Bridge East Jc.
King Edward Bridge West Jc.
St James Bridge Jc.
FELLING
PELAW
North Jc.
South Jc.
Swalwell Branch
DUNSTON ON-TYNE
Norwood J.c.
BENSHAM
SWALWELL
LOW FELL
NEWBIGGIN-BY-THE SEA
NORTH BLYTH (Goods only)
BLYTH
NEWSHAM
N.E.
HARTLEY
SEATON DELAVAL
SEGHILL
HOLYWELL (Goods)
MONKSEATON
WHITLEY BAY
CULLERCOATS
TYNEMOUTH
BACKWORTH
PERCY MAIN
NORTH SHIELDS
HOWDON
WALLSEND
SOUTH SHIELDS
HIGH SHIELDS
WALKER
JARROW
WESTOE LANE
MARSDEN COTTAGE
TYNE DOCK
MARSDEN
HEBBURN
1. WILLINGTON QUAY
2. MOUNT PLEASANT
3. CARVILLE
4. WALKERGATE
Level Crossing
EAST BOLDON
BROCKLEY WHINS
PELAW
BOLDON (Gds)
SOUTHWICK (Gds)
North Dock
HYLTON LANE (Gds)
MONKWEARMOUTH
USWORTH
PALLION
CENTRAL
South Dock
WASHINGTON
HYLTON
MILLFIELD
SUNDERLAND
COXGREEN
Ryhope Grange Jc.
PENSHAW
RYHOPE
RYHOPE EAST
FENCEHOUSES
SEAHAM COLLIERY
SEATON
SEAHAM
LEAMSIDE
MURTON
HETTON
SOUTH HETTON
EASINGTON
PITTINGTON
HASWELL
(Gds)
SHERBURN COL.
HORDEN
ELVET
SHERBURN HOUSE
SHOTTON BRIDGE
BLACKHALL ROCKS
THORNLEY
SHINCLIFFE
HESLEDEN
COXHOE (Goods)
WELLFIELD
TRIMDON
CASTLE EDEN
Cemetery North Jc.
WINGATE
HART
COXHOE BRIDGE
WEST CORNFORTH
Cemetery West Jc.
HARTLEPOOL
FERRYHILL
HURWORTH BURN
WEST HARTLEPOOL
SEATON CAREW
SEDGEFIELD
WYNYARD
BRADBURY
GREATHAM
SEATON SNOOK
THORPE THEWLES
BILLINGHAM
REDCAR
NORTON-ON-TEES
HAVERTON HILL
PORT CLARENCE
STILLINGTON
AYCLIFFE
CARLTON
S. Jc.
Norton E. Jc.
Loco. Shed
North Goods
GRANGETOWN
SALTBURN
SOUTH BANK
MARSKE
Loco Shed
STOCKTON
South Goods
CARGO FLEET
MIDDLESBROUGH
BROTTON
NEWPORT
NORTH SKELTON
SKINNINGROVE
STAITHES
ESTON
BOOSBECK
Darlington Works N.E.R.
NORTH ROAD
THORNABY
GUISBOROUGH
LOFTUS
HINDERWELL
Level Crossing
ORMESBY
PINCHINTHORPE
GRINKLE
KETTLENESS
Loco Shed
FIGHTING COCKS (Gds)
EAGLESCLIFFE
BANK TOP
NUNTHORPE
HUTTON GATE
DINSDALE
YARM
DARLINGTON
SANDSEND
WHITBY WEST CLIFF
WHITBY TOWN
COMMONDALE
Loco. Shed
CROFT SPA
GREAT AYTON
CASTLETON
RUSWARP
KILDALE
DANBY
LEALHOLM
SLEIGHTS
PICTON
STOKESLEY
ERYHOLME (Gds)
Eryholme Jc.
TRENHOLME BAR
INGLEBY
BATTERSBY
EGTON
HAWSKER
GLAISDALE
GROSMONT
ROBIN HOOD'S BAY
SEXHOW
POTTO
COWTON
N.E.
FYLING HALL
WEST ROUNTON GATES
ROSEDALE (Goods)
BECKHOLE
GOATHLAND
RAVENSCAR
WELBURY
Blakey Jc.
DANBY WISKE
BROMPTON
STAINTONDALE
HAYBURN WYKE
Wiske Moor Watertroughs
S
H
I
R
E
TOWN (Goods)
Northallerton Low Jc.
AINDERBY
NORTHALLERTON
South J.c.
CLOUGHTON
LEVISHAM
SCRUTON
Cordio Jc.
SCALBY
LEEMING BAR
SCARBOROUGH (Goods)
NEWBY WISKE
OTTERINGTON
Twenty one
Twenty two

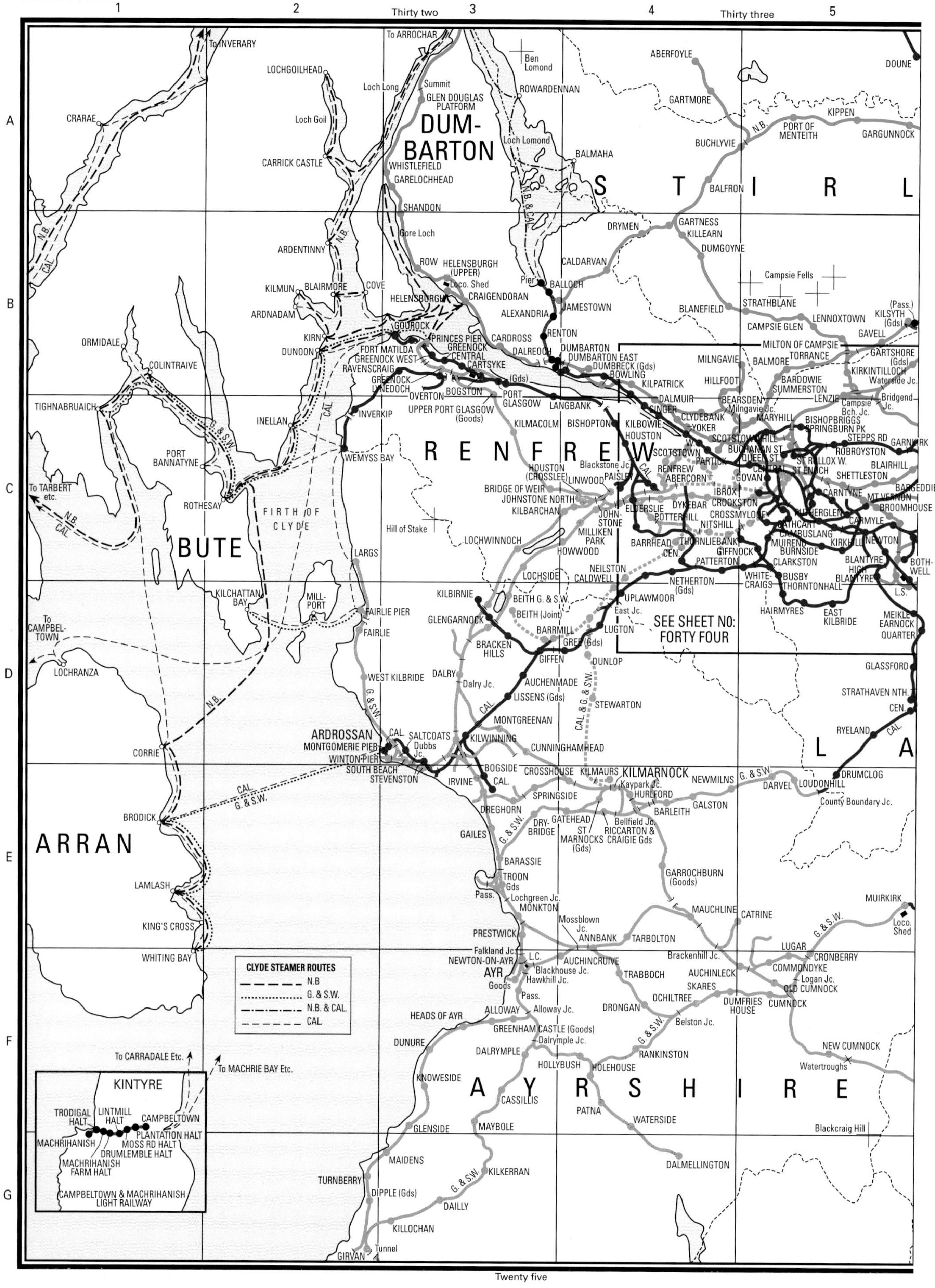

1 2 Thirty two 3 4 Thirty three 5

A B C D E F G

To INVERARY
CRARAE
LOCHGOILHEAD
Loch Goil
CARRICK CASTLE
To ARROCHAR
Loch Long
Summit
GLEN DOUGLAS PLATFORM
DUM-BARTON
WHISTLEFIELD
GARELOCHHEAD
SHANDON
Gore Loch
ROW
HELENSBURGH (UPPER)
Loco. Shed
HELENSBURGH
CRAIGENDORAN
Ben Lomond
ROWARDENNAN
Loch Lomond
BALMAHA
ABERFOYLE
GARTMORE
BUCHLYVIE
PORT OF MENTEITH
KIPPEN
GARGUNNOCK
DOUNE
S T I R L
BALFRON
DRYMEN
GARTNESS
KILLEARN
DUMGOYNE
CALDARVAN
Pier
BALLOCH
JAMESTOWN
ALEXANDRIA
RENTON
CARDROSS
DALREOCH
DUMBARTON
DUMBARTON EAST
DUMBRECK (Gds)
BOWLING
KILPATRICK
DALMUIR
SINGER
Campsie Fells
STRATHBLANE
BLANEFIELD
CAMPSIE GLEN
LENNOXTOWN
KILSYTH (Pass.) (Gds)
GAVELL
MILTON OF CAMPSIE
GARTSHORE (Gds)
TORRANCE
KIRKINTILLOCH
Waterside Jc.
MILNGAVIE
BALMORE
HILLFOOT
BARDOWIE
SUMMERSTON
LENZIE
Campsie Bch. Jc.
Bridgend Jc.
BEARSDEN
Milngavie Jc.
MARYHILL
BISHOPBRIGGS
SPRINGBURN PK
STEPPS RD
GARNKIRK
ARDENTINNY
KILMUN
BLAIRMORE
COVE
ARDNADAM
KIRN
DUNOON
GOUROCK
PRINCES PIER
GREENOCK CENTRAL
CARTSYKE
FORT MATILDA
GREENOCK WEST
RAVENSCRAIG
GREENOCK LYNEDOCH
OVERTON
BOGSTON
(Gds)
PORT GLASGOW
UPPER PORT GLASGOW (Goods)
LANGBANK
BISHOPTON
KILBOWIE
CLYDEBANK
YOKER
SCOTSTOUNHILL
KILMACOLM
HOUSTON
SCOTSTOWN
BUCHANAN ST
QUEEN ST
ROBROYSTON
ST ROLLOX W.
BLAIRHILL
PARTICK
CENTRAL
ST ENOCH
SHETTLESTON
ORMIDALE
COLINTRAIVE
TIGHNABRUAICH
INELLAN
INVERKIP
WEMYSS BAY
R E N F R E W
Blackstone Jc.
HOUSTON (CROSSLEE)
LINWOOD
PAISLEY
RENFREW
ABERCORN
GOVAN
IBROX
CARNTYNE
BARGEDDIE
MT VERNON
BROOMHOUSE
PORT BANNATYNE
G. & S.W.
CAL.
To TARBERT etc.
N.B. CAL.
ROTHESAY
FIRTH OF CLYDE
BUTE
BRIDGE OF WEIR
JOHNSTONE NORTH
KILBARCHAN
JOHN-STONE
ELDERSLIE
DYKEBAR
CROOKSTON
POTTERHILL
CROSSMYLOOF
NITSHILL
RUTHERGLEN
CARMYLE
CATHCART
CAMBUSLANG
KIRKHILL
NEWTON
Hill of Stake
LOCHWINNOCH
MILLIKEN PARK
HOWWOOD
BARRHEAD
CEN.
THORNLIEBANK
GIFFNOCK
MUIREND
BURNSIDE
CLARKSTON
PATTERTON
LARGS
LOCHSIDE
NEILSTON
CALDWELL
NETHERTON (Gds)
WHITE-CRAIGS
BUSBY
THORNTONHALL
BLANTYRE
HIGH BLANTYRE
BOTHWELL
L.S.
KILCHATTAN BAY
MILLPORT
To CAMPBELTOWN
KILBIRNIE
BEITH G. & S.W.
BEITH (Joint)
UPLAWMOOR
East Jc.
HAIRMYRES
EAST KILBRIDE
MEIKLE EARNOCK
QUARTER
FAIRLIE PIER
FAIRLIE
GLENGARNOCK
BARRMILL
LUGTON
SEE SHEET NO: FORTY FOUR
LOCHRANZA
BRACKEN HILLS
GREE (Gds)
GIFFEN
DUNLOP
GLASSFORD
WEST KILBRIDE
DALRY
Dalry Jc.
AUCHENMADE
LISSENS (Gds)
STEWARTON
STRATHAVEN NTH.
CEN.
N.B.
CAL. & G. & S.W.
MONTGREENAN
ARDROSSAN
MONTGOMERIE PIER
CAL.
SALTCOATS
Dubbs Jc.
KILWINNING
CUNNINGHAMHEAD
RYELAND
CAL.
L A
CORRIE
WINTON PIER
SOUTH BEACH
STEVENSTON
IRVINE
BOGSIDE
CAL.
CROSSHOUSE
KILMAURS
KILMARNOCK
Kaypark Jc.
HURLFORD
NEWMILNS
G. & S.W.
DARVEL
LOUDONHILL
DRUMCLOG
County Boundary Jc.
CAL. G. & S.W.
BRODICK
SPRINGSIDE
BARLEITH
GALSTON
DREGHORN
DRY-BRIDGE
GATEHEAD
ST MARNOCKS (Gds)
Bellfield Jc.
RICCARTON & CRAIGIE Gds
GAILES
ARRAN
BARASSIE
TROON
Gds
Pass.
GARROCHBURN (Goods)
LAMLASH
Lochgreen Jc.
MONKTON
MAUCHLINE
CATRINE
MUIRKIRK
Loco. Shed
KING'S CROSS
PRESTWICK
Mossblown Jc.
ANNBANK
TARBOLTON
LUGAR
WHITING BAY
Falkland Jc.
NEWTON-ON-AYR
L.C.
AYR
Blackhouse Jc.
Hawkhill Jc.
Goods
Pass.
AUCHINCRUIVE
TRABBOCH
Brackenhill Jc.
AUCHINLECK
SKARES
CRONBERRY
COMMONDYKE
Logan Jc.
OLD CUMNOCK

CLYDE STEAMER ROUTES

— — — —	N.B
··········	G. & S.W.
—·—·—·—	N.B. & CAL.
- - - - -	CAL.

HEADS OF AYR
ALLOWAY
Alloway Jc.
DRONGAN
OCHILTREE
DUMFRIES HOUSE
CUMNOCK
GREENHAM CASTLE (Goods)
Belston Jc.
DUNURE
DALRYMPLE
Dalrymple Jc.
G. & S.W.
RANKINSTON
NEW CUMNOCK
Watertroughs
To CARRADALE Etc.
To MACHRIE BAY Etc.
HOLLYBUSH
HOLEHOUSE
KNOWESIDE
A Y R S H I R E
CASSILLIS
PATNA
WATERSIDE

KINTYRE
TRODIGAL HALT
LINTMILL HALT
CAMPBELTOWN
PLANTATION HALT
MACHRIHANISH
MOSS RD HALT
DRUMLEMBLE HALT
MACHRIHANISH FARM HALT
CAMPBELTOWN & MACHRIHANISH LIGHT RAILWAY

GLENSIDE
MAYBOLE
Blackcraig Hill
MAIDENS
KILKERRAN
G. & S.W.
DALMELLINGTON
TURNBERRY
DIPPLE (Gds)
DAILLY
KILLOCHAN
Tunnel
GIRVAN

Twenty five

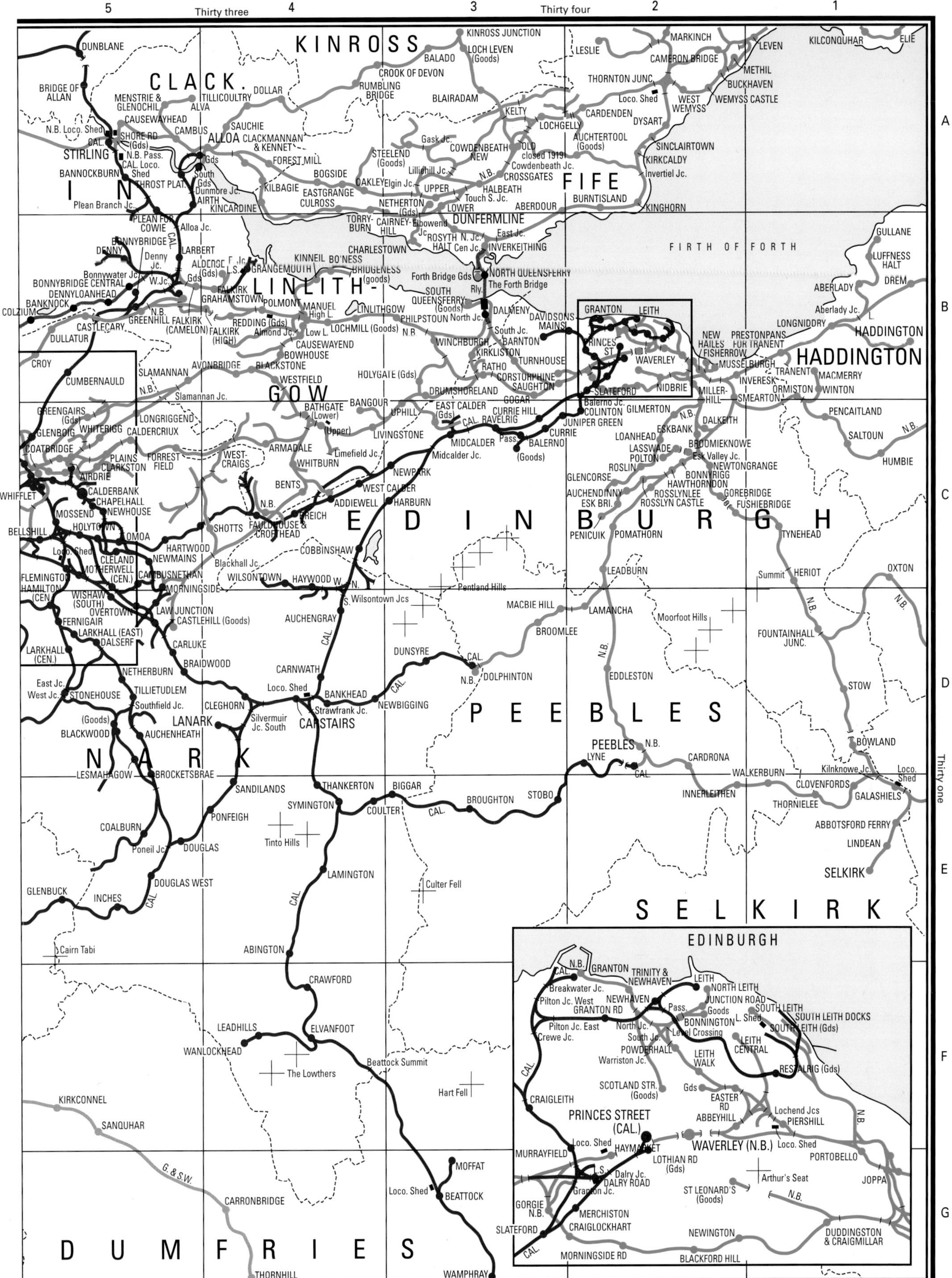

KINROSS

CLACK.

DUNBLANE

BRIDGE OF ALLAN

MENSTRIE & GLENOCHIL
CAUSEWAYHEAD
N.B. Loco. Shed
STIRLING SHORE RD (Gds)
CAL. N.B. Pass.
BANNOCKBURN CAL. Loco. Shed
THROST PLAT. South

PLEAN Branch Jc.
PLEAN FOR COWIE
DENNY
BONNYBRIDGE Denny Jc. W.Jc.
BONNYWATER Jc. Dunmore Jc.
DENNYLOANHEAD AIRTH
BANKNOK Bonnybridge Central
COLZIUM GREENHILL FALKIRK (CAMELON)
CASTLECARY FALKIRK (HIGH)
DULLATUR Almond Jc.
CROY Low L. LOCHMILL (Goods)
CUMBERNAULD N.B. REDDING (Gds)
Slamannan Jc. CAUSEWAYEND BOWHOUSE

TILLICOULTRY
DOLLAR
ALVA
SAUCHIE
ALLOA CLACKMANNAN & KENNET
CAMBUS FOREST MILL
Gds BOGSIDE
KILBAGIE EASTGRANGE
CULROSS
KINCARDINE
AIRTH
TORRYBURN CAIRNEY HILL
CHARLESTOWN
N. QUEENSFERRY

CROOK OF DEVON
RUMBLING BRIDGE
BLAIRADAM
KELTY
STEELEND (Goods) LOCHGELLY
COWDENBEATH NEW
OLD closed 1919
Cowdenbeath Jc. CROSSGATES
HALBEATH
Touch S.C. Jc. ABERDOUR
DUNFERMLINE
ROSYTH N. Jc. East Jc.
Cen Jc. INVERKEITHING
Forth Bridge Gds
The Forth Bridge Rly.
SOUTH QUEENSFERRY
PHILPSTOUN North Jc.

KINROSS JUNCTION (Goods)
LOCH LEVEN (Goods)
LESLIE
MARKINCH
CAMERON BRIDGE
THORNTON JUNC.
Loco. Shed
CARDENDEN WEST WEMYSS
DYSART WEMYSS CASTLE
AUCHTERTOOL SINCLAIRTOWN
KIRKCALDY
Invertiel Jc.
BURNTISLAND
KINGHORN

LEVEN KILCONQUHAR ELIE
METHIL
BUCKHAVEN

FIFE

FIRTH OF FORTH

GULLANE
LUFFNESS HALT
ABERLADY
DREM
Aberlady Jc. LONGNIDDRY HADDINGTON
NEW HAILES PRESTONPANS FOR TRANENT
FISHERROW HADDINGTON
INVERESK MACMERRY
MUSSELBURGH TRANENT ORMISTON WINTON
MILLERHILL SMEARTON.
DALKEITH PENCAITLAND
SALTOUN
HUMBIE
N.B.

LINLITH-

GRANGEMOUTH
GRAHAMSTOWN MANUEL
FALKIRK Kinneil BO'NESS
BRIDGENESS (goods)
POLMONT High L. LINLITHGOW
WINCHBURGH KIRKLISTON RATHO
DALMENY South Jc.
DAVIDSONS MAINS
GRANTON LEITH
PRINCES ST. WAVERLEY
SLATEFORD NIDBRIE
CORSTORPHINE SAUGHTON
TURNHOUSE GOGAR
BALERNO Jc. COLINTON GILMERTON
CURRIE JUNIPER GREEN LOANHEAD ESKBANK
RAVELRIG BALERNO (Goods) LASSWADE Esk Valley Jc.
HOLYGATE (Gds) DRUMSHOREL AN
EAST CALDER CURRIE HILL
BATHGATE (Lower) (Upper) UPHILL MIDCALDER Pass.
LIVINGSTONE MIDCALDER Jc.
BANGOUR
GLENCORSE ROSLIN
AUCHENDINNY ROSSLYNLEE
ESK BRI. ROSSLYN CASTLE
BROOMIEKNOWE
NEWTONGRANGE
BONNYRIGG
HAWTHORNDEN
GOREBRIDGE
FUSHIEBRIDGE

GOW

EDINBURGH

HADDINGTON

GREENGAIRS (Gds)
GLENBOIG WHITERIGG CALDERCRUIX
COATBRIDGE
AIRDRIE PLAINS FORREST FIELD
CLARKSTON WEST CRAIGS
WHIFFLET CALDERBANK ARMADALE BENTS
CHAPELHALL WHITBURN Limefield Jc.
BELLSHILL NEWHOUSE N.C. NEWPARK
MOSSEND BREICH
HOLYTOWN OMOA FAULDHOUSE & CROFTHEAD
Loco. Shed CLELAND SHOTTS ADDIEWELL HARBURN
FLEMINGTON (CEN.) MOTHERWELL NEWMAINS WEST CALDER
HAMILTON (CEN.) CAMBUSNETHAN HARTWOOD
WISHAW (SOUTH) MORNINGSIDE
OVERTOWN WILSONTOWN
FERNIEGAIR WISHAW WILSONTOWN
LARKHALL (EAST) BLACKHALL Jc. HAYWOOD W. N.
DALSERF LAW JUNCTION COBBINSHAW
LARKHALL (CEN.) CASTLEHILL (Goods) S. Wilsontown Jcs
OVERTOWN AUCHENGRAY

PEEBLES

PENICUIK
POMATHORN
LEADBURN
Summit HERIOT
OXTON
FOUNTAINHALL JUNC.
STOW
N.B.

TYNEHEAD

East Jc.
West Jc. STONEHOUSE
Southfield Jc. TILLIETUDLEM
(Goods) CLEGHORN
BLACKWOOD LANARK
AUCHENHEATH
NETHERBURN BRAIDWOOD
NARK CARNWATH
LESMAHAGOW BROCKETSBRAE CARLUKE
SANDILANDS
COALBURN PONFEIGH SYMINGTON
Poneil Jc. Tinto Hills
DOUGLAS
GLENBUCK DOUGLAS WEST LAMINGTON
INCHES Cairn Tabi
ABINGTON

MACBIE HILL LAMANCHA
BROOMLEE Moorfoot Hills
PEEBLES N.B. LYNE CARDRONA
WALKERBURN
INNERLEITHEN
STOBO BROUGHTON
Loco. Shed BANKHEAD
Strawfrank Jc. NEWBIGGING
Silvermuir Jc. South CARSTAIRS
CARNWATH
DOLPHINTON N.B.
DUNSYRE CAL.
THANKERTON BIGGAR
COULTER

CLOVENFORDS
Kilnknowe Jc. Loco. Shed
THORNIELEE GALASHIELS
ABBOTSFORD FERRY
BOWLAND LINDEAN
SELKIRK

SELKIRK

CRAWFORD
LEADHILLS ELVANFOOT
WANLOCKHEAD The Lowthers Beattock Summit
Hart Fell
Culter Fell
Tinto Hills

MOFFAT
KIRKCONNEL Loco. Shed BEATTOCK
SANQUHAR CARRONBRIDGE
G & SW
THORNHILL WAMPHRAY

DUMFRIES

EDINBURGH (inset)

N.B. GRANTON TRINITY & NEWHAVEN
CAL. Breakwater Jc. LEITH NORTH LEITH
Pilton Jc. West NEWHAVEN JUNCTION ROAD
GRANTON RD Pass. SOUTH LEITH
Pilton Jc. East North Jc. Goods Shed SOUTH LEITH DOCKS
Crewe Jc. South Jc. BONNINGTON SOUTH LEITH (Gds)
Level Crossing
POWDERHALL LEITH CENTRAL
Warriston Jc. LEITH WALK
SCOTLAND STR. (Goods) Gds REST ALRIG (Gds)
CRAIGLEITH EASTER RD
PRINCES STREET (CAL.) ABBEYHILL Lochend Jcs
Loco. Shed HAYMARKET PIERSHILL
MURRAYFIELD WAVERLEY (N.B.) Loco. Shed PORTOBELLO
LOTHIAN RD (Gds)
L.S. DALRY ROAD Arthur's Seat JOPPA
GORGIE Dalry Jc. ST LEONARD'S (Goods) DUDDINGSTON & CRAIGMILLAR
N.B. Granton Jc. N.B.
MERCHISTON NEWINGTON
SLATEFORD CRAIGLOCKHART BLACKFORD HILL
MORNINGSIDE RD

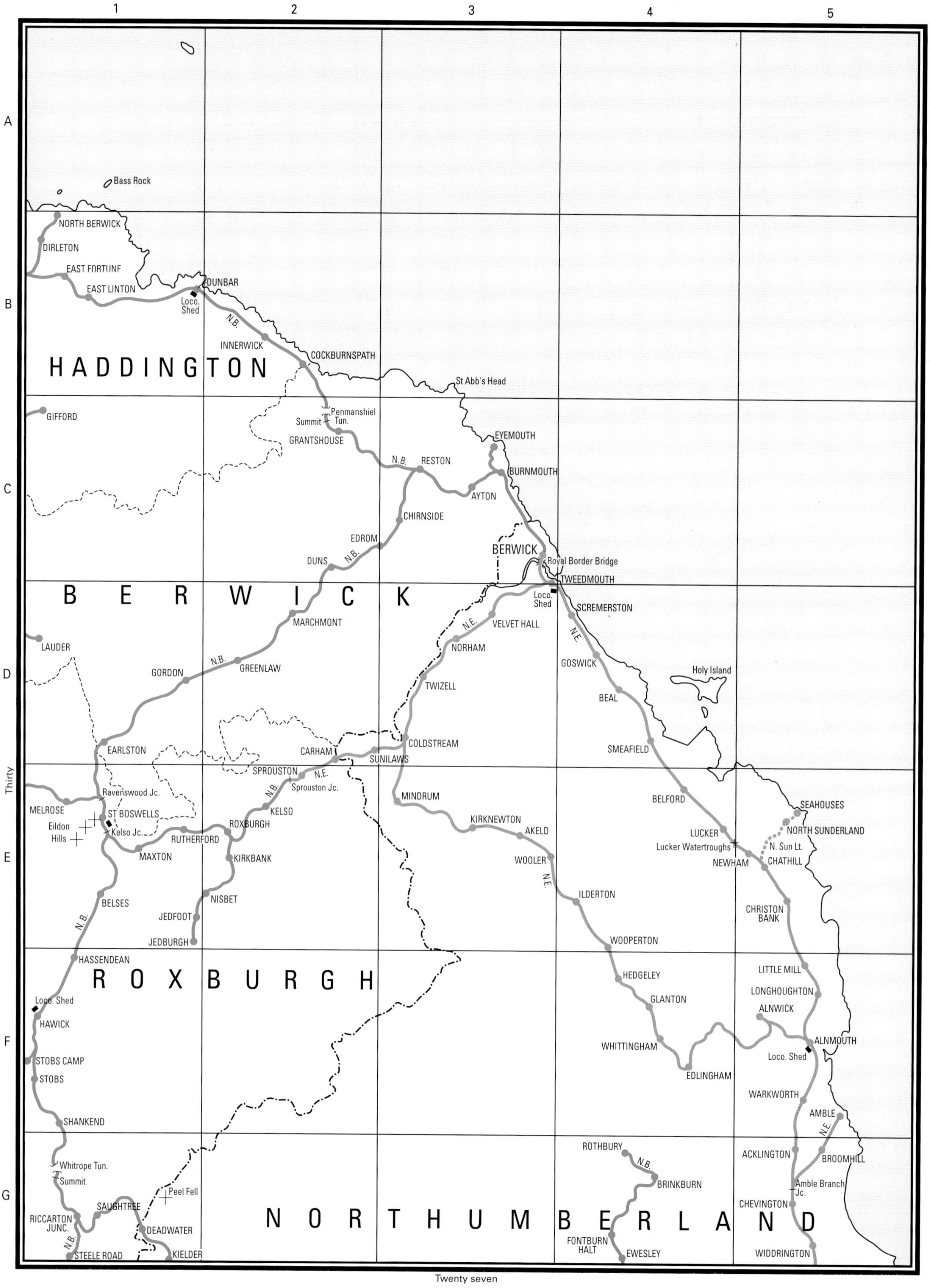

1
2
3
4
5
A
B
C
D
E
F
G
Bass Rock
NORTH BERWICK
DIRLETON
EAST FORTUNE
EAST LINTON
DUNBAR
Loco. Shed
N.B.
INNERWICK
COCKBURNSPATH
HADDINGTON
St Abb's Head
GIFFORD
Summit
Penmanshiel Tun.
GRANTSHOUSE
EYEMOUTH
N.B.
RESTON
BURNMOUTH
AYTON
CHIRNSIDE
EDROM
DUNS
N.B.
BERWICK
Royal Border Bridge
TWEEDMOUTH
Loco. Shed
B E R W I C K
SCREMERSTON
MARCHMONT
N.E.
VELVET HALL
NORHAM
N.E.
LAUDER
GORDON
N.B.
GREENLAW
GOSWICK
Holy Island
TWIZELL
BEAL
EARLSTON
CARHAM
COLDSTREAM
SUNILAWS
SMEAFIELD
Thirty
SPROUSTON
N.E.
Sprouston Jc.
Ravenswood Jc.
MINDRUM
SEAHOUSES
MELROSE
ST BOSWELLS
KELSO
N.B.
BELFORD
Eildon Hills
Kelso Jc.
ROXBURGH
KIRKNEWTON
AKELD
LUCKER
NORTH SUNDERLAND
RUTHERFORD
Lucker Watertroughs
N. Sun Lt.
MAXTON
KIRKBANK
WOOLER
N.E.
NEWHAM
CHATHILL
BELSES
NISBET
ILDERTON
CHRISTON BANK
N.B.
JEDFOOT
JEDBURGH
WOOPERTON
HASSENDEAN
R O X B U R G H
LITTLE MILL
HEDGELEY
LONGHOUGHTON
Loco. Shed
GLANTON
ALNWICK
HAWICK
WHITTINGHAM
ALNMOUTH
Loco. Shed
STOBS CAMP
STOBS
EDLINGHAM
WARKWORTH
SHANKEND
AMBLE
N.E.
Whitrope Tun.
Summit
ROTHBURY
N.B.
ACKLINGTON
BROOMHILL
BRINKBURN
Peel Fell
Amble Branch Jc.
SAUGHTREE
CHEVINGTON
RICCARTON JUNC.
DEADWATER
N O R T H U M B E R L A N D
N.B.
FONTBURN HALT
STEELE ROAD
KIELDER
EWESLEY
WIDDRINGTON
Twenty seven

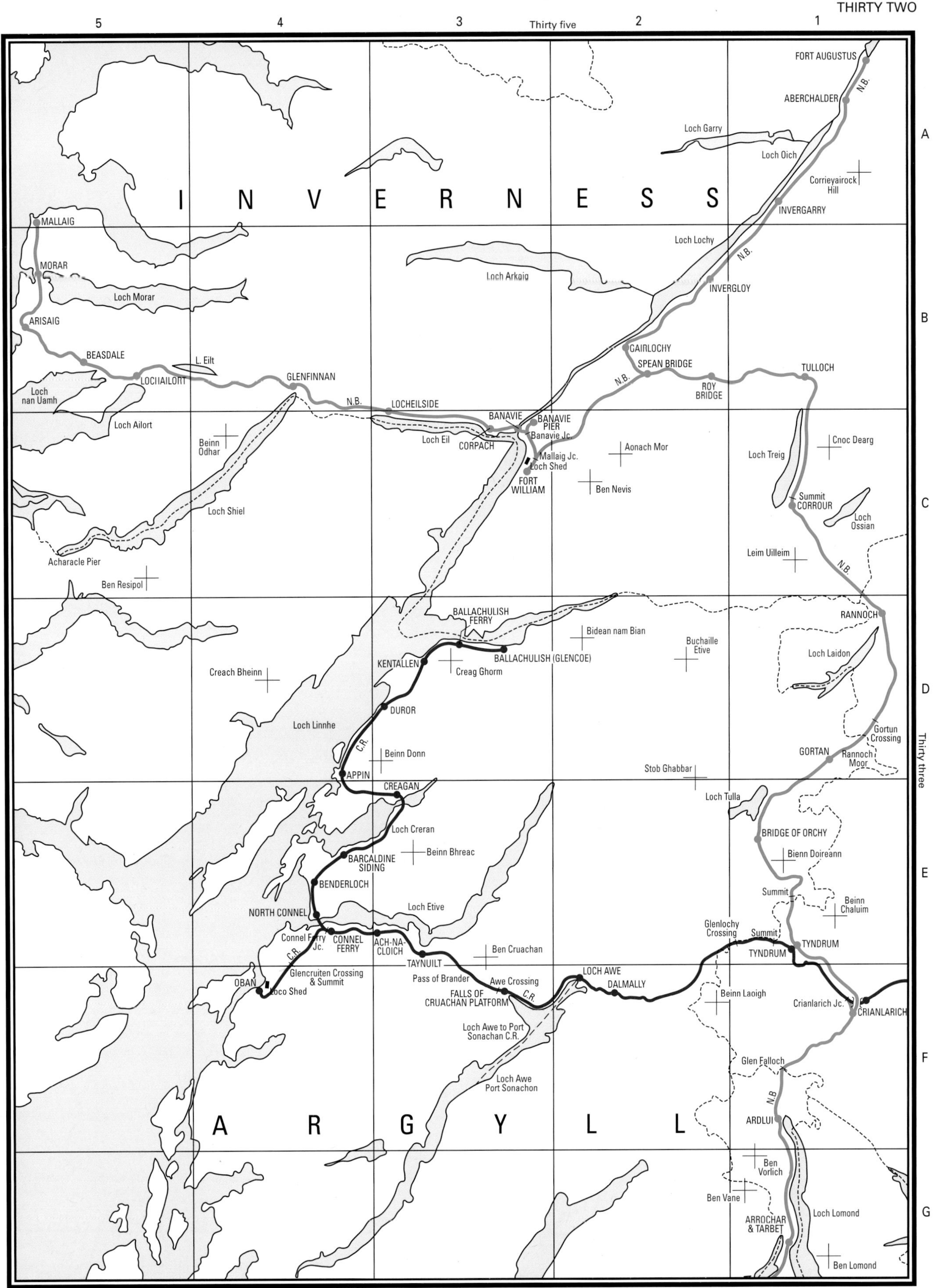

5
4
3
Thirty five
2
1
A
B
C
D
E
F
G
Thirty three
Twenty nine
I N V E R N E S S
A R G Y L L
FORT AUGUSTUS
ABERCHALDER
N.B.
Loch Garry
Loch Oich
Corrieyairock Hill
INVERGARRY
Loch Lochy
INVERGLOY
Loch Arkaig
MALLAIG
MORAR
Loch Morar
ARISAIG
BEASDALE
L. Eilt
LOCHAILORT
GLENFINNAN
Loch nan Uamh
Loch Ailort
LOCHEILSIDE
GAIRLOCHY
SPEAN BRIDGE
ROY BRIDGE
TULLOCH
BANAVIE
BANAVIE PIER
Banavie Jc.
Loch Eil
CORPACH
Mallaig Jc.
Loch Shed
FORT WILLIAM
Aonach Mor
Ben Nevis
Loch Treig
Cnoc Dearg
Summit
CORROUR
Loch Ossian
Beinn Odhar
Loch Shiel
Acharacle Pier
Ben Resipol
Leim Uilleim
RANNOCH
BALLACHULISH FERRY
Bidean nam Bian
BALLACHULISH (GLENCOE)
Buchaille Etive
Loch Laidon
KENTALLEN
Creag Ghorm
Creach Bheinn
DUROR
Loch Linnhe
C.R.
Beinn Donn
APPIN
Gortun Crossing
GORTAN
Rannoch Moor
Stob Ghabbar
CREAGAN
Loch Tulla
Loch Creran
BRIDGE OF ORCHY
BARCALDINE SIDING
Beinn Bhreac
Bienn Doireann
BENDERLOCH
Summit
Beinn Chaluim
NORTH CONNEL
Loch Etive
Glenlochy Crossing
Summit
Connel Ferry Jc.
CONNEL FERRY
ACH-NA-CLOICH
Ben Cruachan
TYNDRUM
TAYNUILT
LOCH AWE
OBAN
Loco Shed
Glencruiten Crossing & Summit
Pass of Brander
Awe Crossing
DALMALLY
FALLS OF CRUACHAN PLATFORM
Beinn Laoigh
Crianlarich Jc.
CRIANLARICH
Loch Awe to Port Sonachan C.R.
Glen Falloch
Loch Awe Port Sonachon
ARDLUI
Ben Vorlich
Ben Vane
Loch Lomond
ARROCHAR & TARBET
Ben Lomond

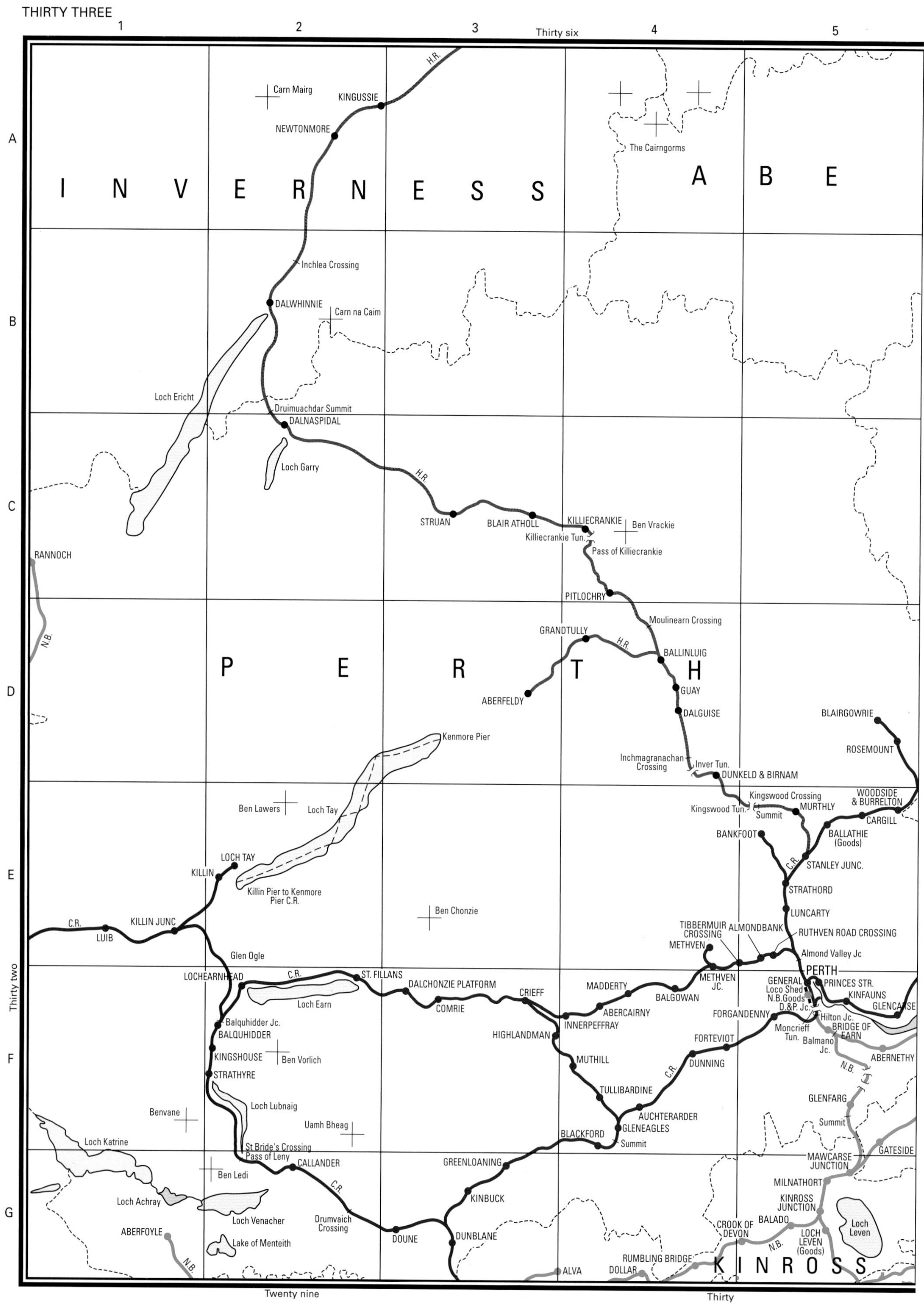
1
2
3
Thirty six
4
5
A
B
C
D
E
F
G
Thirty two
Twenty nine
Thirty
H.R.
Carn Mairg
KINGUSSIE
NEWTONMORE
The Cairngorms
I N V E R N E S S
A B E
Inchlea Crossing
DALWHINNIE
Carn na Caim
Loch Ericht
Druimuachdar Summit
DALNASPIDAL
Loch Garry
H.R.
STRUAN
BLAIR ATHOLL
KILLIECRANKIE
Ben Vrackie
Killiecrankie Tun.
Pass of Killiecrankie
RANNOCH
PITLOCHRY
Moulinearn Crossing
GRANDTULLY
H.R.
BALLINLUIG
N.B.
P E R T H
GUAY
ABERFELDY
DALGUISE
BLAIRGOWRIE
Kenmore Pier
ROSEMOUNT
Inchmagranachan Crossing
Inver Tun.
DUNKELD & BIRNAM
Ben Lawers
Loch Tay
Kingswood Crossing
Kingswood Tun.
Summit
MURTHLY
WOODSIDE & BURRELTON
CARGILL
BANKFOOT
BALLATHIE (Goods)
LOCH TAY
KILLIN
Killin Pier to Kenmore Pier C.R.
C.R.
STANLEY JUNC.
STRATHORD
Ben Chonzie
LUNCARTY
C.R.
LUIB
KILLIN JUNC
TIBBERMUIR CROSSING
ALMONDBANK
RUTHVEN ROAD CROSSING
METHVEN
Glen Ogle
Almond Valley Jc
LOCHEARNHEAD
C.R.
ST. FILLANS
DALCHONZIE PLATFORM
METHVEN JC.
PERTH
GENERAL
Loco Shed
N.B.Goods
D.&P. Jc.
PRINCES STR.
KINFAUNS
GLENCARSE
Loch Earn
CRIEFF
MADDERTY
BALGOWAN
COMRIE
ABERCAIRNY
FORGANDENNY
Balquhidder Jc.
BALQUHIDDER
INNERPEFFRAY
HIGHLANDMAN
Hilton Jc.
Moncrieff Tun.
BRIDGE OF EARN
Balmano Jc.
FORTEVIOT
KINGSHOUSE
Ben Vorlich
MUTHILL
ABERNETHY
STRATHYRE
C.R.
DUNNING
N.B.
Loch Lubnaig
TULLIBARDINE
GLENFARG
Benvane
AUCHTERARDER
Uamh Bheag
GLENEAGLES
Summit
Loch Katrine
BLACKFORD
Summit
St Bride's Crossing
Pass of Leny
CALLANDER
GREENLOANING
MAWCARSE JUNCTION
GATESIDE
Ben Ledi
C.R.
MILNATHORT
KINBUCK
Loch Achray
KINROSS JUNCTION
Drumvaich Crossing
BALADO
Loch Venacher
Loch Leven
ABERFOYLE
CROOK OF DEVON
DOUNE
DUNBLANE
N.B.
LOCH LEVEN (Goods)
Lake of Menteith
RUMBLING BRIDGE
N.B.
ALVA
DOLLAR
K I N R O S S

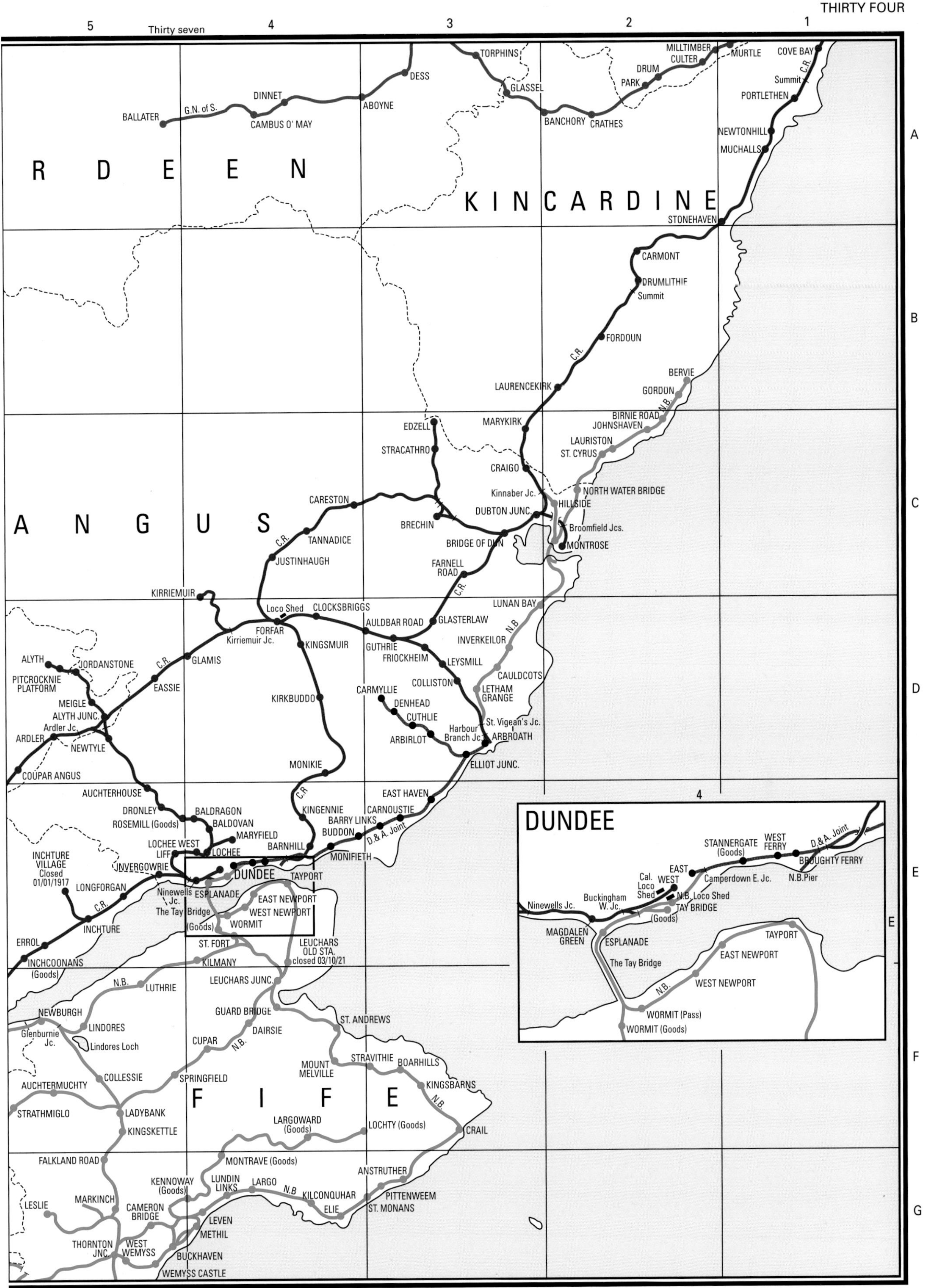
5
Thirty seven
4
3
2
1
A
B
C
D
E
F
G
Thirty
BALLATER
G.N. of S.
DINNET
CAMBUS O' MAY
ABOYNE
DESS
TORPHINS
GLASSEL
BANCHORY
CRATHES
PARK
DRUM
MILLTIMBER
CULTER
MURTLE
COVE BAY
Summit
C.R.
PORTLETHEN
NEWTONHILL
MUCHALLS
R D E E N
KINCARDINE
STONEHAVEN
CARMONT
DRUMLITHIE
Summit
FORDOUN
C.R.
LAURENCEKIRK
BERVIE
GORDON
N.B.
BIRNIE ROAD
JOHNSHAVEN
MARYKIRK
LAURISTON
ST. CYRUS
EDZELL
STRACATHRO
CRAIGO
Kinnaber Jc.
NORTH WATER BRIDGE
HILLSIDE
DUBTON JUNC.
CARESTON
BRECHIN
Broomfield Jcs.
MONTROSE
BRIDGE OF DUN
ANGUS
C.R.
TANNADICE
JUSTINHAUGH
FARNELL ROAD
C.R.
KIRRIEMUIR
Loco Shed
CLOCKSBRIGGS
LUNAN BAY
FORFAR
Kirriemuir Jc.
AULDBAR ROAD
GLASTERLAW
N.B.
INVERKEILOR
KINGSMUIR
GUTHRIE
FRIOCKHEIM
LEYSMILL
ALYTH
JORDANSTONE
GLAMIS
C.R.
CAULDCOTS
PITCROCKNIE PLATFORM
EASSIE
COLLISTON
LETHAM GRANGE
KIRKBUDDO
CARMYLLIE
DENHEAD
MEIGLE
ALYTH JUNC.
CUTHLIE
Ardler Jc.
St. Vigean's Jc.
ARDLER
NEWTYLE
ARBIRLOT
Harbour Branch Jc.
ARBROATH
ELLIOT JUNC.
COUPAR ANGUS
MONIKIE
AUCHTERHOUSE
EAST HAVEN
C.R.
DRONLEY
BALDRAGON
KINGENNIE
CARNOUSTIE
ROSEMILL (Goods)
BALDOVAN
BARRY LINKS
BUDDON
D.& A. Joint
LOCHEE WEST
MARYFIELD
INCHTURE VILLAGE Closed 01/01/1917
LIFF
LOCHEE
BARNHILL
MONIFIETH
INVERGOWRIE
DUNDEE
TAYPORT
LONGFORGAN
Ninewells Jc.
ESPLANADE
EAST NEWPORT
C.R.
The Tay Bridge
WEST NEWPORT
(Goods)
WORMIT
INCHTURE
ERROL
ST. FORT
LEUCHARS OLD STA. closed 03/10/21
INCHCOONANS (Goods)
KILMANY
N.B.
LUTHRIE
LEUCHARS JUNC.
NEWBURGH
GUARD BRIDGE
Glenburnie Jc.
LINDORES
DAIRSIE
ST. ANDREWS
Lindores Loch
CUPAR
N.B.
MOUNT MELVILLE
STRAVITHIE
BOARHILLS
AUCHTERMUCHTY
COLLESSIE
SPRINGFIELD
KINGSBARNS
N.B.
STRATHMIGLO
LADYBANK
FIFE
KINGSKETTLE
LARGOWARD (Goods)
LOCHTY (Goods)
CRAIL
FALKLAND ROAD
MONTRAVE (Goods)
ANSTRUTHER
KENNOWAY (Goods)
LUNDIN LINKS
LARGO
N.B
KILCONQUHAR
PITTENWEEM
LESLIE
MARKINCH
CAMERON BRIDGE
ELIE
ST. MONANS
LEVEN
METHIL
THORNTON JNC.
WEST WEMYSS
BUCKHAVEN
WEMYSS CASTLE
4
DUNDEE
E
STANNERGATE (Goods)
WEST FERRY
D.& A. Joint
BROUGHTY FERRY
EAST
Camperdown E. Jc.
N.B.Pier
Cal. Loco Shed
WEST
Buckingham W. Jc.
N.B. Loco Shed
Ninewells Jc.
TAY BRIDGE
(Goods)
MAGDALEN GREEN
ESPLANADE
TAYPORT
EAST NEWPORT
The Tay Bridge
N.B.
WEST NEWPORT
WORMIT (Pass)
WORMIT (Goods)

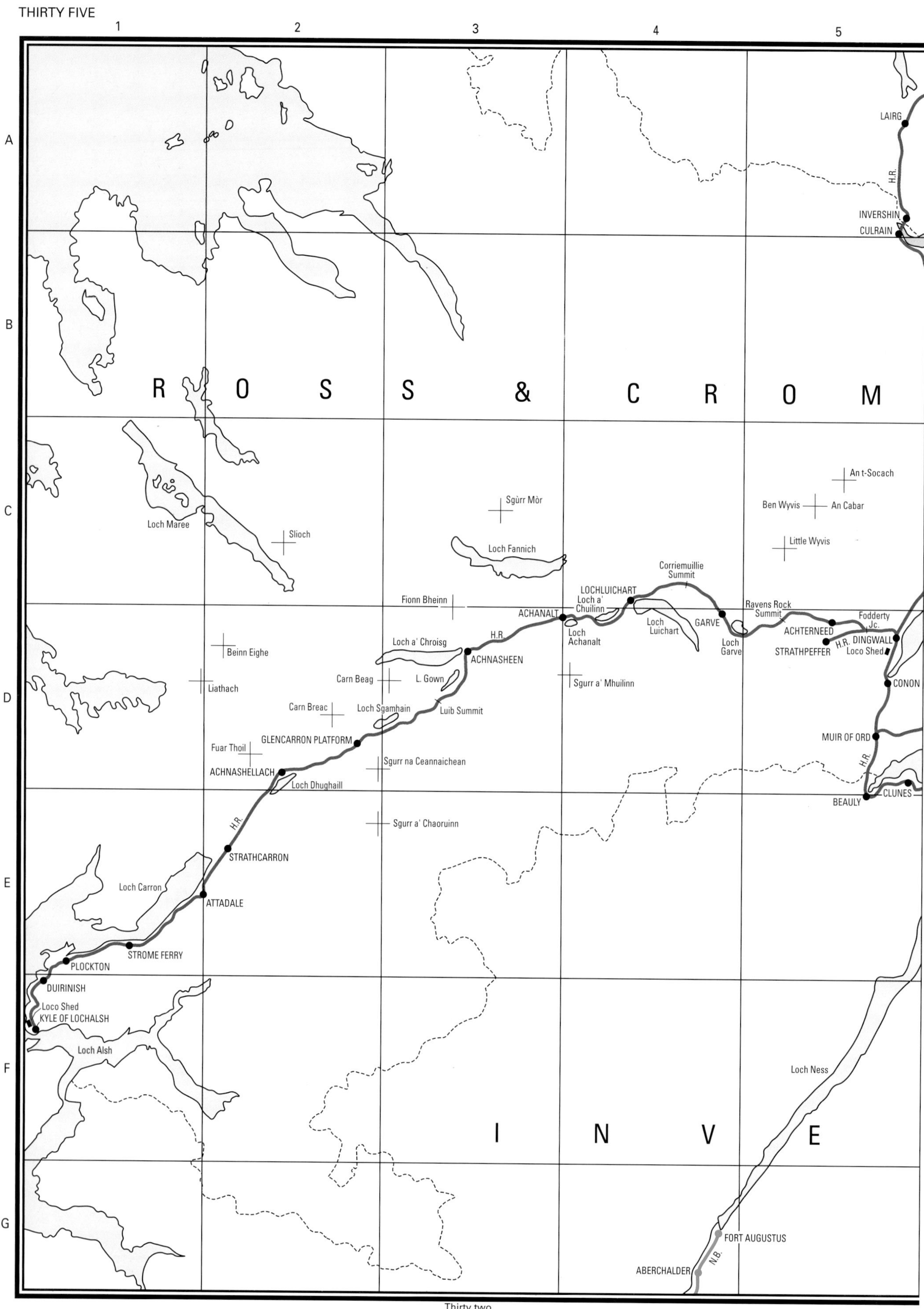
1
2
3
4
5
A
B
C
D
E
F
G
R O S S & C R O M
I N V E
LAIRG
H.R.
INVERSHIN
CULRAIN
An t-Socach
Ben Wyvis
An Cabar
Sgùrr Mòr
Loch Maree
Slioch
Loch Fannich
Little Wyvis
Corriemuillie Summit
LOCHLUICHART
Loch a' Chuilinn
Fionn Bheinn
ACHANALT
Loch Achanalt
Loch Luichart
GARVE
Ravens Rock Summit
Fodderty Jc.
ACHTERNEED
DINGWALL
STRATHPEFFER
Loco Shed
Loch Garve
Loch a' Chroisg
H.R.
ACHNASHEEN
Beinn Eighe
Liathach
Carn Beag
L. Gown
Sgurr a' Mhuilinn
CONON
Carn Breac
Loch Sgamhain
Luib Summit
Fuar Thoil
GLENCARRON PLATFORM
MUIR OF ORD
Sgurr na Ceannaichean
ACHNASHELLACH
Loch Dhughaill
BEAULY
CLUNES
Sgurr a' Chaoruinn
STRATHCARRON
Loch Carron
ATTADALE
STROME FERRY
PLOCKTON
DUIRINISH
Loco Shed
KYLE OF LOCHALSH
Loch Alsh
Loch Ness
FORT AUGUSTUS
N.B.
ABERCHALDER

Thirty two

5
Thirty eight
4
3
2
1
A
B
C
D
E
F
G
Thirty seven
Thirty three
Summit
Acheilidh Crossing
ROGART
BRORA
H.R.
DUNROBIN (Private)
THE MOUND
GOLSPIE
H.R.
CAMBUSAVIE PLATFORM
SKELBO
EMBO
DORNOCH
BONAR BRIDGE
Dornoch Firth
EDDERTON
TAIN
H.R.
A R T Y
FEARN
NIGG
KILDARY
DELNY
ALNESS
INVERGORDON
SHORE
Cromarty Firth
NOVAR
FOULIS
MORAY FIRTH
LOSSIEMOUTH
HOPEMAN
BURGHEAD
COLTFIELD PLATFORM
CALCOTTS
GARMOUTH
URQUHART
SPEY BAY
G.N. of S.
Loco Shed
MOSSTOWIE
ELGIN
H.R.
KINLOSS
ALVES
LHANBRYDE
BALNACOUL
FOCHABERS TOWN
LONGMORN
ORBLISTON JUNCTION
Loco Shed
FORRES
BRODIE
AULDEARN
NAIRN
COLEBURN
BIRCHFIELD PLATFORM
Summit
ORTON
H.R.
FORTROSE
AVOCH
FORT GEORGE
MUNLOCHY
H.R.
GOLLANFIELD JUNC.
ALLANGRANGE
Inverness Firth
REDCASTLE
H.R.
DALCROSS
M O R A Y
DUNPHAIL
Closed
MULBEN
ROTHES
Summit
DANDALEITH
CRAIGELLACHIE
DRUM-MUIR
ALLANFEARN
LENTRAN
CULLODEN MOOR
BUNCHREW
INVERNESS
Loco Sheds
Lochgorm Works H.R.
N A I R N
KNOCKANDO
ABERLOUR
G.N. of S.
Summit
CARRON
DUFFTOWN
BLACKSBOAT
DAVIOT
DAVA
Dava Summit
H.R.
ADVIE
BALLINDALLOCH
Ben Rinnes
MOY
Loch Moy
G.N. of S.
TOMATIN
Carn Glas
CROMDALE
B A N F F
GRANTOWN-ON-SPEY
GRANTOWN-ON-SPEY
H.R.
Slochd Summit
Slochd Crossing
BROOMHILL
CARR BRIDGE
NETHY BRIDGE
BOAT OF GARTEN
R N E S S
AVIEMORE
Loco Shed
Loch Alvie
Monadhlaith Mountains
KINCRAIG
Loch Insh
H.R.

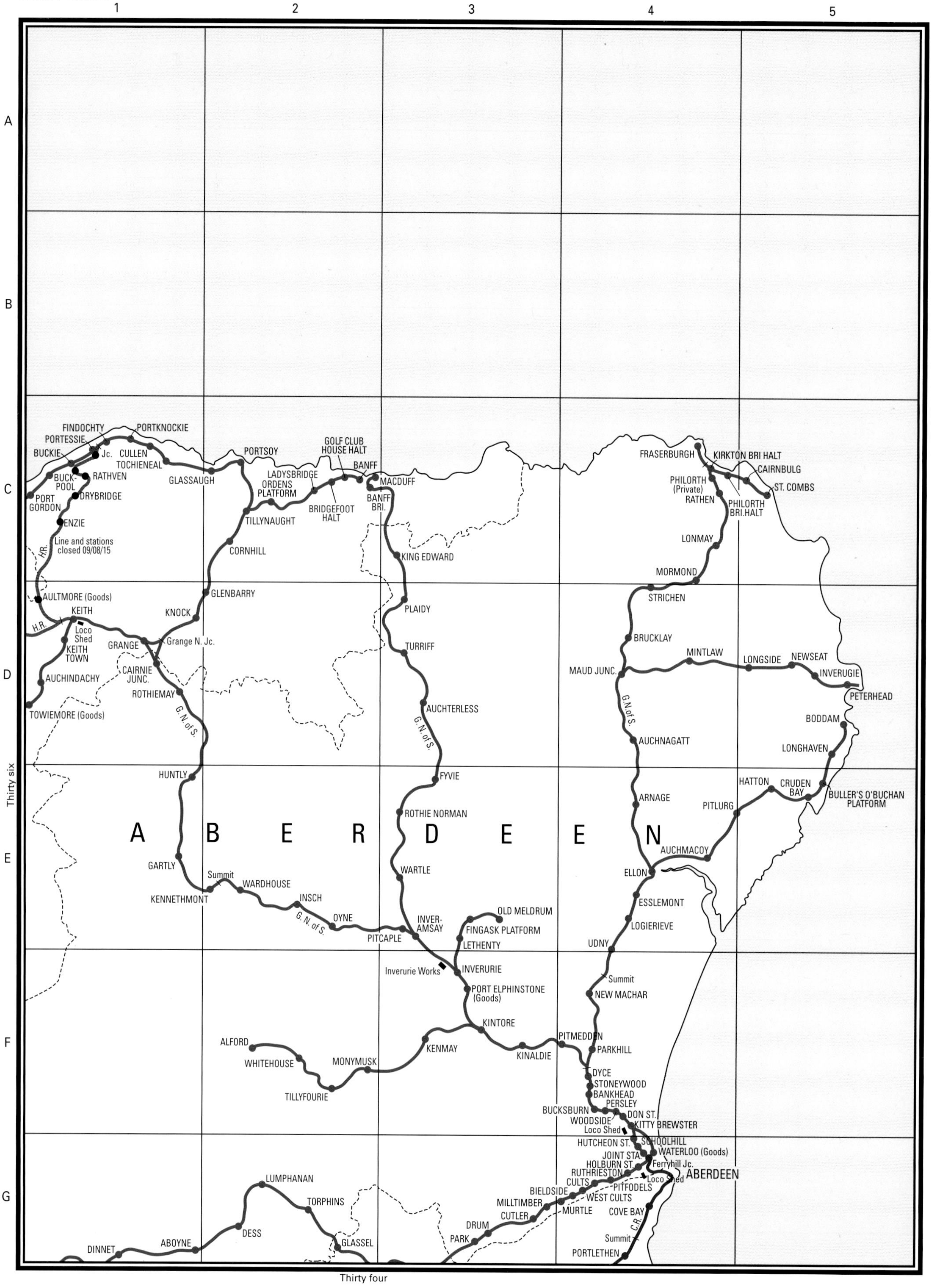

1 2 3 4 5

A

B

C

FINDOCHTY
PORTKNOCKIE
PORTESSIE
BUCKIE
Jc.
CULLEN
TOCHIENEAL
PORTSOY
GOLF CLUB HOUSE HALT
BANFF
BUCK-POOL
RATHVEN
GLASSAUGH
LADYSBRIDGE
ORDENS PLATFORM
MACDUFF
PORT GORDON
DRYBRIDGE
BRIDGEFOOT HALT
BANFF BRI.
TILLYNAUGHT
ENZIE
Line and stations closed 09/08/15
H.R.
CORNHILL
KING EDWARD
FRASERBURGH
KIRKTON BRI HALT
CAIRNBULG
PHILORTH (Private)
RATHEN
ST. COMBS
PHILORTH BRI.HALT
LONMAY
MORMOND
STRICHEN

D

AULTMORE (Goods)
GLENBARRY
PLAIDY
KEITH
H.R.
Loco Shed
KNOCK
KEITH TOWN
GRANGE
Grange N. Jc.
TURRIFF
BRUCKLAY
MINTLAW
LONGSIDE
NEWSEAT
AUCHINDACHY
CAIRNIE JUNC.
MAUD JUNC.
INVERUGIE
ROTHIEMAY
PETERHEAD
TOWIEMORE (Goods)
G.N. of S.
AUCHTERLESS
G.N. of S.
G.N. of S.
BODDAM
AUCHNAGATT
LONGHAVEN

Thirty six

E

HUNTLY
FYVIE
HATTON
CRUDEN BAY
ROTHIE NORMAN
ARNAGE
PITLURG
BULLER'S O'BUCHAN PLATFORM
A B E R D E E N
AUCHMACOY
GARTLY
WARTLE
ELLON
Summit
WARDHOUSE
KENNETHMONT
INSCH
ESSLEMONT
OLD MELDRUM
OYNE
INVER-AMSAY
G. N. of S.
FINGASK PLATFORM
LOGIERIEVE
PITCAPLE
LETHENTY
UDNY
INVERURIE
Inverurie Works
Summit
PORT ELPHINSTONE (Goods)
NEW MACHAR

F

KINTORE
ALFORD
KENMAY
PITMEDDEN
WHITEHOUSE
MONYMUSK
KINALDIE
PARKHILL
DYCE
STONEYWOOD
TILLYFOURIE
BANKHEAD
PERSLEY
BUCKSBURN
DON ST.
WOODSIDE
Loco Shed
KITTY BREWSTER
HUTCHEON ST.
SCHOOLHILL
JOINT STA.
WATERLOO (Goods)
HOLBURN ST.
Ferryhill Jc.
RUTHRIESTON
ABERDEEN

G

LUMPHANAN
CULTS
Loco Shed
PITFODELS
BIELDSIDE
WEST CULTS
TORPHINS
MILLTIMBER
MURTLE
COVE BAY
CUTLER
DESS
DRUM
C.R.
ABOYNE
PARK
Summit
DINNET
GLASSEL
PORTLETHEN

Thirty four

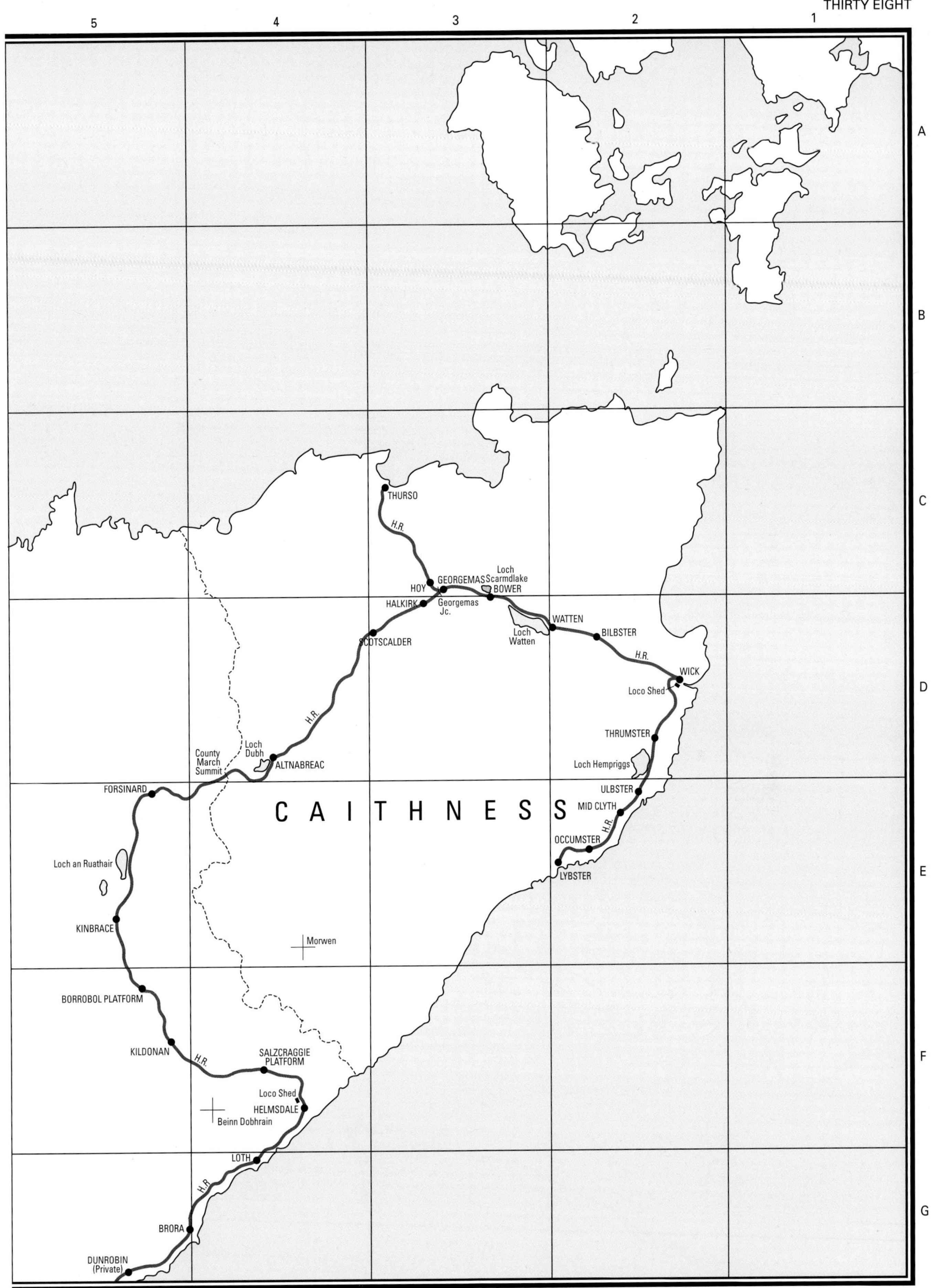
5
4
3
2
1
A
B
C
D
E
F
G
THURSO
H.R.
Loch
Scarmdlake
HOY
GEORGEMAS
BOWER
HALKIRK
Georgemas
Jc.
WATTEN
Loch
Watten
BILBSTER
SCOTSCALDER
H.R.
WICK
Loco Shed
H.R.
THRUMSTER
Loch
Dubh
County
March
Summit
ALTNABREAC
Loch Hempriggs
FORSINARD
ULBSTER
CAITHNESS
MID CLYTH
H.R.
OCCUMSTER
Loch an Ruathair
LYBSTER
KINBRACE
Morwen
BORROBOL PLATFORM
KILDONAN
H.R.
SALZCRAGGIE
PLATFORM
Loco Shed
HELMSDALE
Beinn Dobhrain
LOTH
H.R.
BRORA
DUNROBIN
(Private)
Thirty six

1 Warwick Rd Jc.
2 West Street Jc.
3 SMITHFIELD G.W. Gds
4 WORSHIP STR. (Goods)
5 Minories Jc.
6 ALDGATE EAST
7 HAYDON SQUARE L.N.W. (Goods)
8 GOODMAN'S YARD G.E. (Goods)
9 MINT STR. G.N. (Goods)
10 MINT STR M.R. (Goods)
11 LUDGATE HILL
12 ST PAUL'S S.E. & C.
13 MANSION HOUSE
14 CANNON STREET
15 MONUMENT
16 MARK LANE
17 ST MARY'S
18 WARWICK RD (Goods) L.N.W.
19 WARWICK RD (Goods) G.W.
20 Earls Court Jc.
21 Goods Yard Jc.
22 West London Ext. Jc.
23 KEN. LILLIE BRI. (Gds)
24 TURNHAM GREEN
25 CHISWICK PARK
26 WEST END LANE
27 LADBROKE GROVE
28 WESTBOURNE PARK
29 ROYAL OAK
30 Junction Rd Jc.
31 Highgate Rd Jc.
32 CHALK FARM
33 CAMDEN
34 Hampstead Rd Jc.
35 Kentish Town Jc.
36 CAMDEN TOWN
37 Maiden Lane Jc.
38 St Pancras Jc. (West)
39 KENTISH TOWN
40 St Pancras Jc.
41 North London Incline Jc.
42 ST PANCRAS (Goods)
43 Copenhagen Jc,
44 Copenhagen Tun.
45 MAIDEN LANE (Gds)
46 KINGS CROSS (SUBURBAN)
47 Campbell Road Jc.
48 Upper Abbey Mills Jc.
49 SPITALFIELDS (Goods)
50 Bishopsgate Jc.
51 SPITALFIELDS (Coal)
52 Vallance Road Jc.
53 Borough Market Jc.
54 Metropolitan Jc.
55 Hampstead Tun.
56 St John's WoodTun
57 OLD OAK LANE HALT
58 WEST HAMPSTEAD
59 Primrose Hill Tuns
60 WOOD LANE (WHITE CITY)
61 MAIDEN LANE (Pass.)
62 CALEDONIAN ROAD & BARNSBURY

A L.B.S.C. & Joint
B WEST LONDON Joint
C WEST LONDON EXTENSION Joint
D HAMMERSMITH & CITY Joint
E EAST LONDON Joint
F WHITECHAPEL & BOW Joint
G L.B.S.C. & S.E. & C. Joint
H NORTH & STH. WESTERN JUNC.
J TOTTENHAM & FOREST GATE
K L.N.W. & MID. Joint
L TOTTENHAM & HAMPSTEAD

NOTE:
TO AVOID CONFUSION TUBE RAILWAYS ARE OMITTED AND MET. & MET.-DISTRICT COVERED SECTIONS ARE SHO WN AS SURFACE LINES

5 4 3 2 1

ALEXANDRA PALACE
PALACE GATES (WOOD GREEN)
NOEL PARK & WOOD GREEN
BRUCE GROVE
NORTHUMBERLAND PARK
WALTHAMSTOW (WOOD STR.)
GEORGE LANE
FAIRLOP
G.N.
WOOD GREEN
MUSWELL HILL
WEST GREEN
TOTTENHAM HALE
BLACKHORSE RD
HOE STREET WALTHAMSTOW
SNARESBROOK & WANSTEAD
CHALK FARM
Hampstead Rd Jc.
Primrose Hill Jc.
Loco. Shed
CAMDEN (Goods)
BARKINGSIDE
NEWBURY PARK
HORNSEY
Loco. Shed
N. Jc.
W. Jc.
S. Jc.
ST JAMES' STREET WALTHAMSTOW
WALTHAMSTOW
G.E.
HARRINGAY
SEVEN SISTERS
ST ANN'S RD
SOUTH TOTTENHAM
South Tottenham Jc.
CROUCH END
STROUD GREEN
'L'
HARRINGAY PARK (GREEN LANES)
CROUCH HILL
STAMFORD HILL
Copper Mill Jc.
Hall Farm Jc.
LEYTONSTONE
HORNSEY ROAD
UPPER HOLLOWAY
STOKE NEWINGTON
Clapton Jc.
Lea Bridge Jc.
LEA BRIDGE
LEYTON
LEYTONSTONE
MANOR PARK FOR LITTLE ILFORD
ILFORD
G.E.
FINSBURY PARK
TUFNELL PARK (Gds)
JUNCTION RD
HIGHGATE RD Closed 1918
Loco. Shed
KENTISH TOWN
CLARENCE YARD (Gds)
St Paul's Rd Jc.
HIGHBURY VALE (Gds)
RECTORY ROAD
Gds
CLAPTON
LEYTON
'J'
WANSTEAD PARK
FOREST GATE (Goods)
Forest Gate Jc.
WOOD GRANGE PARK
FOREST GATE
ASHBURTON GROVE (Gds)
DRAYTON PARK
MILDMAY PARK
Western Jc.
KINGSLAND closed 1865
HACKNEY DOWNS
HACKNEY WICK
Loughton Jc.
Chobham Farm Jc.
East Ham Loop Nth Jc.
Barking East Jc.
BARKING
L.T. & S.
CANONBURY
N.L.
Eastern Jc.
HACKNEY
G.N. Gds
MARYLAND POINT
Goods
Canonbury Jc.
DALSTON JUNC.
HOMERTON
VICTORIA PARK
CEN.
STRATFORD
EAST HAM
HIGHBURY & ISLINGTON
CANONBURY & ESSEX ROAD
L.N.W. Gds
LOWER
Sheet Factory Jc.
L.N.W. Goods
Coal
Gasworks Tun.
Loco. Shed
HAGGERSTON
LONDON FIELDS
CARPENTERS RD (Gds)
STRATFORD MARKET (WEST HAM)
HAMPSTEAD HEATH
Highgate Rd Jc.
JUNCTION RD
Junction Rd Jc.
GOSPEL OAK
Carlton Rd Jc.
Kentish Town Jc.
KENTISH TOWN
KENTISH TOWN
YORK ROAD
Goods L.N.W.
ST PANCRAS
KING'S CROSS
OLD STREET
SHOREDITCH
BISHOPSGATE (Gds) H. Level
CAMBRIDGE HEATH
L.N.W. Gds
COBORN RD for OLD FORD
OLD FORD
MID. Gds
Goods
PLAISTOW
UPTON PARK
L.T. & S. Works
Loco. Shed
SOMERS TOWN (Gds)
G.N. Gds Jc.
FARRINGDON STREET
ALDERSGATE STREET
New Inn Yard Jc.
BETHNAL GREEN
E. Jc.
W. Jc.
BOW RD
BOW
L.S.
WEST HAM
Abbey Mills Lower Jc.
MILE END
Gds
BROMLEY
EUSTON
KING'S CROSS (MET.)
MOORGATE ST
LIV. ST MET.
LIVERPOOL STREET
SHOREDITCH
STEPNEY GREEN
Coal
DEVONS RD
PLAISTOW & WEST HAM (Goods)
EUSTON SQUARE
G.N. Gds
BROAD STREET
WHITECHAPEL
BURDETT ROAD
SOUTH BROMLEY
L.N.W.. Goods
HOLBORN VIADUCT
ALDGATE
COMMERCIAL RD Gds (L.T. & S.)
SHADWELL
POPLAR (EAST INDIA)
East India Dock Rd Jc.
L.N.W. Coal
CANNING TOWN
G.E.
BECKTON
FENCHURCH STREET
E.L.
M.R. Coal ROAD
TIDAL BASIN
CONNAUGHT RD
CENTRAL
BLACKFRIARS
TEMPLE
LEMAN ST
E. SMITHFIELD
STEPNEY
LIMEHOUSE
POPLAR
WEST INDIA DOCKS
MILLWALL JUNC.
BLACKWALL
CUSTOM HOUSE
P.L.A. Rly
MANOR WAY
GALLIONS
CHARING CROSS
MET.-DIS.
WESTMINSTER
CANNON STREET
G.E. Goods
WAPPING
SILVERTOWN
MID. Goods
WATERLOO JUNC.
N.L. Coal
ROTHERHITHE
NORTH WOOLWICH
ABBEY WOOD
ST JAMES' PARK
WATERLOO
L.B.S.C.
LONDON BRIDGE
SPA ROAD BERMONDSEY
SOUTH DOCK
MILLWALL DOCKS
G.N. Goods
Angerstein Wharf
PLUMSTEAD
LONDON NECROPOLIS
BRICKLAYERS ARMS (Goods)
SURREY DOCKS
WILLOW WALK (Gds)
SOUTHWARK PK
NORTH GREENWICH
VAUXHALL
ELEPHANT & CASTLE
SOUTH BERMONDSEY
Corbet's Lane Jc.
Deptford Wharf
WOOLWICH ARSENAL
CHARLTON JUNCTION
WOOLWICH DOCKYARD
WESTCOMBE PARK
POPLAR
EAST INDIA DOCKS Goods
NINE ELMS (Goods)
Loco. Shed
North Kent West Jc.
Surrey Canal Jc.
Nth Kent Jc.
DEPTFORD Closed 15/03/15 to19/07/26
MAZE HILL (EAST GREENWICH)
E. India Dock Rd Jc.
High St Jc.
L.N.W. Coal
BLACKWALL Gds
Bricklayers Arms Jc.
WALWORTH RD
Both stations closed 03/04/1916
GREENWICH
GREENWICH PARK
Greenwich Park branch & stations closed 01/01/1917
Blackheath Tunnel
Loco. Shed
SOUTH LAMBETH
W. Gds
Old Kent Rd Jc.
QUEEN'S RD
Down Jc.
Up Jc.
G.E.
POPLAR
CAMBERWELL
PECKHAM RYE
'K'
G.E. Gds
NEW CROSS
BLACKHEATH HILL
MILLWALL JUNC.
L.N.W. Goods
WANDSWORTH ROAD
LOUGHBOROUGH JUNC.
DENMARK HILL
Cow Lane Jc.
NUNHEAD
L.S.
NEW CROSS
ST JOHN'S
G.W. Goods
L.N.W. Goods
MID. Goods
Canterbury Rd Jc.
M.R. Coal
BRIXTON
L.N.W. & M.R. Coal
LEWISHAM JUNC.
Kidbrooke Tunnel
N.L.
N.L Coal
G.N. Goods
G.E.
WELLING
CLAPHAM & NORTH STOCKWELL
EAST BRIXTON
Cambria Rd Jc.
EAST DULWICH
BROCKLEY
Parks Bridge Jc.
BLACKHEATH
KIDBROOKE
S.E. & C.
HONOR OAK
CROFTON PARK
HITHER GREEN
Lee Jc.
Loco Shed
LEE for BURNT ASH
SHOOTERS HILL & ELTHAM PARK
N. Jc.
HERNE HILL
S. Jc.
NORTH DULWICH
LORDSHIP LANE FOR FOREST HILL
HONOR OAK PARK
LADYWELL
WELL HALL FOR NORTH ELTHAM
S.E. & C.
KNIGHT'S HILL (Goods)
Knights Hill Tun.
FOREST HILL FOR LORDSHIP LANE
NEW ELTHAM & POPE STREET
STREATHAM HILL
L.B.S.C.
TULSE HILL
DULWICH
CATFORD BRIDGE
CATFORD
GROVE PARK
ELTHAM & MOTTINGHAM
SIDCUP
Leigham Jc.
SYDENHAM HILL
West Norwood Jc.
WEST NORWOOD
UPPER SYDENHAM
SYDENHAM
Leigham Tuns
GIPSY HILL
Sydenham Tun.
BELLINGHAM
Streatham N. Jc.
Streatham Tun.
STREATHAM
Penge Tun.
LOWER SYDENHAM
CRYSTAL PALACE
PENGE
BECKENHAM HILL
Chislehurst Tun.
ELMSTEAD WOODS
Streatham S.Jc.
STREATHAM COMMON
CRYSTAL PALACE HIGH LEVEL & UPPER NORWOOD
PENGE
KENT HOUSE
NEW BECKENHAM
RAVENSBOURNE
SUNDRIDGE PARK
Streatham Jc.
L.B.S.C.
ANERLEY
New Beckenham Jc.
CHISLEHURST
Chislehurst Jc.
Bromley Jc.
Penge Jc.
BECKENHAM JUNC.
Shortlands Jc.
NORBURY
CLOCK HOUSE
SHORTLANDS
BROMLEY NORTH
St Mary Cray Jc.
Spur Jc.
Bickley Jc.
THORNTON HEATH
NORWOOD JUNC.
ELMER'S END
BROMLEY SOUTH
BICKLEY
ST MARY CRAY
SELHURST
Orpington Jc.
Selhurst Jc.
EDEN PARK
BEDDINGTON LANE HALT
Gloucester Rd Jc.
WOODSIDE & SOUTH NORWOOD
Woodside Jc.
'G'
WEST CROYDON
Windmill Bridge Jc.
CROYDON (ADDISCOMBE ROAD)
WEST WICKHAM
HAYES
ORPINGTON

A B C D E F G

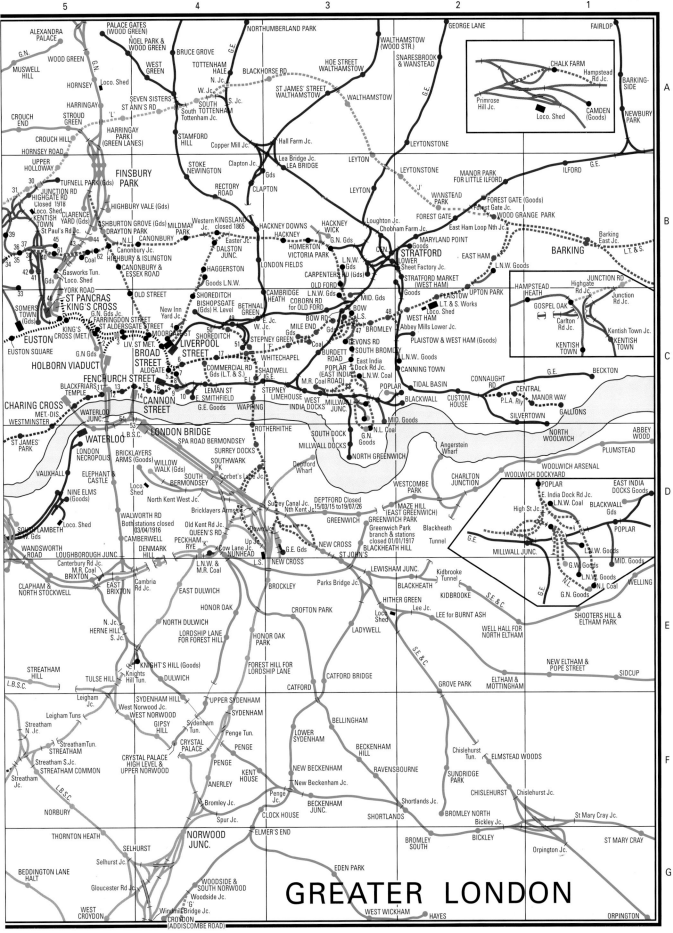

GREATER LONDON

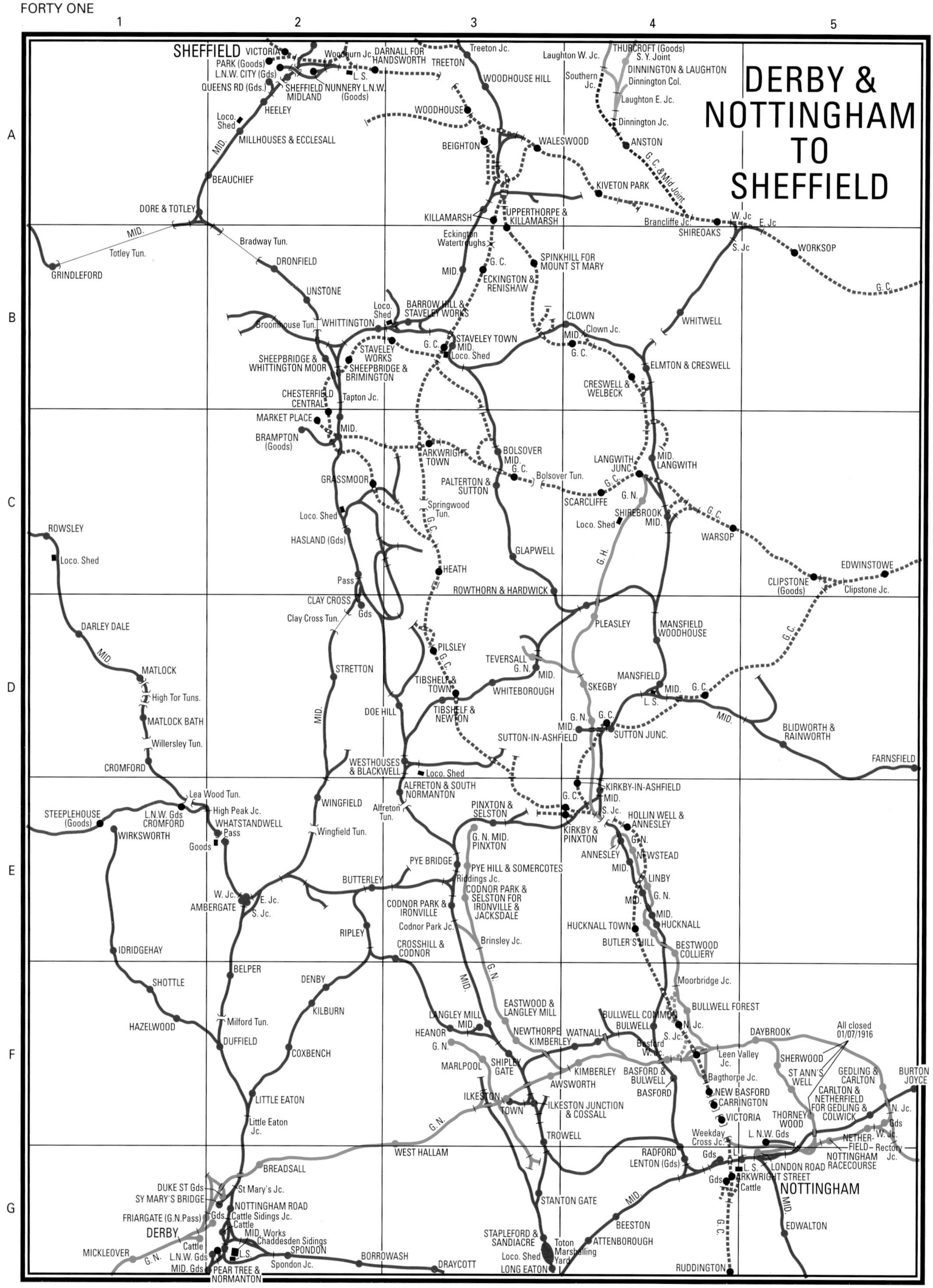

DERBY & NOTTINGHAM TO SHEFFIELD

1
2
3
4
5
A
B
C
D
E
F
G

SHEFFIELD
VICTORIA
PARK (Goods)
L.N.W. CITY (Gds)
QUEENS RD (Gds.)
SHEFFIELD MIDLAND
NUNNERY L.N.W. (Goods)
Woodburn Jc.
DARNALL FOR HANDSWORTH
L.S.
TREETON
Treeton Jc.
WOODHOUSE HILL
Laughton W. Jc.
Southern Jc.
THURCROFT (Goods)
S. Y. Joint
DINNINGTON & LAUGHTON
Dinnington Col.
Laughton E. Jc.
Dinnington Jc.
ANSTON
HEELEY
Loco. Shed
MILLHOUSES & ECCLESALL
MID.
WOODHOUSE
BEIGHTON
WALESWOOD
BEAUCHIEF
KIVETON PARK
G.C.& Mid Joint
DORE & TOTLEY
KILLAMARSH
UPPERTHORPE & KILLAMARSH
Brancliffe Jc.
W. Jc
E. Jc
S. Jc
SHIREOAKS
WORKSOP
MID.
Totley Tun.
Bradway Tun.
GRINDLEFORD
DRONFIELD
Eckington Watertroughs
MID.
G. C.
ECKINGTON & RENISHAW
SPINKHILL FOR MOUNT ST MARY
G.C.
UNSTONE
Loco. Shed
BARROW HILL & STAVELEY WORKS
WHITWELL
Broomhouse Tun.
WHITTINGTON
CLOWN
Clown Jc.
MID.
G. C.
STAVELEY TOWN
G. C.
MID.
Loco. Shed
SHEEPBRIDGE & WHITTINGTON MOOR
STAVELEY WORKS
SHEEPBRIDGE & BRIMINGTON
ELMTON & CRESWELL
CRESWELL & WELBECK
CHESTERFIELD CENTRAL
Tapton Jc.
MARKET PLACE
MID.
BRAMPTON (Goods)
ARKWRIGHT TOWN
BOLSOVER MID.
G. C.
Bolsover Tun.
LANGWITH JUNC.
MID. LANGWITH
GRASSMOOR
PALTERTON & SUTTON
SCARCLIFFE
G.C.
G. N.
G.C.
Springwood Tun.
G.C.
Loco. Shed
SHIREBROOK MID.
Loco. Shed
ROWSLEY
HASLAND (Gds)
WARSOP
Loco. Shed
GLAPWELL
G.H.
EDWINSTOWE
HEATH
CLIPSTONE (Goods)
Clipstone Jc.
Pass
ROWTHORN & HARDWICK
CLAY CROSS
Gds
Clay Cross Tun.
DARLEY DALE
PLEASLEY
MANSFIELD WOODHOUSE
G.C.
PILSLEY
G.C.
TEVERSALL G. N.
MID.
MID
MATLOCK
STRETTON
MANSFIELD
High Tor Tuns.
TIBSHELF & TOWN
WHITEBOROUGH
SKEGBY
L.S.
MID.
G. C.
MATLOCK BATH
DOE HILL
TIBSHELF & NEWTON
MID.
G. N.
G. C.
MID.
MID.
BLIDWORTH & RAINWORTH
Willersley Tun.
SUTTON-IN-ASHFIELD
SUTTON JUNC.
FARNSFIELD
CROMFORD
WESTHOUSES & BLACKWELL
Loco. Shed
ALFRETON & SOUTH NORMANTON
KIRKBY-IN-ASHFIELD
Lea Wood Tun.
G. C.
MID.
S. Jc.
STEEPLEHOUSE (Goods)
L.N.W. Gds CROMFORD
High Peak Jc.
WHATSTANDWELL
Pass
WINGFIELD
Alfreton Tun.
PINXTON & SELSTON
HOLLIN WELL & ANNESLEY
WIRKSWORTH
Goods
Wingfield Tun.
KIRKBY & PINXTON
G. N. MID. PINXTON
ANNESLEY
G.N.
NEWSTEAD
PYE BRIDGE
PYE HILL & SOMERCOTES
MID.
Riddings Jc.
LINBY
BUTTERLEY
W. Jc.
E. Jc.
S. Jc.
AMBERGATE
CODNOR PARK & SELSTON FOR IRONVILLE & JACKSDALE
MID.
G. N.
CODNOR PARK & IRONVILLE
MID.
HUCKNALL
Codnor Park Jc.
HUCKNALL TOWN
RIPLEY
Brinsley Jc.
BUTLER'S HILL
BESTWOOD COLLIERY
IDRIDGEHAY
CROSSHILL & CODNOR
BELPER
DENBY
G. N.
MID.
Moorbridge Jc.
SHOTTLE
EASTWOOD & LANGLEY MILL
BULLWELL FOREST
KILBURN
LANGLEY MILL
MID.
BULLWELL COMMON
All closed 01/07/1916
HAZELWOOD
Milford Tun.
HEANOR
G. N.
NEWTHORPE
KIMBERLEY
WATNALL
BULWELL
N. Jc.
S. Jc.
DAYBROOK
DUFFIELD
Basford W. Jc.
Leen Valley Jc.
SHERWOOD
COXBENCH
MARLPOOL
SHIPLEY GATE
KIMBERLEY
BASFORD & BULWELL
ST ANN'S WELL
GEDLING & CARLTON
BURTON JOYCE
AWSWORTH
Bagthorpe Jc.
BASFORD
NEW BASFORD
CARRINGTON
CARLTON & NETHERFIELD FOR GEDLING & COLWICK
LITTLE EATON
ILKESTON
TOWN
ILKESTON JUNCTION & COSSALL
VICTORIA
THORNEY WOOD
N. Jc.
Gds
Little Eaton Jc.
G. N.
TROWELL
Weekday Cross Jc.
L. N.W. Gds
W. Jc.
NETHERFIELD
Rectory Jc.
WEST HALLAM
RADFORD
LENTON (Gds)
Gds
L.N.
NOTTINGHAM RACECOURSE
BREADSALL
L. S.
LONDON ROAD
Gds
ARKWRIGHT STREET
Cattle
NOTTINGHAM
DUKE ST Gds
St Mary's Jc.
SY MARY'S BRIDGE
NOTTINGHAM ROAD
STANTON GATE
MID.
FRIARGATE (G.N.Pass)
Gds.
Cattle Sidings Jc.
Cattle
G.C.
DERBY
MID. Works
BEESTON
EDWALTON
Chaddesden Sidings
STAPLEFORD & SANDIACRE
ATTENBOROUGH
MICKLEOVER
G. N.
Cattle
L.N.W. Gds
L.S.
SPONDON
BORROWASH
Toton Marshalling Yard
Loco. Shed
MID. Gds
Spondon Jc.
DRAYCOTT
PEAR TREE & NORMANTON
LONG EATON
RUDDINGTON

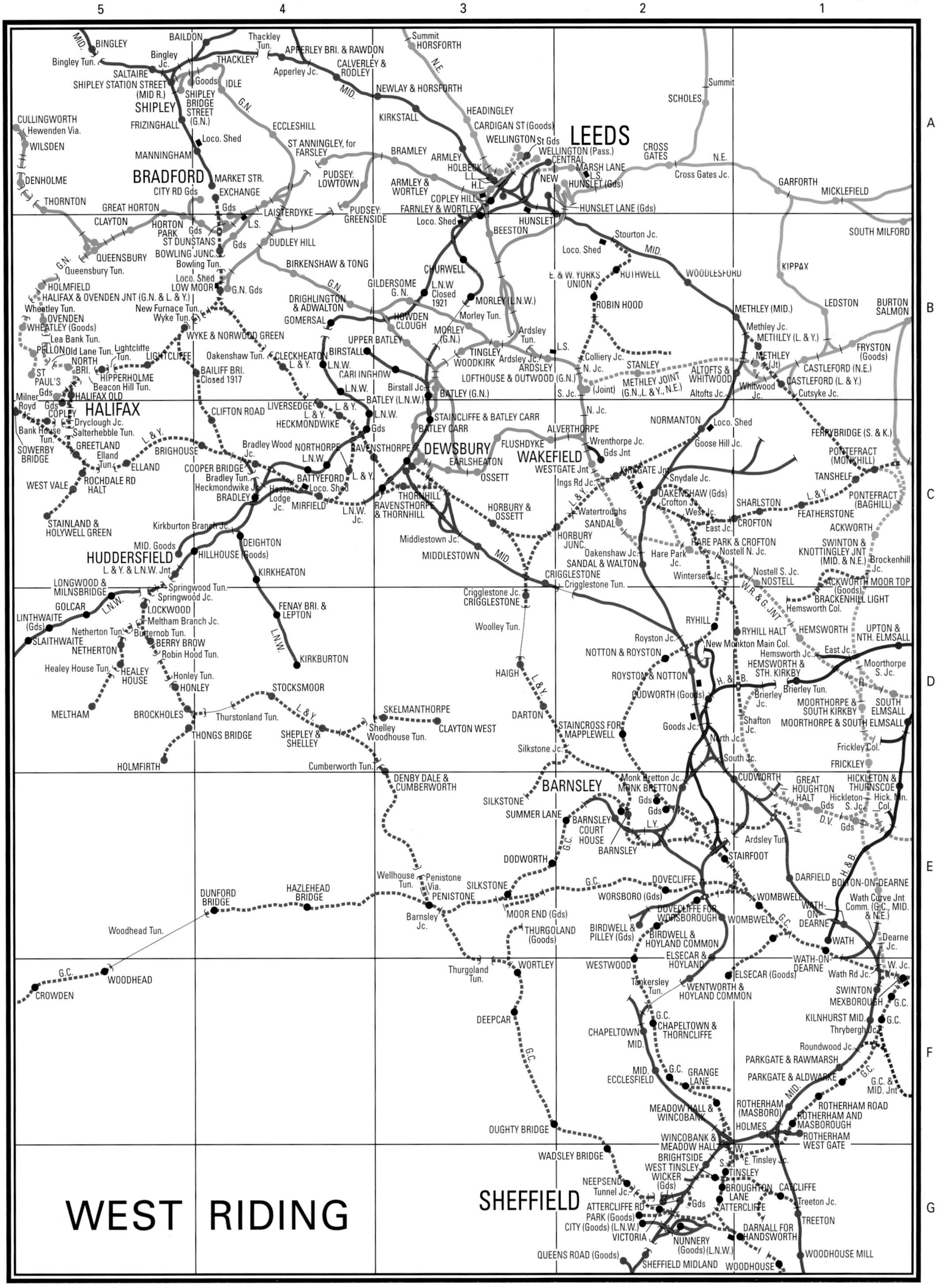

WEST RIDING

5 4 3 2 1
A B C D E F G
LEEDS
BRADFORD
HALIFAX
HUDDERSFIELD
DEWSBURY
WAKEFIELD
BARNSLEY
SHEFFIELD
BINGLEY
BAILDON
Thackley Tun.
APPERLEY BRI. & RAWDON
Summit
HORSFORTH
CALVERLEY & RODLEY
Apperley Jc.
NEWLAY & HORSFORTH
KIRKSTALL
HEADINGLEY
CARDIGAN ST (Goods)
WELLINGTON St Gds
WELLINGTON (Pass.)
CENTRAL
MARSH LANE
NEW
HUNSLET (Gds)
HUNSLET LANE (Gds)
CROSS GATES
Cross Gates Jc.
SCHOLES
GARFORTH
MICKLEFIELD
SOUTH MILFORD
SHIPLEY STATION STREET (MID R.)
SHIPLEY BRIDGE STREET (G.N.)
SALTAIRE
Bingley Tun.
Bingley Jc.
THACKLEY
IDLE
FRIZINGHALL
MANNINGHAM
Loco. Shed
MARKET STR.
EXCHANGE
CITY RD Gds
ECCLESHILL
ST ANNINGLEY, for FARSLEY
BRAMLEY
ARMLEY
HOLBECK
ARMLEY & WORTLEY
COPLEY HILL
FARNLEY & WORTLEY
PUDSEY: LOWTOWN
PUDSEY: GREENSIDE
LAISTERDYKE
CULLINGWORTH
Hewenden Via.
WILSDEN
DENHOLME
THORNTON
GREAT HORTON
CLAYTON
HORTON PARK
ST DUNSTANS
BOWLING JUNC.
Bowling Tun.
QUEENSBURY
Queensbury Tun.
DUDLEY HILL
BIRKENSHAW & TONG
GILDERSOME
CHURWELL
BEESTON
HUNSLET
Stourton Jc.
ROTHWELL
WOODLESFORD
KIPPAX
E. & W. YORKS UNION
ROBIN HOOD
METHLEY (MID.)
LEDSTON
BURTON SALMON
HOLMFIELD
HALIFAX & OVENDEN JNT (G.N. & L. & Y.)
Wheatley Tun.
OVENDEN
WHEATLEY (Goods)
Lea Bank Tun.
PELLON
Old Lane Tun.
Lightcliffe Tun.
NORTH BRI.
ST PAUL'S
HIPPERHOLME
Beacon Hill Tun.
HALIFAX OLD
LOW MOOR
G.N. Gds
New Furnace Tun.
Wyke Tun.
WYKE & NORWOOD GREEN
LIGHTCLIFFE
Oakenshaw Tun.
CLECKHEATON
BAILIFF BRI. Closed 1917
DRIGHLINGTON & ADWALTON
GOMERSAL
HOWDEN CLOUGH
L.N.W Closed 1921
MORLEY (L.N.W.)
Morley Tun.
MORLEY (G.N.)
UPPER BATLEY
BIRSTALL
CARLINGHOW
Birstall Jc.
TINGLEY
WOODKIRK
Ardsley Tun.
Ardsley Jc.
ARDSLEY
LOFTHOUSE & OUTWOOD (G.N.)
Colliery Jc.
STANLEY
METHLEY JOINT (G.N., L. & Y., N.E.)
ALTOFTS & WHITWOOD
Altofts Jc.
Whitwood Jc.
Methley Jc.
METHLEY (L. & Y.)
METHLEY (Jt)
FRYSTON (Goods)
CASTLEFORD (N.E.)
CASTLEFORD (L. & Y.)
Cutsyke Jc.
Milner Royd Jc.
COPLEY
Dryclough Jc.
Salterhebble Tun.
Bank House Tun.
SOWERBY BRIDGE
GREETLAND
Elland Tun.
ELLAND
BRIGHOUSE
CLIFTON ROAD
LIVERSEDGE
HECKMONDWIKE
BATLEY (L.N.W.)
BATLEY (G.N.)
STAINCLIFFE & BATLEY CARR
BATLEY CARR
NORTHORPE L.N.W.
RAVENSTHORPE
FLUSHDYKE
EARLSHEATON
OSSETT
ALVERTHORPE
Wrenthorpe Jc.
Gds Jnt
WESTGATE Jnt
NORMANTON
Loco. Shed
Goose Hill Jc.
FERRYBRIDGE (S. & K.)
PONTEFRACT (MONKHILL)
TANSHELF
PONTEFRACT (BAGHILL)
WEST VALE
ROCHDALE RD HALT
COOPER BRIDGE
Bradley Tun.
Heckmondwike Jc.
BRADLEY
Bradley Wood Jc.
BATTYEFORD
Heaton Lodge Jc.
MIRFIELD
THORNHILL
RAVENSTHORPE & THORNHILL
HORBURY & OSSETT
Ings Rd Jc.
KIRKGATE Jnt
Snydale Jc.
OAKENSHAW (Gds)
Crofton Jc.
West Jc.
East Jc.
Watertroughs
SANDAL
SHARLSTON
CROFTON
FEATHERSTONE
ACKWORTH
STAINLAND & HOLYWELL GREEN
Kirkburton Branch Jc.
DEIGHTON
MID. Goods
L. & Y. & L.N.W. Jnt
HILLHOUSE (Goods)
Middlestown Jc.
MIDDLESTOWN
HORBURY JUNC.
Oakenshaw Jc.
SANDAL & WALTON
Hare Park Jc.
HARE PARK & CROFTON
Nostell N. Jc.
Wintersett Jc.
Nostell S. Jc.
NOSTELL
SWINTON & KNOTTINGLEY JNT (MID. & N.E.)
Brockenhill Jc.
ACKWORTH MOOR TOP (Goods)
BRACKENHILL LIGHT
Hemsworth Col.
KIRKHEATON
CRIGGLESTONE
Crigglestone Jc.
Crigglestone Tun.
LONGWOOD & MILNSBRIDGE
Springwood Tun.
Springwood Jc.
GOLCAR
LINTHWAITE (Gds)
LOCKWOOD
Meltham Branch Jc.
Netherton Tun.
Butternob Tun.
SLAITHWAITE
NETHERTON
BERRY BROW
Robin Hood Tun.
FENAY BRI. & LEPTON
Woolley Tun.
RYHILL
RYHILL HALT
Royston Jc.
NOTTON & ROYSTON
New Monkton Main Col.
HEMSWORTH
UPTON & NTH. ELMSALL
Hemsworth Jc.
East Jc.
HEMSWORTH & STH. KIRKBY
Moorthorpe S. Jc.
Healey House Tun.
HEALEY HOUSE
Honley Tun.
HONLEY
KIRKBURTON
HAIGH
ROYSTON & NOTTON
Brierley Tun.
CUDWORTH (Goods)
Brierley Jc.
MOORTHORPE & SOUTH KIRKBY
SOUTH ELMSALL
MOORTHORPE & SOUTH ELMSALL
MELTHAM
BROCKHOLES
Thurstonland Tun.
STOCKSMOOR
SKELMANTHORPE
DARTON
STAINCROSS FOR MAPPLEWELL
Goods Jc.
Shafton Jc.
THONGS BRIDGE
SHEPLEY & SHELLEY
Shelley Woodhouse Tun.
CLAYTON WEST
North Jc.
Frickley Col.
Silkstone Jc.
South Jc.
FRICKLEY
HOLMFIRTH
Cumberworth Tun.
DENBY DALE & CUMBERWORTH
Monk Bretton Jc.
MONK BRETTON
CUDWORTH
GREAT HOUGHTON HALT
HICKLETON & THURNSCOE
Hickleton S. Jc.
Hick. Mn. Col.
SILKSTONE
SUMMER LANE
Gds
BARNSLEY COURT HOUSE
BARNSLEY
Ardsley Tun.
DODWORTH
STAIRFOOT
Wellhouse Tun.
Penistone Via.
PENISTONE
SILKSTONE
DOVECLIFFE
WORSBORO (Gds)
DARFIELD
BOLTON-ON-DEARNE
Wath Curve Jnt Comm. (G.C., MID. & N.E.)
DUNFORD BRIDGE
HAZLEHEAD BRIDGE
Barnsley Jc.
MOOR END (Gds)
THURGOLAND (Goods)
DOVECLIFFE FOR WORSBOROUGH
WOMBWELL
BIRDWELL & PILLEY (Gds)
BIRDWELL & HOYLAND COMMON
WATH-ON-DEARNE
WATH
Dearne Jc.
Woodhead Tun.
ELSECAR & HOYLAND
ELSECAR (Goods)
Thurgoland Tun.
WORTLEY
WESTWOOD
Tankersley Tun.
WENTWORTH & HOYLAND COMMON
Wath Rd Jc.
W. Jc.
SWINTON
MEXBOROUGH
WOODHEAD
CROWDEN
DEEPCAR
CHAPELTOWN
CHAPELTOWN & THORNCLIFFE
KILNHURST MID.
Thrybergh Jc.
Roundwood Jc.
PARKGATE & RAWMARSH
PARKGATE & ALDWARKE
G.C. & MID. Jnt
ECCLESFIELD
GRANGE LANE
MEADOW HALL & WINCOBANK
ROTHERHAM (MASBORO)
ROTHERHAM ROAD
ROTHERHAM AND MASBOROUGH
HOLMES
ROTHERHAM WEST GATE
OUGHTY BRIDGE
WINCOBANK & MEADOW HALL
WADSLEY BRIDGE
BRIGHTSIDE
WEST TINSLEY
E. Tinsley Jc.
TINSLEY
WICKER (Gds)
NEEPSEND
Tunnel Jc.
BROUGHTON LANE
CATCLIFFE
Treeton Jc.
TREETON
ATTERCLIFFE RD
ATTERCLIFFE
PARK (Goods)
CITY (Goods) (L.N.W.)
VICTORIA
NUNNERY (Goods) (L.N.W.)
DARNALL FOR HANDSWORTH
QUEENS ROAD (Goods)
SHEFFIELD MIDLAND
WOODHOUSE
WOODHOUSE MILL
MID.
G.N.
N.E.
L.N.W.
L. & Y.
L.S.
L.L.
H.L.
G.C.
H. & B.
D.V.
W.R. & G. JNT
L.Y.

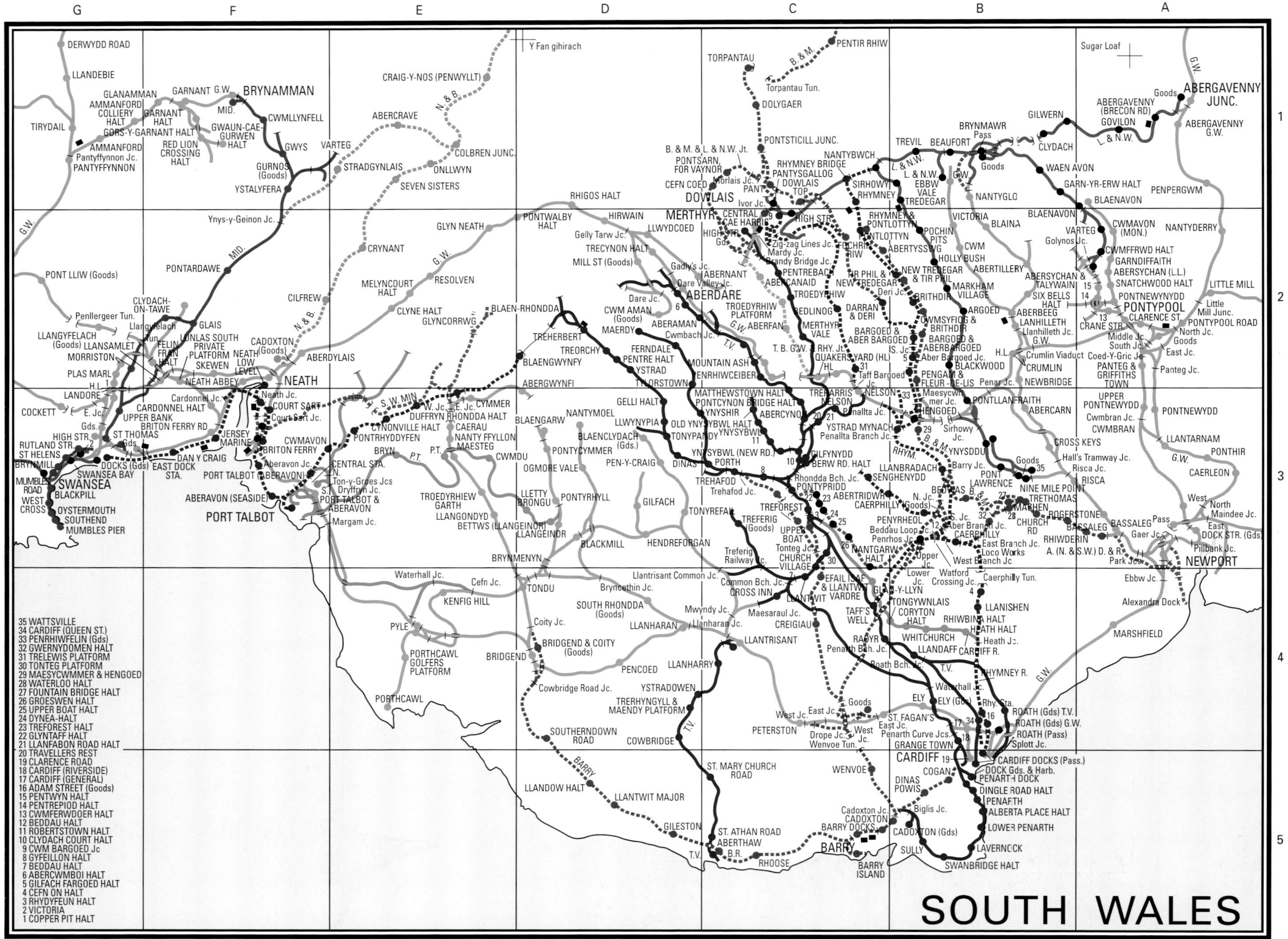
SOUTH WALES
35 WATTSVILLE
34 CARDIFF (QUEEN ST.)
33 PENRHIWFELIN (Gds)
32 GWERNYDOMEN HALT
31 TRELEWIS PLATFORM
30 TONTEG PLATFORM
29 MAESYCWMMER & HENGOED
28 WATERLOO HALT
27 FOUNTAIN BRIDGE HALT
26 GROESWEN HALT
25 UPPER BOAT HALT
24 DYNEA-HALT
23 TREFOREST HALT
22 GLYNTAFF HALT
21 LLANFABON ROAD HALT
20 TRAVELLERS REST
19 CLARENCE ROAD
18 CARDIFF (RIVERSIDE)
17 CARDIFF (GENERAL)
16 ADAM STREET (Goods)
15 PENTWYN HALT
14 PENTREPIOD HALT
13 CWMFERWDOER HALT
12 BEDDAU HALT
11 ROBERTSTOWN HALT
10 CLYDACH COURT HALT
9 CWM BARGOED Jc
8 GYFEILLON HALT
7 BEDDAU HALT
6 ABERCWMBOI HALT
5 GILFACH FARGOED HALT
4 CEFN ON HALT
3 RHYDYFEUN HALT
2 VICTORIA
1 COPPER PIT HALT

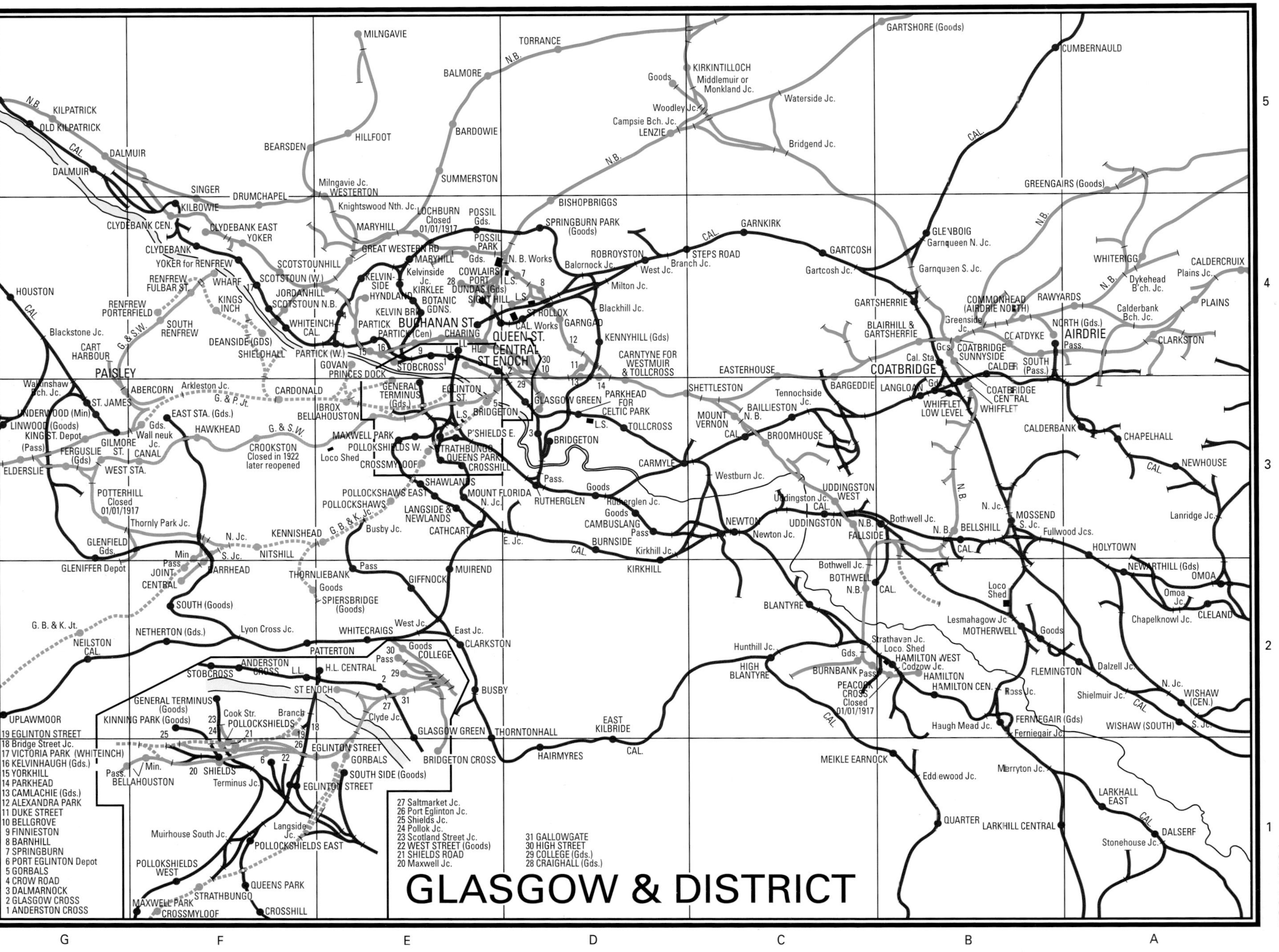
GLASGOW & DISTRICT
19 EGLINTON STREET
18 Bridge Street Jc.
17 VICTORIA PARK (WHITEINCH)
16 KELVINHAUGH (Gds.)
15 YORKHILL
14 PARKHEAD
13 CAMLACHIE (Gds.)
12 ALEXANDRA PARK
11 DUKE STREET
10 BELLGROVE
9 FINNIESTON
8 BARNHILL
7 SPRINGBURN
6 PORT EGLINTON Depot
5 GORBALS
4 CROW ROAD
3 DALMARNOCK
2 GLASGOW CROSS
1 ANDERSTON CROSS
27 Saltmarket Jc.
26 Port Eglinton Jc.
25 Shields Jc.
24 Pollok Jc.
23 Scotland Street Jc.
22 WEST STREET (Goods)
21 SHIELDS ROAD
20 Maxwell Jc.
31 GALLOWGATE
30 HIGH STREET
29 COLLEGE (Gds.)
28 CRAIGHALL (Gds.)
MILNGAVIE
TORRANCE
BALMORE
BARDOWIE
HILLFOOT
BEARSDEN
SUMMERSTON
KILPATRICK
OLD KILPATRICK
DALMUIR
SINGER
DRUMCHAPEL
Milngavie Jc.
WESTERTON
KILBOWIE
CLYDEBANK CEN.
CLYDEBANK EAST
YOKER
CLYDEBANK
YOKER for RENFREW
SCOTSTOUNHILL
SCOTSTOUN (W.)
JORDANHILL
SCOTSTOUN N.B.
WHITEINCH CAL.
RENFREW FULBAR ST.
WHARF
KINGS INCH
RENFREW PORTERFIELD
SOUTH RENFREW
DEANSIDE (GDS)
SHIELDHALL
HOUSTON
Blackstone Jc.
CART HARBOUR
PAISLEY
Walkinshaw Bch. Jc.
ST. JAMES
ABERCORN
Arkleston Jc.
EAST STA. (Gds.)
HAWKHEAD
LINWOOD (Goods)
KING ST. Depot
GILMORE ST.
CANAL
WEST STA.
FERGUSLIE (Gds)
ELDERSLIE
POTTERHILL Closed 01/01/1917
Thornly Park Jc.
GLENFIELD Gds.
GLENIFFER Depot
BARRHEAD
SOUTH (Goods)
NITSHILL
KENNISHEAD
CROOKSTON Closed in 1922 later reopened
CARDONALD
IBROX
BELLAHOUSTON
GOVAN
PRINCES DOCK
MAXWELL PARK
POLLOKSHIELDS W.
Loco Shed
CROSSMYLOOF
POLLOCKSHAWS EAST
POLLOCKSHAWS
Busby Jc.
THORNLIEBANK
SPIERSBRIDGE (Goods)
GIFFNOCK
MURIEND
WHITECRAIGS
PATTERTON
NETHERTON (Gds.)
NEILSTON CAL.
Lyon Cross Jc.
UPLAWMOOR
CLARKSTON
BUSBY
THORNTONHALL
HAIRMYRES
EAST KILBRIDE
KNIGHTSWOOD Nth. Jc.
LOCHBURN Closed 01/01/1917
POSSIL Gds.
POSSIL PARK
MARYHILL
GREAT WESTERN RD
KELVINSIDE
Kelvinside Jc.
HYNDLAND
KIRKLEE
BOTANIC GDNS.
KELVIN BRIDGE
PARTICK
PARTICK (Cen)
PARTICK (W.)
CHARING CROSS
BUCHANAN ST.
QUEEN ST.
COWLAIRS
PORT DUNDAS (Gds)
SIGHTHILL
N. B. Works
ST. ROLLOX
CAL. Works
CENTRAL
ST ENOCH
STOBCROSS
GENERAL TERMINUS (Gds.)
EGLINTON ST.
BRIDGETON
P'SHIELDS E.
STRATHBUNGO
QUEENS PARK
CROSSHILL
SHAWLANDS
MOUNT FLORIDA
LANGSIDE & NEWLANDS
CATHCART
RUTHERGLEN
GLASGOW GREEN
PARKHEAD FOR CELTIC PARK
TOLLCROSS
KENNYHILL (Gds)
CARNTYNE FOR WESTMUIR & TOLLCROSS
GARNGAD
Blackhill Jc.
Milton Jc.
ROBROYSTON
Balornock Jc.
SPRINGBURN PARK (Goods)
BISHOPBRIGGS
STEPS ROAD
Branch Jc.
GARNKIRK
GARTCOSH
Gartcosh Jc.
KIRKINTILLOCH
Middlemuir or Monkland Jc.
Goods
Woodley Jc.
Campsie Bch. Jc.
LENZIE
Waterside Jc.
Bridgend Jc.
GARTSHORE (Goods)
CUMBERNAULD
GREENGAIRS (Goods)
GLENBOIG
Garnqueen N. Jc.
Garnqueen S. Jc.
GARTSHERRIE
BLAIRHILL & GARTSHERRIE
COATBRIDGE
COATBRIDGE SUNNYSIDE
COMMONHEAD (AIRDRIE NORTH)
RAWYARDS
WHITERIGG
Dykehead B'ch. Jc.
CALDERCRUIX
Plains Jc.
PLAINS
Calderbank Bch. Jc.
AIRDRIE
NORTH (Gds.)
CLARKSTON
CALDER
SOUTH (Pass.)
CALDERBANK
CHAPELHALL
NEWHOUSE
Lanridge Jc.
COATBRIDGE CENTRAL
WHIFFLET
WHIFFLET LOW LEVEL
LANGLOAN
BARGEDDIE
EASTERHOUSE
SHETTLESTON
Tennochside Jc.
BAILLIESTON
MOUNT VERNON
BROOMHOUSE
CARMYLE
Westburn Jc.
CAMBUSLANG
Rutherglen Jc.
BURNSIDE
KIRKHILL
Kirkhill Jc.
NEWTON
Newton Jc.
UDDINGSTON
UDDINGSTON WEST
Uddingston Jc.
FALLSIDE
Bothwell Jc.
BOTHWELL
BELLSHILL
MOSSEND
Fullwood Jcs.
HOLYTOWN
NEWARTHILL (Gds)
OMOA
Omoa Jc.
CLELAND
Chapelknowl Jc.
BLANTYRE
HIGH BLANTYRE
Hunthill Jc.
BURNBANK
Strathaven Jc.
Loco. Shed
HAMILTON WEST
Codzow Jc.
HAMILTON
HAMILTON CEN.
PEACOCK CROSS Closed 01/01/1917
Lesmahagow Jc.
MOTHERWELL
Loco Shed
FLEMINGTON
Dalzell Jc.
Shielmuir Jc.
WISHAW (CEN.)
WISHAW (SOUTH)
Ross Jc.
FERNIEGAIR (Gds)
Ferniegair Jc.
Haugh Mead Jc.
MEIKLE EARNOCK
Eddlewood Jc.
QUARTER
LARKHILL CENTRAL
Merryton Jc.
LARKHALL EAST
DALSERF
Stonehouse Jc.
G. B. & K. Jt.
STOBCROSS
ANDERSTON CROSS
H.L. CENTRAL
ST ENOCH
GENERAL TERMINUS (Goods)
KINNING PARK (Goods)
POLLOCKSHIELDS
SHIELDS
BELLAHOUSTON
GORBALS
SOUTH SIDE (Goods)
EGLINTON STREET
GLASGOW GREEN
BRIDGETON CROSS
Clyde Jc.
COLLEGE
Muirhouse South Jc.
POLLOKSHIELDS EAST
POLLOKSHIELDS WEST
QUEENS PARK
STRATHBUNGO
MAXWELL PARK
CROSSMYLOOF
CROSSHILL

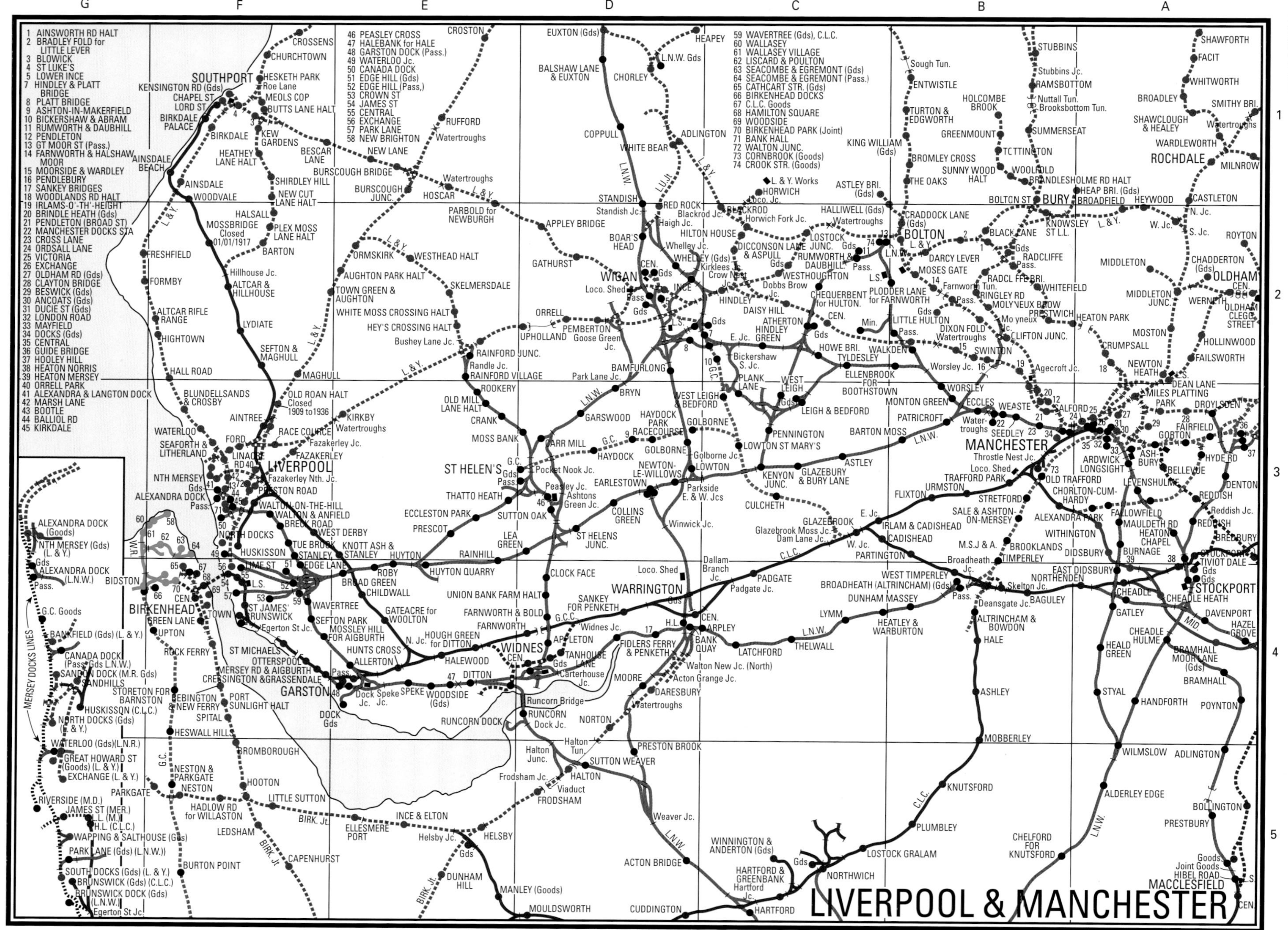
LIVERPOOL & MANCHESTER
1 AINSWORTH RD HALT
2 BRADLEY FOLD for LITTLE LEVER
3 BLOWICK
4 ST LUKE'S
5 LOWER INCE
7 HINDLEY & PLATT BRIDGE
8 PLATT BRIDGE
9 ASHTON-IN-MAKERFIELD
10 BICKERSHAW & ABRAM
11 RUMWORTH & DAUBHILL
12 PENDLETON
13 GT MOOR ST (Pass.)
14 FARNWORTH & HALSHAW MOOR
15 MOORSIDE & WARDLEY
16 PENDLEBURY
17 SANKEY BRIDGES
18 WOODLANDS RD HALT
19 IRLAMS-O'-TH'-HEIGHT
20 BRINDLE HEATH (Gds)
21 PENDLETON (BROAD ST)
22 MANCHESTER DOCKS STA
23 CROSS LANE
24 ORDSALL LANE
25 VICTORIA
26 EXCHANGE
27 OLDHAM RD (Gds)
28 CLAYTON BRIDGE
29 BESWICK (Gds)
30 ANCOATS (Gds)
31 DUCIE ST (Gds)
32 LONDON ROAD
33 MAYFIELD
34 DOCKS (Gds)
35 CENTRAL
36 GUIDE BRIDGE
37 HOOLEY HILL
38 HEATON NORRIS
39 HEATON MERSEY
40 ORRELL PARK
41 ALEXANDRA & LANGTON DOCK
42 MARSH LANE
43 BOOTLE
44 BALLIOL RD
45 KIRKDALE
46 PEASLEY CROSS
47 HALEBANK for HALE
48 GARSTON DOCK (Pass.)
49 WATERLOO Jc.
50 CANADA DOCK
51 EDGE HILL (Gds)
52 EDGE HILL (Pass,)
53 CROWN ST
54 JAMES ST
55 CENTRAL
56 EXCHANGE
57 PARK LANE
58 NEW BRIGHTON
59 WAVERTREE (Gds), C.L.C.
60 WALLASEY
61 WALLASEY VILLAGE
62 LISCARD & POULTON
63 SEACOMBE & EGREMONT (Gds)
64 SEACOMBE & EGREMONT (Pass.)
65 CATHCART STR. (Gds)
66 BIRKENHEAD DOCKS
67 C.L.C. Goods
68 HAMILTON SQUARE
69 WOODSIDE
70 BIRKENHEAD PARK (Joint)
71 BANK HALL
72 WALTON JUNC.
73 CORNBROOK (Goods)
74 CROOK STR. (Goods)

Gazetteer

This Gazetteer to the Atlas is divided into six parts, in the following order:

1. List of abbreviations used to represent the various companies owning and/or using the various stations, meeting at junctions, etc
2. Index to tunnels named on the maps
3. Index to watertroughs that appear on the maps
4. Index to principal summits named on the maps
5. Index to principal bridges and viaducts marked on the maps
6. Index to stations, junctions, etc

Stations with dual titles
Dual titles are only used for stations having the word '&' in such title: they are not cross-indexed and only appear under the first name, e.g. Dunkeld & Birnam only appears under the letter 'D'. In the case of dual titles joined by the word 'for', only the first name is shown.

Stations sub-titled
When the sub-title is characteristic, it is indexed in its own right, in addition to the main title, e.g. Norwich is indexed generally under 'N' and also under 'T' as Thorpe (Norwich). Similar entries include the various 'Victorias', Paragon (Hull), Warrior Square (St Leonards), etc. Non-characteristic titles like 'Central', 'Exchange', 'North', 'New', etc, are not directly entered as such, if at all, but when shown they follow the name of the place, e.g. Barnsley (Exchange), Leeds (New).

Plurality of stations at a single place
Where two companies each have their own station(s) at any given place, the companies' initials are separated by '&' thus: Bedford, LNW & Mid; Tunbridge Wells, LBSC & SEC. When three or more companies have stations in a place, a comma (,) separates the first two or more, e.g. Cymmer, GW, RSB & SWM.

Joint stations are shown with the initials of the owning partners or of the Joint undertaking if it has a specific name, e.g. Cosham, LBSC&LSWJt.; Ludlow, S&H.

Ownership and users of stations
Stations used by more than one company, in so far as passenger traffic is concerned, are shown with the owning company or companies in bolder type, followed by other users shown within brackets, as under (the ramifications of goods workings are too complex to be included):
Aberdeen (Pass), **Cal&GNSJt** (NB)
Branksome, **LSW**(SD)
Crewe, **LNW**(GW/NS)

In some instances, a 'foreign' user has been shown as a matter of interest even though such user may have ceased slightly earlier than 1922. It has also been shown in those cases where an absorbed company appears in its own right on the maps, e.g. Bridgend, **GW**(BRY), the Barry Railway having been absorbed by the GWR prior to the general grouping.

Joint stations used by other companies in addition to the Joint owning partners are shown thus, the joint partners not being individually shown:
Ackworth, **SK**(GN/GC)
Carlisle, **CJC**(G&SW/M&C/Mid/NB/NE)
Knutsford, **CLC**(LNW)

Details of the component partners of all Joint undertakings will be found against the appropriate title in the list of abbreviations.

Joint services using junction or other stations that are purely the property of one or other of the joint partners (the joint line having been terminated at some point thereof) are not shown against such stations unless the Joint Company actually runs its own trains, e.g.: SD *is* shown against Bath, Broadstone, etc, since the Somerset & Dorset Joint did work trains through between Bath and Bournemouth.
QYM *is not* shown against Quaker's Yard or Merthyr since the Quaker's Yard & Merthyr Joint had no rolling stock or locomotives and was merely a section of the GW and Rhymney joint property lying between Quaker's Yard and Merthyr (GW).
CKP *is* shown against Penrith since the Cockermouth, Keswick & Penrith Company's trains, although worked by the L&NW, nevertheless arrived and departed Penrith in their own right, and were not in any sense 'Joint'.

An exception to this method has been made in the case of the Birkenhead Joint, which, although owning neither rolling stock nor locomotives and whose line terminated at Walton Jc (Warrington), has been shown against certain L&NW stations between Warrington and Manchester Exchange by virtue of the joint service operated between Chester and Manchester, worked variously by L&NW and GW trains.

Line junctions are shown in italics. Those situated on individual companies' lines that can be readily identified by an adjoining or nearby station on the same name are not generally indexed, but those that form a meeting point of two or more companies are shown thus:
Acton Wells Jc, NSW/GW/LNW/Mid
Bopeep Jc, LBSC/SEC

Where is it on the map?
Example from Index: Abermule, Cam, 14B2. Answer: on map 14 in the square found by following section B across until it meets the vertical column No 2.

The assistance of the BTC Archivist, Mr L. C. Johnson, and his staff in making available timetables and other documents of the period is gratefully acknowledged.

1 List of Abbreviations

In the case of Joint or Subsidiary Lines with individual titles, the owning or leasing partners or companies are indicated in brackets immediately after the title.

AD	Alexandra (Newport & South Wales) Docks & Railway
AJ	Axholme Joint (LY and NE)
AN	Ashby & Nuneaton Joint (LNW and Midland)
BAC	Bere Alston & Calstock Light (PDSW)
BC	Bishop's Castle
BJ	Birkenhead Joint (GW and LNW)
BL	Brackenhill Light
BM	Brecon & Merthyr
BPGV	Burry Port & Gwendraeth Valley
BRY	Barry
BWHA	Bideford, Westward Ho! & Appledore
Cal	Caledonian
Cam	Cambrian
Car	Cardiff
CE	Clifton Extension (GW and Midland)
CJC	(Carlisle) Citadel Station Joint Committee (Cal and LNW)
CKP	Cockermouth, Keswick & Penrith
CL	Corringham Light
CLC	Cheshire Lines Committee (GC, GN and Midland)
CM	Campbeltown & Machrihanish Light
CMDP	Cleobury Mortimer & Ditton Priors Light
CO	Croydon & Oxted Joint (LBSC and SEC)
Cor	Corris
CRY	Croesor
CVH	Colne Valley & Halstead
CWJ	Cleator & Workington Junction
D&A	Dundee & Arbroath Joint (Cal and NB)
D&B	Dumbarton & Balloch Joint (Cal and NB)
Dist	Metropolitan District
DJ	(Carlisle) Dentonholme Joint Committee (G&SW, Midland and NB)
DV	Dearne Valley
DVL	Derwent Valley Light
Eas	Easingwold
ECH	Easton & Church Hope (GW and LSW)
EK	East Kent Light
EL	East London (GE, LBSC, Met, Met Dist, and SEC)
ELB	Edenham & Little Bytham
EWY	East & West Yorkshire Union
FB	Forth Bridge Railway Co (GN, Midland, NB and NE)
Fest	Festiniog
Fur	Furness
FYN	Freshwater, Yarmouth & Newport
GBK	Glasgow, Barrhead & Kilmarnock Joint (Cal and G&SW)
GC	Great Central
GE	Great Eastern
GN	Great Northern
GNS	Great North of Scotland
G&P	Glasgow & Paisley Joint (Cal and G&SW)
G&SW	Glasgow & South Western
GTC	(Carlisle) Goods Traffic Committee (Cal, G&SW, LNW and Midland)
GV	Gwendraeth Valley
GVT	Glyn Valley Tramway
GW	Great Western
HB	Hull & Barnsley
H&C	Hammersmith & City (GW and Met)
HHL	Halifax High Level (GN and LY)
HJ	Halesowen Joint (GW and Midland)
H&O	Halifax & Ovenden Joint (GN and LY)
HR	Highland
IMR	Isle of Man Railway
IW	Isle of Wight Railway
IWC	Isle of Wight Central Railway
K&B	Kilsyth & Bonnybridge Joint (Cal and NB)
KE	Knott End
KES	Kent & East Sussex
LB	Lynton & Barnstaple
LBSC	London, Brighton & South Coast
LC	Liskeard & Caradon (GW)
LE	London Electric
LL	Liskeard & Looe (GW)
LM	Llanelly & Mynydd Mawr
LNW	London & North Western
LOR	Liverpool Overhead
LSW	London & South Western
LTS	London, Tilbury & Southend
LU	Lancashire & Yorkshire & Lancashire Union Joint (LNW and LY)
LY	Lancashire & Yorkshire
Mawd	Mawddwy Light (Cambrian)
M&C	Maryport & Carlisle
MDHB	Mersey Docks & Harbour Board
ME	Manx Electric
Mer	Mersey
Met	Metropolitan
MGN	Midland & Great Northern Joint (GN and Midland)
Mid	Midland
MJ	Methley Joint (GN, LY and NE)
MSJA	Manchester South Junction & Altrincham (GC and LNW)
MSL	Mid-Suffolk Light
MSW	Midland & South Western Junction
Mum	Swansea & Mumbles
NB	North British

N&B	Neath & Brecon
NE	North Eastern
NL	North London
NS	North Staffordshire
NSJ	Norfolk & Suffolk Joint (GE and MGN)
NSL	North Sunderland Light
NSW	North & South Western Junction (LNW, Midland and NL)
NU	North Union Joint (LNW and LY)
NV	Nidd Valley
NWNG	North Wales Narrow Gauge
OAGB	Oldham, Ashton-under-Lyne & Guide Bridge (GC and LNW)
OAT	Oxford & Aylesbury Tramroad (Met&GCJt)
O&I	Otley & Ilkley Joint (Midland and NE)
PCB	Portmadoc, Croesor & Beddgelert
PDJ	Princes Dock Joint (Cal, G&SW and NB)
PDSW	Plymouth, Devonport & South Western Junction
PL	Preston & Longridge Joint (LNW and LY)
PLA	Port of London Authority
PT	Port Talbot Railway and Docks
P&W	Portpatrick & Wigtownshire Joint (Cal, G&SW, LNW and Midland)
PWY	Preston & Wyre (LNW and LY)
QYM	Quaker's Yard & Merthyr Joint (GW and Rhymney)
RCT	Rye & Camber Tramway
Rhy	Rhymney
RKF	Rowrah & Kelton Fell
RSB	Rhondda & Swansea Bay
SBH	Snailbeach District Railways
SD	Somerset & Dorset Joint Committee (LSW and Midland)
SEC	South Eastern & Chatham
S&H	Shrewsbury & Hereford Joint (GW and LNW)
SHD	Sheffield District Railway (GC and Midland)
SK	Swinton & Knottingley (Midland and NE)
SL	Selsey Light
S&M	Shropshire & Montgomeryshire Light
SMJ	Stratford-on-Avon & Midland Junction
SMR	Snowdon Mountain Railway
SSM	South Shields, Marsden & Whitburn Colliery
SVW	Severn & Wye Joint (GW and Midland)
SWD	Southwold
SWM	South Wales Mineral
SWN	Shrewsbury & Wellington Joint (GW and LNW)
SWP	Shrewsbury & Welshpool Joint (GW and LNW)
SYJ	South Yorkshire Joint (GC, GN, LY, Midland and NE)
Tal	Talyllyn
Tan	Tanat Valley Light (Cambrian)
TBJ	Taff Bargoed Joint (GW and Rhymney)
TFG	Tottenham & Forest Gate (LTS and Midland)
THJ	Tottenham & Hampstead Junction (GE and Midland)
TV	Taff Vale
Van	Van Light (Cambrian)
VR	Vale of Rheidol (Cambrian)
VT	Vale of Towy Joint (GW and LNW)
WB	Whitechapel & Bow Joint (LTS and Met District)
WCE	Whitehaven, Cleator & Egremont Joint (Furness and LNW)
WCJ	Wath Curve Joint Committee (GC, Midland and NE)
WCP	Weston, Clevedon & Portishead
Wir	Wirral
WL	West London Joint (GW and LNW)
W&L	Welshpool & Llanfair Light (Cambrian)
WLE	West London Extension Joint (GW, LNW, LBSC and LSW)
WM	Wrexham & Minera Joint (GW and LNW)
WP	Weymouth & Portland Joint (GW and LSW)
WRG	West Riding & Grimsby Joint (GC and GN)
WSC	Woodside & South Croydon (LBSC and SEC)
WT	Wantage Tramway
WUT	Wisbech & Upwell Tramway

2 Index to Tunnels

Tunnel	Railway	Map ref
Abbotscliff	SEC	6D2
Alderton	GW	9G3
Alfreton	Mid	16C4/41E3
Ampthill	Mid	10C1
Ardsley	Mid	21F3/42E1
Ardsley	GN	42B3
Armathwaite	Mid	27D1
Arnworth	LY	45B2
Asfordby	Mid	16E3
Askham	GN	16A3
Balcombe	LBSC	5E3
Bangor	LNW	19D2
Bank House	LY	21E2/42C5
Barnsdale (South Kirkby)	HB	26E4
Baron Wood	Mid	27D1
Beacon Hill	LY	42B5
Belmont (Bangor)	LNW	19D2
Betchworth	LBSC	5D2
Bincombe	GW	3F3
Bingley	Mid	21D2/42A5
Birkett	Mid	27F2
Blackheath	SEC	40D2
Blaenrhondda	RSB	7B5/43E2
Blea Moor	Mid	24A1
Bletchingley	SEC	5D3
Bodorgan	LNW	19D1
Bolsover	GC	41C3
Bopeep	SEC	6F5
Bowling	LY	42B4
Box	GW	3A4
Bradley	LNW	42C4
Bradway	Mid	16A5/41B2
Bramhope	NE	21D3
Brierley	HB	47D1
Brislington	GW	3A3/8C1
Brooksbottom	LY	45B1
Broomhouse	Mid	16A5/41 B2
Brownqueen	GW	1D3
Buckhorn Weston	LSW	3D3
Buckshead	GW	1E1
Burdale	NE	22B5
Buriton	LSW	4D2
Butternob	LY	42D2
Caerphilly	Rhy	43B4
Campden	GW	9C5
Castle Hill	LY	21E1
Catesby	GC	10B4
Charlton	SEC	6D2
Chatham	SEC	6B5
Chee Tor	Mid	15A5
Chilcompton	SD	3B3/8E1
Chislehurst	SEC	40F2
Christleton	LNW	15B1
Clarborough	GC	16A2
Clay Cross	Mid	41D2
Clayton	LBSC	5F3
Combe Down	SD	3B3/8D1
Copenhagen	GN	40B5
Corbridge	NE	27C4
Corby	Mid	16G1
Cowburn	Mid	15A5
Cressbrook	Mid	15A5
Crick	LNW	10A3
Crigglestone	Mid	21E3/42D2
Crimple	NE	21C3
Culgaith	Mid	27E1
Cumberworth	LY	21F2/42D3
Dainton	GW	2D3
Denaby	HB	26F4
Devonshire	SD	3B3/8D1
Dinmore	S&H	9B1
Dove Holes	Mid	15A4
Drewton	HB	27D4
Elland	LY	42C5
Elstree	Mid	11G2
Festiniog	LNW	19E3
Fisherton	LSW	4C5
Fort Pitt	SEC	6B5
Gas Works (King's Cross)	GN	40B5
Gillingham (Kent)	SEC	6B5
Girvan	G&SW	29G2
Gisburn	LY	24C1
Glaston	Mid	16F1
Glenfield	Mid	16F4
Greet	GW	9D4
Grimston	Mid	16E3
Grove	SEC	5D5
Guston	SEC	6D2
Haddon	Mid	15B5
Hadley North	GN	11G2
Hadley South	GN	11G2
Halton	BJ	45D5
Hampstead	GC	39B5
Harbour (Dover)	SEC	6D2
Hastings	SEC	6F5
Haverstock Hill	Mid	39B5
Haywards Heath	LBSC	5E3
Headstone	Mid	15B5
Healey House	LY	42D5
Helm	Mid	27F2
Hickleton	HB	42E1
High Tor	Mid	16B5/41D1
Honiton	LSW	2A1

Honley	LY	42D5
Horsfall	LY	21E1
Hunsbury Hill	LNW	10B2
Hunting Butts	GW	9D4
Inver	HR	33D4
Kensal Green	LNW	39C4
Kidbrook	SEC	40E2
Killiecrankie	HR	33C4
Kilsby	LNW	10A4
Kingswood	HR	33E5
Kirton	GC	22F4
Kitsonwood	LY	20A1
Knighton	Mid	16F3
Knights Hill	LBSC	40E5
Lazonby	Mid	27D1
Lea Bank	H&O	42B5
Lea Wood	Mid	16B5/41E1
Leigham	LBSC	40F5
Lightcliffe	LY	42B5
Linslade	LNW	10D1
Litchfield	LSW	4B3
Litton	Mid	15A5
Llandegai	LNW	19D2
Llanderfal	GW	19F5
Llangyfelach	GW	43G2
Lord's	GC	39C5
Lydden	SEC	6D2
Manton	Mid	16F2
Marley	GW	2D4
Martello	SEC	6D2
Merstham	LBSC & SEC	5C3
Mickleham	LBSC	5C2
Middle Hill	GW	3A4
Milford (Derbys)	Mid	16C5/41F2
Millwood	LY	21E1
Moncrieff	Cal	33F5
Moorcock	Mid	27G2
Morley	LNW	21E3/42B3
Mossdale Head	Mid	27G3
Mountfield	SEC	6E5
Mount Pleasant	SEC	6F5
Netherton	LY	42D5
New Furnace	LY	42B4
Northchurch	LNW	10E1
North Stoke	LBSC	5F1
Nuttall	LY	45B1
Oakenshaw	LY	42B4
Old Lane	H&O	42B5
Ore	SEC	6F5
Pansbourne	GN	11F2
Patcham	LBSC	5F3
Peascliffe	GN	16D1
Penge	SEC	40F4
Penllergaer	GW	43G2
Penmaenrhos	LNW	19D4
Penmanshiel	NB	31C2
Polhill	SEC	5C4
Polperro	GW	1E1
Popham	LSW	4C3
Potters Bar	GN	11G2
Preston Hall	SEC	6C5
Primrose Hill	LNW	39B5
Priory	SEC	6D2
Queensbury	GN	42B5
Redhill	LBSC	5C3
Rise Hill	Mid	24A1/27G2
Robin Hood	LY	21E2/42D5
Royal George	LNW	21F1
St Anne's Wood	GW	3A3/8C1
St John's Wood	GC	39B5
Salterhebble	LY	42C5
Saltwood	SEC	6D2
Sandling	SEC	6D3
Sapperton	GW	9F4
Saxelby	Mid	16E3
Scout	LNW	21F1
Seaton	Mid	16F1
Selling	SEC	6C3
Sevenoaks	SEC	5C4
Severn	GW	8C2/9F1-G1
Shakespeare	SEC	6D2
Sharnbrook	Mid	10B1
Shelley Woodhouse	LY	42D4
Shillamill	LSW	1C5
Shillingham	GW	1D5
Shotlock Hill	Mid	27G2
Shugborough	LNW	15E4
Sodbury	GW	9G3
Somerhill	SEC	5D5
Sough	LY	20A2/24E2/24F1/45B1
Spittal	GW	13G1
Springwood (Derbys)	GC	41C3
Springwood (Yorks)	LNW&LYJt	42C5
Standedge	LNW	21F1
Stanton	Mid	16D3
Stockingford	Mid	16F5
Stoke	GN	16D1
Stowe Hill	LNW	10B3
Strawberry Hill	SEC	5D5
Streatham	LBSC	40F5
Sugar Loaf	HB	27D4
Summit (Littleborough)	LY	21E1
Sydenham	SEC	40F4

Taitlands	Mid	24B1
Tankersley	Mid	21F3/42F2
Thackley	Mid	42A4
Thurgoland	GC	21F3/42F3
Thurstonland	LY	21F2/42D4
Torpantau	B&M	8A5/14G3/43C1
Totley	Mid	16A5/41B1
Treverrin	GW	1D3
Twerton	GW	3B3/8D1
Wadhurst	SEC	5E5
Waller's Ash	LSW	4C3
Waste Bank	Mid	27E1
Watford (Herts)	LNW	11G1
Watford (Northants)	LNW	10A3
Weasel Hall	LY	21E1
Weedley	HB	27D4
Wellhouse	LY	21F3/42E3
Wells	SEC	5D5
Welwyn North	GN	11F2
Welwyn South	GN	11F2
Wenvoe	BRY	43C4
Wheatley	HHL	42B5
Whitehall	GW	8G5
White House Farm	GW&GCJt	5A1/10F2
Whitrope	NB	31G1
Wickwar	Mid	8B1/9F2
Willersley	Mid	16B5/41D1
Wing	Mid	16F2
Wingfield	Mid	16C5/41E2
Winsor Hill	SD	3C2/8E1
Winterbutlee	LY	21E1
Woodhead	GC	21F2/42E5
Woolley	LY	42D3
Wyke	LY	21E2/42B4

3 Index to Watertroughs

Aber	LNW	19D3
Aldermaston	GW	4A3
Aynho	GW	10C4
Brock	LNW	24D3
Castlethorpe	LNW	10C2
Charlbury	GW	10D5
Charwelton	GC	10B4
Chester	LNW	20D4
Creech (Durston)	GW	8F3
Diggle	LNW	21F1
Dillicar	LNW	27F1
Eccles	LNW	45B3
Eckington	GC	16A4/41B2
Exminster	GW	2B3
Fairwood (Westbury)	GW	3B4
Ferryside (Carmarthen)	GW	7A2
Flint	LNW	20D5
Garsdale	Mid	24A1/27G2
Goring	GW	4A2/10G3
Halebank	LNW	45E4
Hademore	LNW	15E5
Haselour	Mid	15F5
Hest Bank	LNW	24B3
Holbrook Park (Rugby)	LNW	10A4
Hoscar	LY	20B3/24F3/45E1
Ipswich	GE	12D3
Keynsham	GW	3A3/8D1
Kirkby	LY	20B4/24F3/45E3
Langley (Knebworth)	GN	11E2
Lapworth	GW	9A5
Lea Road (Salwick)	PWY	24D3
Lostock Jc	LY	24F2/45C2
Loughborough	Mid	16E4
Lucker	NE	31E4
Luddendenfoot	LY	21E1
Ludlow	S&H	9A1
Magor	GW	8B2
Melton Mowbray	Mid	16E2
Moore	LNW	45D4
Muskham (Newark)	GN	16B2
Newbold (Rugby)	LNW	10A4
New Cumnock	G&SW	29F5
Oakley	Mid	10B1/11C1
Prestatyn	LNW	19C5
Rufford	LY	20A3/24E3/45E1
Scrooby	GN	21G5
Smithy Bridge	LY	21E1/45A1
Sowerby Bridge	LY	21E1
Tivetshall	GE	12A3/18G3
Wakefield	LY	42C2
Walkden	LY	45B2
Werrington	GN	17F2
Whitmore	LNW	15C3/20F1
Wiske Moor (Northallerton)	NE	28D5

4 Index to Summits

Aisgill	Mid	27G2
Amersham	Met&GCJt	10F1
Beattock	Cal	30F4
Corriemuille	HR	35C4
Corrour	NB	32C1
County March	HR	38D4
Dainton	GW	2D3
Dava	HR	36E3
Desborough	Mid	10A2/16G2
Druimuachdair	HR	33B2
Dutchlands	Met&GCJt	10E2
Elsenham	GE	11E4
Falahill	NB	30C1
Glenoglehead	Cal	33E2
Hewish	LSW	3E1
Honiton	LSW	2A2
Ingrave	GE	5A5
Lickey Incline	Mid	9A4
Luib	HR	35D3
Masbury	SD	3B2/8E1
Mortehoe	LSW	7E1
Peak Forest	Mid	15A4
Penmanshiel	NB	31C2
Raven's Rock	HR	35D5
Sapperton	GW	9F4
Shap	LNW	27F1
Sharnbrook	Mid	10B1
Shenfield & Hutton	GE	11G4
Slochd	HR	36F4
Stainmore	NE	27F3
Stoke	GN	16D1
Talerddig	Cam	14B4
Templecombe	LSW	8G1
Tyndrum	Cal & NB	32E1
Wendover	Met&GCJt	10E2
Whiteball	GW	8G5
Whitrope	NB	31G1
Wrangaton	GW	2D5

5 Index to Bridges and Viaducts

Barmouth	Cam	13A5
Belah	NE	27F3
Britannia Tubular Bridge	LNW	19D2
Chearsley	GW&GCJt	10E3
Chirk	GW	20F4
Crumlin	GW	8B4/43B2
Dee	GW	20F4
Dinting	GC	21F1
Forth Bridge	FB	30B3
Halton	BJ	15A1/20D3/45D5
Hawarden Swing Bridge	GC	20D4
Hewenden	GN	42A5
High Level Bridge (Gateshead)	NE	28 (inset)
King Edward Bridge (Newcastle-on-Tyne)	NE	28 (inset)
Kings Ferry Bridge	SEC	6B4
Mottram	GC	21G1
Ouse	LBSC	5E3
Penistone	LY	42E3
Royal Albert Bridge (Saltash)	GW	1D5
Royal Border Bridge	NE	31C3
Runcorn	LNW	45D4
Scotswood (Newcastle-on-Tyne)	NE	28 (inset)
Severn	SVW	8A1/9E2
Solway	Cal	26B2
Stonehouse	GW	9E3
Southborough	SEC	5D5
Tay Bridge	NB	34E4
Welland	Mid	16F1
Welwyn	GN	11F2

6 Index of Locations

Note: The following references are to the original atlas map numbers, not page numbers. Thus Abbey station's reference of 15E1 refers to square E1 in map number 15, which is on page 54. To find the page number for each map, refer to the list on page 5.

Abbey (Shrewsbury), S&M, 15E1
Abbey for West Dereham, GE, 11A5; 17F5
Abbey Foregate Plat, SWN, 15E1
Abbey Mills Jcs, LTS & GE, 40C2
Abbey Street (Nuneaton), Mid, 16F5
Abbey Town, NB, 26C2
Abbey Wood, SEC, 5B4; 40D1
Abbeydore, GW, 14F1
Abbeyhill, NB, 30 (inset)
Abbots Ripton, GN, 11B2
Abbotsbury, GW, 3F2
Abbotsford Ferry, NB, 30C1
Abbotsham Road, BWHA, 7F2
Abbotswood Jc, Mid/GW, 9C3
Aber Bargoed Jc, BM, 43B2
Aber Branch Jc, BM/Rhy, 43B3
Aber, LNW, 19D3
Aberaman, TV, 8B5; 43D2
Aberangell, Mawd, 14A4
Aberavon (Seaside), RSB, 7B4; 43F3
Aberavon Jc, RSB/PT, 43F3
Aberayron, GW, 13D4
Aberayron Jc, GW, 13E5
Aberbargoed & Bargoed, Rhy(BM), 8B4; 43B2
Aberbeeg, GW, 8B4; 43B2
Aberbran, N&B (Mid), 14F4
Abercairny, Cal, 33F4
Abercanaid, QYM, 8A5; 43C2
Abercarn, GW, 8B4; 43B3
Aberchalder, NB, 32A1; 35G4
Abercorn (Paisley), G&SW, 29C4; 44F3
Abercrave, N&B(Mid), 7A4; 43El
Abercwmboi Halt, TV, 43C2
Abercynon, TV, 8B5; 43C3
Aberdare, GW & TV, 8B5; 43D2
Aberdeen (Goods), Cal & GNS, 37G4
Aberdeen (Pass), Cal&GNSJt(NB), 37G4
Aberdour, NB, 30A3
Aberdovey, Cam, 13B5
Aberdylais, GW, 7B4; 43F2
Aberedw, Cam, 14E3
Abererch, Cam, 19F1
Aberfan, QYM, 8B5; 43C2
Aberfeldy, HR, 33D3
Aberffrwd, VR, 14C5
Aberfoyle, NB, 29A4; 33G1
Abergavenny, GW & LNW, 8A3; 43A1
Abergavenny Junc, GW(LNW), 8A3; 43A1
Abergele, LNW, 19D4
Abergwili, LNW, 13G4
Abergwynfi, GW, 7B5; 43D3
Abergynolwyn, Tal, 13B5
Aberlady Jc, NB, 30B1
Aberlady, NB, 30B1
Aberllefeni, Cam, 14A5
Aberlour, GNS, 36D1
Abermule, Cam, 14B2
Abernant, GW, 8A5; 43D2
Abernethy, NB, 33F5
Abersychan, GW, 8A4; 43A2
Abersychan & Talywain, LNW(GW), 8A4; 43A2
Aberthaw, BRY & TV, 8D5; 43C5
Abertillery, GW, 8A4; 43B2
Abertridwr, Rhy, 8B4; 43C3
Abertysswg, BM, 43C2
Aberystwyth, Cam&GWJt & VR, 13C5
Abingdon, GW, 10F4
Abington, Cal, 30E4
Aboyne, GNS, 34A4; 37G1
Aby, GN, 17A3
Accrington, LY, 24E1
Ach-na-cloich, Cal, 32E3
Achanalt, HR, 35D4
Acheilidh Crossing, HR, 36A5
Achmacoy, GNS, 37E4
Achnasheen, HR, 35D3
Achnashellach, HR, 35D2
Achterneed, HR, 35D5
Acklington, NE, 31G5
Ackworth, SK(GC/GN), 21 E4; 42C1
Ackworth Moor Top (Goods), BL, 42C1
Acle, GE, 18F2
Acocks Green & South Yardley, GW, 9A5; 15G5
Acrefair, GW, 20F5
Acton, GW & NSW, 5B2; 39C3
Acton Bridge, LNW, 15A1; 20D3; 45D5
Acton Grange Jc, BJ/LNW, 15A1; 20C3; 45D4
Acton Lane Jcs, LSW/Dist, 39D3
Acton Town, Dist, 39D3
Acton Wells Jc, NSW/GW/LNW/Mid, 39C3
Adam Street Goods (Cardiff), Rhy, 43B4
Adderbury, GW, 10C4
Adderley (Salop), GW, 15C2; 20F2
Adderley Park, LNW, 13C4
Addiewell, Cal & NB, 30C4
Addingham, Mid, 21C2
Addison Rd (Kensington), WL(H&C/LBSC/LSW), 39D4
Addlestone, LSW, 5C2
Adisham, SEC, 6C2
Adlestrop, GW, 9D5
Adlington (Ches), LNW(NS), 15A3; 20C1; 45A5
Adlington (Lancs), LY, 20A2; 24F2; 45D1
Admaston, SWN, 15E2
Advie, GNS, 36E2
Adwick Jc, WRG, 21F4
Afon Wen, Cam(LNW), 19F1
Agecroft Jc, LY, 45B2
Aichengray, Cal, 30D4
Aichnagatt, GNS, 37D4
Ainderby, NE, 21A3; 28G5
Ainsdale, LY (LNW), 20A4; 24F4; 45F1
Ainsdale Beach, CLC, 20A4; 24F4; 45F1
Ainsworth Rd Halt, LY, 45B2
Aintree, LY & CLC, 20B4; 24F4; 45F3
Airbank Jc, M&C, 26D2
Airdrie, Cal & NB, 30C5; 44B4
Airdrie North (Goods), NB, 44B4
Airdrie South (Pass), Cal, 44B4
Aire Jc, HB/GC&HBJt, 21E5
Airmyn & Rawcliffe, NE, 21E5
Airth, Cal, 30A5
Akeld, NE, 31E3
Akeman Street, GC, 10E3
Albert Dock (Hull), NE, 22A1 (inset)
Albert Road Halt, LSW, 1 (inset)
Alberta Place Halt, TV, 43B5
Albion, LNW, 13B2 (inset)
Albrighton, GW, 15F3
Alcester, Mid(GW), 9B4
Aldeburgh, GE, 12C2
Aldeby, GE, 12A2; 18F1
Alderbury Jc, LSW, 4D5
Alderley Edge, LNW, 15A3; 20D1; 45A5
Aldermaston, GW, 4A3
Alderse (Goods), NB, 30B4
Aldersgate Street, Met (Dist/GN/GW/Mid/H&C), 40C5
Aldershot (North Camp) & South Farnborough, SEC, 4B1; 5C1
Aldershot Town, LSW(SEC), 4B1
Aldgate, Met(Dist), 40C4
Aldgate East, Dist&MetJt(H&C), 40C4
Aldin Grange for Bearpark, NE, 27D5
Aldridge, Mid, 15F4
Alexandra Dock (Hull), NE, 22E3
Alexandra Dock (Liverpool), LNW & Mid, 45F3 and inset
Alexandra Dock (Newport), AD, 8C3; 43A4
Alexandra Palace, GN(NL), 40A5
Alexandra Park (Glasgow), NB, 44D4
Alexandra Park (Manchester), GC, 45A3
Alexandria, D&B, 29B3
Alford (Aberdeenshire), GNS, 37F2
Alford (Lincs), GN, 17A3
Alford Halt (Som), GW, 3C2; 8F1
Alfreton & South Normanton, Mid, 16C4; 41E3
Algarkirk, GN, 17D2
All Saints (Clevedon), WCP, 3A1; 8C3
Allanfearn, HR, 36D5
Allangrange, HR, 36D5
Allbrook Jc, LSW, 4D3
Allendale, NE, 27C3
Aller Jc, GW, 2C3
Allerton (Lancs), LNW & CLC, 45E4
Allerton (Yorks), NE, 21C4
Alloa Jc, Cal, 30B5
Alloa, NB(Cal), 30A4
Alloa South (Goods), Cal, 30A5
Alloway, G&SW, 29F3
Alloway Jc, G&SW, 29F3
Almeley, GW, 14E1
Almond Jc, NB, 30B4
Almond Valley Jc, Cal, 33E5
Almondbank, Cal, 33E4
Alne, NE(Eas), 21B4
Alness, HR, 36C5

Alnmouth, NE, 31F5
Alnwick, NE, 31F5
Alperton, Dist, 39B2
Alresford (Essex), GE, 12E4
Alresford (Hants), LSW, 4C3
Alrewas, LNW, 15E5
Alsager, NS, 15C3; 20E1
Alsager Road, NS, 15C3; 20E1
Alsop-en-le-Dale, LNW, 15C5
Alston, NE, 27D2
Altanabreac, HR, 38D4
Altcar & Hillhouse, CLC(LY), 20B4; 24F4; 45F2
Altcar Rifle Range, LY(LNW), 20B4; 24F4; 45F2
Althorne, GE, 6A4; 12G5
Althorp Park, LNW, 10B3
Althorpe, GC, 22F5
Altofts & Whitwood, Mid, 21E3; 42B1
Altofts Jc, Mid/NE, 42B2
Alton (Hants), LSW, 4C2
Alton (Staffs), NS, 15C4
Altrincham & Bowdon, MSJA(CLC), 15A3; 20C1; 24G1; 45B4
Alva, NB, 30A5; 33G3
Alvechurch, Mid, 9A4
Alverstone, IWC, 4F3
Alverthorpe, GN, 21E3; 42C3
Alves, HR, 36C2
Alvescot, GW, 10E5
Alyth Junc, Cal, 34D5
Ambergate, Mid, 16C5; 41G1
Ambergate East Jc, Mid, 16C5
Ambergate South Jc, Mid, 16C5
Ambergate West Jc, Mid, 16C5
Amberley, LBSC, 5F1
Amble, NE, 31F5
Amble Branch Jc, NE, 31G5
Amersham, Met&GCJt, 10F1
Amesbury, LSW, 4C5
Amesbury Jc, LSW, 4C5
Amisfield, Cal, 26A3
Amlwch, LNW, 19C1
Ammanford, GW, 7A4; 43G1
Ammanford Colliery Halt, GW, 43G1
Amotherby, NE, 22E5
Ampleforth, NE, 21A5
Ampthill, Mid, 10C1; 11D1
Ancaster, GN, 16C1; 17C1
Ancoats (Goods), Mid, 45A3
Anderston Cross, Cal, 44E4; 44F2 (inset)
Andover Junc, LSW(MSW), 4C4
Andover Town, LSW(MSW), 4C4
Andoversford & Dowdeswell, MSW, 9D4
Andoversford, GW(MSW), 9D4
Anerley, LBSC, 40F4
Angel Road, GE, 5A3
Angerstein Wharf, SEC, 40D2
Angerton, NB, 27A4
Angmering, LBSC, 5F2
Annan, G&SW & Cal, 26B2
Annbank, G&SW, 29E4
Annesley, Mid, 41E4 ***see also*** Hollin Well
Annfield Plain, NE, 27C5
Annitsford, NE, 27B5
Ansdell & Fairhaven, PWY, 20A4; 24E4
Anston, GC&MidJt, 16A4; 41A4
Anstruther, NB, 34G3
Apethorne Jc, GC&MidJt/CLC, 21G1
Apperley Bridge & Rawdon, Mid, 21D2; 42A4
Apperley Jc, Mid, 42A4
Appin, Cal, 32D4
Appleby (Lincs), GC, 22F4
Appleby (Westmorland), Mid & NE, 27E2
Appledore (Devon), BWHA, 7F2
Appledore (Kent), SEC, 6E4
Applehurst Jc, WRG/NE, 21E5
Appleton, LNW, 45D4
Appley Bridge, LY, 20B3; 24F3; 45D2
Arbirlot, D&A, 34D3
Arbroath, D&A, 34D3
Archcliffe Jc, SEC, 6D2
Arddleen, Cam, 14A2
Ardingly, LBSC, 5E3
Ardleigh, GE, 12E4
Ardler Jc, Cal, 34D5
Ardley, GW, 10D4
Ardlui, NB, 32F1
Ardrossan, G&SW & Cal, 29D3
Ardsley, GN(GC), 21E3; 42B3
Ardsley Jc, GN, 42B3
Ardwick, GC, 20B1; 24F1; 45A3
Arenig, GW, 19F4
Argoed, LNW, 8B4; 43B2
Arisaig, NB, 32B5
Arkholme, Fur&MidJt, 24B2
Arkleston Jc, G&P/G&SW, 44F3
Arksey, GN(NE), 21F5
Arkwright Street (Nottingham), GC, 16D4; 41G4
Arkwright Town, GC, 16B4; 41C3
Arlecdon, CWJ, 26E3
Arlesey & Shefford Road, GN, 11D2
Arley (Worcs), GW, 9A2
Arley & Fillongley, Mid, 16G5
Armadale, NB, 30C4
Armathwaite, Mid, 27D1
Armitage, LNW, 15E5
Armley & Wortley, GN(LY) & Mid, 21D3 and inset C1; 42A3
Arnage, GNS, 37E4
Arnside, Fur, 24A3
Arpley (Warrington), LNW, 15A2; 20C2; 24G2; 45D4
Arram, NE, 22D4
Arrochar & Tarbet, NB, 32G1
Arthington, NE, 21D3
Arthog, Cam, 13A5
Arundel, LBSC, 5F1
Ascot, LSW, 4A1; 5B1
Ascott-under-Wychwood, GW, 10D5
Asfordby, Mid, 16E3
Ash, SEC (LSW), 4Bl; 5C1
Ash Green, LSW, 4B1; 5C1
Ash Jc, SEC/LSW, 4B1; 5C1
Ash Town, EK, 6C2
Ashbourne, LNW&NSJt, 15C5
Ashburton, GW, 2C4
Ashburton Grove Goods, GN, 40B5
Ashburton Jc, GW, 2D4
Ashbury, GC, 20B1; 24F1; 45A3
Ashbury, LSW, 1B5
Ashby Magna, GC, 16G4
Ashby-de-la-Zouch, Mid(LNW), 16E5
Ashchurch, Mid, 9D3
Ashcott, SD, 3C1; 8E2
Ashdon Halt, GE, 11D4
Ashendon Jcs, GW&GCJt/GC, 10E3
Ashey, IWC, 4F3
Ashford (Kent), SEC, 6D4
Ashford (Middx), LSW, 5B2
Ashford Works, SEC, 6D3
Ashington, NE, 27A5
Ashley (Ches), CLC, 15A3; 20C1, 24G1; 45B4
Ashley & Weston (Northants), LNW, 16F2
Ashley Hill, GW, 8C1 and inset 3F1; 24G1
Ashley Hill Jc, GW/Mid, 3G1 (inset)
Ashperton, GW, 9C2
Ashtead, LSW&LBSCJt, 5C2
Ashton (Devon), GW, 2C3
Ashton (Lancs), OAGB, LY, GC & LNW, 21F1 and inset A2; ***see also*** Dukinfield
Ashton-in-Makerfield, GC, 45D3
Ashton Jc (Bristol), GW, 3 (inset)
Ashton Moss Jcs, LNW & LY/GC, 21 (inset)
Ashton-under-Hill, Mid, 9C4
Ashton's Green Jc, LNW, 45D3
Ashurst, LBSC, 5D4
Ash Vale, LSW, 4B1; 5C1 ***see also*** Aldershot (North Camp)
Ashwater, LSW, 1B5
Ashwell (Rutland), Mid, 16E2
Ashwell & Morden (Cambs), GN, 11D2
Ashwellthorpe, GE, 12A3; 18F3
Askam, Fur, 24B5
Askern, LY(GN), 21E5
Askern Jc, GN/LY, 21F5
Askrigg, NE, 21A1; 27G3
Aslockton, GN, 16C2
Aspall & Thorndon, MSL, 12C3
Aspatria, M&C, 26D3
Aspley Guise Halt, LNW, 10C1
Astley, LNW(BJ), 20B2; 24G2; 45C3
Astley Bridge (Goods), LY, 20B2; 24F2; 45C1
Aston (Warwicks), LNW, 13B4; 15G5
Aston Botterell Siding, CMDP, 15G2
Aston-by-Stone, NS, 15D3; 20F1
Aston Curve Jc, Mid, 13C4
Aston Rowant, GW, 10F3
Aswarby & Scredingham, GN, 17D1
Athelney Jc, GW, 3D1; 8F3
Athelney, GW, 3D1; 8F3
Atherstone, LNW, 16F5
Atherton, LY & LNW, 20B2; 24F2; 45C2
Attadale, HR, 35E2
Attenborough Jc, Mid, 16D4
Attenborough, Mid, 16D4; 41G4
Attercliffe, GC, 21G4; 42G2
Attercliffe Road, Mid, 42G2
Attleborough, GE, 12A4; 18F4
Attlebridge, MGN, 18E3
Auchendinny, NB, 30C2

Auchenheath, Cal, 30D5
Auchenmade, Cal, 29D3
Auchincruive, G&SW, 29F4
Auchindachy, GNS, 37D1
Auchinleck, G&SW, 29F5
Auchmacoy, GNS, 37E4
Auchnagatt, GNS, 37D4
Auchterarder, Cal, 33F4
Auchterhouse, Cal, 34E5
Auchterless, GNS, 37D3
Auchtermuchty, NB, 34F5
Auchtertool (Goods), NB, 30A2
Audenshaw Jc, OAGB, 21A2 (inset)
Audlem, GW, 15C2; 20F2
Audley, NS, 15C3; 20E1
Audley End, GE, 11E4
Aughengray, Cal, 30D4
Aughton Park Halt, LY, 20B4; 24F3; 45E2
Auldbar Road, Cal, 34D3
Auldearn, HR, 36D3
Auldgirth, G&SW, 26A4
Aultmore, HR, 37D1
Authorpe, GN, 17A3
Aviemore, HR, 36F3
Avoch, HR, 36D5
Avon Lodge, LSW, 4E5
Avonbridge, NB, 30B4
Avoncliff Halt, GW, 3B4
Avonmouth, GW & CE, 3A2; 8C2; 9G1
Avonside Wharf (Goods), Mid, 3 (inset)
Avonwick, GW, 2D4
Awre for Blakeney, GW, 8A1; 9E2
Awsworth, GN, 16C4; 41F3
Axbridge, GW, 3B1; 8E3
Axminster, LSW, 2B1
Aycliffe, NE, 28E5
Aylesbury, GW&GCJt/Met&GCJt, 10E2; LNW, 10E2
Aylesbury GW&GCJt Comm Jcs, GW&GCJt, 10E2
Aylesbury Met&GC Jc, GW&GCJt,10E2
Aylesbury North Jc, GW&GCJt, 10E2
Aylesford, SEC, 6C5
Aylsham, GE & MGN, 18D3
Aynho, GW, 10D4
Aynho Park Plat, GW, 10D4
Ayot, GN, 11F2
Ayr, G&SW, 29F3
Aysgarth, NE, 21A1; 27G4
Ayton, NB, 31C3

Backworth, NE, 28B5
Bacton, GW, 14F1
Bacup, LY, 20A1; 24E1
Badminton, GW, 9G3
Baggrow, M&C, 26D2
Baghill (Pontefract), SK(GC/GN), 21E4; 42C1
Bagillt, LNW, 20D5
Bagshot, LSW, 4A1; 5C1
Bagthorpe Jc, GC/GN, 41F4
Baguley, CLC, 20C1; 24G1; 45B4
Bagworth & Ellistown, Mid, 16E4
Baildon, Mid, 21D2; 42A4
Bailey Gate, SD, 3E4
Bailiff Bridge, LY, 21E2; 42B4
Baillieston, Cal, 44C3
Bainton, NE, 22C4
Baker Street, Met(Dist/GW/H&C), 39C5
Bakewell, Mid, 15B5
Bala, GW, 19F4
Bala Junc, GW, 19F4
Balado, NB, 30A3; 33G5
Balcombe, LBSC, 5E3
Baldersby, NE, 21A3
Balderton, GW, 20E4
Baldock, GN, 11E2
Baldovan, Cal, 34E4
Baldragon, Cal, 34E4
Balerno, Cal, 30C3
Balfron, NB, 29A4
Balgowan, Cal, 33F4
Balham & Upper Tooting, LBSC(LNW), 5B3; 39E5
Balham Jc, LBSC, 39E5
Ballabeg, IMR, 23C2
Ballachulish, Cal, 32D3
Ballachulish Ferry, Cal, 32D3
Ballasalla, IMR, 23C2
Ballater, GNS, 34A5
Ballathie (Goods), Cal, 33E5
Ballaugh, IMR, 23A2; 25G4
Ballindalloch, GNS, 36E2
Ballingham, GW, 9D1
Ballinluig, HR, 33D4
Balliol Road, LNW, 45F3 ***see also*** Bootle (Lancs)
Balloch, D&B, 29B3
Balloch Pier, D&B, 29B3
Bally Jc, GN/GC, 21F5
Balmano Jc, NB, 33F5
Balmore, NB, 29B5; 44E5
Balnacoul, HR, 36C1
Balne, NE, 21E5
Balne Moor (Goods), HB, 21E5
Balornock Jc, Cal, 44D4
Balquhidder, Cal, 33F2
Balquhidder Jc, Cal, 33F2
Balshaw Lane & Euxton, LNW, 20A3; 24E2; 45D1
Bamber Bridge, LY, 20A3; 24E2
Bamford, Mid, 15A5
Bamfurlong, LNW, 20B2; 24F2; 45D2
Bampton (Devon), GW, 7G5
Bampton (Oxon), GW, 10E5
Banavie, NB, 32C3
Banavie Jc, NB, 32C3
Banavie Pier, NB, 32C3
Banbury, GW(GC) & LNW(SMJ), 10C4
Banbury Jc, GC/GW, 10C4
Banbury Line Jc, GW/Mid, 9D3
Banchory, GNS, 34A3
Banff, GNS, 37C2
Banff Bridge, GNS, 37C2
Bangor, LNW, 19D2
Bangor-on-Dee, Cam, 20F4
Bangour, NB, 30C4
Bank Hall, LY, 45F3
Bank Quay (Warrington), LNW(BJ) & LNW, 45D4
Bank Top (Burnley), LY, 24D1
Bank Top (Darlington), NE, 28F5
Bankfield (Liverpool) Goods, LY, 45 (inset)
Bankfoot, Cal, 33E5
Bankhead (Aberdeen), GNS, 37F4
Bankhead (Lanark), Cal, 30D4
Banknock, K&B, 30B5
Banks, LY, 20A4; 24E3
Bannister Green Halt, GE, 11E5
Bannockburn, Cal, 30A5
Banstead, LBSC, 5C3
Baptist End Halt, GW, 13C1
Barassie G&SW, 29E3
Barber's Bridge, GW, 9D2
Barbon, LNW, 24A2
Barcaldine Siding, CR, 32E4
Barcombe, LBSC, 5F4
Barcombe Mills, LBSC, 5F4
Bardney, GN, 17B1
Bardon Hill, Mid, 16E4
Bardon Mill, NE, 27B2
Bardowie, NB, 29B5; 44E5
Bardsey, NE, 21D3
Bare Lane, LNW, 24B3
Bare Lane Jc, LNW, 24B3
Bargeddie, NB, 29C5; 44C4
Bargoed & Aberbargoed, BM, 8B4; 43B2
Barham, SEC, 6C2
Barking, LTS(Dist/Mid), 5A4; 40B1
Barking East Jc, LTS, 40B1
Barkingside, GE, 40A1
Barkston, GN, 16C1
Barlaston & Tittensor, NS, 15D3; 20F1
Barlby Jc, NE, 21D5
Barleith, G&SW, 29E4
Barlow, NE, 21D5
Barmby, HB, 21E5
Barming, SEC, 6C5
Barmouth, Cam, 13A5
Barmouth Jc, Cam, 13A5
Barnack, GN, 17F1
Barnard Castle, NE, 27E4
Barnby Dun, GE(NE), 21F5
Barnby Moor & Sutton, GN, 16A3
Barnes, LSW, 5B3; 39E4
Barnes Bridge, LSW, 39D3
Barnetby, GC, 22F3
Barnham, GE, 12B5
Barnham Jc, LBSC, 5F1
Barnhill (Dundee), Cal, 34E4
Barnhill Jc, NB, 44D4
Barnhurst, SEC, 5B4
Barnoldswick, Mid, 21 (inset)
Barnsley, GC & LY, 42E2
Barnsley Court House, Mid(GC), 42E2
Barnsley Jc, GC, 21F3, 42E3
Barnstaple, GW, LSW & LB, 7F3
Barnstaple Junction, LSW(GW), 7F3
Barnstaple Town, LSW & LB, 7F3
Barnstone, GN&LNWJt, 16D2
Barnt Green, Mid, 9A4
Barnton, Cal, 30B3
Barnwell, GE, 11C3
Barnwell, LNW, 11A1; 16G1; 17G1

Barons Court, Dist, 39D4
Baron's Lane Halt, GE, 12G5
Barr Road Jc, GN, 16D1
Barracks, Mid, 24D1
Barras, NE, 27F3
Barrasford, NB, 27B3
Barrhead, GBK, Cal & G&SW, 44F2
Barrhill, G&SW, 25A3
Barrmill, GBK & Cal, 29D3
Barrow, CLC, 15B1; 20D3
Barrow, Fur, 24B5
Barrow Haven, GC, 22E3
Barrow Hill & Staveley Works, Mid, 16A4; 41B3 *see also* Staveley Works
Barrow on Soar & Quorn, Mid, 16E3
Barrs Court (Hereford), S&H(Mid), 9C1
Barrs Court Jc, GW, 9C1
Barrs Court Jc North, GW, 9C1
Barry, BRY, 8D4; 43C5;
Barry Docks, BRY, 43C5
Barry Island, BRY, 8D4; 43C5
Barry Jc, MB/BRY, 8B4; 43B3
Barry Links, D&A, 34E3
Bartlow, GE, 11D4
Barton (Goods) (Hereford), GW, 9C1
Barton (Goods) (Yorks), NE, 27F5
Barton (Lincs), GC, 22E4
Barton & Broughton, LNW, 24D3
Barton & Walton, Mid(LNW), 13A5
Barton Hill, NE, 22B5
Barton-le-Street, NE, 22B5
Barton Moss, LNW, 20B2; 24F2; 45B2
Baschurch, GW, 14A1; 20G4
Basford (Notts), Mid, 41F4
Basford & Bulwell, GN, 16C4; 41F4
Basingstoke, LSW(GW) & GW, 4B3
Bason Bridge, SD, 3B1; 8E3
Bassaleg, GW(LNW), 8C3; 43A3
Bassenthwaite Lake, CKP, 26E2
Bath, GW & Mid(SD), 3A3; 8D1
Bathampton, GW, 3A3
Bathgate, NB, 30C4
Batley, LNW & GN, 21E3; 42B3
Batley Carr, GN, 42C3 *see also* Staincliffe
Battersby, NE, 28F4
Battersea, WLE, 5B3; 39E5 and inset E3
Battersea Park, LBSC, 39D5 and inset E4
Battersea Pier Jc, LBSC, 39E4 (inset)
Battle, SEC, 6F5
Battlesbridge, GE, 6A5; 11G5
Battyeford, LNW, 42C4
Bawtry Jc, GN, 21G5
Baxenden, LY, 20A1; 24E1
Bay Horse, LNW, 24C3
Baynards, LBSC, 5D2
Bayswater, Met(Dist), 39C5
Bengeworth, Mid, 9C4
Beaconsfield, GW&GCJt, 5A1; 10F1
Beal, NE, 31D4
Bealings, GE, 12D3
Beamish, NE, 27C5
Beanacre Halt, GW, 3A4
Bearley GW, 9B5
Bearsden, NB, 29B4; 44E5
Bearstead & Thurnham, SEC, 6C5
Beasdale, NB, 32B5
Beattock, Cal, 30G3
Beauchief, Mid, 16A5; 41A2
Beaufort, LNW, 8A4; 43B1
Beaulieu Road, LSW, 4E4
Beauly, HR, 35D5
Beaumont's Halt, Mid, 11F1
Bebington & New Ferry, BJ, 20C4; 24G4; 45F4
Bebside, NE, 27A5
Beccles, GE, 12A2; 18G2
Beccles Swing Bridge, GE, 12A2; 18F1
Beckenham Hill, SEC, 40F3
Beckenham Junc, SEC, 40F3
Beckermet, WCE, 26F3
Beckfoot, RE, 26F2
Beckford, Mid, 9C4
Beckhole, NE, 28F2
Beckingham, GN&GEJt, 22G5
Beckton, GE, 5B4; 40C1
Bedale, NE, 21A3; 27G5
Beddau Halt, Rhy, 43B3
Beddau Halt, TV, 43C4
Beddau Loop Jc, Rhy, 43B3
Beddgelert, NWNG, 19E2
Beddington Lane Halt, LBSC, 40G5
Bedford, Mid & LNW, 10C1; 11D1
Bedford North Jc, Mid, 10C1; 11D1
Bedhampton Halt, LBSC, 4E2
Bedlington, NE, 27A5
Bedlinog, TBJ, 8B5; 43C2
Bedminster, GW, 3G1 (inset)
Bedminster Jc, GW, 3G1 (inset)
Bedwas, BM, 8B4; 43B3
Bedwellty Pits, LNW, 8A4
Bedworth, LNW, 16G5
Bedwyn, GW, 4A5
Beechburn, NE, 27D5
Beeston (Notts), Mid, 16D4; 41G4
Beeston (Yorks), GN(GC), 21D3; 42B3
Beeston Castle & Tarporley, LNW, 15B1; 20E3
Beeston Tor, NS, 15C5
Beighten, GC, 16A4; 41A3
Beith, G&SW & GBK, 29D3
Bekesbourne, SEC, 6C2
Belford, NE, 31E4
Belgrave & Birstall, GC, 16E3
Bell Busk, Mid, 21C1
Bell Green, LNW, 10A3
Bellahouston, G&SW, 44E3 and inset G1
Belle Vue, GC&MidJt, 20C1; 45A3
Bellfield Jc, G&SW, 29E4
Bellgrove, NB, 44D4
Bellingham (Kent), SEC, 40F3
Bellingham (Northumb), NB, 27A3
Bellshill, Cal & NB, 30C5; 44B3
Bellwater Jc, GN, 17C3
Belmont (Surrey), LBSC, 5C3
Belper, Mid, 16C5; 41F2
Belses, NB, 31E1
Belston Jc, G&SW, 29F4
Belton (Lincs), AJ, 22F5
Belton (Norfolk), GE, 18F1
Beltring & Bainbridge Halt, SEC 5D5
Beluncle Halt, SEC, 6B5
Belvedere, SEC, 5B4
Belvoir Jc, GN, 16D2
Bembridge, IW, 4F2
Bempton, NE, 22B3
Ben Rhydding, O&I, 21C2
Benderloch, Cal, 32E4
Benfleet, LTS, 6A5
Bengeworth, Mid, 9C4
Beningborough, NE, 21C4
Bensham, NE, 27C5; 28 (inset)
Bentham, Mid, 24B2
Bentley (Hants), LSW, 4C1
Bentley (Suffolk), GE, 12D4
Bentley Jc, GC, 21F5
Benton, NE, 27B5
Bents, NB, 30C4
Bentworth & Lasham, LSW, 4C2
Benwick Goods, GE, 11A3; 17G3
Bere Alston, LSW/BAC, 1D5
Bere Ferrers, LSW, 1D5
Berkeley, SVW, 8B1; 9F2
Berkeley Road, Mid & SVW, 8B1; 9F2
Berkhamsted, LNW, 10E1
Berkswell, LNW, 9A5
Berney Arms, GE, 18F1
Berrington, GW, 15F1
Berrington & Eye, S&H, 9B1
Berry Brow, LY, 21E2; 42D5
Bervie, NB, 34B2
Berw Road Halt, TV, 43C3
Berwick (Sussex), LBSC, 5F4
Berwick-on-Tweed, NE&NBJt, 31C3
Berwig Halt, GW, 20E5
Berwyn, GW, 20F5
Bescar Lane, LY, 20A4; 24E3; 45F1
Bescot, LNW, 13A3; 15F4
Bessacar Jc, SYJ/DV, 21F5
Bestwood Colliery, GN, 16C4; 41E4
Beswick (Goods), Mid, 45A3
Betchworth, SEC, 5C2
Bethesda, LNW, 19D2
Bethnal Green, GE, 40C4
Betley Road, LNW, 15C2; 20E2
Bettisfield, Cam, 20F3
Bettws (Llangeinor), PT, 7B5; 43D3 *see also* Llangeinor
Bettws Garmon, NWNG, 19E2
Bettws-y-Coed, LNW, 19E4
Beverley, NE, 22D3
Beverley Jc, NE, 22D3
Beverley Road (Hull), HB, 22 (inset)
Bewdley, GW, 9A3
Bexhill, LBSC & SEC, 6F5
Bexley, SEC, 5B4
Bexleyheath, SEC, 5B4
Bicester, GW & LNW, 10D3
Bickershaw & Abram, GC, 45C2
Bickershaw Jcs, LNW, 45C2
Bickleigh, GW, 2D5
Bickley, SEC, 40G2

Bickley Jc, SEC, 40G2
Biddenden, KES, 6D4
Biddulph, NS, 15B3; 20E1
Bideford, LSW & BWHA, 7F2
Bidford-on-Avon, SMJ, 9B5
Bidston (Goods), GC & Wir, 20C4; 24G5; 45F4
Bidston (Pass), Wir(GC), 20C4; 24G5; 45F4
Bieldside, GNS, 37G4
Biggar, Cal, 30E3
Biggleswade, GN, 11D2
Biglis Jc, BRY/TV, 8D4; 43B5
Bilbster, HR, 38D2
Billacombe, GW, 2D5
Billericay, GE, 5A5; 11G5
Billing, LNW, 10B2
Billingborough & Horbling, GN, 17D1
Billinge Green Halt, LNW, 15B2; 20D2
Billingham-on-Tees, NE, 28E4
Billingshurst, LBSC, 5E2
Bilson (Goods), GW & SVW, 8A1; 9E2
Bilston, GW, 15F4; 13A1 *see also* Ettingshall Road
Bilton Road Jc, NE, 21C3
Binegar, SD, 3B2; 8E1
Bingham, GN, 16C3
Bingham Road (Notts), GN&LNWJt, 16D3
Bingley, Mid, 21D2; 24F1; 42A5
Bingley Jc, Mid, 42A5
Binton, SMJ, 9B5
Birch Vale, GC&MidJt, 15A4; 21G1
Birchfield Plat, GNS, 36D1
Birchills, LNW, 15F4
Birchington-on-Sea, SEC, 6B2
Birdbrook, CVH, 11D5
Birdingbury, LNW, 10A4
Birdwell & Hoyland Common, GC, 21F3; 42E2
Birdwell & Pilley (Goods), Mid, 21F3; 42E2
Birkdale, LY(LNW), 20A4; 24E4; 45F1
Birkdale Palace, CLC, 20A4; 24E4; 45F1
Birkenhead, BJ, CLC, GC, GW, LNW, Mer, Wir, 20C4; 24G4; 45F4
Birkenhead Park, Wir, 45F4
Birkenshaw & Tong, GN, 21D2; 42B4
Birmingham (Goods), GW, LNW & Mid, 13 (inset) and 15G4
Birmingham (Pass), GW & LNW&MidJt, 13 (inset) and 15G4
Birmingham Curve Jc, Mid, 15E5
Birnie Road, NB, 34C2
Birstall (Yorks), LNW, 21E2; 42B4
Birstall Jc, LNW, 42B3
Birstwith, NE, 21C3
Birtley, NE, 27C5
Bishop Auckland, NE, 27E5
Bishop's Castle, BC, 14C1
Bishop's Castle Railway, BC, 14C1
Bishop's Cleeve, GW, 9D4
Bishop's Lydeard, GW, 8F4
Bishop's Nympton & Molland, GW, 7F5
Bishops Road, GW&MetJt, 39C2 (inset)
Bishop's Stortford, GE, 11E3
Bishop's Waltham, LSW, 4D3
Bishopbriggs, NB, 29C5; 44D4
Bishopsbourne, SEC, 6C2
Bishopsgate, GE, 40C4
Bishopsgate Jc, GE/EL&NL, 40C4
Bishopstone, LBSC, 5G4
Bishopton, Cal, 29C4
Bisley Camp, LSW, 5C1
Bispham, PWY, 24D4
Bittaford Platform, GW, 2D5
Bitterley, S&H, 9A1
Bitterne, LSW, 4E4
Bitton, Mid, 3A3; 8D1
Blaby, LNW, 16F4
Black Bank, GE, 11A4; 17G4
Black Bull, NS, 15C3; 20E1
Black Dog Siding, GW, 3A5
Black Dyke, NB, 26C3
Black Lane (Radcliffe), LY, 20B2; 24F1; 45B2
Blackburn, LY(LNW/Mid), 24D2
Blackford Hill, NB, 30 (inset)
Blackford, Cal, 33F4
Blackfriars, Dist(Met), 40C5
Blackhall Jc, NB, 30C4
Blackhall Rocks, NE, 28D4
Blackheath (London), SEC, 5B4; 40E2
Blackheath Hill, SEC, 5B4; 40D3
Blackhill, NE, 27C4
Blackhill Jc, Cal, 44D4
Blackhorse Road, TFG, 40A3
Blackhouse Jc, G&SW, 29F3
Blackmill, GW, 7B5; 43D3
Blackmoor, LB, 7E4
Blackpill, Mum, 43G3
Blackpool, PWY, 24D4
Blackrod, LY, 20B2; 24F2; 45C2
Blackrod Jc, LY, 45C2
Blacksboat, GNS, 36E2
Blackstone, NB, 30B4
Blackstone Jc, Cal, 44G4
Blackthorn, GW, 10D3
Blackwall (Goods), GN, 40C3 and inset D1
Blackwall (Pass), GE, 5B4; 40C2
Blackwater (IoW), IWC, 4F3
Blackwater & Camberley, SEC, 4B1 *see also* Camberley & York Town
Blackwell (Worcs), Mid, 9A4
Blackwell Mill Halt, Mid, 15A5
Blackwood (Lanark), Cal, 30D5
Blackwood (Mon), LNW, 8B4; 43B2
Blacon, GC, 20D4
Blaenau Festiniog, LNW, GW & Fest, 19F3
Blaenavon, GW & LNW(GW), 8A4; 43A1
Blaenclydach (Goods), GW, 8B5; 43D3
Blaengarw, GW(PT), 7B5; 43D3
Blaengwynfi, RSB, 7B5; 43D2
Blaenplwyf Halt, GW, 13E5
Blaenrhondda, RSB, 7B5; 43D2
Blagdon, GW, 3B2; 8D2
Blaina, GW, 8A4; 43B2
Blair Atholl, HR, 33C3
Blairadam, NB, 30A3
Blairgowrie, Cal, 33D5
Blairhill & Gartsherrie, NB, 29C5; 44B4 *see also* Gartsherrie
Blake Hall, GE, 11G4
Blake Street, LNW, 15F5
Blakeney (Goods), GW, 8A1; 9E2
Blakesley, SMJ, 10C3
Blakey Jc, NE, 28F3
Blandford, SD, 3E4
Blanefield, NB, 29B4
Blankney & Metheringham, GN&GEJt, 16B1; 17B1
Blantyre, Cal, 29C5; 44C2
Blaydon, NE(NB), 27B5 and 28 inset
Blaydon East Jc, NE, 28 (inset)
Blaydon North Jc, NE, 28 (inset)
Blaydon South Jc, NE, 28 (inset)
Bleadon & Uphill, GW, 3B1; 8D3
Blean & Tyler Hill Halt, SEC, 6C3
Bleasby, Mid, 16C3
Bledlow, GW, 10F2
Bledlow Bridge Halt, GW, 10F2
Blencow, CKP, 26E1
Blenheim & Woodstock, GW, 10E4
Bletchington, GW, 10E4
Bletchley, LNW, 10D2
Blidworth & Rainworth, Mid, 16B3; 41D5
Blisworth, LNW & SMJ, 10B3
Blockley, GW, 9C5
Blodwell Junc, Cam, 14A2; 20G5
Blowers Green, GW, 13B1
Blowick, LY, 20A4; 24E4; 45F1
Bloxham, GW, 10C4
Bloxwich, LNW, 15F4
Blue Anchor, GW, 8E5
Blundellsands & Crosby, LY(LNW), 20B4; 24F4; 45F3
Blunham, LNW, 11D1
Blunsdon, MSW, 9F5
Bluntisham, GE, 11B3
Blyth, NE, 28A5
Blythburgh, SWD, 12B2
Blythe Bridge, NS, 15C4
Blyton, GC, 22G5
Boar's Head, LNW & LU, 20B3; 24F2; 45D2
Boarhills, NB, 34F3
Boat of Garten, HR(GNS), 36F3
Boddam, GNS, 37D5
Bodfari, LNW, 19D5
Bodiam, KES, 6E5
Bodmin, GW & LSW, 1D3
Bodmin Road, GW, 1D3
Bodorgan, LNW, 19D1
Bognor, LBSC, 5G1
Bogside (Fife), NB, 30A4
Bogside (Renfrew), Cal & G&SW, 29E3
Bogston, Cal, 29B3
Boldon (Goods), NE, 28C5
Bollington, GC&NSJt, 15A4; 45A5
Bollo Lane Jc, LSW/NSW, 39D3
Bolsover, GC & Mid, 16B4; 41C3
Bolton, LY(Mid), LY & LNW, 20B2; 24F1; 45B2
Bolton Abbey, Mid, 21C1
Bolton-le-Sands, LNW, 24B3
Bolton-on-Dearne, SK(GC), 21F4; 42E1
Bolton Percy, NE(LY/GN), 21D4
Bolton Street (Bury), LY, 20B1; 24F1; 45B1

Bonar Bridge, HR, 36B5
Boncath, GW, 13F3
Bo'ness, NB, 30B4
Bonnington, Cal & NB, 30 (inset)
Bonnybridge, Cal, K&B & NB, 30B5
Bonnybridge Central, Cal, K&B & NB, 30B5
Bonnyrigg, NB, 30C2
Bonnywater Jc, Cal/K&B, 30B5
Bontnewydd, GW, 14A5; 19G3
Bookham, LSW, 5C2
Boosbeck, NE, 28E3
Boot, RE, 26F2
Bootham Jc, NE, 21C5 and inset A4
Bootle (Cumb), Fur, 24A5; 26G3
Bootle (Lancs), LY, 45F3 ***see also*** Balliol Rd
Bopeep Jc, SEC/LBSC, 6F5
Bordesley, GW, 13C4; 15G5
Bordesley Jc, GW, 13C4
Bordon, LSW, 4C1
Borough Market Jc, SEC, 40C4
Boroughbridge, NE, 21B4
Borrobol Platform, HR, 38F5
Borrowash, Mid, 16D4; 41G2
Borth, Cam, 13C5
Borwick, Fur&MidJt, 24B3
Boscarne Jc, LSW/GW, 1D3
Boscombe, LSW, 3F5
Bosham, LBSC, 4E1
Bosley, NS, 15B3; 20D1
Boston, GN, 17C3
Boston Manor, Met & Dist, 39D2
Botanic Gardens (Glasgow), Cal, 44E4
Botanic Gardens (Hull), NE, 22 (inset)
Bothwell, Cal & NB, 29C5; 44C2
Bothwell Jc, Cal, 44B3
Bothwell Jc, NB, 44C2
Botley, LSW, 4E3
Bott Lane Halt, LY, 21 (inset); 24D1
Bottesford, GN, 16D2
Bottesford N, E, S & W Jcs, GN, 16C2
Botteslow Jc, NS, 15C3
Bottisham & Lode, GE, 11C4
Boughrood & Llyswen, Cam, 14F3
Boughton, GC, 16B3
Boultham Jc, GN&GEJt, 16B1
Bourne, GN(Mid/MGN), 17E1
Bourne East Jc, GN, 17E1
Bourne End, GW, 5A1; 10G2
Bourne West Jc, GN, 17E1
Bournemouth Central, LSW, 3F5; West, LSW(SD), 3F5
Bournville, Mid, 9A4; 15G4
Bourton-on-the-Water, GW, 9D5
Bovey for Islington, GW, 2C4
Bow (Devon), LSW, 2B4
Bow (London), NL & LNW, 40C3
Bow Brickhill Halt, LNW, 10D2
Bow Road, WB & GE, 40C3
Bow Street, Cam, 13C5
Bowbridge Crossing Halt, GW, 9E3
Bower, HR, 38C3
Bowes, NE, 27F4
Bowes Park, GN 5A3
Bowhouse, NB, 30B4
Bowland, NB, 30D1
Bowling, Cal & NB, 29B4
Bowling Junc, LY, 42B4
Bowness, Cal, 26C2
Box, GW, 3A4
Box Hill & Burford Bridge, LBSC, 5C2
Box Hill, SEC, 5C2
Boxford, GW, 4A4
Boxmoor & Hemel Hempsted, LNW, 10E1; 11F1 ***see also*** Hemel Hempsted
Boyce's Bridge, WUT, 17F4
Braceborough Spa, GN, 17E1
Bracebridge (Goods), GN, 16B1
Brackenhill Jc (Ayrshire), G&SW, 29E4
Brackenhill Jc (Yorks), SK(GC/GN), 21E4
Brackenhill Light Railway, BL, 42D1
Brackenhills, Cal, 9D3
Brackley, LNW, 10C3
Brackley Central, GC, 10C3
Bracknell, LSW, 4A1
Bradbury, NE, 28E5
Bradfield, GE, 12E4
Bradford (Goods), GN, LY, & Mid, 21D2; 42A4
Bradford (Pass), 21D2; 42A4
Bradford Jcs, GW, 3B4
Bradford-on-Avon, GW, 3B4
Brading Junc, IW, 4F3
Bradley (Yorks), LNW(LY), 42C4
Bradley Fold, LY, 20B2; 24F1; 45B2
Bradley Wood Jc, LY, 21E2; 42C4
Bradnop, NS, 15C4
Bradwell, LNW, 10C2
Brafferton, NE, 21B4
Braidwood, Cal, 30D5
Braintree & Bocking, GE, 11E5
Braithwaite, CKP, 26E2
Braithwell Jc, HB&GCJt/GC&Mid&HBJt, 21G5
Bramber, LBSC, 5F2
Brambledown Halt, SEC, 6B4
Bramford, GE, 12D4
Bramhall, LNW(NS), 15A3; 20C1; 45A4
Bramhall Moor Lane (Goods), Mid, 45A4
Bramley (Hants), GW, 4B2
Bramley (Yorks), GN(LY), 21D3; 42A3
Bramley & Wonersh, LBSC, 5D1
Brampford Speke, GW, 2B3
Brampton (Suffolk), GE, 12B2; 18G2
Brampton Goods (Chesterfield), Mid, 16B5; 41C2
Brampton Halt, NS, 20F1
Brampton Junc (Cumb), NE, 27C1
Brampton Town (Cumb), NE, 27C1
Bramwith (Goods), WRG, 21F5
Brancepeth, NE, 27D5
Brancliffe Jc, GC/GC&MidJt, 16A4; 41A4
Brandlesholme Road Halt, LY, 45B1
Brandon (Durham), NE, 27D5
Brandon (Norfolk), GE, 11A5; 17G5
Brandon & Wolston, LNW, 10A5
Brandy Bridge Jc, TV/GW&TVJt, 43C2
Branksome, LSW(SD), 3F5
Bransford Road, GW, 9B3
Branston (Staffs), Mid, 15E5
Branston & Heighington, GN&GEJt, 16B1; 17B1
Branston Jc, Mid, 15E5
Bransty (Whitehaven), Fur&LNWJt, 26E4
Branthwaite, WCE, 26E3
Brasted, SEC, 5C4
Bratton Fleming, LB, 7E3
Braughing, GE, 11E3
Braunston, LNW, 10B4
Braunston & Willoughby, GC, 10B4
Braunton, LSW(GW), 7F3
Braystones, Fur, 26F3
Brayton, M&C(Cal), 26D2
Brayton East Jc, NE, 21D5
Brayton North Jc, NE, 21D5
Breadsall, GN, 16D5; 41G2
Breakwater Jc, Cal, 30 (inset)
Breamore, LSW, 4D5
Brechin, Cal, 34C3
Breck Road, LNW, 20C4; 24G4; 45F3
Brecon, BM (Cam/Mid/N&B), 14F3
Brecon Curve Jc (Hereford), GW/Mid, 9C1
Brecon Road (Abergavenny), LNW, 43A1
Bredbury, GC&MidJt, 21G1; 45A3
Bredon (Worcs), Mid, 9C3
Breich, Cal, 30C4
Brent (Devon), GW, 2D4
Brent Jc (Cricklewood), Mid, 39B4
Brent Jc (Willesden), LNW, 39C3
Brent Knoll, GW, 3B1; 8E3
Brentford, LSW & GW, 5B2; 39D2
Brentford Lane Jc, LSW, 39D3
Brentham, GW, 39C2
Brentor, LSW, 1C5
Brentwood & Warley, GE, 5A5
Bretby, Mid, 16E5
Brettell Lane, GW, 15G3
Breydon Jc, GE, 18F1
Bricket Wood, LNW, 11G1
Bricklayers Arms Goods, SEC, 40D4
Bricklayers Arms Jc, LBSC, 40D4
Bridestowe, LSW, 2B5
Bridge, SEC, 6C3
Bridge of Allan, Cal, 30A5
Bridge of Dee, G&SW, 26C5
Bridge of Dun, Cal, 34C3
Bridge of Earn, NB, 33F5
Bridge of Orchy, NB, 32E1
Bridge of Weir, G&SW, 29C3
Bridge Street (Northampton), LNW, 10B2
Bridge Street Jc (Glasgow), Cal/G&P, 44F2 (inset)
Bridgefoot, WCE, 26E3
Bridgefoot Halt, GNS, 37C2
Bridgend, GW(BRY), 7C5; 43D4
Bridgend & Coity (Goods), BRY, 43D4
Bridgend Jc, NB, 29B5; 44C5
Bridgeness, NB, 30B4
Bridgeton, Cal, 44D3
Bridgeton Cross, Cal, 44E1
Bridgeton Cross, Cal & NB(G&SW), 44D3
Bridgnorth, GW, 15F2
Bridgwater, GW & SD, 3C1; 8F3
Bridlington, NE, 22B3
Bridport for Lyme Regis, GW, 3F1

Brierfield, LY, 24D1
Brierley Hill, GW, 15G3
Brierley Jc, HB/DV, 21E4; 42D1
Brigg, GC, 22F4
Brigham, LNW&M&CJt, 26E3
Brighouse, LY, 21E2; 42C4 *see also* Clifton Road
Brightlingsea, GE, 12F4
Brighton, LBSC, 5F3
Brighton Road (Birmingham), Mid, 13D4
Brighton Works, LBSC, 5F3
Brightside, Mid, 21G3; 42G2
Brill & Ludgershall, GW, 10E3
Brill, OAT, 10E3
Brimington, Mid, B2
Brimscombe, GW, 9F3
Brimscombe Bridge Halt, GW, 9F3
Brimsdown, GE, 5A3; 11G3
Brindle Heath (Goods), LY, 45B3
Brinkburn, NB, 31G4
Brinklow, LNW, 10A4
Brinkworth, GW, 9G4
Brinscall, LU, 20A2; 24E2
Brinsley Jc, GN 41E3
Brislington, GW, 3A2; 8D1
Bristol, GW/Mid, GW & Mid, 3A2 and inset; 8C1/2
Bristol Road, WCP, 3A1; 8D3
Britannia, LY, 20A1
Brithdiri, Rhy, 8B4; 43B2 *see also* Cwmsyfiog
Briton Ferry Road, GW, 43F3
Briton Ferry, GW, RSB & SWM, 7B4; 43F3
Brixham, GW, 2D3
Brixton, SEC 5B3; 40E5
Brixton Coal Depot, Mid, 40E5
Brixton Road (Devon), GW, 2E5
Brixworth, LNW, 10A2
Broad Clyst, LSW, 2B3
Broad Green, LNW, 20C4; 45E4
Broad Street (London), NL & LNW, 5A3; 40C4
Broad Street (Pendleton), LY, 45B3
Broadfield, LY, 20B1; 24F1; 45A2
Broadheath Jc, LNW/CLC, 45B4
Broadheath, LNW, 20C2; 24G2; 45B4
Broadley LY, 20A1; 45A1
Broadstairs, SEC, 6B1
Broadstone, WCP, 3A1; 8D3
Broadstone Jc, LSW(SD), 3F5
Broadway, GW, 9C4
Brock, LNW, 24D3
Brockenhill Jc, SK(GC/GN)/ind, 42C1
Brockenhurst, LSW, 4E4
Brocketsbrae, Cal, 30D5
Brockford & Wetheringsett, MSL, 12C4
Brockholes, LY, 21F2; 42D5
Brocklesby, GC, 22E3
Brockley, LBSC, 40E3
Brockley Whins, NE, 28C5
Brodie, HR, 36D3
Bromborough, BJ, 20C4; 45F5
Bromfield (Cumb), Cal, 26D2
Bromfield (Salop), S&H, 9A1
Bromford Bridge, Mid, 15G5
Bromham & Rowde, GW, 3B5
Bromley (London), LTS(Dist), 40C3
Bromley Cross, LY, 20A2; 24E1; 45B1
Bromley Jc (Norwood), LBSC/SEC, 40F4
Bromley North (Kent), SEC, 5B4; 40F2
Bromley South (Kent), SEC, 5B4; 40G2
Bromley Spur Jc, SEC/LBSC, 40F4
Brompton (Yorks), NE, 28G5
Brompton & Fulham Goods, LNW, 39D4
Bromsgrove, Mid, 9A4
Bromshall (Goods), NS, 15D4
Bromyard, GW, 9B2
Brondesbury, LNW(NL), 39B4 *see also* Kilburn, Met
Brondesbury Park, LNW(NL), 39B4
Bronwydd Arms, GW, 13G4
Brookland, SEC, 6E4
Brooklands, MSJA(CLC), 20C1; 24G1; 45B3
Brooksby, Mid, 16E3
Brookwood Cemetery (London Necropolis Co), 5C1
Brookwood Cemetery (London Necropolis Co), LSW, 5C1
Brookwood, LSW, 5C1
Broom (Junc), Mid(SMJ), 9B4
Broome, LNW, 14C1
Broomfield Jc, Cal/NB, 34C2
Broomfleet, NE(GC), 22E4
Broomhill (Inverness), HR, 36F3
Broomhill (Northumb), NE, 31G5
Broomhouse, NB, 29C5; 44C3
Broomieknowe, NB, 30C2
Broomielaw (Durham), NE, 27E4
Broomlee, NB, 30D3
Brora, HR, 36A4; 38G5
Brotton, NE, 28E3
Brough, NE(GC/LNW), 22E4
Broughton, LNW, 20D4
Broughton (Peebles), Cal, 30E3
Broughton Astley, Mid, 16G4
Broughton Cross, LNW, 26E3
Broughton Gifford Halt, GW, 3B4
Broughton-in-Furness, Fur, 24A5
Broughton Lane, GC, 42G2
Broughty Ferry, D&A, 34E1 (inset)
Browndown Halt, LSW, 4E3
Brownhills, LNW & Mid, 15F4
Broxbourne & Hoddesdon, GE, 11F3
Broxbourne Jc, GE, 11F3
Broxton, LNW, 15C1; 20E3
Bruce Grove, GE, 40A4
Brucklay, GNS, 37D4
Brundall, GE, 18F2
Brunswick (Liverpool) Goods, CLC, 20C4; 24G4; 45F4 and inset
Brunswick Dock (Liverpool) Goods, LNW, 45F4 and inset
Bruton, GW, 3C3; 8F1
Brymbo, GW(LNW) & GC, 20E4
Brymbo West Crossing Halt, GW, 20E4
Bryn (Glam), PT, 7B5; 43E3
Bryn (Lancs), LNW, 20B3; 24F2; 45D3
Bryn Teify, GW, 13F4
Brynamman, GW & Mid, 7A4; 43F1
Bryncethin Jc, GW, 7C5; 43D4
Brynglas, Tal, 13B5
Bryngwyn (Carnarvon), NWNG, 19E2
Bryngwyn Halt (Montgomery), Cam, 14A2
Brynkir, LNW, 19F2
Brynmawr, LNW(GW), 8A4; 43B1
Brynmenyn, GW, 7C5; 43D3
Brynmill, Mum, 43G3
Bubwith, NE, 21D5
Buccleuch Dock Jc, Fur, 24B5
Buchanan Street (Glasgow), Cal, 29C5; 44E4
Buchlyvie, NB, 29A4
Buckden, Mid, 11C2 *see also* Offord
Buckenham, GE, 18F2
Buckfastleigh, GW, 2D4
Buckhaven, NB, 30A2; 34G5
Buckhurst Hill, GE, 5A4
Buckie, GNS & HR, 37C1
Buckingham, LNW, 10D3
Buckingham West Jc, Cal, 34E2 (inset)
Buckland Jc, SEC, 6D2
Buckley, GC, 20D5 *see also* Padeswood
Buckley Junc, GC, 20D4
Bucknall & Northwood, NS, 15C3
Bucknell, LNW, 14D1
Buckpool, GNS, 37C1
Bucksburn, GNS, 37F4
Buddon, D&A, 34E4
Bude, LSW, 1A4
Budleigh Salterton, LSW, 2C2
Bugle, GW, 1D2
Bugsworth, Mid, 15A4
Buildwas, GW, 15F2
Builth Road High Level, LNW, 14E3
Builth Road Low Level, Cam, 14E5
Builth Wells, Cam, 14E3
Bulford, LSW, 4C5
Bulford Camp, LSW, 4C5
Bulkington, LNW, 16G5
Bullers o' Buchan Platform, GNS, 37E5
Bullgill, M&C, 26D3
Bullgill Jc, M&C, 26D3
Bullo Pill, GW, 8A1; 9E2
Bulwell, Mid, 16C4; 41F4 *see also* Basford
Bulwell Common, GC, 16C4; 41F4
Bulwell Forest, GN, 16C4; 41F4
Bunchrew, HR, 36D5
Bungalow Town Halt, LBSC, 5F2
Bungay, GE, 12A2; 18G2
Buntingford, GE, 11E3
Burbage (Goods), GW, 4A5
Burdale, NE, 22B5
Burdett Road, GE(LTS), 40C3
Bures, GE, 12E5
Burgess Hill, LBSC, 5E3
Burgh (Cumb), NB, 26C1
Burgh (Lincs), GN, 17B4
Burghclere, GW, 4B3
Burghead, HR, 36C2
Burleigh Street (Goods) (Hull), HB, 22 (inset)
Burlescombe, GW, 2A2; 8G5
Burlington Road Halt, PWY, 24D4
Burn Hill, NE, 27D4

Burn Naze Halt, PWY, 24D4
Burnage, LNW, 45A3
Burnbank, NB, 44C2
Burneside, LNW, 27G1
Burngullow, GW, 1D2
Burnham (Som), SD, 3B1; 8E3
Burnham Beeches, GW, 5B1
Burnham Market, GE, 18D5
Burnham-on-Crouch, GE, 6A4; 12G5
Burnley, LY, 24D1
Burnmouth, NB, 31C3
Burnside (Westmorland), LNW, 27G1
Burnside, Cal, 29C5; 44D3
Burnstones, NE, 27C2
Burnt House (Goods), GE, 11A3; 17G3
Burnt Mill, GE, 11F3
Burntisland, NB, 30A2
Burrington, GW, 3B2; 8D2
Burry Port, BPGV, 7B2 *see also* Pembrey, GW
Burscough Bridge, LY, 20A4; 24F3; 45E1
Burscough Junc, LY, 20B4; 24F3; 45E1
Bursledon, LSW, 4E3
Burslem, NS, 15C3; 20E1
Burston, GE, 12B3
Burton & Holme, LNW, 24B3
Burton Agnes, NE, 22B3
Burton Joyce, Mid, 16C3; 41F5
Burton Lane Jc, NE, 21C5 and inset A4
Burton-on-Trent (Goods), Mid, GN & LNW, 15D5 and inset
Burton-on-Trent (Pass), Mid(GN/LNW/NS), 15D5 and inset
Burton Point, GC, 20D4; 45F5
Burton Salmon, NE(GN), 21E4; 42B1
Burwarton, CMDP, 15G2
Burwell, GE, 11C4
Bury (Lancs), LY, 20B1; 24F1; 45B1/2
Bury St Edmunds, GE, 12C5
Busby, Cal, 29C5; 44E2
Busby Jc, Cal/GBK, 44E3
Bush Hill Park, GE, 5A3; 11G3
Bushbury (Goods), LNW, 15F3
Bushbury Jc, LNW/GW, 15F3
Bushey & Oxhey, LNW, 5A2; 11G1
Bushey Lane Jc, LY, 20B3; 24F3; 45E2
Butler's Hill, GN, 16C4; 41E4
Butterknowle (Goods), NE, 27E4
Butterley, Mid, 16C5; 41E2
Butterton, MS, 15B5
Buttington, Cam & SWP, 14A2
Butts Jc, LSW, 4C2
Butts Lane Halt, LY, 20A4; 24E4; 45F1
Buxted, LBSC, 5E4
Buxton, LNW & Mid, 15A4
Buxton Lamas, GE, 18E3
Byers Green, NE, 27D5
Byfield, SMJ, 10B4
Byfleet & Woodham, LSW, 5C1
Byker, NE, 28 (inset)
Bynea (Carmarthenshire), GW, 7B3

Cadbury Road, WCP, 3A1; 8C2
Cadeleigh, GW, 2A3
Cadishead, CLC, 20C2; 24G2; 45C3
Cadoxton, BRY(TV), 8D4; 43B5
Cadoxton Goods (Neath), N&B, 43F2
Cadoxton Jc, BR, 43C5
Cae Harris, TBJ, 43C2
Caerau, GW, 7B5; 43E3
Caergwrle Castle, GC, 20E4
Caerleon, GW, 8B3; 43A3
Caerphilly, Rhy(AD), 8C4; 43B3
Caerphilly East Branch Jc, BM/RHY, 43B3
Caerphilly Locomotive Works, Rhy, 43B3
Caerphilly Lower Branch Jc, BM, 43B3
Caerphilly Upper Branch Jc, BM/RHY, 43B3
Caerphilly West Branch Jc, RHY, 43B3
Caersws, Cam, 14C3
Caerwys, LNW, 20D5
Caffyns Halt, LB, 7E4
Cairn Valley Jc, G&SW, 26B4
Cairnbuig, GNS, 37C5
Cairneyhill, NB, 30A3
Cairnie Junc, GNS, 37D1
Caister-on-Sea, MGN, 18E1
Caister Road Jc, MGN, 18F1
Calbourne & Shalfleet, FYN, 4F4
Calcotts, GNS, 36C1
Caldarvan, NB, 29B4
Calder, Cal, 44B4
Calderbank, Cal, 30C5; 44A3
Calderbank Branch Jc, NB, 44A4
Caldercruix, NB, 30C5; 44B4
Caldon Low Halt, NS, 15C4
Caldwell, GBK, 29D4
Caldy, BJ, 20C5; 24G5
Caledonian Rd & Barnsbury, NL(LNW), 40B5
Callander, Cal, 33G2
Callerton, NE, 27B5
Callington, BAC, 1C5
Callowland, LNW, 11G1
Calne, GW, 3A5
Calstock, BAC, 1C5
Calthwaite, LNW, 27D1
Calveley, LNW, 15B1; 20E3
Calverley & Rodley, Mid, 21D2; 42A4
Calvert, GC, 10D3
Cam, Mid, 8B1; 9F2
Camber, RCT, 6E4
Camberley & York Town, LSW, 4B1 *see also* Blackwater, SEC
Camborne, GW, 1E5 (inset)
Cambria Road Jc, LBSC/SEC, 40E4
Cambridge (Goods), GE, GN, LNW & Mid, 11C3
Cambridge (Pass), GE(GN/LNW/Mid), 11C3
Cambridge Heath, GE, 40C4
Cambus, NB, 30A5
Cambus o' May, GNS, 34A4
Cambusavie Platform, HR, 36A4
Cambuslang, Cal, 29C5; 44D3
Cambusnethan, Cal, 30C5
Camden Goods, LNW, 40C5 and inset A1
Camden Town, NL(LNW), 40B5
Camel's Head Halt, LSW, 1 (inset)
Camelford, LSW, 1B3
Camelon, NB(Cal), 30B5
Camelon (Goods), NB & Cal, 30B5
Cameron Bridge, NB, 30A2; 34G5
Camerton (Cumb), LNW, 26E3
Camerton (Som), GW, 3B3; 8D1
Camlachie (Goods), NB, 44D4
Camp Hill, Mid, 13C4
Camp Hill Jc, Mid, 3C4
Campbell Road Jc, LTS/WB, 40C3
Campbeltown, CM, 29 (inset)
Campden, GW, 9C5
Camperdown East Jc, NB/D&A, 34E2 (inset)
Campsie Branch Jc, NB, 29B5; 44D5
Campsie Glen, NB, 29B5
Canada Dock (Liverpool), LNW, 45F3 and inset
Canal (Inverness), HP, 36E5
Canal (Paisley), G&P, 29C4; 44F3
Canal Jc (Carlisle), NB, 26C1
Canning Town, GE & LNW, 40C2
Cannock, LNW, 15E4
Cannon Street (Hull), HB, 22 (inset)
Cannon Street (London), SEC & Dist&MetJt, 40C4
Cannon's Marsh (Goods), GW, 3 (inset)
Canonbie, NB, 26B1
Canonbury, NL, 40B4
Canonbury (Essex Road), GN, 40B5
Canonbury Jc, GN/NL, 40B5
Canterbury, SEC, 6C3
Canterbury Road Jc, SEC, 40E5
Cantley, GE, 18F2
Capel, GE, 12D4
Capel Bangor, VR, 13C5
Capenhurst, BJ, 20D4; 45F5
Carbean, GW, 1D2
Carbis, GW, 1D2
Carbis Bay, GW, 1F4 (inset)
Carcroft, WRG, 21F4
Cardenden, NB, 30A2
Cardiff (Goods), GW, TV, Rhy & LNW, 8C4; 43B4/5
Cardiff (Pass), GW(BRY/TV), Rhy(Car) & TV, 8C4; 43B4/5
Cardiff Docks (Pass), TV, 8C4; 43B5
Cardigan, GW, 13E2
Cardigan Jc, GW, 7A1; 13G2
Cardigan Road Goods (Leeds), NE, 42A3
Cardington, Mid, 11D1
Cardonald, G&P, 44F3
Cardonnel Halt, GW, 43F3
Cardonnel Jc, GW/RSB, 43F3
Cardrona, NB, 30D2
Cardross, Cal, 29B3
Careston, NB, 34C4
Cargill, Cal, 33E5
Cargo Fleet, NE, 28E4
Carham, NE, 31D2
Carisbrooke Halt, FYN, 4F3
Cark & Cartmel, Fur, 24B4
Carlinghow, LNW, 42B3
Carlisle (Goods), Cal, LNW, M&C, Mid, NB, NE, & DJ, 26C1
Carlisle (Pass), CJC(G&SW/M&C/Mid/NB/NE), 26C1
Carlton (Durham), NE, 28E5

Carlton (Yorks), HB, 21E5
Carlton & Netherfield for Gedling & Colwick, Mid, 16C3; 41F5 *see also* Netherfield, GN
Carlton Colville, GE, 12A1; 18G1
Carlton-on-Trent, GN, 16B2
Carlton Road Jc, Mid, 39B5; 40C1 (inset)
Carluke, Cal, 30D5
Carmarthen Junc, GW, 13G4
Carmarthen Town, GW(LNW), 7A2; 13G4
Carmont, Cal, 34B2
Carmuirs Jcs, Cal/NB, 30B5
Carmyle, Cal, 29C5; 44D3
Carmyllie, D&A, 34D3
Carn Brea, GW, 1E5 (inset)
Carnaby, NE, 22B3
Carnarvon, LNW, 19D2
Carnforth (Goods), Fur&LNW&MidJt, 24B3
Carnforth (Pass), Fur&LNWJt(Mid), 24B3
Carno, Cam, 14B4
Carnoustie, D&A, 34E3
Carntyne for Westmuir & Tollcross, NB, 29C5; 44D3
Carnwath, Cal, 30D4
Carpenders Park, LNW, 5A2
Carpenters Road Goods, GE, 40B3
Carr Bridge, HR, 36F3
Carr Lane Halt, KE, 24C4
Carr Mill, LNW, 20B3; 24F3; 45D3
Carrington, GC, 41F4
Carrog, GW, 20F5
Carron, GNS, 36G2
Carronbridge, G&SW, 30G4
Carshalton, LBSC, 5C3
Carstairs, Cal, 30D4
Cart Harbour (Paisley), G&SW, 44G4
Carterhouse Jc, LNW, 45D4
Cartsyke, Cal, 29B3
Carville, NE, 28B5
Cassillis, G&SW, 29F3
Castle (Lancaster), LNW(Mid), 24C3
Castle (Northampton), LNW, 10B2
Castle Ashby & Earls Barton, LNW(Mid), 10B2
Castle Bar Park Halt, GW, 39C2
Castle Bromwich, Mid, 15G5
Castle Bytham, Mid(MGN), 16E1; 17E1
Castle Caereinion, W&L, 14B3
Castle Cary (Som), GW, 3C2; 8F1
Castle Cary Jc, GW, 3C3; 8F1
Castle Donington & Shardlow, Mid, 16D4
Castle Douglas, G&SW, 26C5
Castle Douglas Branch Jc, G&SW, 26B3
Castle Eden, NE, 28D5
Castle Hills Jc, WRG, 21F4
Castle Howard, NE, 22B5
Castle Jc, NE, 28 (inset)
Castle Kennedy, P&W, 25C2
Castle Mill, GVT, 20F5
Castlecary (Dunbarton), NB, 30B5
Castleford, NE(LY/GN) & LY, 21E4; 42B1
Castlehill (Goods), NB, 30D5
Castlethorpe, LNW, 10C2
Castleton (Lancs), LY, 20B1; 24F1; 45A1
Castleton (Yorks), NE, 28F3
Castletown, IMR, 23C2
Castor, LNW, 11A1; 17F1
Catcliffe, SHD, 21G4; 42G1
Caterham, SEC, 5C3
Catfield, MGN, 18E2
Catford, SEC, 40E3
Catford Bridge, SEC, 40E3
Cathcart, Cal, 29C5; 44E3
Cathcart Street (Birkenhead), BJ, 45F4
Cathcart Street (Greenock), Cal, 29B3
Caton, Mid, 24B3
Catrine, G&SW, 29E5
Cattal, NE, 21C4
Catterick Bridge, NE, 27F5
Cattewater Jc, GW/LSW, 1 (inset)
Cattewater Harbour, LSW, 1A2
Cattle Sidings Jc, Mid, 41G2
Cauldcots, NB, 34D3
Causeland, LL, 1D4
Causewayend, NB, 30B4
Causewayhead, NB, 30A5
Cavendish, GE, 11D5
Cawood, NE, 21D5
Cawston, GE, 18E3
Caythorpe, GN, 16C1
Cayton, NE, 22A3
Cefn, GW, 20F4
Cefn Coed, BM&LNWJt, 8A5; 43C1
Cefn Jc, GW/PT, 7C5; 43E4
Cefn On Halt, Rhy, 43B4
Cefn-y-bedd, GC, 20E4
Ceint, LNW, 19D2
Cemetery North Jc, NE, 28D4
Cemetery West Jc, NE, 28D4
Cemmaes, Mawd, 14B4
Cemmes Road, Cam, 14B5
Central (Royal Albert Docks), PLA(GE), 40C2
Cerist, Van, 14C4
Cerney & Ashton Keynes, MSW, 9F4
Chacewater, GW, 1E1 and inset E5
Chadderton (Goods), LY, 45A2
Chaddesden Sidings, Mid, 41G2
Chalcombe Road Platform, GC, 10C4
Chalder, SL, 4E1
Chalfont & Latimer, Met&GCJt, 10F1
Chalford, GW, 9F3
Chalk Farm, NL, 39B5; 40A1 (inset)
Challoch Jc, P&W, 25C3
Challow, GW, 10F5
Chaloners Whin Jc, NE, 21C5 and inset A5
Chandlers Ford, LSW, 4D4
Chapel Lane, S&M, 14A1
Chapel Street (Southport), LY(LNW), 20A4; 24E4; 45F1
Chapel-en-le-Frith, Mid & LNW, 15A4
Chapelhall, Cal, 30C5; 44A3
Chapelknowle Jc, Cal, 44A2
Chapelton, LSW, 7F3
Chapeltown, Mid, 21F3; 42F2
Chapeltown & Thorncliffe, GC, 21F3; 42F2
Chappel & Wakes Colne, GE(CVH), 12E5
Chard, GW&LSWJt, 3E1
Chard Junc, LSW, 2A1; 3E1
Charfield, Mid, 8B1; 9F2
Charing, SEC, 6C4
Charing Cross (Glasgow), NB, 44E4
Charing Cross (London), SEC & Dist(Met), 5B3; 40C5
Charlbury, GW, 10D5
Charlestown (Ashton), LY(LNW), 21A2 (inset)
Charlestown (Fife), NB, 30B3
Charlton Halt (Oxon), LNW, 10E4
Charlton Junc (Kent), SEC, 5B4; 40D2
Charlton Kings, GW(MSW), 9D4
Charlton Mackrell, GW, 3D2; 8F2
Chartham, SEC, 6C3
Chartley, GN, 15D4
Charwelton, GC, 10B4
Chatburn, LY, 24D1
Chatham, SEC, 6B5
Chathill, NE(NSL), 31E5
Chatteris, GN&GEJt, 11A3; 17G3
Chatterley, NS, 15C3; 20E1
Cheadle (Ches), CLC & LNW, 20C1; 45A4
Cheadle (Staffs), NS, 15C4
Cheadle Heath, Mid, 43A4
Cheadle Hulme, LNW(NS), 15A3; 24G1; 45A4
Cheam, LBSC, 5C3
Checker House, GC, 16A3
Cheddar, GW, 3B1; 8E2
Cheddington, LNW, 10E1
Cheddleton, NS, 15C4
Chedworth, MSW, 9E4
Cheesewring Quarry, LC, 1C4
Chelfham, LB, 7F3
Chelford for Knutsford, LNW, 15A3; 20D1; 45B5
Chellaston & Swarkstone, Mid, 16D5
Chelmsford, GE, 11F5
Chelsea & Fulham, WLE, 5B3; 39D5
Chelsea Basin Jc, WLE, 39D5
Chelsfield, SEC, 5C4
Cheltenham, GW, Mid & Mid(MSW), 9D4
Cheltenham Race Course, GW, 9D4
Cheltenham South & Leckhampton, GW(MSW), 9D4
Chepstow, GW, 8B2; 9F1
Chequerbent for Hulton, LNW, 45C2
Cheriton Halt, SEC, 6D2
Cherry Burton, NE, 2D4
Cherry Tree, LY(LNW), 20A2; 24E2
Chertsey, LSW, 5B1
Chesham, Met&GCJt, 10F1
Cheshunt, GE, 11G3
Chester, CLC, GC & LNW, 20D4
Chester Jc, LNW, 15C2; 20E2
Chester-le-Street, NE, 27C5
Chester North Gate, CLC, 20D4
Chester Road, LNW, 15F5
Chesterfield Central, GC, 41B2
Chettisham, GE, 11B4
Chevening Halt, SEC, 5C4
Chevington, NE, 31G5
Chichester, LBSC & SL, 4E1
Chigwell Lane, GE, 11G3
Chigwell, GE, 5A4
Chilcompton, SD, 3B3; 8E1

Childwall, CLC, 20C4; 24G3; 45E5
Chilham, SEC 6C3
Chilsworthy, BAC, 1C5
Chiltern Green, Mid, 11F1
Chilworth & Albury, SEC, 5D1
Chingford, GE, 5A4, 11G3
Chinley, Mid, 15A5
Chinley East Jc, Mid, 15A4
Chinley North Jc, Mid, 15A4
Chinley South Jc, Mid, 15A4
Chinnor, GW, 10F2
Chippenham, GW, 3A4
Chippenham Jc, GE, 11C4
Chipping Norton, GW, 10D5
Chipping Sodbury, GW, 8C1; 9G2
Chipstead, SEC, 5C3
Chirk, GW & GVT, 20F4
Chirnside, NB, 31C3
Chiseldon & Chenies, MSW, 11G1
Chiselhurst, SEC, 40F2
Chiselhurst Jc, SEC, 40F2
Chislet Colliery Halt, SEC, 6C2
Chiswick & Grove Park, 39D3
Chittening Factory Platform, GW, 8C2; 9G1
Chobham Farm Jc, GE, 40B3
Chollerton, NB, 27B3
Cholsey & Moulsford, GW, 10C4
Choppington, NE, 27A5
Chorleywood & Chenies, Met&GCJt, 5A1; 10F1
Chorlton, CLC, 20C1
Chorlton, LNW, 24G1
Chorlton-cum-Hardy, CLC, 45B3
Christchurch, LSW, 4F5
Christon Bank, NE, 31E5
Christow, GW, 2B4
Christs Hospital (West Horsham), LBSC, 5E2
Chudleigh, GW, 2C3
Church & Oswaldtwistle, LY, 24E1
Church Fenton, NE(GC/GN/LY), 21D4
Church Road (Garston), LNW, 20C4
Church Road (Mon), BM, 8B4; 43B3
Church Road (Warwicks), Mid, 13C3; 15G4
Church Stretton, S&H, 14B4
Church Village, TV, 8C5; 43C3
Churchbury, GE, 5A3; 11G3
Churchdown, GW&Mid, 9D3
Churchill & Blakedown, GW, 9A3
Churchtown, LY, 20A4; 24E4; 45F1
Churn, GW, 10G4
Churston, GW, 2D3
Churwell, LNW, 21D3; 42B3
Chwilog, LNW, 19F1
Chwilog, LNW, 19F1
Cilfrew, N&B, 7B4; 43F2
Cilfynydd, TV, 8B5; 43C3
Ciliau-Aeron, GW, 13E4
Cilmery, LNW, 14E3
Cinderford, GW & SVW, 8A1; 9E2
Cirencester, GW & MSW, 9F4
City Basin Jc (Exeter), GW, 2B3
City Road Goods (Bradford), GN, 42A4
Clackmannan & Kennet, NB, 30A4
Clacton-on-Sea & Southcliff, GE, 12F3
Clandon, LSW, 5C1
Clapham (Yorks), Mid, 24B1
Clapham & North Stockwell (London), SEC(LBSC), 40E5
Clapham Junc (London), LSW, LBSC(LNW) & WLE, 5B3; 39E5 and inset F3
Clapton, GE, 40B4
Clapton Jc, GE, 40B4
Clapton Road, WCP, 3A1; 8C2
Clarbeston Jc, GW, 13G1
Clarbeston Road, GW, 13G1
Clarborough Jc, GC, 16A2
Clare, GE, 11D5
Clarence Road (Cardiff), GW(BRY/TV), 43B4
Clarence Street (Pontypool), GW, 43A2
Clarence Yard Goods, GN, 40B5
Clarkston (Lanark), NB, 30C5; 44A4
Clarkston (Renfrew), Cal, 29C5; 44E2
Clatford, LSW(MSW), 4C4
Claverdon, GW, 9B5
Claxby & Usselby, GC, 22G3
Clay Cross, Mid, 16B5; 41C; 2D2
Claydon (Bucks), LNW, 10D3
Claydon (Suffolk), GE, 12D4
Claygate & Claremont, LSW, 5C2
Claypole, GN, 16C2
Clayton, GN, 21D2; 42B5
Clayton Bridge, LY, 45A3
Clayton West, LY, 21F3; 42D3
Cleator Moor, WCE & CWJ, 26F3
Cleckheaton, LY & LNW, 21E2; 42B4
Cledford Bridge Halt, LNW, 15B2; 20D2
Clee Hill, S&H, 9A1
Cleethorpes, GC, 22F2
Cleeve, Mid, 9D3
Clegg Street (Oldham), OAGB(LY), 21D1 (inset); 45A2
Cleghorn, Cal, 30D4
Cleland, Cal, 30C5; 44A2
Clenchwarton, MGN, 17E4
Cleobury Mortimer, GW & CMDP, 9A2
Cleobury North Crossing, CMDP, 15G2
Cleobury Town, CMDP, 9A2
Clevedon, GW & WCP, 3A1; 8D3
Clevedon (All Saints), 3A1; 10F1
Clevedon East, WCP, 3A1; 8D3
Cliburn, NE, 27E1
Cliddesden, LSW, 4B2
Cliff Common, NE & DVL, 21D5
Cliffe, SEC, 6B5
Clifford, GW, 14E2
Clifton (Derbys), NS, 15C5
Clifton (Westmorland), NE, 27E1
Clifton & Lowther, LNW, 27E1
Clifton Bridge, GW, 3A2 and inset
Clifton Down, CE, 3 (inset); 3A2; 8C2
Clifton Junc (Lancs), LY, 20B1; 24F1; 45B2
Clifton Maybank (Goods), GW, 3E2; 8G2
Clifton Maybank Jc, GW, 3D2
Clifton Mill, LNW, 10A4
Clifton-on-Trent, GC, 16B2
Clifton Road (Brighouse), LY, 21E2; 42C4
Clipston & Oxendon, LNW, 10A3; 16G3
Clipstone (Goods), GC, 16B3; 41C5
Clipstone Jc, GC/ind, 16B3; 41C5
Clitheroe, LY(Mid), 24D1
Clock Face, LNW, 20C3; 24G3; 45D4
Clock House, SEC, 40F4
Clocksbriggs, Cal, 34D4
Closeburn, G&SW, 26A4
Clough Fold, LY, 20A1; 24E1
Cloughton, NE, 28G1
Clovenfords, NB, 30E1
Clown, GC & Mid, 16A4; 41B4
Clown Jc, GC/Mid, 41B4
Clunes, HR, 35D5
Clutton, GW, 3B3; 4D1
Clydach (Brecknock), LNW, 8A4; 43B1
Clydach Court Halt, TV, 43C3
Clydach-on-Tawe, Mid & GW, 7B4; 43F2
Clyde Jc, G&SW, 44E2 (inset)
Clydebank, Cal, 29C4; 44F4
Clydebank Central, NB, 44F4
Clydebank East, NB, 29C4; 44F4
Clynderwen, GW, 13G2
Clyne Halt, GW, 43E2
Clyst St Mary & Digby Halt, LSW, 2C3
Coal Yard Jc (Clapham), LNW/WLE, 39E4 (inset)
Coalbrookdale, GW, 15F2
Coalburn, Cal, 30E5
Coaley Junc, Mid, 8B1; 9E2
Coalpit Heath, GW, 8C1; 9G2
Coalport, GW & LNW, 15F2
Coalville, Mid & LNW, 16E4
Coanwood, NE, 27C2
Coatbridge, Cal & NB, 30C5; 44B4
Coatbridge Sunnyside, NB, 44B4
Coatdyke, NB, 44B4
Coates (Glos), GW, 9F4
Cobbinshaw, Cal, 30C4
Cobham for Stoke d'Abernon, LSW, 5C2
Coborn Road, GE, 40C3
Cobridge, NS, 15C3; 20E1
Cockburnspath, NB, 31B2
Cockerham Cross Halt, KE, 24C3
Cockermouth, LNW&CKPJt (M&C), 26E3
Cockett, GW, 7B3; 43G3
Cockfield (Durham), NE, 27E4
Cockfield (Suffolk), GE, 12C5
Cocking, LBSC, 4D1
Cockley Brake Jc, LNW/SMJ, 10C2
Codford, GW, 3C5
Codnor Park, GN, 16C4; 41E3
Codnor Park & Selston for Ironville & Jacksdale, Mid, 16C4; 41E3
Codnor Park Jc, Mid/GN, 41E3
Codsall, GW, 15F3
Codzow Jc, Cal, 44B2
Coed Poeth, GW, 20E5
Coed Talon, LNW, 20E5
Coed-y-Gric Jc, GW, 8B3; 43A2
Cogan, BRY, 8C4; 43B5
Cogie Hill Halt, KE, 24C3
Cogload Jc, GW, 8F3
Coity Jc, GW/BRY, 7C5; 43D4

Coke Ovens Jc, GE/NSJ, 12A1; 18F1
Colbren Junc, N&B(Mid), 7A5; 43E1
Colby, IMR, 23C2
Colchester, GE, 12E4
Cold Norton, GE, 12G5
Coldham, GE, 17F3
Coldham Lane Jc, GE, 11C3
Coldstream, NE, 31D3
Cole Green, GN, 11F2
Cole, SD, 3C3; 8F1
Coleburn, GNS, 36D1
Coleford for Staurton, SVW & GW, 8A1; 9E1
Coleford Jc, LSW, 2B4
Colehouse Lane, WCP, 3A1; 8D3
Coleshill, Mid, 15G5
Colfin, P&W, 25C2
Colinton, Cal, 30C2
College Goods (Glasgow), G&SW, 44D4 and inset E2
Collessie, NB, 34F5
Colliery Jc, EWY/GN, 42B2
Collingbourne, MSW, 4B5
Collingham, Mid, 16B2
Collingham Bridge, NE, 21C4
Collins Green, LNW, 20C3; 24G2; 45D3
Colliston, Cal, 34D3
Colnbrook, GW, 5B1; 10G1
Colne, Mid, 21 (inset); 24D1
Colne, LY&MidJt, 21 (inset)
Coltfield Platform, HR, 36C2
Coltishall, GE, 18E3
Colwall, GW, 9C2
Colwich, LNW&NSJt, 15E4
Colwyn Bay, LNW, 19D4
Colyford, LSW, 2B1
Colyton, LSW, 2B1
Colzium, K&B, 30B5
Combe Hay Halt, GW, 3B3; 8D1
Combpyne, LSW, 2B1
Commercial Road Goods, LTS, 40C4
Common Branch Jc, TV, 43C4
Commondale, NE, 28F3
Commondyke, G&SW, 29F5
Commonhead (Airdrie North), NB, 44B4
Compton, GW, 10G4
Comrie, Cal, 33F3
Conder Green, LNW, 24C3
Condover, S&H, 15F1
Congleton, NS(LNW), 15B3; 20D1
Congleton Upper Jc, NS, 15B3; 20E3
Congresbury, GW, 3A1; 8D3
Coningsby, GN, 17C2
Conisborough, GC(Mid), 21F4
Coniston, Fur, 26G1
Connah's Quay, LNW, 20D4
Connah's Quay & Shotton, GC, 20D4
Connah's Quay East Jc, GC, 20D4
Connah's Quay North Jc, GC, 20D4
Connaught Road, PLA(GE), 40C2
Connel Ferry, Cal, 32E4
Connel Ferry Jc, Cal, 32E4
Conon, HR, 35D5
Cononley, Mid, 21C1
Consall, NS, 15C4
Consett, NE, 27C4
Constable Burton, NE, 21A2; 27G5
Conway Morfa, LNW, 19D3
Conwil, GW, 13G4
Cooden Beach Halt, LBSC, 6G5
Cook Street Branch, G&SW, 44F2 (inset)
Cookham, GW, 5A1; 10G2
Cooksbridge, LBSC, 5F4
Coombe, LL, 1D4
Coombe Lane, WSC, 5C3
Coombes Holloway Halt, GW, 13D1
Cooper Bridge, LY, 21E2; 42C4
Cop Lane Halt, LY, 20A3; 24E3
Copenhagen Jc, GN, 40B5
Copgrove, NE, 21B3
Copley, LY, 21E2; 42C5
Copley Hill, LNW, 42A3
Copmanthorpe, NE(GN), 21C5
Copper Mill Jc, GE, 40A4
Copper Pit Halt, GW, 43G2
Copperas Hill, CWJ, 26E3
Copplestone, LSW, 2A4
Coppull, LNW, 20A3; 24E2; 45D1
Copyhold Jc, LBSC, 5E3
Corbet's Lane Jc, LBSC/SEC, 40D4
Corbridge, NE(NB), 27C4
Corby (Lincs), ON, 16D1; 17E1
Cordio Jc, ME, 21A3; 28G5
Corfe Castle, LSW, 3G5
Corfe Mullen Jc, SD, 3F5
Corkickle (Whitehaven), Fur, 26E4
Cornbrook Goods, CLC, 45B3
Cornhill, GNS, 37C2
Cornholme, LY, 20A1; 21E1
Cornwood, GW, 2D5
Corpach, NB, 32C3
Corpusty & Saxthorpe, MGN, 18D4
Corringham, CL, 6A5
Corringham Light Railway, CL, 6A5
Corris, Cor, 14B5
Corrour, NB, 32C1
Corsham, GW, 3A4
Corstorphine, NB, 30B3
Corton, NSJ, 12A1; 18F1
Corwen, GW(LNW), 19F5
Coryates, GW, 3F3
Coryton, CL, 6A5
Coryton (Devon), GW, 1C5
Coryton Halt (Glam), Car, 43B4
Cosham, LSW&LBSCJt, 4E2
Cosham Jc, LBSC/LSW, 4E2
Cossington, SD, 3C1; 8E3
Cotehill, Mid, 27C1
Cotham, GN, 16C2
Cotherstone, NE, 27E4
Coton Hill (Goods), GW, 15E1
Cottam, GC, 16A2
Cottesmore, Mid, 16E1
Cottingham, NE, 22D3
Cottingham Jc, NE, 22D3; 22A2 (inset)
Cottingwith, DVL, 21D5
Coughton, Mid, 9B4
Coulsdon & Cane Hill, SEC, 5C3
Coulsdon & Smitham Downs, LBSC, 5C3
Coulter, Cal, 30E4
Coundon, NE, 27E5
Coundon Road, LNW, 10A5
Counter Drain, MGN, 17E2
Countesthorpe, Mid, 16F3
County Boundary Jc, Cal/G&SW, 29E5
County School, GE, 18E4
Coupar Angus, Cal, 34D5
Court Sart, RSB, 7B4; 43F3
Court Sart Jc, SWM, 43F3
Cove Bay, Cal, 34A1; 37G4
Coventry, LNW, 10A5
Cow Lane Jc, LBSC/SEC, 40D4
Cowbit, GN&GEJt, 17E2
Cowbridge, TV, 8C5; 43D4
Cowbridge Road Jc, BRY/GW, 43D4
Cowden, LBSC, 5D4
Cowdenbeath Jc, NB, 30A3
Cowdenbeath New, NB, 30A3
Cowes, IWC, 4F3
Cowlairs, NB, 44D4
Cowley, GW, 5A2; 10G1
Cowley Bridge Jc, GW/LSW, 2B3
Cowton, NE, 28F5
Coxbench, Mid, 16C5; 41F2
Coxgreen, NE, 28C5
Coxhoe (Goods), NE, 28D5
Coxhoe Bridge, NE, 28D5
Coxlodge, NE, 27B5
Coxwold, NE, 21A4
Craddock Lane (Bolton) Goods, LY, 45B2
Cradley Heath & Cradley, GW, 15G2
Cradoc, N&B (Mid), 14F4
Craig-y-Nos (Penwyllt), NAB(Mid), 7A5; 43E1
Craigellachie, GNS, 36D1
Craigendoran, NB, 29B3
Craigendoran Pier, NB, 29B3
Craighall Goods, NB, 44E4
Craigleith, Cal, 30 (inset)
Craiglockhart, NB, 30 (inset)
Craigo, Cal, 34C3
Crail, NB, 34F3
Crakehall, NE, 21A3; 27G5
Cramlington, NE, 27B5
Cranbrook, SEC, 6D5
Crane Street (Pontypool), GW, 8B4; 43A2
Crane Street Jc, LNW/Mid, 15E3 (inset)
Cranford (Northants), Mid, 10A1
Crank, LNW, 20B3; 24F3; 45E3
Cranleigh, LBSC, 5D2
Cranley Gardens, GN(NL), 39A5
Cranmore, GW, 3C3; 8E1
Cransley, Mid, 10A2
Crathes, GNS, 34A2
Craven Arms & Stokesay, S&H(BC), 14C1
Crawford, Cal, 30F4
Crawley, LBSC, 5D3
Cray, N&B(Mid), 14G4
Crayford, SEC, 5B4
Creagan, Cal, 32E3
Credenhill, Mid, 9C1; 14F1

Crediton, LSW, 2B4
Creech Jc, GW, 8F4
Creetown, P&W, 25C4
Creigiau, BRY, 8C5; 43C4
Cressage, GW, 15F1
Cressing, GE, 11F5
Cressington & Grassendale, CLC, 20C4; 45F4
Cresswell (Staffs), NS, 15D4
Creswell & Welbeck, GC, 16B4; 41B3
Crew Green, S&M, 14A1
Crewe, LNW(GW/NS), 15C2; 20E2
Crewe Jc, Cal, 30 (inset)
Crewe North-South Jc, LNW, 20E2
Crewe Wharf (Goods), NS, 15B2; 20E2
Crewe Works, LNW, 15B2; 20E2
Crewkerne, LSW, 3E1
Crews Hill, GN, 11G2
Crianlarich Jc, NB/Cal, 32F1
Crianlarich, Cal & NB, 32F1; 33F1
Criccieth, Cam, 19F2
Cricklade, GW, 9F4
Cricklewood, Mid, 5A3; 39B4
Crieff, Cal, 33F3
Criggion, S&M, 14A2
Crigglestone, LY & Mid, 21E3; 42C3/D3
Crigglestone Jc, LY, 42D3
Crimple Jc, NE, 21C3
Croesor Railway, CRY, 19F2
Croft, LNW, 16F4
Croft Spa, NE, 28F5
Crofton, LY, 21E4; 42C1 ***see also*** Hare Park
Crofton Jc, LY/WRG, 42C2
Crofton Park, SEC, 40E3
Cromdale, GNS, 36E2
Cromer, GE, 18D3
Cromer Beach, MGN, 18D3
Cromer Jc, GE, 18D3
Cromford, Mid & LNW, 16B5; 41D1/E1
Cromwell Curve Jcs, Dist, 39D5
Cronberry, G&SW, 29E5
Crook, NE, 27D5
Crook of Devon, NB, 30A3; 33G4
Crook Street (Bolton) Goods, LNW, 45C2
Crookston, G&SW, 29C4; 44F3
Cropredy, GW, 10C4
Crosby (IoM), IMR, 23B2
Crosby Garrett, Mid, 27F2
Cross Gates (Yorks), NE, 21D3; 42A2
Cross Gates Jc, NE, 21D3; 42A2
Cross Hands, GW & LM, 7A3
Cross Hill, GBK, 44 (inset)
Cross Inn, TV, 8C5; 43C4
Cross Keys, GW, 8B4; 43B3
Cross Lane, LNW(BJ), 45B3
Crossens, LY, 20A4; 24E4; 45F1
Crossfield (Goods), WCE, 26F3
Crossford, G&SW, 26A4
Crossgates (Fife), NB, 30A3
Crosshill, Cal, 44E3 and inset F1
Crosshill & Codnor, Mid, 16C4; 41F3
Crosshouse, G&SW, 29E4
Crossmichael, P&W, 26B5
Crossmyloof, GBK, 29C5; 44E3 and inset F1
Croston, LY, 20A3; 24E3; 45E1
Crouch End, GN(NL), 40A5
Crouch Hill, THJ(LTS), 40A5
Crow Nest Jc, LY, 45C2
Crow Park, GN, 16B2
Crow Road, Cal, 44E4
Crowborough & Jarvis Brook, LBSC, 5E5
Crowcombe, GW, 8F4
Crowden, GC, 21F2; 42F5
Crowborn Jc, GC, 21A2 (inset)
Crowhurst, SEC, 6F5
Crowburst Jc, LBSC/CO, 5D4
Crowle, AJ, 22E5
Crowle, GC, 22F5
Crown Street (Liverpool) Goods, LNW, 45F4
Crown Street Halt, NS, 20F2
Crowthorn Jc, LNW/OAGB, 21A2 (inset)
Croxall, Mid, 15E5
Croxdale, NE, 27D5
Croxley Green, LNW, 5A2; 11G1
Croy, NB, 30B1
Croydon (Addiscombe Road), SEC, 40G4
Cruckmeole Jc, SWP, 14A1
Cruckton, S&M, 14A1
Cruden Bay GNS, 37E5
Crudgington, GW, 15E2
Crumlin, GW, 8B4; 43B2
Crumpsall, LY, 20B1; 24F1; 45A2
Crymmych Arms, GW, 13F2
Crynant, N&B, 7A5; 43E2
Crystal Palace, LBSC(LNW), 5B3; 40F4
Crystal Palace High Level & Upper Norwood, SEC, 5B3; 40F4
Cuckoo Jc, MGN, 17E2
Cuddington, CLC, 15D2; 20D2; 45D5
Cudworth, Mid(HB/LY) & HB, 21F3/4; 42D2/E2
Cuffley & Goff's Oak, GN, 11G2
Culcheth, GC, 20C2; 24G2; 45C3
Culgaith, Mid, 27E1
Culham, GW, 10F4
Culkerton, GW, 9F3
Cullen, GNS, 37C1
Cullercoats, NE, 28B5
Cullingworth, GN, 21D1; 42A5
Culloden Moor, HR, 36D4
Cullompton, GW, 2A2
Culmstock, GW, 2A2; 8G5
Culrain, HR, 35A5
Culross, NB, 30A4
Culter, GNS, 34A2; 37G3
Cults, GNS, 37G4
Culworth, GC, 10C4
Culworth Jc, GC, 10C4
Cumbernauld, Cal, 30B5; 44B5
Cummersdale, M&C, 26C1
Cummertrees, G&SW, 26B3
Cumnock, G&SW, 29F5
Cumwhinton, Mid, 26C1
Cunninghamhead, G&SW, 29D3
Cupar, NB, 34F4
Currie, Cal, 30C3
Currie Hill, Cal, 30C3
Currock Jc, MC, 26C1 and inset
Curry Rivell Jc, GW, 3D1; 8F3
Curthwaite, M&C, 26C1
Curve Jc (Crewe), LNW, 20E2
Curzon Street, LNW, 13C4
Curzon Street Jc, LNW/Mid, 13C4
Custom House, GE, 40C2
Cuthlie, D&A, 34D3
Cutler, GNS, 34A2; 37G3
Cutler's Green Halt, GE, 11E4
Cutsyke Jc, LY/NB, 42B1
Cuxton, SEC, 5B5
Cwm, GW, 8A4; 43B2
Cwm Bargoed Jc, TBJ, 43C2
Cwm Blawd, LM, 7A3
Cwm Mawr, BPGV, 7A3
Cwm Prysor, GW, 19F4
Cwm-y-Glo, LNW, 19E2
Cwmaman, GW, 8B5; 43D2
Cwmavon (Glam), RSB, 7B4; 43F3
Cwmavon (Mon), GW, 8A4; 43A2
Cwmbran, GW, 8B3; 43A3
Cwmbran Jc, GW, 43A3
Cwmdu, PT, 7B5; 43E3
Cwmffrwd Halt, GW, 43A2
Cwmffrwdoer Halt, GW, 43A2
Cwmllynfell, Mid, 7A4; 43F1
Cwmsyfiog & Brithdir, BM, 43B2 ***see also*** Brithdir
Cyfronydd, W&L, 14B3
Cymmer, GW, RSB & SWM, 7B5; 43E3
Cynghordy, LNW, 14F5
Cynheidre, LM, 7A3
Cynonville Halt, RSB, 43E3
Cynwyd, GW, 19F5

Dacre, NE, 21B2
Dagenham, LTS, 5A4
Dagenham Dock, LTS, 5A4
Daggons Road, LSW, 3E5
Dailly, G&SW, 29G3
Daimler Halt, LNW, 10A5
Dairsie, NB, 34F4
Dairycoates (Goods), HB, 22 (inset)
Daisy Bank, GW, 13A1
Daisy Hill, LY, 20B2; 24F2; 45C2
Daisyfield, LY, 24D2
Dalbeattie, G&SW, 26C4
Dalchonzie Platform, Cal, 33F3
Dalcross, HR, 36D4
Dalegarth, RE, 26F2
Dalguise, HR, 33D4
Dalkeith, NB, 30C2
Dallam Branch Jc, LNW, 45D4
Dallow Lane Wharf, LNW, 15D5 (inset)
Dalmally, Cal, 32F2
Dalmarnock, Cal, 44D3
Dalmellington, G&SW, 29G4
Dalmeny, NB, 30B3
Dalmuir, Cal & NB, 29B4; 44G5
Dalnaspidal, HR, 33C2
Dalreoch, D&B, 29B3
Darby End Halt, GW, 13C1
Dalry, G&SW, 29D3

Dalry Jc, Cal, 30 (inset)
Dalry Jc, G&SW, 29D3
Dalry Road, Cal, 30 (inset)
Dalrymple, G&SW, 29F3
Dalrymple Jc, G&SW, 29F3
Dalserf, Cal, 30D5; 44A1
Dalston (Cumb), M&C, 26C1
Dalston Junc (London), NL(LNW), 40B4
Dalton, Fur, 24B4
Dalwhinnie, HR, 33B2
Dalzell Jc, Cal, 44A2
Dam Lane Jc, CLC, 20C2; 24G2; 45C3
Damems, Mid, 21D1
Dan-y-Graig, RSB, 7B4; 43F3
Danby, NE, 28F3
Danby Wiske, NE, 28G5
Dandaleith, GNS, 36D1
Danzey for Tanworth, GW, 9A5
Darcy Lever, LY, 45B2
Dare Jc, GW, 43D2
Dare Valley Jc, TV, 43D2
Daresbury, BJ, 15A1; 20C3; 45D4
Darfield, Mid, 21F4; 42E1
Darlaston, LNW, 13A2; 15F4
Darley, NE, 21C2
Darley Dale, Mid, 16B5; 41D1
Darlington, NE, 28F5
Darlington Works, NE, 28F5
Darnall for Handsworth, GC, 16A3; 21G4; 41A2; 42G1
Darran & Deri, Rhy(BM), 8B4; 43C2
Darras Hall, NE, 27B5
Darsham, GE, 12B2
Dartford, SEC, 5B5
Dartmouth (ferry service for Kingswear), GW, 2E3
Darton, LY, 21F3; 42D3
Darvel, G&SW, 29E5
Darwen, LY(Mid), 20A2; 24E2
Datchet, LSW, 5B1; 10G1
Dauntsey, GW, 9G4
Dava, HR, 36E3
Davenport, LNW, 15A3; 20C1; 21G1; 45A4
Daventry, LNW, 10B3
Davidson's Mains, Cal, 30B2
Daviot, HR, 36E4
Dawlish, GW, 2C3
Dawlish Warren, GW, 2C3
Day's Bridge Jc, GW, 3 (inset)
Daybrook, GN, 16C3; 41F5
Dduallt, Fest, 19F3
Deadwater, NB, 27A1; 31G1
Deal, SEC, 6C1
Dean, LSW, 4D5
Dean Lane, LY, 20B1; 24F1; 45A2
Deansgate Jc (Altrincham), CLC/MSJA, 45B4
Deanside (Goods), G&P, 44F4
Dearham Bridge, M&C, 26D3
Dearham, M&C, 26D3
Dearne Jc, SK, 21F4; 42E1
Deepcar, GC, 21F3; 42F3
Deepdale, PL & PWY, 24D3
Deepfields & Coseley, LNW, 13A1; 15F4
Deeping St James, GN, 17F2
Defford, Mid, 9C3
Defiance, GW, 1D5
Deganwy, LNW, 19C3
Deighton, LNW, 21E2; 42C4
Delabole, LSW, 1C3
Delamere, CLC, 15B1; 20D3
Delny, HR, 36C5
Delph, LNW, 21F1
Denaby, DV & HB, 21F4
Denbigh, LNW, 19D5
Denby Dale & Cumberworth, LY, 21F3; 42E3
Denby, Mid, 16C5; 41F2
Denham, GW&GCJt, 5A1; 10G1
Denham Golf Club Platform, GW&GCJt, 5A1; 10F1
Denhead, D&A, 34D3
Denholme, GN, 21D2; 42A5
Denmark Hill, LBSC(SEC), 40E4
Denny, Cal, 30B5
Denny Jc, Cal/K&B, 30B5
Dennyloanhead, K&B, 30 B5
Denstone Crossing, NS, 15C5
Dent, Mid, 24A1
Denton (Lancs), LNW(LY), 20C1; 21G1; 45A3
Denton Jc, LNW, 21G1
Denton Siding, GN, 16D2
Denver, GE, 11A4; 17F4
Deptford, SEC, 40D3
Deptford Wharf, LBSC, 40D3
Derby, Mid(LNW/NS) & GN, 16D5; 41G2
Derby Road (Ipswich), GE, 12D3
Dereham, GE, 18E4
Deri Jc, BM/Rhy, 8B4; 43C3
Derry Ormond, GW, 13E5
Dersingham, GE, 17D5
Derwen, LNW, 19E5
Derwenthaugh (Goods), NE, 28 (inset)
Derwydd Road, GW(LNW), 7A4; 13G5; 43G1
Desborough & Rothwell, Mid, 10A2; 16G2
Desford, Mid, 16F4
Dess, GNS, 34A3; 37G2
Detton Road Siding, CMDP, 9A2
Devil's Bridge, VR, 14C5
Devizes, GW, 3B5
Devonport, GW & LSW, 1D5 and inset
Devonport Jc, GW/LSW, 1A1 (inset)
Devons Road, NL & LNW, 40C3
Devynock & Sennybridge, N&B(Mid), 14F4
Dewsbury, GN, LNW, LY & Mid, 21E3; 42C3
Dewton Halt, LBSC, 6G5
Dicconson Lane & Aspull, LY, 20B2; 24F2; 45C2
Didcot, GW, 10F4
Didcot N & E Jcs, GW, 10F5
Didcot West Curve Jc, GW, 10F4
Didsbury, Mid, 20C1; 24G1; 45A3
Digby, GN&GEJt, 17C1
Diggle, LNW, 21F1
Diglake Jc, NS, 15C3; 20E1
Dinas (Merioneth), Fest, 19F3
Dinas (Rhondda), TV, 43D3
Dinas Junc (Carnarvon), LNW & NWNG, 19E2
Dinas Mawddwy, Mawd, 14A4
Dinas Powis, BRY, 8D4; 43B5
Dingestow, GW, 8A2; 9E1
Dingle Road Halt, TV, 43B5
Dingwall, HR, 35D5
Dinmore, S&H, 9B1
Dinnet, GNS, 34A4; 37G1
Dinnington & Laughton, SYJ, 16A4; 21G4; 41A4
Dinnington Colliery, SYJ, 41A4
Dinnington Jc, SYJ/GC&MidJt, 16A4; 21C4; 41A4
Dinnington South Jc, SYJ/GC&MidJt, 16A4
Dinsdale, NE, 28F5
Dinting, GC, 21G1
Dinton, LSW, 3C5
Dinwoodie, Cal, 26A3
Dipple (Goods), G&SW, 29G2
Dirleton, NB, 31B1
Disley, LNW, 15A4
Diss, GE, 12B4
Distington, WCE&CWJJt, 26E3
Ditchford, LNW, 10A1
Ditchingham, GE, 12A2; 18G2
Ditton, LNW, 15A1; 20C3; 24G3; 45E4
Ditton Priors, CMDP, 15G1
Dixon Fold, LY, 45B2
Dobbs Brow Jc, LY, 45C2
Dock Jc (Ely), GE, 11B4
Dock Street (Newport) Goods, GW, 43A3
Docking, GE, 17D5
Docks Branch Jc (Maryport), LNW, 26D3
Dockyard Halt, GW, 1A1
Doddington & Harby, GC, 16B2
Dodworth, GC, 21F3; 42E3
Doe Hill, Mid, 16B4; 41D3
Dogdyke, GN, 17C2
Dolau, LNW, 14D3
Doldowlod, Cam, 14D4
Doleham Halt, LBSC, 6E5
Dolgelley, GW(Cam), 14A5
Dolgoch, Tal, 13B5
Dollar, NB, 30A4; 33G4
Dollis Hill, Met, 39B4
Dolphinton, Cal & NB, 30D3
Dolwen, Cam, 14C4
Dolwyddelen, LNW, 19E3
Dolygaer, BM, 8A5; 43C1
Dolyhir, GW, 14E2
Dolywern, GVT, 20F5
Don Street, GNS, 37F4
Doncaster (Goods), GN, GC & Mid, 21F5 and inset G2
Doncaster (Pass), GN(GC/GE/LY/Mid/NE) & GC&HBJt, 21F5 and inset G2
Doncaster Works, GN, 21F5
Donington-on-Bain, GN, 17A2
Donington Road, GN&GEJt, 17D2
Donisthorpe, AN, 16E5
Donnington, LNW, 15E2
Dorchester, GW & LSW, 3F3
Dorchester Jc, GW/WP, 3F3
Dore & Totley, Mid, 16A5; 41A1
Dore South Jc, Mid, 16A5
Dorking, LBSC & SEC, 5C2

Dormans, LBSC, 5D4
Dornoch, HR, 36B4
Dornock, G&SW, 26B2
Dorrington, S&H, 14B1; 15F1
Dorstone, GW, 14F1
Doublebois, GW, 1D4
Douglas (IoM), IMR & ME, 23C2
Douglas (Lanark), Cal, 30E5
Douglas Derby Castle (IoM), MER, 23B3
Douglas West, Cal, 30E5
Doune, Cal, 33G3
Dousland, GW, 2C5
Dove Holes, LNW, 15A4
Dove Jc, NS/GN, 15D5
Dovecliffe, GC, 42E2
Dovecliffe for Worsborough, LY, 42E1
Dover, SEC, 6D2
Dover Marine, SEC, 6D2
Dover Priory, SEC, 6D2
Dovercourt Bay, GE, 12E3
Dovey Junc, Cam, 14B5
Dowlais, BM, LNW & TBJ, 8A5; 43C2
Dowlais Top, BM, 8A5; 43C1
Dowlow Halt, LNW, 15B5
Downfield Crossing Halt, GW, 9E3
Downham, GE, 17F4
Downton, LSW, 4D5
Doxey Rd (Goods), GN, 15E3
Dragon Jc, NE, 21C3
Drax, HB, 21E5
Drax Hales, NE, 21E5
Draycott (Derbys), Mid, 16D4; 41G3
Draycott (Som), GW, 3B2; 8 E2
Drayton (Norfolk), MGN, 18E3
Drayton (Sussex), LBSC, 4E1; 5F1
Drayton Green (Ealing) Halt, GW, 39C1
Drayton Jc, LNW/GN&LNWJt, 16G2
Drayton Park, GN, 40B5
Dreghorn, G&SW, 29E3
Drem, NB(NE), 30B1
Driffield, NE, 22C4
Drigg, Fur, 26F3
Drighlington & Adwalton, GN, 42B4
Droitwich, GW(Mid), 9B3
Droitwich Road (Goods), Mid, 9B3
Dronfield, Mid, 16A5; 41B2
Drongan, G&SW, 29F4
Dronley, Cal, 34E5
Drope Jc, BRY, 43C4
Droxford, LSW, 4D2
Droylsden, LY & LNW, 21F1 and inset A2; 45A3
Drum, GNS, 34A2; 37G3
Drumburgh, NB, 26C2
Drumchapel, NB, 44F4
Drumclog, Cal, 29E5
Drumlemble Halt, CM, 29 (inset)
Drumlithie, Cal, 34B2
Drummuir, GNS, 36D1
Drumshoreland, NB, 30B3
Drumvaich Crossing, Cal, 33G2
Drws-y-Nant, GW, 14A5; 19G4
Drybridge (Ayrshire), G&SW, 29E3; 37C1
Drybrook Road, SVW, 8A1; 9E2
Dryclough Jc, LY, 42C5
Dryffryn Jc, GW, 43E3
Drymen, NB, 29B4
Drypool (Goods), NE, 22 (inset)
Drysllwyn, LNW, 7A3; 13G5
Dubbs Jc, G&SW, 29D3
Dubton Junc, Cal, 34C3
Ducie Street Goods (Manchester), GC, 45A3
Dudbridge, Mid, 9E3
Dudding Hill Goods, Mid, 39B4
Duddingston & Craigmillar, NB, 30 (inset)
Dudley, GW, LNW(GW) & Mid, 13B2; 15G4
Dudley Hill, GN, 21D2; 42B4
Dudley Port, LNW, 13B2; 15G4
Dudworth (Goods), HB, 42D2
Duffield, Mid, 16C5; 41F2
Duffryn Rhondda Halt, RSB, 43E3
Dufftown, GNS, 36E1
Duffws, Fest, 19F3
Duirinish, HR, 35F1
Duke Street (Derby) Goods, GN, 41G2
Duke Street (Glasgow), NB, 44D4
Dukeries Junc, GN & GC, 16B2
Dukinfield, GC, 21A2 (inset)
Dukinfield & Ashton, LNW, 21A2 (inset)
Dulingham, GE, 11C4
Dullator, NB, 30B5
Dulverton, GW, 7F5
Dulwich, SEC, 40E4
Dumbarton, D&B, 29B3
Dumbarton (East), Cal, 29B4
Dumbreck (Goods), NB, 29B4
Dumfries, G&SW(Cal), G&SW & Cal, 26B3
Dumfries House, G&SW, 29F4
Dumgoyne, NB, 29B4
Dunball, GW, 3C1; 8E3
Dunbar, NB(NE), 31BI
Dunblane, Cal, 30A5; 33G3
Dunbridge, LSW, 4D4
Dunchurch, LNW, 10A4
Dundee (East), D&A, 34E4
Dundee (Tay Br), NB, 34E4
Dundee (West), Cal, 34E4
Dunfermline, NB, 30A3
Dunford Bridge, GC, 21F2; 42E4
Dungeness, SEC, 6E3
Dunham, GE, 18E5
Dunham Hill, BJ, 15A1; 20D3; 45E5
Dunham Massey, LNW, 15A2; 20C2; 24G2; 45B4
Dunhampstead (Goods), Mid, 9B3
Dunkeld & Birnham, HR, 33D4
Dunkerton, GW, 3B3; 8D1
Dunkerton Colliery Halt, GW, 3B3; 8D1
Dunlop, GBK, 29D4
Dunmere Halt, LSW, 1D3
Dunmore Jc, Cal, 30A5
Dunmow, GE, 11E4
Dunning, Cal, 33F4
Dunnington, DVL, 21C5
Dunnington Halt, DVL, 21C5
Dunphail, HR, 36D3
Dunragit, P&W, 25C2
Dunrobin (private), HR, 36A4; 38G5
Duns, NB, 31C2
Dunsbear (workmen), SR, 1A5
Dunscore, G&SW, 26A4
Dunsland Cross, LSW, 1A5
Dunstable (Goods), GN & LNW, 10D1; 11E1
Dunstable (Pass), GN(LNW) & LNW(GN), 10D1; 11E1
Dunstable Church Street, GN, 10D1; 11E1
Dunstall Park, GW, 15F3
Dunster, GW, 8E5
Dunston Jc, NE, 28 (inset)
Dunston-on-Tyne, NE, 28 (inset)
Dunston Staiths, NE 28 (inset)
Dunsyre, Cal, 30D3
Dunton Green, SEC, 5C4
Dunure, G&SW, 29F3
Dunvant, LNW, 7B3
Durham, NE, 27D5
Durham Ox Jc (Lincoln), GN/GC, 16B1 and inset; 17B1
Durley Halt, LSW, 4D3
Durnsford Road, 39F5
Duror, Cal, 32D3
Dursley, Mid, 8B1; 9F2
Durston, GW, 3D1; 8F3
Dyce, GNS, 37F4
Dyffryn Jc, PT, 43E3
Dyffryn, Cam, 13A5; 19G2
Dyke Junc Halt, LBSC, 5F3
Dykebar, Cal, 29C4
Dykehead Branch Jc, NB, 44A4
Dymock, GW, 9D2
Dynea Halt, AD, 43C3
Dysart, NB, 30A2
Dyserth, LNW, 19D5

Eaglescliffe, NE, 28E5
Ealing Broadway, GW, Dist & LE, 5B2; 39C2
Ealing Common, Dist, 39C3
Eamont Bridge Jc, LNW/NE, 27E1
Earby, Mid, 21C1; and inset
Eardington, GW, 15G2
Eardisley, Mid(GW), 14E2
Earith Bridge, GE, 11B3
Earlestown, LNW(BJ), 20C3; 24G2; 45D3
Earley, SEC(LSW), 4A2
Earls Colne, CVH, 12E5
Earls Court, Dist(LNW), 39D5
Earls Court Jc, Dist/WL/WLE, 39D4
Earlsfield for Summerstown, LSW, 5B3; 39E5
Earlsheaton, GN, 42C3
Earlston, NB, 31D1
Earlswood, LBSC, 5D3
Earlswood Lakes, GW, 9A5
Earsham, GE, 12A2; 18G2
Earswick, NE, 21C5
Easington, NE, 28D5
Easingwold, Eas, 21B4
Eassie, Cal, 34D5
East Acton, GW, 39C3
East Anstey, GW, 7F5
East Barkwith, GN, 17A2
East Boldon, NE, 28C5

East Brixton, LBSC, 40E5
East Budleigh, LSW, 2B2
East Calder (Goods), NB, 30C3
East Croydon, LBSC(SEC/LNW), 5C3
East Didsbury, LNW, 45A4
East Dulwich, LBSC, 40E4
East Farleigh, SEC, 6C5
East Finchley, GN(NL), 5A3; 39A5
East Fortune, NB, 31B1
East Garston, GW, 4A4; 10G5
East Gate Jc (Colchester), GE, 12E5
East Grinstead, LBSC, 5D4
East Halton, GC, 22E3
East Ham, LTS(Dist/Mid), 40B2
East Ham Loop North Jc, LTS, 40B2
East Horndon, LTS, 5A5
East India Dock Road Jc, NL, 40D1 (inset); 40C3
East India Docks Goods, GE, 40C2 and inset D1
East Jc (Colwich), LNW, 15E4
East Kent Light Railway, EK, 6C2
East Kilbride, Cal, 29D5; 44D2
East Langton, Mid, 16F3
East Leake, GC, 16D4
East Linton, NB, 31B1
East Malling Halt, SEC, 6C5
East Minster-on-Sea, SEC, 6B4
East Newport, NB, 34E4
East Norton, GN&LNWJt, 16F2
East Putney, LSW(Dist), 39E4
East Rudham, MGN, 18D5
East Smithfield Goods, GE, 40C4
East Southsea, LSW&LBSCJt, 4E2
East Street (Bridport), GW, 3F1
East Suffolk Jc, GE, 12D3
East Ville, GN, 17C3
East Winch, GE, 17E5
Eastbourne, LBSC, 5G5
Eastbury, GW, 4A4; 10G5
Eastchurch, SEC, 6B4
Eastcote, Met(Dist), 39Bl
Easter Road (Goods), NB, 30 (inset)
Easterhouse, NB, 44C3
Eastgate, NE, 27D3
Eastgrange, NB, 30A4
Easthaven, D&A, 34E3
Eastleigh & Bishopstoke, LSW(GW), 4D3
Eastleigh South Jc, LSW, 4D3
Eastleigh Works, LSW, 4D3
Eastoft, AJ, 22E5
Easton, ECH, 3G3
Easton Court, S&H, 9A1
Easton Lodge, GE, 11E4
Eastry, EK, 6C2
Eastry South, EK, 6C2
Eastwood (Yorks), LY, 21E1
Eastwood & Langley Mill, GN, 41F3 *see also* Langley Mill
Eaton, BC, 14C1
Ebberston, NE, 22A4
Ebbsfleet & Cliffsend Halt, SEC, 6B1
Ebbw Jc (Newport, Mon), GW, 8C3; 43A4
Ebbw Vale, GW & LNW, 8A4; 43B1
Ebchester, NE, 27C4
Ebdon Lane, WCP, 3A1; 8D3
Ebley Crossing Halt, GW, 9E3
Ecclefechan, Cal, 26B2
Eccles, LNW(BJ), 45B3
Eccles Road, GE, 12A4; 18G4
Ecclesfield, Mid & GC, 21G3; 42F2
Eccleshill, GN, 21D2; 42A4
Eccleston Park, LNW, 20C3; 24G3; 45E3
Eckington (Worcs), Mid, 9C3
Eckington & Renishaw, GC & Mid, 16A4; 41B3
Ecton, NS, 15B5
Edale, Mid, 15A5
Edderton, HR, 36B5
Eddleston, NB, 30D2
Eddlewood Jc, Cal, 44B1
Eden Park, SEC, 5B3; 40G3
Eden Valley Jc, LNW/NE, 27E1
Edenbridge, LBSC & SEC, 5D4
Edenbridge Town, LBSC, 5D4
Edenham & Little Bytham Railway, ELB, 16E1
Edge Hill, LNW, 45F4
Edge Lane, LNW, 45F4
Edgebold, S&M, 14A1; 15E1
Edgware, GN, 5A2
Edgware Road, Met(Dist/GW/H&C), 39C5
Edinburgh, Cal & NB, 30B2 and inset
Edington & Bratton, GW, 3B4
Edington Junc, SD, 3C1; 8E3
Edlingham, NE, 31F4
Edlington (Goods), DV, 21G2 (inset)
Edmondthorpe & Wymondham, Mid(MGN), 16E2
Edrom, NB, 31C2
Edwalton, Mid, 16D3; 41G5
Edwinstowe, GC, 16B3; 41C5
Edzell, Cal, 34C3
Efail Isaf, BRY, 8C5; 43C4
Effingham Junc, LSW, 5C2
Egerton Street Jc, CLC, 45F4 and inset G5
Eggesford, LSW, 2A5; 7G4
Egginton, NS&GNJt, 16D5
Egham, LSW, 5B1
Eglinton Street, Cal, GAP & G&SW, 44E3 and inset F1
Egloskerry, LSW, 1B4
Egremont (Cumberland), WCE, 26F3
Egton, NE, 28F2
Elbowend Jc, NB, 30B3
Elburton Cross, GW, 2E5
Elderslie, G&SW, 29C4; 44G3
Elephant & Castle, SEC, 40D5
Elford, Mid, 15E5
Elgin, GNS & HR, 36C2
Elgin Jc (Fife), NB, 30A3
Elham, SEC, 6D2
Elie, NB, 30A1; 34G4
Elland, LY, 21E2; 42C5
Elland Jc, LY, 42C5
Ellenbrook for Boothtown, LNW, 45B2
Ellerby, NE, 22D3
Ellesmere, Cam, 20F4
Ellesmere Port, BJ, 20D4; 45E5
Ellingham, GE, 12A2; 18G2
Elliot Junc, D&A, 34D3
Ellon, GNS, 37E4
Elmbridge, WUT, 17F4
Elmers End, SEC, 5B3; 40G4
Elmesthorpe, LNW(Mid), 16F4
Elmore Halt, LSW, 4E3
Elmstead Woods, SEC, 40F2
Elmswell, GE, 12C4
Elmton & Creswell, Mid, 16A4; 41B4 *see also* Creswell, GC
Elrington, NE, 27C3
Elsecar (Goods), GC, 42F2
Elsecar & Hoyland Common, Mid, 21F3; 42F2 *see also* Wentworth
Elsenham, GE, 11E4
Elsham, GC, 22F4
Elslack, Mid, 21C1; and inset
Elsted, LSW, 4D1
Elstree, Mid, 5A2; 11G2
Elswick, NE(NB), 28 (inset)
Eltham & Mottingham, SEC, 5B4; 40E2
Elton (Northants), LNW, 11A1; 17G1
Elton & Orston (Notts), GN, 16C2
Elvanfoot, Cal, 30F4
Elvet, NE, 28D5
Elvington (Kent), EK, 6C2
Elvington (Yorks), DVL, 21C5
Ely (Cambs), GE, 11B4
Ely (Glam), GW(BRY) & TV, 8C4; 43B4
Embleton, CKP, 26E2
Embo, HR, 36A4
Embsay, Mid, 21C1
Emerson Park Halt, LTS, 5A5
Emneth, GE, 17F4
Emsworth, LBSC, 4E1
Enborne Jc, GW, 4A3
Enderby, LNW&MidJt, 16F4
Endon, NS, 15C4
Enfield, GN, 5A3; 11G2
Enfield Lock, GE, 11G3
Enfield Town, GE, 5A3; 11G3
Enthorpe, NE, 22C4
Entwistle, LY, 20A2; 24E2; 45B1
Enzie, HR, 37C1
Epping, GE, 11G3
Epsom, LSW & LBSC, 5C2;
Epsom Downs, LBSC, 5C3
Epworth, AJ, 22F5 *see also* Haxey, GN&GEJt
Erdington, LNW, 15F5
Eridge, LBSC, 5D5
Erith, SEC, 5B4
Errol, Cal, 34E5
Erwood, GW, 14F3
Eryholme (Goods), NE, 28F5
Eryholme Jc, NE, 28F3
Escrick, NE, 21D5
Esgairgeiliog, Corris, 14B5
Esher & Claremont, LSW, 5B2; 39G1
Esholt, Mid(NE), 21D2
Esk Valley Jc, NB, 30C2
Eskbank, NB, 30C2
Eskbridge, NB, 30C2

Eskdale Green, RE, 26F2
Eskett (Goods), WCE, 26E3
Eskett Jc, WCE, 26E3
Eskmeals, Fur, 26G3
Esplanade (Dundee), NB, 34E4
Esplanade (Ryde, IoW), LSW&LBSCJt(IW/IWC), 4F3
Essendine, GN, 16E1; 17E1
Esslemont, GNS, 37E4
Eston, NE, 28E4
Etchingham, SEC, 6E5
Etherley, NE, 27E5
Etruria, NS, 15C3; 20F1
Ettingshall Rd & Bilston, LNW, 15F4 *see also* Bilston, GW
Ettington, SMJ, 10C5
Etwall, GN, 16D5
Euston, LNW, 5A3; 40C5
Euston Square, Met(Dist/GW/H&C), 40C5
Euxton (Goods), LY, 20A3; 24E2; 45D1 *see also* Balshaw Lane
Euxton Jc, LNW/LY, 20A3; 24E3
Eveningham, NE, 22D5
Evenwood, NE, 27E5
Evercreech (New), SD, 3C3; 8E1
Evercreech Junc, SD, 3C3; 8F1
Evershot, GW, 3E2
Evesham, GW & Mid, 9C4
Ewell, LSW & LBSC, 5C3
Ewesley, NB, 27A4; 31G4
Ewood Bridge, LY, 20A1; 24E1
Exchange (Liverpool), LY, 45F4 and inset G5
Exeter, GW(LSW), GW & LSW, 2B3
Exminster, GW, 2B3
Exmouth, LSW, 2C2
Exmouth Jc, LSW, 2B3
Exning Road Halr, GE, 11C4
Eyarth, LNW, 19E5; 20E5
Eydon Road Platform, GC, 10C4
Eye (Suffolk), GE, 12B3
Eye Green, MGN, 17F2
Eyemouth, NB, 31C3
Eynsford, SEC, 5C5
Eynsham, GW, 10E4
Eythorne, EK, 6C2

Facit, LY, 20A1; 24E1; 45A1
Factory Jc, SEC, 39F4 (inset)
Failsworth, LY, 20 B1; 45A2
Fairbourne, Cam, 13A5
Fairfield, GC, 45A3
Fairford, GW, 9F5
Fairlie, G&SW, 29D2
Fairlie Pier, G&SW, 29D2
Fairlop, GE, 5A4; 40A1
Fakenham, GE & MGN, 18D5
Falcon Jc, LBSC, 39F2 (inset)
Falcon Lane Goods, LNW, 39F3 (inset)
Falkirk, NB & Cal, 30B4
Falkirk (High), NB, 30B4
Falkirk Grahamstown, NB, 30B4
Falkland Jc, G&SW, 29F3
Falkland Road, NB, 34G5
Fallowfield, GC, 20C1; 24G1; 45A3
Falls of Cruachan Platform, CR, 32F3
Fallside, Cal, 44C3
Falmer, LBSC, 5F3
Falmouth, GW, 1F1
Falstone, NB, 27A2
Fambridge, GE, 6A4; 12G5
Fangfoss, NE, 22C5
Fareham, LSW, 4E3
Faringdon (Berks), GW, 10F5
Farington (Lancs), NU, 20A3; 24E3
Farlington, LBSC, 4E2
Farnborough, LSW & SEC, 4B1
Farncombe, LSW, 5D1
Farnell Road, Cal, 34C3
Farnham, LSW, 4C1
Farnham Jc, LSW, 4B1
Farningham Road & Sutton-at-Hone, SEC, 5B5
Farnley & Wortley, LNW, 21D3 and inset; 42A3
Farnsfield, Mid, 16B3; 41D5
Farnworth, CLC, 45D4
Farnworth & Bold, LNW, 20C3; 24G3; 45D4
Farnworth & Halshaw Moor, LY, 20B2; 24F1; 45B2
Farringdon (Goods) (Hants), LSW, 4C2
Farringdon Street, Met(Dist/GN/GW/Mid/H&C), 40C5
Farthinghoe, LNW(SMJ), 10C4
Fauldhouse & Crofthead, Cal & NB, 30C4
Faversham, SEC, 6C3
Faversham Jc, SEC, 6C3
Fawkham for Hartley & Longfield, SEC, 5B5
Fawley (Hereford), GW, 9D1
Fay Gate, LBSC, 5D3
Fazakerley, LY, 20B4; 24G4; 45F3
Fazakerley Jc, LY, 45F3
Fazakerley North Jc, LY, 45F3
Fearn, HR, 36B4
Featherstone, LY, 21E4; 42C1
Featherstone Park, NE, 27C2
Feeder Bridge Jc, GW, 3 (inset)
Felin Fach, GW, 13E5
Felin Foel, LM, 7B3
Felin Fran Halt, GW, 7B4; 43F2
Felin Hen, LNW, 19D2
Felixstowe, GE, 12E3
Felling, NE, 28 (inset)
Felmingham, MGN, 18D3
Felstead, GE, 11E5
Feltham, LSW, 5B2
Feltham Jc, LSW, 39E1
Fenay Bridge & Lepton, LNW, 21E2; 42D4
Fencehouses, NE, 28C5
Fenchurch Street, GE(LTS), 5B3; 40C4
Fencote, GW, 9B1
Fen Ditton Halt, GE, 11C3
Feniscowles, LU, 20A2; 24E2
Fenn's Bank, Cam, 15D1; 20F3
Fenny Bentley (Goods), LNW, 15C5
Fenny Compton, GW & SMJ, 10B4
Fenny Stratford, LNW, 10D2
Fenton, NS, 15C3; 20F1
Fenton Manor, NS, 15C3; 20F1
Ferguslie (Paisley) Goods, Cal & G&SW, 44G3
Ferndale, TV, 8B5; 43D2
Fernhill Heath, GW(Mid), 9B3
Ferniegair (Goods), Cal, 30D5; 44B2
Ferniegair Jc, Cal, 4B2
Ferriby, NE(GC), 22E4
Ferry (Cambs), MGN, 17E3
Ferry (Sussex), SL, 4F1
Ferrybridge for Knottingley, SK(GC/GN), 21E4; 42C1 *see also* Knottingley
Ferryhill (Durham), NE, 28D5
Ferryhill Jc (Aberdeen), Cal/GNS, 37G4
Ferryside, GW, 7A2
Festiniog, GW, 19F3
Festiniog Railway, Fest, 19F3
Ffairfach, GW(LNW), 13G5
Ffridd Gate, Cam, 14B5
Ffrith, WM, 20E4
Fidlers Ferry & Penketh, LNW, 15A1; 20C3; 24G3; 45D4
Fighting Cocks (Goods), NE, 28F5
Filey, NE, 22A3
Filleigh, GW, 7F4
Filton Junc, GW, 8Cl; 9G1
Finchley (Church End), GN(NL), 5A3; 39A5
Finchley Road, Met & Mid, 39B5
Finchley Road & Frognal, LNW(NL), 39B5
Findochty, GNS, 37C1
Finedon, Mid, 10A2
Fingask Platform, GNS, 37E3
Finghall Lane, NE, 21A2; 27G5
Finmere, GC, 10D3
Finnieston, NB, 44E4
Finningham, GE, 12C4
Finningley, GN&GEJt, 21F5
Finsbury Park, GN(NL), 5A3; 40B5
Firsby, GN, 17B3
Firsby South Jc, GN, 17B3
Fish Ponds, Mid, 3A3; 8C1
Fishbourne Halt, LBSC, 4E1
Fisherrow (Goods), NB, 30B2
Fishersgate Halt, LBSC, 5F3
Fishguard & Goodwick, GW, 13F1
Fishguard Harbour, GW, 13F1
Fiskerton, Mid, 16C3
Fittleworth, LBSC, 5E1
Five Ways (Staffs), LNW, 15E4
Five Mile House, GN, 17B1
Fladbury, GW, 9C4
Flamborough, NE, 22B3
Flax Bourton, GW, 3A2; 8D2
Flaxton, NE, 21B5
Flecknoe, LNW, 10B4
Fledborough, GC, 16B2
Fleet (Hants), LSW, 4B1
Fleet (Lincs), MGN, 17E3
Fleet Jc, GE, 12A2; 18F1
Fleetwood, PWY & LY, 24C4
Flemington, Cal, 30C5; 44A2
Fletton (Goods), GN, 11A2; 17G2
Flimby, LNW, 26D3
Flint, LNW, 20D5
Flitwick, Mid, 10D1; 11E1
Flixton, CLC, 20C2; 45B3

Flordon, GE, 12A3; 18F3
Floriston, Cal, 26C1
Flushdyke, GN, 21E3; 42C3
Fochabers Town, HR, 36C1
Fochriw, BM, 8A5; 43C2
Fockerby, AJ, 22E5
Fodderty Jc, HR, 35D5
Foggathorpe, NE, 22D5
Foleshill, LNW, 10A5; 16G5
Foley Park Halt, GW, 9A3
Folkestone, SEC Central, 6D2; Harbour, 6D2; Junction, 6D2
Fontburn Halt, NB, 27A4; 31G4
Forcett Depot, NE, 27F5
Forcett Jc, NE, 27E5
Ford & Crossgates (Salop), S&M, 14A1
Ford (Devon), LSW & GW, 1D5 and inset
Ford (Lancs), LY, 20B4; 24G4; 45F3
Ford Bridge, S&H, 9B1
Ford Green, NS, 15C3; 20E1
Ford Junc (Sussex), LBSC, 5F1
Forden, Cam, 14B2
Fordham, GE, 11B4
Fordingbridge, LSW, 4E5
Fordoun, Cal, 34B2
Foregate Street (Worcester), GW, 9B3
Forest Gate, GE, 40B2
Forest Gate Jc, GE/LTS, 40B2
Forest Hall, NE, 27B5
Forest Hill, LBSC, 40E4
Forest Mill, NB, 30A4
Forest Row, LBSC, 5D4
Forfar, Cal, 34D4
Forgandenny, Cal, 33F5
Forge Mills, Mid, 15F5
Forge Valley, NE, 22A4
Formby, LY(LNW), 20B4; 24F4; 45G2
Forncett, GE, 12A3; 18G3
Forres, HR, 36D3
Forrestfield, NB, 30C5
Forsinard, HR, 38E5
Fort Augustus, NB, 32A1; 35G4
Fort Brockhurst, LSW, 4E3
Fort George, HR, 36D4
Fort Gomer Halt, LSW, 4E3
Fort Matilda, Cal, 29B3
Fort William, NB, 32C3
Forteviot, Cal, 33F4
Fortrose, HR, 36D5
Forty Hill, GE, 11G3
Foryd, LNW, 19C5
Foryd Jc, LNW, 19C5
Foryd Pier, LNW, 19C5
Foss Cross, MSW, 9E4
Foss Island Jc, NE, 21A4 (inset)
Foss Islands (Goods), NE, 21A4 (inset)
Fotherby Halt, GN, 17A3; 22G2
Foulis, HR, 36C5
Foulridge, Mid, 21 (inset); 24D1
Foulsham, GE, 18E4
Fountain Bridge Halt, BM(Rhy), 43B3
Fountainhall Junc, NB, 30D1
Four Ashes, LNW, 15E3
Four Crosses, Cam, 14A2
Four Oaks, LNW, 15F5
Fourstones, NE, 27B3
Fowey, GW, 1D3
Foxdale, IMR, 23B2
Foxfield, Fur, 24A5
Foxhall Jc, GW, 10F4
Foxton, GE(GN), 11D3
Framlingham, GE, 12C3
Frankton, Cam, 20F4
Fransham, GE, 18E5
Frant, SEC, 5D5
Fraserburgh, GNS, 37C4
Fratton, LSW&LBSCJt, 4E2
Fremington, LSW, 7F3
French Drove, GN&GEJt, 17F3
Freshfield, LY(LNW), 20B4; 24F4; 45G2
Freshford, GW, 3B3
Freshwater, FYN, 4F4
Friargate (Derby), GN, 16D5; 41G2
Friary (Plymouth), LSW, 1 (inset)
Friary Jc, GW/LSW, 1 (inset)
Friary N, S & W Jcs, GW, 1 (inset)
Frickley, SK(GC), 21F4; 42D1
Frickley Colliery, SK(GC), 42D1
Friden (Goods), LNW, 15B5
Friezland, LNW, 21F1
Frimley, LSW, 4B1; 5C1
Frinton-on-Sea, GE, 12E3
Friockheim, Cal, 34D3
Frisby, Mid, 16E3
Frittenden Road, KES, 6D5
Fritwell & Somerton, GW, 10D4
Frizinghall, Mid, 21D2; 42A5
Frizington, WCE, 26F3
Frocester, Mid, 9E3
Frodingham & Scunthorpe, GC, 22F4 *see also* Scunthorpe
Frodsham, BJ, 15A1; 20D3; 45D5
Frodsham Jc, BJ/LNW, 15A1; 20D3; 45D5
Frome, GW, 3C3
Frongoch, GW, 19F4
Frosterley, NE, 27D4
Fryston (Goods), NE, 21E4; 42B1
Fulbar Street (Renfrew), G&SW, 44F4
Fulbourne, GE, 11C4
Fullerton, LSW(MSW), 4C4
Fullwood Jcs, Cal, 44B3
Fulwell (Middx), LSW, 5B2; 39F1
Fulwell & Westbury (Bucks), LNW, 10D3
Furness Abbey, Fur, 24B5
Furness Vale, LNW, 15A4
Fushiebridge, NB, 30C2
Fyling Hall, NE, 28F1
Fyvie, GNS, 37E3

Gadly's Jc, GW/TV, 8A5; 43D2
Gaer Jc, GW, 43A3
Gaerwen, LNW, 19D2
Gailes, G&SW, 29E3
Gailey, LNW, 15E3
Gainford, NE, 27E5
Gainsborough, GC & GN&GEJt, 16A2; 22G5
Gainsborough N & S Jcs, GC/GN&GEJt, 16A2; 22G5
Gairlochy, NB, 32B2
Gaisdale, NE, 28F2
Galashiels, NB, 30E1
Galgate, LNW, 24C3
Gallions, PLA(GE), 40C1
Gallowgate, G&SW, 44 (inset)
Galston, G&SW, 29E4
Galton Jc, GW, 13C2
Gamlingay, LNW, 11D2
Gannow Jc, LY, 24D1
Ganton, NE, 22A4
Gara Bridge, GW, 2D4
Garelochhead, NB, 29A3
Garforth, NE, 21D4; 42A1
Gargrave, Mid, 21C1
Gargunnock, NB, 29A5
Garlieston, P&W, 25D4
Garmouth, GNS, 36C1
Garn-yr-erw, LNW(GW), 43B1
Garnant, GW, 7A4; 43F1
Garnant Halt, GW, 43F1
Garndiffaith, LNW, 43A2
Garneddwen, Cor, 14A5
Garngad, NB, 44D4
Garnkirk, Cal, 29C5; 44C4
Garnqueen North Jc, Cal, 44B4
Garnqueen South Jc, Cal/NB, 44B4
Garrochburn (Goods), G&SW, 29E4
Garstang & Catterall, LNW(KE), 24D3
Garstang Town, KE, 24D3
Garston, CLC & LNW, 20C4; 45E4
Garston Dock, LNW, 20C4; 45E4
Garswood, LNW, 20B3; 24F3; 45D3
Gartcosh, Cal, 44C4
Gartcosh Jc, Cal, 44C4
Garth, LNW, 14E4
Garth & Van Road, Van, 14C4
Gartly, GNS, 37E1
Gartmore, NB, 29A4
Gartness, NB, 29B4
Garton, NE, 22C4
Gartsherrie Cal, 44B4 *see also* Blairhill
Gartshore (Goods), NB, 29B5; 44B5
Garve, HR, 35C4
Gascoigne Wood Jc, NE, 21D4
Gask Jc, NB, 30A3
Gasworks Jc, LSW, 3F5
Gateacre, CLC, 20C4; 24G3; 45E4
Gatehead, G&SW, 29E4
Gatehouse-of-Fleet, P&W, 25C5
Gateshead, NE, 28 (inset)
Gateside, NB, 33F5
Gatewen Halt, GW, 20E4
Gathurst, LY, 20B2; 24F3; 45D2
Gatley, LNW, 45A4
Gatwick Racecourse, LBSC, 5D3
Gavell, NB, 29B5
Gayton Road, MGN, 17E5
Geddington, Mid, 16G2
Gedling & Carlton, GN, 16C3; 41F5
Gedney, MGN, 17E3

Geldeston, GE, 12A2; 18G2
Gelli Halt, TV, 43D3
Gelly Tarw Jc, GW, 8A5; 43D2
General Terminus Goods (Glasgow), Cal, 44E3 and inset F2
George Lane, GE, 5A4; 40A2
Georgemas, HR, 38C3
Georgemas Jc, HR, 38C3
Gerrards Cross, GW&GCJt, 5A1; 10F1
Gidea Park, GE, 5A4;
Giffen, Cal, 29D3
Giffnock, Cal, 44E2
Gifford, NB, 31C1
Giggleswick, Mid, 24B1
Gildersome, GN & LNW, 21D3; 42B3
Gileston, BRY, 8D5; 43D5
Gilfach, GW, 8B5; 43D3
Gilfach Fargoed Halt, Rhy, 43B2
Gillett's Crossing Halt, PWY, 24D4
Gillfoot (Goods), WCE, 26
Gilling, NE, 21A5
Gillingham (Dorset), LSW, 3D4
Gillingham (Kent), SEC, 6B5
Gilmerton, NB, 30C2
Gilmour Street (Paisley), G&P, 44G3
Gilnockie, NB, 26B1
Gilsland, NE, 27B1
Gilwern, LNW, 8A4; 43B1
Gipsy Hill, LBSC(LNW), 40F4
Girvan, G&SW, 29G2
Gisburn, LY, 24C1
Glais, Mid, 7B4; 43F2
Glaisdale, NE, 28F2
Glaisgill, NE, 27F2
Glamis, Cal, 34D5
Glan Conway, LNW, 19D4
Glan-y-Llyn, Car, 43C4
Glanamman, GW, 7A4; 43F1
Glandyfi, Cam, 14B5
Glanrafon, VR, 13C5
Glanrhyd, VT, 14G5
Glanton, NE, 31F4
Glanyrafon, Tan, 14A2; 20G5
Glapwell, Mid, 16B4; 41C3
Glasbury-on-Wye, Mid, 14F2
Glasgow (Goods), Cal, GBK, G&P, G&SW, & NB, 29 –; 44 –
Glasgow (Pass), Cal, G&SW & NB, 29 –; 44 –
Glasgow Cross, Cal, 44D4 and inset E2
Glasgow Green, Cal, 44D3 and inset E2
Glassaugh, GNS, 37C2
Glassel, GNS, 34A3; 37G2
Glassford, Cal, 29D5
Glasson Dock, LNW, 24C3
Glasson Plat, NB, 26C2
Glasterlaw, Cal, 34D3
Glastonbury & Street, SD, 3C2; 8E2
Glazebrook & Bury Lane, CLC, 20C2; 45C3
Glazebrook Moss Jc, CLC/GC, 20C2; 24G2; 45C3
Glazebury, LNW(BJ), 20B2; 24G2; 45C3
Glemsford, GE, 12D5
Glen Douglas Platform, 29A3
Glen Parva, LNW, 16F4
Glenbarry, GNS, 37D1
Glenboig, Cal, 30C5; 44B4
Glenbuck, Cal, 30E5
Glenburnie Jc, NB, 34F5
Glencarron Platform, HR, 35D2
Glencarse, Cal, 33F5
Glencorse, NB, 30C2
Glencruiten Crossing, Cal, 32E4
Glendon & Rushton, Mid, 10A2; 16G2
Glendon South Jc, Mid, 10A2; 16A2
Gleneagles, Cal, 33F4
Glenfarg, NB, 33F5
Glenfield (Leicester), Mid, 16F4
Glenfield Goods (Paisley), Cal, 44G3
Glenfinnan, NB, 32B4
Glengarnock, G&SW & Cal, 29D3
Gleniffer (Goods), G&SW, 44G2
Glenluce, P&W, 25C3
Glenside, G&SW, 29F3
Glenwhilly, G&SW, 25B2
Glodwick Road (Oldham), LNW(GC), 21F1 and inset D1
Glodwick Road, LNW, 21D1
Glogue, GW, 13F3
Glossop, GC, 21G1
Gloucester, GW & Mid, 9E3
Gloucester Road (London), Dist & Met(Dist), 39D5
Glyn Abbey, BPGV, 7A2
Glyn Neath, GW, 7A5; 43E2
Glyn Valley Tramway, GVT, 20F5
Glynceiriog, GVT, 20F5
Glyncorrwg, SWM, 43E2
Glynde, LBSC, 5F4
Glyndyfrdwy, GW, 20F5
Glyntaff Halt, AD, 43C3
Gnosall, LNW, 15E3; 20G2
Goathland, NE, 28F2
Gobowen, GW, 20F4
Gobowen Jc, 20F4
Godalming, LSW, 5D1
Godley, GC & CLC, 21G1
Godmanchester, GN&GEJt(Mid), 11B2
Godshill, IWC, 4G3
Godstone, SEC, 5D3
Godwin's Halt, Mid, 10G1; 11F1
Gogar, NB, 30B3
Golant, GW, 1D3
Golborne, LNW & GC, 20B2; 24F2; 45D3
Golborne Jc, LNW, 20B2; 24F1; 45D3
Golcar, LNW, 21E2; 42D5
Golden Grove, LNW, 13G5
Golden Hill Platform (Pembroke), GW, 7D2
Goldhawk Road, H&C, 39D4
Goldsborough, NE, 21C4
Golf Club House Halt, GNS, 37C2
Golf Club Platform, LBSC, 5F3
Golfa, W&L, 14B2
Gollanfield Junc, HR, 36D4
Golspie, HR, 36A4
Golynos Jc, GW/LNW, 43A2
Gomersal, LNW, 21E2; 42B4
Gomshall & Shere, SEC, 5D2
Goole, NE(GC/LY), 22E5
Goonbell Halt, GW, 1E1
Goonhavern Halt, GW, 1D1
Goose Green Jc, LNW, 45D2
Goose Hill Jc, Mid/LY, 42C2
Goostrey, LNW, 15B3; 20D1
Gorbals, GBK, 44E3 and inset E1
Gordon, NB, 31D1
Gorebridge, NB, 30C2
Goring & Streatley, GW, 10G3
Goring-by-Sea, LBSC, 5F2
Gorleston Links Halt, GE, 18F1
Gorleston North, NSJ, 18F1
Gorleston-on-Sea, NSJ, 18F1
Gors-y-Garnant Halt, GW, 43G1
Gorseinon, LNW, 7B3
Gortan, NB, 32D1
Gortan Crossing, NB, 32D1
Gorton, GC, 45A3
Gosberton GN&GEJt, 17D2
Gosford Green, LNW, 10A5
Gospel Oak, LNW(NL) & THJ, 39B5; 40C1 (inset)
Gosport, LSW, 4E2
Goswick, NE, 31D4
Gotham, GC, 16D4
Gotham Jc, GC, 16D4
Gotherington, GW, 9D4
Goudhurst, SEC, 6D5
Gourdon, NB, 34B2
Gourock, Cal, 29B3
Govan, G&P, 29C4; 44E4
Govilon, LNW, 8A4; 43A1
Gowdall Jc, HB, 21E5
Gowerton, LNW, 7B3
Goxhill, GC, 22E3
Grace Dieu Halt, LNW, 16E4
Grafham, Mid, 11B1
Grafton & Burbage, MSW, 4B5
Grafton Jc, GW/MSW, 4B5
Grahamston (Falkirk), NB(Cal), 30B4
Grain Crossing Halt, SEC, 6B4
Grainsby Halt, GN, 22F2
Grampound Road, GW, 1E2
Grandborough Road, Met&GCJt, 10D3
Grandtully, HR, 33D4
Grane Road (Goods), LY, 20A1; 24E1
Grange, GNS, 7D1
Grange Court, GW, 8A1; 9E2
Grange Lane, GC, 42F2
Grange North Jc, GNS, 37D1
Grange Park, GN, 5A3, 11G2
Grange-over-Sands, Fur, 24B3
Grange Road, LBSC, 5D3
Grangemouth, Cal(NB), 30B4
Grangetown (Glam), TV(BRY), 8C4; 43C4
Grangetown (Yorks), NE, 28
Grantham, GN, 16D1
Granton, Cal & NB, 30B2 and inset
Granton Jc, Cal/NB, 30 (inset)
Granton Road, Cal, 30 (inset)
Grantown-on-Spey, HR & GNS, 36F3
Grantshouse, NB, 31C2

Grasscroft, LNW, 21F1
Grassington & Threshfield, Mid, 21B1
Grassmoor, GC, 16B5; 41C2
Grassmoor Jc, GE/GN&GEJt, 11A3; 17F3
Grateley, LSW, 4C5
Gravel Hill, GW, 1D1
Gravelly Hill, LNW, 15F5
Graveney (Goods), SEC, 6C3
Gravesend Central, SEC, 5B5
Gravesend West Street, SEC, 5B5
Grayrigg, LNW, 27G1
Grays, LTS, 5B5
Great Alne, GW, 9B5
Great Ayton, NE, 28F4
Great Barr, LNW, 13B3; 15F4
Great Barr/Perry Barr North Jc, LNW, 13B3
Great Bentley, GE, 12E4
Great Bridge, GW & LNW, 13B2 (inset)
Great Bridgeford, LNW(NS), 15D3; 20G1
Great Broughton (Goods), CWJ, 26D3
Great Chesterford, GE, 11D4
Great Coates, GC, 22F2
Great Dalby, GN&LNWJt, 16E2
Great Eastern Goods (Smithfield), GE, 40C4
Great Glen, Mid, 16F3
Great Harwood, LY, 24D1
Great Harwood Jc, LY, 24D2
Great Haywood Halt, NS, 15E4
Great Horton, GN, 21D2; 42A5
Great Houghton, DV, 42E1
Great Howard Street (Liverpool) Goods, LY, 45 (inset)
Great Linford, LNW, 10C2
Great Longstone for Ashford, Mid, 15B5
Great Malvern, GW(Mid), 9C3
Great Missenden, Met&GCJt, 10F2
Great Moor Street (Bolton), LNW, 45C2
Great Ormesby, MGN, 18E1
Great Ponton, GN, 16D1
Great Portland Street, Met(Dist/GW/H&C), 39C5
Great Shefford, GW, 4A4; 10G5
Great Somerford, GW, 9G4
Great Western Road (Glasgow), NB, 44E4
Greatham, NE, 28E4
Gree (Goods), Cal, 29D4
Green Ayre (Lancaster), Mid, 24B3
Green Lane, Mer, 45F4
Green Lane Jc, GW, 39C1 (inset)
Green Road, Fur, 24A5
Green's Siding, GW, 14F2
Greenfield, LNW, 21F1
Greenford, GW, 5A2; 39B1
Greengairs (Goods), NB, 30C5; 44A5
Greenham Castle (Goods), G&SW, 29F3
Greenhead, NE, 27B2
Greenhill, Cal, 30B5
Greenhithe, SEC, 5B5
Greenlaw, NB, 31D2
Greenloaning, Cal, 33G3
Greenmount, LY, 20A1; 24E1; 45B1
Greenock, Cal & G&SW, 29B3
Greenock West, Cal, 29B3
Greenodd, Fur, 24A4
Greenside (Pudsey), GN, 21D2; 42A4
Greenside Jc (Coatbridge), NB, 44B4
Greenwich, SEC, 5B4; 40D3
Greenwich Park, SEC, 40D3
Greetland, LY, 21E2; 42C5
Greetwell Jc, GN/GN&GEJt, 16B1; 17B1
Grendon Underwood Jc, GC, 10D3
Gresford, GW, 20E4
Gresley, Mid(LNW), 16E5
Gretna, Cal & NB, 26B1
Gretna Green, G&SW, 26B1
Gretna Jc, NB, 26B1
Gretton (Northants), Mid, 16F1
Gretton Hall (Glos), GW, 9D4
Griffith's Crossing, LNW, 19D2
Grimes Hall & Wythall Halt, GW, 9A5
Grimes Hill Platform, GW, 9A5
Grimethorpe, Mid&GCJt & DV, 21F4
Grimoldby, GN, 17A3; 22G1
Grimsargh, PL, 24D2
Grimsby Docks, GC(GN), GC & GN, 22F2
Grimsby Town, GC(GN), GC & GN, 22F2
Grimston, Mid, 16E3
Grimston Road, MGN, 17E5
Grimstone & Frampton, GW, 3F3
Grindleford, Mid, 16A5; 41B1
Grindley, GN, 15D4
Grindon, NS, 15C5
Grinkle, NE, 28E3
Gristhorpe, NE, 22A3
Groeslon, LNW, 19E2
Groeswen Halt, AD, 43C3
Grogley Halt, LSW, 1D2
Groombridge, LBSC, 5D5
Grosmont, NE, 28F2
Grotton, LNW, 21F1
Grove Ferry, SEC, 6C2
Grove Jc, SEC/LBSC, 5D5
Grove Park, SEC, 5B4; 40E2
Grovesend, LNW, 7B3
Guard Bridge, NB, 34F4
Guay, HR, 33D4
Guestwick, MGN, 18D4
Guide Bridge, GC(LNW) & LNW, 21A2 (inset); 45A3
Guild Street Jc, Mid, 15D5
Guildford, LSW(LBSC&SEC), 5C1
Guisborough, NE, 28E3
Guiseley, Mid(NE), 21D2
Gullane, NB, 30B1
Gunheath, GW, 1D2
Gunhouse Wharf, GC, 22F5
Gunnersbury, LSW(Dist/NL), 39D3
Gunness (Goods), GC, 22F5
Gunnislake, BAC, 1C5
Gunton, GE, 18D3
Gurnos (Goods), Mid, 7A4; 43F1
Guthrie, Cal, 34D3
Guyhirne, GN&GEJt, 17F3
Gwaun-cae-Gurwen Halt, GW, 43F1
Gwernydomen Halt, BM(Rhy), 43B3
Gwersyllt & Wheatsheaf, GC, 20E4
Gwersyllt Hill Halt, GW, 20E4
Gwinear Road, GW, 1(inset)
Gwyddelwern, LNW, 19F5
Gwys, Mid, 7A4; 43F1
Gyfeillon Halt, TV, 43C3
Gypsy Hill, LBSC, 40F4

Habrough, GC, 22E3
Hackbridge, LBSC, 5C3; 39G5
Hackney Downs, GE, 5A3; 40B4
Hackney, NL, 40B3
Hackney Wick Goods, GN, 40B3
Haddenham (Bucks), GW&GCJt, 10E3
Haddenham (Cambs), GE, 11B3
Haddington, NB, 30B1
Haddiscoe, GE, 12A2; 18F1
Hadham, GE, 11F3
Hadleigh, GE, 12D4
Hadley, LNW, 15E2
Hadley Wood, GN(NL), 11G2
Hadlow Road, BJ, 20D4; 45F5
Hadnall, LNW, 15E1; 20G3
Hadneld, GC, 21G1
Haggerston, NL, 40B4
Hagley, GW, 9A3
Hagley Road, LNW, 13C3
Haigh, LY, 21F3; 42D3
Haigh Jc, LNW/LU, 20B3; 24F2; 45D2
Hailsham, LBSC, 5F5
Hairmyres, Cal, 29D5; 44D1
Hainton Street Halt, GN, 22F2
Halbeath, NB, 30A3
Hale, CLC(LNW), 20C1; 24G1; 45B4
Halebank, LNW, 15A1; 20C3; 45E4
Halesowen, GW(Mid), 9A4; 15G4
Halesworth, GE & SWD, 12B2
Halewood, CLC, 15A1; 20C3; 24G3; 45E4
Halifax, LY(GN), LY, HO, HHL & GN, 21E2; 42B5/C5
Halkirk, HR, 38D3
Hall Farm Jc, GE, 40A3
Hall Green, GW, 9A5; 15G5
Hall Road, LY(LNW), 20B4; 24F4; 45F2
Hall Royd Jc, LY, 21E1
Hallaton, GN&LNWJt, 16F2
Hallatrow, GW, 3B3; 8D1
Halling, SEC, 6C5
Hallington, GN, 17A2; 22G2
Halliwell (Goods), LY, 45B1
Halls Tramway Jc, GW, 8B4; 43B3
Halmerend, NS, 15C3; 20E1
Halsall, LY, 20B4; 24F4; 45F2
Halstead (Essex), CVH, 11E5
Halton (Ches), BJ, 15A1; 20D3; 45D5
Halton (Lancs), Mid, 24B3
Halton, Mid, 24B3
Halton Holgate, GN, 17B3
Halton Jc (Ches), LNW, 15A1; 20C3; 45D5
Haltwhistle, NE, 27B2
Halwill Junc & Beaworthy, LSW, 1B5
Ham Bridge Halt, LBSC, 5F2
Ham Lane, WCP, 3A1; 8D3
Ham Mill Crossing Halt, GW, 9F3
Ham Street & Orlestone, SEC, 6D4

Hambleton, NE, 21D5
Hamilton Square (Birkenhead), Mer, 45F4
Hamilton, Cal & NB, 30D5; 44B2
Hammersmith & Chiswick, NSW, 39D3
Hammersmith Branch Jcs, GW & NSW, 39D3
Hammersmith Broadway, Dist & H&C, 39D4
Hammerton, NE, 21C4
Hammerwich, LNW, 15F4
Hampden Park, LBSC, 5F5
Hampole, WRG, 21F4
Hampstead Heath, LNW(NL), 39B5; 40C1 (inset)
Hampstead Norris, GW, 4A3; 10G4
Hampstead Road Jc, LNW, 40A1 (inset)
Hampsthwaite, NE, 21C3
Hampton, LSW, 5B2; 39F1
Hampton Court, LSW, 5B2; 39G2
Hampton Court Jc, LSW, 5B2, 9G1
Hampton-in-Arden, LNW & Mid, 9A5; 15G5
Hampton Loade, GW, 15G2
Hampton Wick, LSW, 39F2
Hamworthy (Goods), LSW, 3F5
Hamworthy Junc, LSW, 3F5
Handborough, GW, 10E4
Handforth, LNW, 15A3; 20C1; 45A4
Handsworth & Smethwick, GW, 13B3
Handsworth Jc, LNW, 13B3
Handsworth Wood, LNW, 13B3
Hanley, NS, 15C3; 20E1
Hannington, GW, 9F5
Hanwell & Elthorne, GW, 5B2; 39C2
Hanwood, SWP, 9A4; 14A1; 15E1
Hapton, LY, 24D1
Harborne, LNW, 13C3; 15G4
Harborne Jc, LNW, 13C3
Harbour Branch Jc (Arbroath), Cal/NB, 34D3
Harburn, Cal, 30C3
Harby & Stathern, GN&LNWJt, 16D2
Hardham Jc, LBSC, 5F1
Hardingham, GE, 18F4
Hardwick Road (Goods), MGN, 17E5
Hare Park & Crofton, WRG, 21E3; 42C2 *see also* Crofton
Hare Park Jc, 42C2
Harecastle, NS, 15C3; 20E1
Haresfield, Mid, 9E3
Hareston, GE, 12B3; 18G3
Harker, NB, 26C1
Harlech, Cam, 19F2
Harlesden, LNW(LE) & Mid, 39B3
Harlesford, GE, 12C2
Harling Road, GE, 12A4; 18G4
Harlington (Beds), Mid, 10D1; 11E1
Harlington (Yorks), DV, 21F4
Harlow, GE, 11F3
Harmston, GN, 16B1
Harold Wood, GE, 5A5
Harpenden, Mid & GN, 11F1
Harpenden Jc, Mid, 11F1
Harperley, NE, 27D4
Harpur Hill, LNW, 15B4
Harrietsham, SEC, 6C4
Harringay, GN(NL), 40A5
Harringay Park, THJ(LTS), 40A5
Harrington, LNW, 26E3
Harringworth, Mid, 16F1
Harrogate, NE(Mid/GN), 21C3
Harrow & Wealdstone, LNW(LE), 5A2; 39A2
Harrow-on-the-Hill, Met&GCJt, 5A2; 39A2
Harston, GE(GN), 11D3
Hart, NE, 28D4
Hartfield, LBSC, 5D4
Hartford, LNW, 15B2; 20D2; 45C5
Hartford & Greenbank, CLC(LNW), 15B2; 20D2; 45C5
Hartford Jc, CLC/LNW, 45C5
Hartington, LNW, 15B5
Hartlebury, GW, 9A3
Hartlepool, NE, 28D4
Hartley, NE, 28B5
Harton Road, GW, 15G1
Harts Hill, GW, 15G3
Hartshill & Basford Halt, NS, 20F1
Hartwood, Cal, 30C5
Harty Road Halt, SEC, 6B3
Harvington, Mid, 9C4
Harwich, GE, 12E3
Hasland (Goods), Mid, 16B5; 41C2
Haslemere, LSW, 4C1
Haslingden, LY, 20A1; 24E1
Hassall Green, NS, 15B3; 20E1
Hassendean, NB, 31F1
Hassocks, LBSC, 5F3
Hassop, Mid, 15B5
Hastings, SEC(LBSC), 6F5
Haswell, NE, 28D5
Hatch, GW, 3D1; 8G3
Hatch End, LNW(LE), 5A2
Hatfield (Herts), GN, 11F2
Hatfield Moor Depot, AJ, 22F5
Hatfield Peverel, GE, 11F5
Hatherley Curve Jc, GW, 9D3
Hathern, Mid, 16D4
Hathersage, Mid, 15A5
Hatton (Aberdeen), GNS, 37E5
Hatton (Warwicks), GW, 9B5
Haugh Mead Jc, Cal, 44B2
Haughley, GE & MSL, 12C4
Haughton, LNW, 15E3; 20G1
Havant, LBSC(LSW), 4E2
Haven Street, IWC, 4F3
Havenhouse, GN, 17B4
Haverfordwest, GW, 7C2
Haverhill, GE & CVH, 11D5
Haverthwaite, Fur, 24A4
Haverton Hill, NE, 28E4
Hawarden, GC, 20D4
Hawes, Mid&NEJt, 27G3
Hawes Junction & Garsdale, Mid(NE), 24A1; 27G2
Hawick, NB, 31F1
Hawkesbury Lane, LNW, 16G5
Hawkhead, G&SW, 44F3
Hawkhill Jc, G&SW, 29F3
Hawkhurst, SEC, 6E5
Haworth, Mid, 21D1
Hawsker, NE, 28F2
Hawthornden, NB, 30C2
Haxby, NE, 21C5
Haxey & Epworth, GN&GEJt, 22F5
Haxey Junc, AJ, 22F5
Haxey Town, AJ, 22F5
Hay, Mid(GW), 14F2
Hayburn Wyke, NE, 28G1
Haydock, GC, 20B3; 24F3; 45D3
Haydock Park Racecourse, GC, 45D3
Haydon Bridge, NE, 27B3
Haydon Square Goods, LNW, 40C4
Haydons Road, LBSC&LSWJt, 39F5
Hayes (Kent), SEC, 5C4; 40G2
Hayes & Harlington (Middx), GW, 5B2
Hayfield, GC&MidJt, 15A4; 21G1
Hayle, GW, 1E4 (inset)
Hayling Island, LBSC, 4E2
Haymarket (Edinburgh), NB, 30 (inset)
Haywards Heath, LBSC, 5E3
Haywood, Cal, 30C4
Hazel Grove, LNW & Mid, 15A4; 20C1; 21G1; 45A4
Hazelwell, Mid, 9A4
Hazelwood, Mid, 16C5; 41F1
Hazlehead Bridge, GC, 21F2; 42E4
Heacham, GE, 17D5
Headcorn, SEC & KES, 6D5
Headingley, NE, 21D3; 42A3
Heads Nook, NE, 27C1
Heads of Ayr, G&SW, 29F3
Heald Green, LNW, 15A3; 20C1; 24G1; 45A4
Healey House, LY, 21F2; 42D5
Healing, GC, 22F2
Heanor, Mid & GN, 16C4; 41F3
Heap Bridge (Goods), LY, 20B1; 24F1; 45A1
Heapey, LU, 20A2; 24E2; 45D1
Heath (Derbys), GC, 16B4; 41C3
Heath Halt (Glam), Car, 43B4
Heath Jc, Rhy/Car, 8C4; 43B4
Heath Park Halt, Mid, 10E1; 11F1
Heath Town Jc, LNW, Mid, 15E3 (inset)
Heather & Ibstock, AN, 16E5
Heathey Lane Halt, LY, 20A4; 24E4; 45F1
Heathfield (Devon), GW, 2C4
Heathfield (Sussex), LBSC, 5E5
Heatley & Warburton, LNW, 15A1; 20C2; 24G2; 45C4
Heaton, NE, 28 (inset)
Heaton Chapel, LNW, 45A3
Heaton Lodge Jc, LY/LNW, 42C4
Heaton Mersey, Mid, 20C1; 24G1; 45A4
Heaton Norris, LNW, 45A3
Heaton Park, LY, 20B1; 24F1; 45A2
Hebburn, NE, 28B5
Hebden Bridge, LY, 21E1
Heck, NE, 21E5
Heckington, GN, 17C2
Heckmondwike, LY & LNW, 21E2; 42C4
Heckmondwike Jc, LNW, 42C4
Heddon-on-the-Wall, NE, 27B5
Hedgeley, NE, 31F4
Hednesford, LNW, 15E4
Hedon, NE, 22E3
Heeley, Mid, 16A5; 41A2

Heighington (Durham), NE, 27E5
Hele & Bradninch, GW, 2A3
Helensburgh, NB, 29B3
Helensburgh Upper, NB, 29B3
Hellaby (Goods), GC&Mid&HBJt, 21G4
Hellesdon, MGN, 18F3
Hellifield, Mid(LY) & Mid, 24C1
Hellingly, LBSC, 5F5
Hellingly Hospital, HH, 5F5
Helmdon, GC & SMJ, 10C3
Helmsdale, HR, 38F4
Helmshore, LY, 20A1; 24E1
Helmsley, NE, 21A5
Helpringham, GN&GEJt, 17D1
Helpston, Mid, 17F1
Helsby, BJ & CLC, 15A1; 20D3; 45E5
Helston, GW, 1F5 (inset)
Hemel Hempsted, Mid, 10E1; 11F1 *see also* Boxmoor
Hemingborough, NE, 21D5
Hemsby, MGN, 18E1
Hemsworth, WRG, 21E4; 42D1
Hemsworth & South Kirkby, HB, 21E4; 42D1
Hemsworth Colliery, BL, 42D1
Hemsworth Jc, HB/WRG, 42D1
Hemyock, GW, 2A2; 8G4
Henbury, GW, 8C2; 9G1
Hendon, Mid, 5A3; 39A4
Hendreforgan, GW, 8B5; 43D3
Henfield, LBSC, 5F2
Hengoed, GW & Rhy, 8B4; 43B3 *see also* Maesycwmmer
Henham Halt, GE, 11E4
Heniarth, W&L, 14B3
Henley-in-Arden, GW, 9B5
Henley-on-Thames, GW, 10G2
Henllan, GW, 13F4
Henlow, Mid, 11E1
Hensall Jc, LY&GNJt/H&B, 21E5
Hensall, LY, 21E5
Henstridge, SD, 3D3; 8G1
Henwick (Worcs), GW, 9B3
Hepscott, NE, 27A5
Hereford (Goods), S&H, GW & Mid, 9C1
Hereford (Pass), S&H(Mid), 9C1
Heriot, NB, 30C1
Hermitage, GW, 4A3
Herne Bay, SEC, 6B2
Herne Hill, SEC, 5B3; 40E5
Herriard, LSW, 4C2
Hertford, GN & GE, 11F2
Hertford Cowbridge, GN, 11F2
Hertingfordbury, GN, 11F2
Hesketh Bank & Tarleton, LY, 20A3; 24E3
Hesketh Park, LY, 20A4; 24E4; 45F1
Hesleden, NE, 28D5
Heslerton, NE, 22A4
Hessay, NE, 21C4
Hessle, NE(GC), 22E4
Hessle Road Jc, NE, 22E3; 22A2 (inset)
Hest Bank, LNW, 24B3
Hest Bank N & S Jcs, LNW, 24B3
Heston Hounslow, Met & Dist, 39D1
Heswall, BJ, 20C5
Heswall Hills, GC, 20C4; 45F4
Hethersett, GE, 18F3
Hetton, NE, 28D5
Hever, LBSC, 5D4
Heversham, Fur, 24A3
Hexham, NE(NB), 27B3
Hexthorpe Jc, GC, 21G2
Heyford, GW, 10D4
Heys Crossing Halt, LY(LNW), 20B3; 24F3; 45E2
Heysham Harbour, Mid, 24C3
Heytesbury, GW, 3C4
Heywood, LY, 20B1; 24F1; 45A1
Hibel Road (Macclesfield), LNW(NS), 15A3; 20D1; 45A5
Hickleton & Thurnscoe, HB, 21F4; 42E1
Hickleton South Jc, SK/DV, 21F4; 42E1
High Barnet, GN(NL), 5A3
High Blantyre, Cal, 29C5; 44C2
High Field, NE, 22D5
High Halden Road, KES, 6D4
High Halstow Halt, SEC, 6B5
High Harrington, CWJ, 26E3
High Lane, GC&NSJt, 15A4; 21G1
High Level Bridge (Gateshead), NE, 28 (inset)
High Peak Jc, Mid/LNW, 16C5; 41E1
High Rocks Halt, LBSC, 5D5
High Shields, NE, 28B5
High Street (Glasgow), NB, 44D4 and inset E2
High Westwood, NE, 27C4
High Wycombe, GW&GCJt, 10F2
Higham (Kent), SEC, 6B5
Higham (Suffolk), GE, 11C5
Higham Ferrers, Mid, 10A1
Higham-on-the-Hill, AN, 16F5
Highams Park, GE, 5A4
Highbridge, GW & SD, 3B1; 8E3
Highbury & Islington, NL(LNW), 40B5
Highbury Vale Goods, GN, 40B5
Highclere, GW, 4B3
Higher Buxton, LNW, 15A4
Highgate, GN(NL), 5A3; 39A5
Highgate Platform, CKP, 26E1
Highgate Road, Mid(LTS) & THJ, 40B5
Highgate Road Jc, Mid/THJ(LTS), 40C1 (inset)
Highlandman, Cal, 33F3
Highley, GW, 9A2; 15G2
Hightown, LY(LNW), 20B4; 24F4; 45F2
Highworth, GW, 9F5
Hildenborough, SEC, 5D5
Hilgay, GE, 11A4; 17F4
Hill End, GN, 11F2
Hillfoot, NB, 29B4; 44E5
Hillhouse Goods (Yorks), LNW, 21E2; 42C4
Hillhouse Jc (Lancs), LY/CLC, 20B4; 24F4; 45F2
Hillington, MGN, 17E5
Hillside (Kincard), NB, 34C2
Hilton House, LY, 20B2; 24F2; 45C2
Hilton Jc, Cal/NB, 33F5
Hincaster Jc, LNW/Fur, 24A3
Hinckley, LNW(Mid), 16F4
Hinderwell, NE, 28E2
Hindley, LY, 20B2; 24F2; 45C2
Hindley & Amberswood (Goods), LNW, 45D2
Hindley & Platt Bridge, GC, 20B2; 24F2; 45D2 *see also* Platt Bridge
Hindley Green, LNW, 45C2
Hindlow, LNW, 15B5
Hindolvestone, MGN, 18D4
Hinton (Glos), Mid, 9C4
Hinton Admiral, LSW, 4F5
Hipperholme, LY, 42B5
Hirwain, GW, 8A5; 43D2
Histon, GE(Mid), 11C3
Hitchin, GN(Mid), GN & Mid, 11E2
Hither Green, SEC, 40E3
Hixon, NS, 15D4
Hockerill Halt, GE, 11E4
Hockley (Birmingham), GW, 13C3; 15G4
Hockley (Essex), GE, 6A5
Hoddesdon Jc, LY(LNW), 20A2; 24E2
Hoddlesdon (Goods), LY, 20A2; 24E1
Hodnet, GW, 15D2; 20G2
Hoe Street (Walthamstow), GE, 40A3
Hoghton, LY, 20A2; 24E2
Holbeach, MGN, 17E3
Holbeck, GN(LY/GC) & Mid(NE), 21C2 (inset); 42A3
Holborn Viaduct, SEC, 5B3; 40C5
Holburn Street, GNS, 37G4
Holcombe Brook, LY, 20A1; 24E1; 45B1
Holehouse, G&SW, 29F4
Holes Bay Jc, LSW, 3F5
Holgate Bridge Jc, NE, 21C5 and inset A4
Holkham, GE, 18C5
Holland Arms, LNW, 19D1
Holland Road Halt, LBSC, 5F3
Hollin Well & Annesley, GC, 41E4
Hollingbourne, SEC, 6C5
Hollins (Goods), LY, 20A2; 24E2
Hollinswood (Goods), GW, 15E2
Hollinwood, LY, 45A2
Holly Bush (Mon), LNW, 8A4; 43B2
Hollybush (Ayr), G&SW, 29F4
Holme (Hunts), GN, 11A2; 17G2
Holme (Lancs), LY, 24D1
Holme (Yorks), NE, 22D5
Holme Hale, GE, 18F5
Holme Lacy, GW, 9C1
Holmes, Mid, 21G4; 42F1
Holmes Chapel, LNW, 15B3; 20D1
Holmfield, H&O, 21D2; 42B5
Holmfirth, LY, 21F2; 42D5
Holmsley, LSW, 4E5
Holmwood, LBSC, 5D2
Holsworthy, LSW, 1A4
Holt (Norfolk), MGN, 18D4
Holt Junc, GW, 3B4
Holtby, NE, 21C5
Holton, GC, 22F3
Holton-le-Clay, GN, 22F2
Holton Village Halt, GN, 22F2
Holwell (Goods), Mid, 16E3
Holygate (Goods), NB, 30B3
Holyhead, LNW, 19B2
Holytown, Cal, 30C5; 44A3

Holywell (North) Goods, NE, 28B5
Holywell Junc, LNW, 20D5
Holywell Town, LNW, 20D5
Holywood, G&SW, 26A4
Homersfield, GE, 12A3; 18G3
Homerton, NL, 40B3
Honeybourne, GW, 9C5
Honeybourne Line Jc, GW/Mid, 9D3
Honing, MGN, 18D2
Honington, GN, 16C1
Honiton, LSW, 2A2
Honley, LY, 21F2; 42D5
Honor Oak, SEC, 40E4
Honor Oak Park, LBSC, 40E4
Hoo Jc, SEC, 6B5
Hook, LSW, 4B2
Hook Norton, GW, 10D5
Hookagate, S&M, 15E1
Hoole, LY, 20A3; 24E3
Hooley Hill, LNW, 21A2 (inset); 45A3
Hooton, BJ, 20D4; 45F5
Hope (Derbys), Mid, 15A5
Hope & Pen-y-ffordd, LNW, 20E4
Hope Exchange (Flint), GC & LNW, 20E4
Hope Village, GC, 20E4
Hopeman, HR, 36C2
Hopton, NSJ, 12A1; 18F1
Hopton Heath, LNW, 14C1
Horbury & Ossett, LY, 21E3; 42C3 *see also* Ossett, GN
Horbury Junc, LY, 21E3; 42C2
Horden, NE, 28D4
Horderley, BC, 14C1
Horeb, LM, 7A3
Horham, MSL, 12B3
Horley, LBSC, 5D3
Hornby, Mid, 24B2
Horncastle, GN, 17B2
Hornchurch, LTS, 5A5
Horninglow, NS(GN), 15C5 (inset)
Horninglow Jc, NS, 15D5
Horninglow Wharf, Mid, 15D5 (inset)
Hornsea, NE, 22C2
Hornsea Bridge, NE, 22C2
Hornsey, GN(NL), 40A5
Hornsey Road, THJ(LTS), 40B5
Horrabridge, GW, 1C5
Horringford, IWC, 4F3
Horrocksford, LY, 24D1
Horrocksford Jc, LY, 24D1
Horsebridge, LSW(MSW), 4C4
Horsehay & Dawley, GW, 15F2
Horsforth, NE, 21D3; 42A3 *see also* Newlay
Horsham, LBSC, 5E2
Horsley, LSW, 5C2
Horsleyfield Jc, GW/LNW, 13B2
Horsmonden, SEC, 6D5
Horsted Keynes, LBSC, 5E3
Horton, Mid, 24B1
Horton Park, GN, 21D2; 42B5
Horwich, LY, 20B2; 24F2; 45C1
Horwich Fork Jc, LY, 45C2
Hoscar, LY, 20B3; 24F3; 45E1
Hothfield, SEC, 6D4
Hotwells, CE, 3 (inset)
Hough Green, CLC, 15A1; 20C3; 24G3; 45E4
Hougham, GN, 16C1
Hounslow & Whitton, LSW & Dist, 5B2; 39D1/E1
Hounslow Barracks, Dist & Met, 39D1
Hounslow Jc, LSW, 39E1
Houston (Crosslee), Cal & G&SW, 29C4; 44G4
Hove, LBSC, 5F3
Hovingham Spa, NE, 21B5
How Mill, NE, 27C1
Howden Clough, GN, 42B3
Howdon, NE, 28B5
Howe Bridge, LNW, 20B2; 24F2; 45C2
Howsham, GC, 22F3
Howwood, G&SW, 29C4
Hoy, HR, 38C3
Hoylake, Wir, 20C5; 24G5
Hubbert's Bridge, GN, 17C2
Hucknall, Mid & GN, 16C4; 41E4
Hucknall Town, GC, 16C4, 41E4
Huddersfield, LNW&LYJt & Mid, 21E2; 42C5
Hugglescote, AN, 16E4
Hull, NE(GC/LNW/LY), NE & HB, 22D3/E3 and inset
Hullavington, GW, 9G3
Hulme End, NS, 15B5
Humber Rd Jc (Coventry), LNW, 10A5
Humber Rd Jc (Lincs), GC, 22E3
Humberstone, GN, 16F3
Humberstone Road, Mid, 16F3
Humbie, NB, 30C1
Humshaugh, NB, 27B3
Huncoat, LY, 24D1
Hundred End, LY, 20A4; 24E3
Hungerford, GW, 4A4
Hunmanby, NE, 22B3
Hunnington, HJ, 9A4; 15G4
Hunslet (Goods), GN & NE, 21D3; 42A2
Hunslet (Pass), Mid(LY), 21D3; 42B2
Hunslet Branch Jc, NE, 21D3
Hunslet Lane (Goods), Mid, 21D3 and inset C2; 42A2
Hunstanton, GE, 17D5
Hunston, SL, 4E1
Hunt's Cross, CLC, 20C4; 45E4
Hunthill Jc, Cal, 44C2
Huntingdon, GN, GN&GEJt & Mid, 11B2
Huntly, GNS, 37E1
Hunwick, NE, 27D5
Hurdlow, LNW, 15B5
Hurlford, G&SW, 29E4
Hurn, LSW, 4E5
Hurst Green Halt, CO, 5C4
Hurst Green Jc, LBSC/CO, 5C4
Hurstbourne, LSW, 4B4
Hurworth Burn, NE, 28D5
Husborne Crawley Halt, LNW, 10C1
Huskisson (Liverpool), CLC, 45F3 and inset
Husthwaite Gate, NE, 21B4
Hutcheon Street, GNS, 37F4
Hutton (Lancs) & Howick, LY, 20A3; 24E3
Hutton Cranswick, NE, 22C4
Hutton Gate, NE, 28E3
Huttons Ambo, NE, 22B5
Huyton, LNW, 20C3; 24G3; 45E4
Huyton Quarry, LNW, 20C3; 24G3; 45E4
Hyde, GC&MidJt, 21G1
Hyde Junc, GC&MidJt, 21G1
Hyde Road, GC, 45A3
Hykeham, Mid, 16B1
Hylton, NE, 28C5
Hylton Lane (Goods), NE, 28C5
Hyndland, NB, 44E4
Hythe (Essex), GE, 12E4
Hythe (Kent), SEC, 6D3

Ibrox, G&P, 29C4; 44E3
Icknield Port Road, LNW, 13C3
Ide, GW, 2B3
Idle, GN, 21D2; 42A4
Idridgehay, Mid, 16C5; 41E1
Ifield Halt, LBSC, 5D3
Ilderton, NE, 31E4
Ilford, GE, 5A4; 40B1
Ilfracombe, LSW(GW), 7E3
Ilkeston, GN, 16C4; 41F3
Ilkeston Junc & Cossall, Mid, 16C4; 41F3
Ilkeston Town, Mid, 16C4; 41F3
Ilkley, Mid & O&I, 21C2
Ilminster, GW, 3D1; 8G3
Immingham, GC, 22E3
Immingham Dock (Goods), GC, 22E2
Ince (Lancs), LY, 45D2 *see also* Lower Ince
Ince & Elton, BJ, 20D3; 45E5
Inchcoonans (Goods), Cal, 34E5
Inches, Cal, 30E5
Inchlea Crossing, HR, 33B2
Inchmagranachan Crossing, HR, 33D4
Inchture, Cal, 34E5
Inchture Village, Cal, 34E5
Ingatestone, GE, 11G4
Ingersby, GN, 16F3
Ingestre, GN, 15D4 *see also* Weston (Staffs)
Ingham, GE, 12B5
Ingleby, NE, 28F4
Ingleton, Mid(LNW), 24B2
Ingrow, Mid & GN, 21D1
Ings Road Jc, LY/GN, 42C2
Innerleithen, NB, 30E2
Innerpeffray, Cal, 33F4
Innerwick, NB, 31B2
Insch, GNS, 37E2
Instow, LSW, 7F3
Inveramsay, GNS, 37E3
Inveresk, NB, 30B2
Invergarry, NB, 32A2
Invergloy, NB, 32B2
Invergordon, HR, 36C5
Invergowrie, Cal, 34E5
Inverkeilor, NB, 34D3
Inverkeithing, NB, 30B3
Inverkip, Cal, 29C2
Inverness, HR, 36E5
Invershin, HR, 35A5
Inverugie, GNS, 37D5

Inverurie, GNS, 37F3
Inworth, GE, 12F5
Ipstones, NS, 15C4
Ipswich, GE, 12D3
Irchester, Mid, 10B1
Irchester Jc, Mid, 10B1
Irlam & Cadishead, CLC, 20C2; 24G2; 45C3
Irlams-o'th-Height, LY, 45B2
Iron Acton, Mid, 8C1; 9G2
Iron Bridge & Broseley, GW, 15F2
Irongray, G&SW, 26A4
Irthlingborough, LNW, 10A1
Irton Road, RE, 26F3
Irvine, G&SW & Cal, 29E3
Isfield, LBSC, 5F4
Isham & Burton Latimer, Mid, 10A2
Isleham, GE, 11B4
Isleworth, LSW, 39D2
Islip, LNW, 10E4
Itchen Abbas, LSW, 4C3
Itchingfield Jc, LBSC, 5E2
Ivor Jc, BM/LNW, 43C1
Ivybridge, GW, 2D5

Jamage Jc, NS, 15C3; 20E1
James Street, Mer, 45G5 (inset)
Jamestown, NB, 29B3
Jarrow, NE, 28B5
Jedburgh, NB, 31E1
Jedfoot, NB, 31E1
Jersey Marine, RSB, 7B4; 43F3
Jervaulx, NE, 21A2; 27G5
Jesmond, NE, 27B5, 28 (inset)
Joan Croft Jc, NE, 21F5
John o' Gaunt, GN&LNWJt, 16E2
Johnshaven, NB, 34C2
Johnston, GW, 7C1
Johnstone, G&SW, 29C4
Johnstone North, G&SW, 29C4
Johnstown & Hafod, GW, 20F4
Jones' Drove (Goods), GE, 11A3; 17G3
Joppa, NB, 30 (inset)
Jordanhill, NB, 44E4
Jordanstone, Cal, 34D5
Junction Road (London), THJ(LTS), 40B5 and inset C1
Junction Road, NB, 30 (inset)
Junction Road (Sussex), KES, 6E5
Junction Road Jc, Mid/THJ(LTS), 40C1 (inset)
Juniper Green, Cal, 30C3
Justinhaugh, Cal, 34C4

Kaypark Jc, G&SW, 29E4
Keadby (Goods), GC, 22F5
Kearsley, LY, 20B2; 24F1; 45B2
Kearsney, SEC, 6D2
Keele, NS, 15C3; 20F1
Kegworth, Mid, 16D4
Keighley, Mid(GN), Mid & GN, 21D1
Keinton Mandeville, GW, 3D2; 8F2
Keith, GNS & HR, 37D1
Keith Town, GNS, 37D1
Kelmarsh, LNW, 10A2
Kelmscott & Langford, GW, 9F5; 10F5
Kelso, NB(NE), 31E2
Kelso Jc, NB, 31E1
Kelston, Mid, 3A3; 8D1
Kelton Fell Colliery, RKF, 26E3
Kelty, NB, 30A3
Kelvedon, GE, 12F5
Kelvedon Low Level, GE, 12F5
Kelvin Bridge, Cal, 44E4
Kelvinhaugh (Goods), Cal&NBJt, 44E4
Kelvinside, Cal, 44E4
Kelvinside Jc, Cal, 44E4
Kemble Junc, GW, 9F4
Kemp Town, LBSC, 5F3
Kempston & Elstow Halt, LNW, 10C1; 11D1
Kempston Hardwick Halt, LNW, 10C1; 11D1
Kempston Rd Jc, Mid, 10C1; 11D1
Kempton Park, LSW, 39F1
Kemsing, SEC, 5C5
Kendal, LNW(Fur), 24A3; 27G1
Kenfig Hill, GW, 7C5; 43E4
Kenilworth, LNW, 10A5
Kenilworth Jc, LNW, 10A5
Kenley, SEC, 5C3
Kenmay, GNS, 37F3
Kennethmont, GNS, 37E2
Kennett, GE, 11C5
Kennington Jc (Oxon), GW, 10E4
Kennishead, GBK, 44E3
Kennoway (Goods), NB, 34G5
Kennybill, (Goods), Cal, 44D4
Kensal Green, LNW(LE), 39C4
Kensal Green Jc, LNW, 39B4
Kensal Rise, LNW(NL), 39B4
Kensington (Addison Rd), WL(H&C/LBSC/LSW), 5B3; 39D4
Kensington High Street (Coal), Mid, 39D5
Kensington High Street (Pass), Dist & Met(Dist), 39D5
Kensington Road Goods (Southport), LY, 45F1
Kent & East Sussex Light Railway, KES, 6E4
Kent House, SEC, 40F4
Kentallen, Cal, 32D3
Kentish Town, Mid(LTS/GE) & LNW(NL), 5A3; 40B5 and inset C1
Kentish Town Jc, Mid, 40C1 (inset)
Kenton (Middx), LNW(LE), 39A2
Kenton (Northumb), NE, 27B5
Kenton (Suffolk), MSL, 12C3
Kenton for Northwick Park, LNW, 39A2
Kents Bank, Fur, 24B3
Kenyon Junc, LNW(BJ), 20C2; 24G2; 45C3
Kerne Bridge, GW, 8A2; 9D1
Kerry, Cam, 14C2
Kershope Foot, NB, 27A1
Keswick, CKP, 26E2
Ketley, GW, 15E2
Ketley Jc, GW/LNW, 15C2; 20E2
Kettering, Mid, 10A2
Kettering Jc, Mid, 10A2
Kettleness, NE, 28E2
Ketton, Mid(LNW), 16F1; 17F1
Kew Bridge, LSW(NL), 39D3
Kew Gardens (Lancs), LY, 20A4; 24E4; 45F1
Kew Gardens (London), LSW(Dist/NL), 39D3
Keyham (Devonport), GW, 1D5 and inset
Keyingham, NE, 22E2
Keymer Jc, LBSC, 5E3
Keynsham, GW, 3A3; 8D1
Kibworth, Mid, 16F3
Kidbrooke, SEC, 40E2
Kidderminster, GW, 9A3
Kidlington, GW, 10E4
Kidsgrove, NS, 15C3; 20E1
Kidsgrove Halt, NS, 15C3; 20E1
Kidwelly, GW, 7A2
Kielder, NB, 27A1; 31G1
Kilbagie, NB, 30A4
Kilbarchan, G&SW, 29C4
Kilbirnie, Cal & G&SW, 29D3
Kilbowie, Cal, 29C4; 44F4
Kilburn (Derbys), Mid, 16C5; 41F2
Kilburn & Brondesbury (Met), 39B4
Kilburn & Maida Vale, LNW(NL), 39B5
Kilconquhar, NB, 30A1; 34G4
Kildale, NE, 28F3
Kildary, HR, 36C4
Kildonan, HR, 38F5
Kildwick & Crosshills, Mid, 21C1
Kilgerran, GW, 13F3
Kilgetty, GW, 7D3
Kilkerran, G&SW, 29G3
Kilknowe Jc, NB, 30D1
Killamarsh, GC & Mid, 16A4; 41A3 *see also* Upperthorpe
Killay, LNW, 7B3
Killearn, NB, 29B4
Killiecrankie, HR, 33C4
Killin, Cal, 33E2
Killin Junc, Cal, 33E1
Killingholme, GC, 22E3
Killingworth, NE, 27B5
Killochan, G&SW, 29G3
Killywhan, G&SW, 26B4
Kilmacolm, G&SW, 29C3
Kilmany, NB, 34E4
Kilmarnock, G&SW & GBK, 29E4
Kilmaurs, G&SW, 29D4
Kilnhurst, Mid & GC, 21 F4; 42F1
Kilnwick Gate (Goods), NE, 22C4
Kilpatrick, NB, 29B4; 44G5
Kilsby & Crick, LNW, 10A4
Kilsyth, K&B & NB, 29B5
Kilwinning, G&SW & Cal, 29D3
Kimberley Park, GE, 18F4
Kimberley, GN & Mid, 16C4; 41F4
Kimbolton, Mid, 11B1
Kimbridge Jc, LSW, 4D4
Kinaldie, GNS, 37F3
Kinbrace, HR, 38E5
Kinbuck, Cal, 33G3
Kincardine, NB, 30A4
Kincraig, HR, 33A3; 36G4
Kineton, SMJ, 10C5
Kinfauns, Cal, 33F5
King Edward, GNS, 37C3

King George Dock (Goods) (Hull), NE&HBJt, 22E3
King Street Goods (Paisley), G&SW, 44G3
King William (Goods), LY, 20A2; 24E1; 45B1
King's Cross, GN & Met(Dist/GW/GN/Mid/ H&C), 5A3; 40C5
King's Inch, G&P, 44F4
King's Langley & Abbot's Langley, LNW, 11G1
King's Lynn, GE(MGN), 17E4
King's Norton, Mid, 9A4
King's Sutton, GW, 10C4
King's Worthy, GW, 4C3
King's Heath, Mid, 9A4; 15G4
Kingennie, Cal, 34E4
Kingham, GW, 9D5
Kinghorn, NB, 30A2
Kingsbarns, NB, 34F3
Kingsbridge, GW, 2E4
Kingsbury, Mid, 15F5
Kingscliffe, LNW, 11A1; 16F1; 17F1
Kingscote, LBSC, 5D4
Kingshouse, Cal, 33F2
Kingskerswell, GW, 2D3
Kingskettle, NB, 34F5
Kingsland, (Hereford), GW, 14D1
Kingsland, NL, 40B4
Kingsland Eastern Jc, NL, 40B4
Kingsland Western Jc, NL, 40B4
Kingsley & Froghall, NS, 15C4
Kingsley Halt, LSW, 4C1
Kingsmuir, Cal, 34D4
Kingston (Surrey), LSW, 5B2; 39F2
Kingston (Sussex) (Goods), LBSC, 5F3
Kingston Crossing Halt, GW, 10F3
Kingston Road, WCP, 3A1; 8D3
Kingston Street (Hull) (Goods), NE, 22 (inset)
Kingswear, GW, 2D3
Kingswood & Burgh Heath, SEC, 5C3
Kingswood Crossing, HR, 33E5
Kingswood Jc, GW, 3 (inset)
Kingthorpe, GN, 17B1
Kington, GW, 14E2
Kingussie, HR, 33A2
Kinloss, HR, 36C2
Kinnaber Jc, Cal/NB, 34C3
Kinneil, NB, 30B4
Kinnerley Junc, S&M, 14A1
Kinnersley, Mid, 14E1
Kinnerton, LNW, 20E4
Kinning Park Goods, Cal, 44F2 (inset)
Kinross Junc, NB, 30A3; 33G5
Kintbury, GW, 4A4
Kintore, GNS, 37F3
Kipling Cotes, NE, 22D4
Kippax, NE, 21D4; 42B1
Kippen, NB, 29A5
Kirby Cross, GE, 12E3
Kirby Moorside, NE, 21A5
Kirby Muxloe, Mid, 16F4
Kirby Park, BJ, 20C5; 24G5
Kirk Michael, IMR, 23B2; 25G4
Kirk Sandall Jc, GC/SYJ, 21F5 and inset
Kirk Smeaton, HB, 21E4
Kirkandrews, NB, 26C1
Kirkbank, NB, 31E2
Kirkbride, NB, 26C2
Kirkbuddo, Cal, 34D4
Kirkburton, LNW, 21E2; 42D4
Kirkburton Branch Jc, LNW, 42C4
Kirkby (in-Furness), Fur, 23A4
Kirkby (Lancs), Fur, 24A5
Kirkby (Lancs), LY, 20B4; 24F3; 45E3
Kirkby & Pinxton, GC, 16C4; 41E4 ***see also*** Pinxton
Kirkby-in-Ashfield, Mid &GC, 16C4; 41E4
Kirkby Lonsdale, LNW, 24B2
Kirkby Stephen, NE, 27F2
Kirkby Stephen & Ravenstonedale, Mid, 27F2
Kirkby Thore, NE, 27E2
Kirkcaldy, NB, 30A2
Kirkconnel, G&SW, 30F5
Kirkcowan, P&W, 25C3
Kirkcudbright, G&SW, 26C5
Kirkdale, LY, 45F3
Kirkgate (Wakefield), LY&GNJt, 21E3; 42C2
Kirkgunzeon, G&SW, 26B4
Kirkham & Wesham, PWY, 24D3
Kirkham Abbey, NE, 22B5
Kirkheaton, LNW, 21E2; 42C4
Kirkhill, Cal, 29C5; 44D3
Kirkhill Jc, Cal, 44D3
Kirkinner, P&W, 25C4
Kirkintilloch, NB, 29B5; 44C5
Kirkland, G&SW, 26A5
Kirklee, Cal, 44E4
Kirkley (Goods), GE, 12A1; 18G1
Kirklington & Edingley, Mid, 16B3
Kirkliston, NB, 30B3
Kirknewton, NE, 31E3
Kirkpatrick, Cal, 26B2
Kirkstall, Mid, 21D3; 42A3
Kirriemuir, Cal, 34D4
Kirriemuir Jc, Cal, 34D4
Kirtlebridge, Cal, 26B2
Kirton, GN, 17D2
Kirton Bridge Halt, GNS, 37C4
Kirton Lindsey, GC, 22F4
Kittybrewster, GNS, 37F4
Kiveton Park, GC, 16A4; 41A4
Knapton (Yorks), NE, 22B4
Knaresborough, NE, 21C3
Knebworth, GN, 11F2
Knight's Hill Goods, LNW, 40E4
Knighton, LNW, 14D2
Knighton Jcs, Mid, 16F3
Knighton South Jc, LNW/Mid, 16F3
Knightswood North Jc, NB, 44E4
Knightwick, GW, 9B2
Knitsley, NE, 27C5
Knock, GNS, 37D1
Knockando, GNS, 36E2
Knockholt, SEC, 5C4
Knott End, KE, 24C4
Knottingley for Ferrybridge, LY&GNJt, 21E4; 42C1 ***see also*** Ferrybridge
Knotty Ash & Stanley, CLC, 45E3 ***see also*** Stanley (Lancs)
Knowesgate, NB, 27A4
Knoweside, G&SW, 29F3
Knowle & Dorridge, GW, 9A5
Knowle Platform, LSW, 4D3
Knowlton, EK, 6C2
Knowsley Street (Bury), LY, 20B1; 24F1; 45B2
Knucklas, LNW, 14D2
Knutsford, CLC(LNW), 15A2; 20D2; 45B5
Knutton Halt, NS, 20F1
Knypersley Halt, NS, 15B3; 20E1
Kyle of Lochalsh, HR, 35F1

Lacock Halt, GW, 3A4
Ladmanlow (Goods), LNW, 15B4
Ladybank, NB, 34F5
Ladysbridge, GNS, 37C2
Ladywell, SEC, 40E3
Laindon, LTS, 5A5
Laira Halt, GW, 1 (inset)
Laira Jc (Plymouth), GW, 1 (inset)
Lairg, HR, 35A5
Laisterdyke, GN(LY), 21D2; 42A4
Lakenheath, GE, 11A5; 17G5
Lamancha, NB, 30D2
Lambley, NE, 27C2
Lambourn, GW, 4A4; 10G5
Lamesley, NE, 27C5
Lamington, Cal, 30E4
Lampeter, GW, 13E5
Lamphey, GW, 7D2
Lamplugh, WCE, 26E3
Lamport, LNW, 10A2
Lanark, Cal, 30D4
Lancaster, LNW(Mid), LNW & Mid, 24C3
Lanchester, NE, 27D5
Lancing, LBSC, 5F2
Landore, GW, 7B4; 43G3
Langbank, Cal, 29B3
Langford (Som), GW, 3B2; 8D2
Langford (Essex), GE, 12F5
Langho, LY, 24D2
Langholm, NB, 26A1
Langley (Bucks), GW, 5B1
Langley (Northumb), NE, 27C3
Langley Green & Rood End, GW, 13C2; 15G4
Langley Jc, GN, 11E2
Langley Mill, Mid, 41F3 ***see also*** Eastwood, GN
Langloan, Cal, 44B3
Langport (East and West), GW, 3D1; 8F3
Langrick, GN, 17C2
Langside & Newlands, Cal, 44E3
Langside Jc, Cal/GBK, 44F1 (inset)
Langston, LBSC, 4E2
Langwathby, Mid, 27D1
Langwith, Mid, 16B4; 41C4
Langwith Junc, GC(GN), 16B4; 41C4
Langworth, GC, 16A1; 17A1
Lanridge Jc, Cal, 44A3
Lansdown (Cheltenham), Mid(MSW), 9D3
Lapford, LSW, 2A4
Lapworth, GW, 9A5
Larbert, Cal(NB), 30B5

Largo, NB, 34G4
Largoward (Goods), NB, 34F4
Largs, G&SW, 29C2
Larkhall (Central), Cal, 30D5; 44B1
Larkhall (East), Cal, 30D5; 44A1
Lartington, NE, 27E4
Lasswade, NB, 30C2
Latchford, LNW, 15A2; 20C2; 24G2; 45C4
Latchley, BAC, 1C5
Latchmere Jcs, WLE, 39E5 and inset E3
Latimer Road, H&C, 39C4
Lauder, NB, 31D1
Laughton East Jc, SYJ, 41A4
Laughton West Jc, SYJ, 41A4
Launceston, LSW & GW, 1B4
Launton, LNW, 10D3
Laurencekirk, Cal(NB), 34B2
Lauriston, NB, 34C2
Lavant, LBSC, 4E1
Lavenham, GE, 12D5
Lavernock, TV, 8D4; 43B5
Laverton Halt, GW, 9C4
Lavington, GW, 3B5
Law Junc, Cal, 30D5
Lawley Bank, GW, 15E2
Lawley Street (Goods), Mid, 13C4
Lawrence Hill, GW, 3 (inset)
Lawrence Hill Jc, Mid, 3G1 (inset)
Lawton, NS, 15B3; 20E1
Laxey, ME, 23B3
Laxfield, MSL, 12B3
Layerthorpe, DVL, 21C5 and inset A5
Lazonby & Kirkoswald, Mid, 27D1
Lea, GN&GEJt, 16A2; 22G5
Lea Bridge, GE, 5A3; 40B3
Lea Bridge Jc, GE, 40B3
Lea Green, LNW, 20C3; 24G3; 45D3
Lea Road (Preston), PWY, 24D3
Leadburn, NB, 30C2
Leadenham, GN, 16C1
Leadgate, NE, 27C5
Leadhills, Cal, 30F4
Leagrave, Mid, 10D1; 11E1
Lealholm, NE, 28F3
Leamington Spa, GW & LNW, 10B5
Leamside, NE, 28D5
Leasowe, Wir, 20C5; 24G5
Leatherhead, LSW & LBSC, 5C2
Leaton, GW, 14A1; 15E1
Lechlade, GW, 9F5
Ledbury, GW, 9C2
Ledsham, BJ, 20D4; 45F5
Ledston, NE, 21E4; 42B1
Lee (Kent), SEC, 5B4; 40E2
Lee Jc, SEC, 40E2
Lee-on-the-Solent, LSW, 4E3
Leebotwood, S&H, 14B1; 15F1
Leeds (Goods), GN, LNW&LYJt, Mid & NE, 21B2 (inset); 42A2/3
Leeds (Pass), Central: GN, LY, LNW, NE; New: LNW&NEJt; Wellington: Mid(LY), 21B2 (inset); 42A2/3
Leegate, M&C, 26D2
Leek, NS, 15C4
Leeming Bar, NE, 21A3; 28G5
Leen Valley Jc, GN, 16C3; 41F4
Lees, LNW, 21F1
Legacy, GW, 20E4
Legbourne Road, GN, 17A3
Leicester (Goods), Mid, GC, GN & LNW, 16F3
Leicester (Pass), Mid(LNW/MGN), GC &GN, 16F3
Leicester Jc (Burton-on-Trent), Mid, 15E5 and inset
Leigh (Staffs), NS, 15D4
Leigh & Bedford, LNW, 20B2; 24F2; 45C3
Leigh Court, GW, 9B3
Leigh-on-Sea, LTS, 6A5
Leigham Jc, LBSC, 40E5
Leighton Buzzard, LNW, 10D1
Leiston, GE, 12C2
Leith, Cal & NB, 30B2 and inset
Leith Central, NB, 30 (inset)
Leith Walk (Goods), Cal, 30 (inset)
Lelant, GW, 1E4 (inset)
Leman Street, GE, 40C4
Lemington, NE, 27B5
Lenham, SEC, 6C4
Lennoxtown, NB, 29B5
Lenton (Goods), Mid, 16D4; 41G4
Lentran, HR, 36D5
Lenwade, MGN, 18E4
Lenzie, NB, 29B5; 44D5
Leominster, S&H, 9B1
Leominster Jc (Worcester), GW, 9B3
Leslie, NB, 30A1; 34G5
Lesmahagow, Cal, 30D5
Lesmahagow Jc, Cal, 44B2
Letchworth, GN, 11E2
Letham Grange, NB, 34D3
Lethenty, GNS, 37E3
Letterston, GW, 13F1
Letterston Jc, GW, 13F1
Leuchars Junc, NB, 34F4
Leuchars Old, NB, 34E4
Leven, NB, 30A1; 34G4
Levenshulme, LNW, 20C1; 24G1; 45A3
Leverton, GC, 16A2
Levisham, NE, 22A5; 28G2
Lewes, LBSC, 5F4
Lewes Road, LBSC, 5F3
Lewisham Junc, SEC, 40E3
Lewknor Bridge Halt, GW, 10F3
Leyburn, NE, 21A2; 27G5
Leycett, NS, 15C3; 20F1
Leyland, NU, 20A3; 24E3
Leysdown, SEC, 6B3
Leysmill, Cal, 34D3
Leyton, GE & TFG, 40B3
Leytonstone, GE & TFG, 5A4; 40A2/B2
Lezayre, IMR, 23A3; 25C4
Lhanbryde, HR, 36C1
Lichfield (City), LNW, 15E5
Lichfield (Trent Valley), LNW, 15E5
Lidlington, LNW, 10C1
Liff, Cal, 34E5
Lifford, Mid, 9A4
Lifton, GW, 1B5
Lightcliffe, LY, 21E2; 42B5
Lightmoor Platform, GW, 15F2
Lilbourne, LNW, 10A4
Lillie Bridge Goods, WLE, 39D4
Lilliehill Jc, NB, 30A3
Lime Street (Liverpool), LNW, 20C4; 24G4; 45F4
Limefield Jc, Cal, 30C4
Limehouse, GE, 40C3
Limpley Stoke, GW, 3B3
Linacre Road, LY, 45F3
Linby, Mid & GN, 16C4; 41E4
Lincoln (Goods), GC, GN & Mid, 16B1 and inset
Lincoln (Pass), GN(GC/GE) & Mid, 16B1 and inset
Lindal, Fur, 24B4
Lindean, NB, 30E1
Lindores, NB, 34F5
Linefoot, MC, 26D3
Lingfield, LBSC, 5D4
Lingwood, GE, 18F2
Linley, GW, 15F2
Linlithgow, NB, 30B4
Linthwaite (Goods), LNW, 21E2; 42D5
Lintmill Halt, CM, 29 (inset)
Linton, GE, 11D4
Lintz Green, NE, 27C5
Linwood (Goods), Cal, 29C4; 44G3
Lion's Holt Halt, LSW, 2C3
Liphook, LSW, 4D1
Lipson Jc, GW, 1 (inset)
Lipson Vale Halt, GW, 1 (inset)
Liscard & Poulton, Wir(GC), 45F3
Liskeard, GW & LL, 1D4
Liss, LSW, 4D1
Lissens (Goods), Cal, 29D3
Litchfield (Hants), GW, 4B3
Little Bytham, GN, 16E1; 17E1
Little Bytham Jc, Mid/MGN, 16E1; 17E1
Little Eaton, Mid, 16C5; 41F2
Little Eaton Jc, Mid, 16C5; 41F2
Little Hulton, LY, 45B2
Little Kimble, GW&GCJt, 10E2
Little Mill, GW, 8B3; 43A2
Little Mill Jc, GW, 8B3; 43A2
Little Mill, NE, 31F5
Little Salkeld, Mid, 27D1
Little Somerford, GW, 9G4
Little Steeping, GN, 17B3
Little Sutton, BJ, 20D4; 45F5
Little Weighton, HB, 22D4
Littleborough, LY, 21E1
Littleham, LSW, 2C2
Littlehampton, LBSC, 5G1
Littlehampton Jc, LBSC, 5F1
Littlehaven Halt, LBSC, 5E2
Littlemore, GW, 10F4
Littleport, GE, 11A4; 17G4
Littleton & Badsey, GW, 9C4
Littleworth, GN, 17E2
Liverpool (Goods), CLC, GC, LNW, LY & Mid, 20 –; 24 –; 45 –

Liverpool (Pass), Central: CLC & Mer; Exchange: LY(Mid); Lime Street: LNW, 20 –; 24 –; 45 –
Liverpool Road (Chester), GC, 20D4
Liverpool Road Halt, NS, 20F1
Liverpool Street (London), GE & Met(Dist/GW/H&C), 5A3; 40C4
Liversedge, LNW & LY, 21E2; 42B4/C4
Livingston, NB, 30C4
Llanaber Halt, Cam, 13A5
Llanarthney, LNW, 13G5
Llanbadarn, VR, 13C5
Llanbedr & Pensarn, Cam, 19G2
Llanbedr Goch, LNW, 19C2
Llanberis, LNW & SM, 19E2
Llanbethery Halt, TV, 43C5
Llanbister Road, LNW, 14D2
Llanbradach, Rhy, 8B4; 43B3
Llanbrynmair, Cam, 14B4
Llandaff, TV, 8C4; 43B4
Llandderfel, GW, 19F5
Llandebie, GW(LNW), 7A3; 43G1
Llandenny, GW, 8A3
Llandilo, GW(LNW), 13G5
Llandilo Bridge, LNW, 13G5
Llandinam, Cam, 14C3
Llandovery, VT, 14F5
Llandow Halt, BRY, 43D5
Llandre, Cam, 13C5
Llandrillo, GW, 19F5
Llandrindod Wells, LNW, 14D3
Llandrinio Road, S&M, 14A2
Llandudno, LNW, 19C3
Llandudno Junc, LNW, 19D4
Llandulas, LNW, 19D4
Llandyssil, GW, 13F4
Llanelly, GW & LM(BPGV), 7B3
Llanelly Queen Victoria Road, LM, 7B3
Llanerch-Ayron Halt, GW, 13D4
Llanerchymedd, LNW, 19C1
Llanfabon Road Halt, TV, 43C3
Llanfair, LNW, 19D2
Llanfair Caereinion, W&L, 14B3
Llanfairfechan, LNW, 19D3
Llanfalteg, GW, 13G2
Llanfechain, Cam, 14A2; 20G5
Llanfyllin, Cam, 14A3
Llanfynydd, WM, 20E4
Llanfyrnach, GW, 13F3
Llangadock, VT, 14F5
Llangammarch Wells, LNW, 14E4
Llangedwyn, Tan, 14A2; 20G5
Llangefni, LNW, 19D1
Llangeinor, GW, 7B5; 43D3 *see also* Bettws
Llangennech, GW, 7B3
Llanglydwen, GW, 13G2
Llangollen, GW, 20F5
Llangonoyd, GW, 7B5; 43E3
Llangunllo, LNW, 14D2
Llangwyllog, LNW, 19C1
Llangybi (Cardigan), GW, 13E5
Llangybi (Carnarvon), LNW, 19F1
Llangyfelach, GW, 7B4; 43G2
Llangyfelach (Goods), GW, 43G2
Llangynog, Tan, 19G5
Llanharan, GW, 8C5; 43D4
Llanharry, TV, 8C5; 43C4
Llanhilleth, GW, 8B4; 43B2
Llanhilleth Jc, GW, 43B2
Llanidloes, Cam, 14C4
Llanilar, GW, 13D5
Llanishen, Rhy, 8C4; 43B4
Llanmorlais, LNW, 7B3
Llanpumpsaint, GW, 13F4
Llanrhaiadr, LNW, 19E5
Llanrhaiadr Mochnant, Tan, 14A3; 20G5
Llanrhystyd Road, GW, 13C5
Llanrwst & Trefriw, LNW, 19E4
Llansamlet, GW, 7B4; 42F2
Llansantffraid, Cam, 14A2
Llansilin Road, Tan, 14A2; 20G5
Llantarnam, GW, 8B3 ; 43A3
Llantrisant, GW(TV) & TV, 8C5; 43C4
Llantrisant Common Jc, TV/GW, 43C4
Llantwit Major, BRY, 8D5; 43D5
Llanuwchllyn, GW, 19G4
Llanvihangel (Mon), GW, 8A3; 14G1
Llanwern, GW, 8B3
Llanwit, TV, 8C5; 43C4
Llanwnda, LNW, 19E2
Llanwrda, VT, 14F5
Llanwrtyd Wells, LNW, 14E4
Llanyblodwell, Tan, 14A2; 20G5
Llanybylher, GW, 13F5
Llan-y-Cefn, GW, 13G2
Llanymynech, Cam & S&M, 14A2; 20G4
Lletty Brongu, PT, 7B5; 43D3
Llong, LNW, 20E5
Llwydcoed, GW, 8A5; 43D2
Llwyn Gwern, Corris, 14B5
Llwyngwril, Cam, 13A5
Llwynypia, TV, 8B5; 43D3
Llynclys, Cam, 14A2; 20G4
Llysfaen, LNW, 19D4
Loanhead, NB, 30C2
Loch Awe, Cal, 32F2
Loch Leven (Goods), NB, 30A3; 33G5
Loch Skerrow, P&W, 25B5
Loch Tay, Cal, 33E2
Lochailort, NB, 32B5
Lochanhead, G&SW, 26B4
Locharbriggs, Cal, 26A3
Lochburn, NB, 44E4
Lochearnhead, Cal, 33F2
Lochee, Cal, 34E4
Lochee West, Cal, 34E4
Locheilside, NB, 32B3
Lochend Jcs, NB, 30 (inset)
Lochgelly, NB, 30A3
Lochgorm Works, HR, 36E5
Lochgreen Jc, G&SW, 29E3
Lochluichart, HR, 35C4
Lochmaben, Cal, 26A3
Lochmill, NB, 30B4
Lochmill (Goods), NB, 30B4
Lochside, G&SW, 29C3
Lochty Goods, NB, 34F4
Lochwinnoch, G&SW, 29C3
Lockerbie, Cal, 26A3
Lockington, NE, 22C4
Lockwood, LY, 21E2; 42D5
Loddington, Mid, 10A2
Loddiswell, GW, 2E4
Lodge Hill, GW, 3B2; 8E2
Lofthouse & Outwood, GN(GC) & MJ, 21E3; 42B2
Lofthouse-in-Nidderdale, NV, 21B2
Loftus, NE, 28E3
Logan Jc, G&SW, 29F5
Logiereve, GNS, 37E4
Login, GW, 13G2
Londesborough, NE, 22D5
Londesborough Road, NE, 22A3
London, 5 –; 39 –; 40 –
London Bridge, LBSC & SEC, 5B3; 40D4
London Fields, GE, 40B4
London Necropolos, LN, 40G5
London Road (Guildford), LSW, 5C1
London Road (Manchester), LNW(NS), GC & MSJA, 20B1; 24F1; 45A3
London Road (Nottingham), GN(LNW), 41G5
London Road (Brighton), LBSC, 5F3
London Road Jc (Derby), Mid, 16D5
Long Buckby, LNW, 10B3
Long Clawson & Hose, GN&LNWJt, 16D2
Long Eaton, Mid, 16D4; 41G3
Long Marston, GW, 9C5
Long Marton, Mid, 27E2
Long Melford, GE, 12D5
Long Preston, Mid, 24C1
Long Stanton, GE(Mid), 11C3
Long Stow (Goods), Mid, 11B1
Long Sutton (Lincs), MGN, 17E3
Long Sutton & Pitney (Som), GW, 3D1; 8F2
Long Witton, NB, 27A4
Longcliffe (Goods), LNW, 15C5
Longdon Road, GW, 9C5
Longdown, GW, 2B3
Longfield Halt for Pindon & Westwood, SEC, 5B5
Longford & Exhall, LNW, 10A5; 16G5
Longforgan, Cal, 4E5; 34E5
Longhaven, GNS, 37D5
Longhedge Jc, WLE/SEC, 39E3 (inset)
Longhope, GW, 8A1; 9E2
Longhoughton, NE, 31F5
Longhurst, NE, 27A5
Longmorn, GNS, 36D2
Longniddry, NB, 30B1
Longparish, LSW, 4C4
Longport, NS, 15C3; 20E1
Longridge, PL, 24D2
Longriggend, NB, 30C5
Longside, GNS, 37D5
Longsight, LNW, 45A3
Longton, NS, 15C3; 20F1
Longton Bridge, LY, 20A3; 24E3
Longtown, NB, 26B1
Longville, GW, 15F1
Longville Jc, LNW/GN, 11A1; 17F2
Longwood & Milnsbridge, LNW, 21E2; 42D5
Lonlas South Private Platform, Mid, 43F2

Lonmay, GNS, 37C4
Looe, LL, 1D4
Lord Street (Southport), CLC, 20A4; 24E3; 45F1
Lord's Bridge, LNW, 11C3
Lordship Lane for Forest Hill, SEC, 40E4
Lossiemouth, GNS, 36C1
Lostock Gralam, CLC, 15A2; 20D2; 45C5
Lostock Hall, LY, 20A3; 24E3
Lostock Junc, LY, 20B2; 24F2; 45C2
Lostwithiel, GW, 1D3
Loth, HR, 38G4
Lothian Road (Goods), Cal, 30F2 (inset)
Loudounhlll, G&SW, 29E5
Loudwater, GW, 5A1; 10F2
Loughborough, Mid, GC & LNW, 16E4
Loughborough Junc, SEC, 40E5
Loughor, GW, 7B3
Loughton, GE, 5A4; 11G3
Loughton Jc, GE, 40B3
Louth, GN, 17A3; 22G2
Loversall Carr Jc, GN/DV, 21F5
Low Bentham (Goods), Mid, 24B2
Low Ellers Jc, SYJ, 21F2
Low Fell, NE, 27C5 and 28 (inset)
Low Gill, LNW, 27G1
Low Moor, LY(GN), LY & GN, 21E2; 42B4
Low Row, NE, 27C1
Low Street, LTS, 5B5
Lowca, CWJ, 26E3
Lowdham, Mid, 16C3
Lower Darwen, LY, 20A2; 24E2
Lower Edmonton, GE, 5A3
Lower Ince, GC, 45D2 ***see also*** Ince (Lancs)
Lower Penarth, TV, 8D4; 43B5
Lower Sydenham, SEC, 40F3
Lowesby, GN, 16F2
Lowestoft, GE(MGN), 12A1; 18G1
Lowestoft Line Jc, MGN, 18F1
Lowestoft North, NSJ, 12A1; 18F1
Lowthorpe, NE, 22C3
Lowton, LNW, 20C2; 24G2; 45D3
Lowton St Mary's, GC, 45C3
Lowtown (Pudsey), GN, 21D2; 42A4
Lubenham, LNW, 16G3
Lucas Terrace, GW, 1 (inset)
Lucas Terrace Halt, LSW, 1A2
Lucker, NE, 31E4
Luckett, BAC, 1C5
Ludborough, GN, 22G2
Luddendenfoot, LY, 21E1
Luddington, AJ, 22E5
Ludgate Jc, LSW, 39E3 (inset)
Ludgershall (Wilts), MSW, 4B5
Ludlow, S&H, 9A1
Luffenham, Mid(LNW), 16F1
Luffness Halt, NB, 30B1
Lugar, G&SW, 29F5
Lugton, Cal & GBK, 29D4
Luib, Cal, 33E1
Lumphanan, GNS, 37G2
Lunan Bay, NB, 34D3
Luncarty, Cal(HR), 33E5
Lundin Links, NB, 34G4
Lunlas South Private Platform, GW, 43F2
Lustleigh, GW, 2C4
Luthrie, NB, 34F5
Luton, Mid & GN(LNW), 11E1
Luton Hoo, GN, 11F1
Lutterworth, GC, 10 A4; 16G4 ***see also*** Ullesthorpe
Luxulyan, GW, 1D3
Lybster, HR, 38E2
Lydbrook Junc, GW & SVW, 8A2; 9E1
Lydd, SEC, 6E3
Lydford, LSW & GW, 1C5
Lydham Heath, BC, 14C1
Lydiate, CLC, 20B4; 24F4; 45F2
Lydney, GW, 8B1; 9F2
Lydney Junc, SVW, 8B1; 9E2
Lydney Town, SVW, 8A1; 9E2
Lydstep, GW, 7D2
Lye, GW, 9A3; 15G3
Lyghe Halt, SEC, 5D5
Lyme Regis, LSW, 3F1
Lyminge, SEC, 6D3
Lymington Jc, LSW, 4D4
Lymington Pier, LSW, 4F4
Lymington Town, LSW, 4F4
Lymm, LNW, 20C2; 24G2; 45C4
Lympstone, LSW, 2C3
Lyndhurst Road, LSW, 4E4
Lyne, Cal, 30D2
Lynedoch, G&SW, 29B3
Lyneside, NB, 26B1
Lynton, LB, 7E4
Lyon Cross Jc, Cal, 44F2
Lyonshall, GW, 14E1
Lytham, PWY, 20A4; 24E4

Mablethorpe, GN, 17A4
Macbie Hill, NB, 30D3
Macclesfield (Goods), LNW&NSJt & GC&NSJt, 15A3; 20D1; 45A5
Macclesfield Central, NS, 15A3; 20D1; 45A5
Macclesfield, Hibel Road, LNW(NS), 15A3; 20D1; 45A5
Macduff, GNS, 37C2
Machen, BM(Rhy), 8B4; 43B3
Machrihanish, CM, 29 (inset)
Machrihanish Farm Halt, CM, 29 (inset)
Machynlleth, Cam & Cor, 14B5
Macmerry, NB, 30B1
Madderty, Cal, 33F4
Madeley (Salop), GW, 15F2
Madeley (Staffs), LNW, 15C3; 20F1
Madeley Jc, GW, 15E2
Madeley Market, LNW, 15F2
Madeley Road, NS, 15C3; 20F1
Maenclochog, GW, 13F2
Maentwrog Road, GW, 19F3
Maerdy, TV, 8B5; 43D2
Maesaraul Jc, TV/GW, 43C4
Maesbrook, S&M, 14A2; 20C4
Maesteg, GW & PT, 7B5, 43E3
Maesycrugiau, GW, 13F4
Maesycwmmer & Hengoed, BM, 43B3 ***see also*** Hengoed
Maesycwmmcr Jc, BM/GW, 43B3
Magdalen Green (Dundee), Cal, 34E2 (inset)
Magdalen Road, GE, 17F4
Maghull, LY, 20B4; 24F4; 45F2 ***see also*** Sefton
Magor, GW, 8C3
Maiden Lane (Goods), LNW, 40B5
Maiden Lane (Pass), NL, 40B5
Maiden Newton, GW, 3F2
Maidenhead, GW, 4A1; 5B1; 10G2
Maidens, G&SW, 29G3
Maidstone, SEC, 6C5
Maindee Jcs, GW, 8B3; 43A3
Malden, LSW, 5B3; 39F3
Maldon East & Heybridge, GE, 12F5
Maldon West, GE, 12F5
Malins Lee, LNW, 15E2
Mallaig, NB, 32A5
Mallaig Jc, NB, 32C3
Malling, SEC, 5C5
Mallwyd, Mawd, 14A4
Malmesbury, GW, 9F3
Malpas, LNW, 15C1; 20E3
Maltby, SYJ, 21G4
Malton, NE, 22B5
Malvern Link, GW, 9C3
Malvern Road (Cheltenham), GW, 9D4
Malvern Wells, GW & Mid, 9C3
Manchester (Goods), CLC, GC, GN, LNW, LY & Mid, 20 –; 24 –; 45 –
Manchester (Pass), 20 –; 24 –; 45 –; Central: CLC Exchange: LNW(BJ); London Road: LNW(NS), GC & MSJA; Victoria: LY(LNW/Mid), 20B1; 24F1; 45A3
Manchester Docks, LY, 45B3
Manchester Line Jc, LNW, 15C2; 20E2
Manchester Road (Burnley), LY, 24D1
Manea, GE, 11A3; 17G4
Mangotsfield, Mid, 3A3; 8C1; 9G2
Manley Goods, CLC, 15B2; 20D3; 45E5
Manningham, Mid(NE), 21D2; 42A4
Manningtree, GE, 12E4
Manningtree N & E Jcs, GE, 12E4
Manod, GW, 19F3
Manor Park for Little Ilford, GE, 40E2
Manor Way, PLA(GE), 40C1
Manorbier, GW, 7D2
Manors, NE, 28 (inset)
Mansfield, Mid(GC) & GC, 16B4; 41D4
Mansfield Woodhouse, Mid(GC), 16B4; 41D4
Mansion House, Dist(Met), 40C5
Manton, Mid, 16F2
Manuel, NB, 30B4
Marazion, GW, 1F4 (inset)
March, GE, 11A3; 17F3
March N, S & W Jcs, GE, 11A3; 17F5
Marchington, NS(GN), 15D5
Marchmont, NB, 31D2
Marchwiel, Cam, 20E4
Marden, SEC, 6D5
Mardock, GE, 11F3
Mardy Jc, GW/GW&TVJt, 43C2
Marefield N, S & W Jcs, GN/GN&LNWJt, 16F2

Marfleet, NE, 22D3
Margam Jc, GW/PT, 7B4; 43F3
Margaretting Halt, GE, 11G5
Margate, SEC, 6B1
Marishes Road, NE, 22A5
Mark Lane, Dist&MetJt, 40C4
Mark's Tey, GE, 12E5
Market Bosworth, AN, 16F5
Market Drayton, GW(NS), 15D2; 20F2
Market Drayton Jc (Nantwich), LNW/GW, 15C2; 20E2
Market Drayton Jc (Wellington), SWN/GW, 15E2
Market Harborough, LNW & Mid, 16G2
Market Place (Chesterfield), GC, 16B5; 41C2
Market Rasen, GC, 17A1; 22G3
Market Street (Bradford), Mid(NE), 42A4
Market Weighton, NE, 22D4
Markham Village, LNW, 43B2
Markinch, NB, 30A2; 34G5
Marlborough, GW & MSW, 4A5
Marlborough Road, Met, 39B5
Marlow, GW, 10G2
Marlpool, GN, 16C4; 41F3
Marple, GC&MidJt, 21G1 ***see also*** Rose Hill
Marron West Jc, LNW/WCE, 26E3
Marsden (Durham), SSM, 28B5
Marsden (Yorks), LNW, 21F1
Marsden Cottage, SSM, 28B5
Marsh Brook, S&H, 14C1; 15G1
Marsh Farm Jc, S&H/GW, 14C1; 15G1
Marsh Gate (Goods), GC, 21G2 (inset)
Marsh Gibbon & Poundon, LNW, 10D3
Marsh Jc, GE, 12A1; 18F1
Marsh Lane (Lancs), LY, 45F3
Marsh Lane (Yorks), NE, 21D3; 42A2
Marsh Mills, GW, 2D5
Marshfield, GW, 8C3; 43A4
Marshland Jc, NE/AJ, 22E5
Marske, NE, 28E3
Marston Gate, LNW, 10E2
Marston Green, LNW, 15G5
Marston Magna, GW, 3D2; 8G1
Marston Moor, NE, 21C4
Martham, MGN, 18E1
Martock, GW, 3D2; 8G2
Marton, LNW, 10A5
Marton Jc, LNW, 10B5
Maryfield (Dundee), Cal, 34E4
Maryhill, Cal & NB, 29C5; 44E4
Marykirk, Cal, 34C3
Maryland Point, GE, 40B2
Marylebone, GC, 5A3; 39C5
Maryport, M&C(LNW), 26D3
Marytavy & Blackdown, GW, 1C5
Masbury, SD, 3C2; 8E1
Masham, NE, 21A3
Massingham, MGN, 18E5
Matlock, Mid, 16B5; 41D1
Matlock Bath, Mid, 16B5; 41D1
Matthews Town Halt, TV, 43C3
Mauchline, G&SW, 29E4
Maud Junc, GNS, 37D4
Maud's Bridge (Goods), GC, 22F5
Mauldeth Road, LNW, 45A3
Mawcarse Junc, NB, 33G5
Maxton, NB, 31E1
Maxwell Park, Cal, 44E3 and inset
Maxwelltown, G&SW, 26B4
May Hill (Monmouth), GW, 8A2; 9E1
Maybole, G&SW, 29F3
Mayfield (Manchester), LNW, 45A3
Mayfield (Sussex), LBSC, 5E5
Maze Hill (East Greenwich), SEC, 40D3
Meadow Hall & Wincobank, GC, 42F2 ***see also*** Wincobank
Mealsgate, M&C, 26D2
Measham, AN, 16E5
Medge Hall, GC, 22F5
Medina Wharf, IWC, 4F3
Medina Wharf (Goods), IWC, 4F3
Medstead, LSW, 4C2
Meigle, Cal, 34D5
Meikle Earnock, Cal, 29D5; 44B1
Meir, NS, 15C4
Melangoose Mill, GW, 1D2
Melbourne, Mid, 16D5
Melcombe Regis, WP, 3G3
Meldon, NB, 27A5
Meldon Jc, LSW, 2B5
Meldreth & Melbourn, GN, 11D3
Meledor Mill, GW, 1D2
Meliden, LNW, 19C5
Melksham, GW, 3A4
Melling, Fur&MidJt, 24B2
Mellis, GE, 12B4
Mells Road, GW, 3B3; 8E1
Melmerby, NE, 21A3
Melrose, NB, 31E1
Meltham, LY, 21F2; 42D5
Meltham Branch Jc, LY, 42D5
Melton, GE, 12D3
Melton Constable, MGN, 18D4
Melton Jc, Mid, 16E2
Melton Mowbray, Mid(MGN) & GN&LNWJt, 16E2
Melverley, S&M, 14A1
Melyncourt Halt, GW, 43E2
Menai Bridge, LNW, 19D2
Mendlesham, MSL, 12C4
Menheniot, GW, 1D4
Menston, Mid(NE), 21D2
Menstrie & Glenochil, NB, 30A5
Menthorpe Gate, NE, 21D5
Meole Brace, S&M, 14B1; 15E1
Meols, Wir, 20C5
Meols Cop, LY, 20A4; 24E4; 45F1
Meopham, SEC, 5B5
Merchiston, Cal, 30 (inset)
Merrybent Jc, NE, 27E5
Merryton Jc, Cal, 44B1
Mersey Road & Aigburth, CLC, 45F4
Merstham, SEC, 5C3
Merstone, IWC, 4F3
Merthyr, GW(BM/LNW/TV) & TV, 8A5; 43C2
Merthyr Vale, TV, 8B5; 43C2
Merton Abbey, LBSC&LSWJt, 39F5
Merton Park, LBSC&LSWJt, 39F4
Methil, NB, 30A2; 34G4
Methley, Mid(LY), LY & MJ, 21E4; 42B1
Methley Jc, GN&LY&NEJt/LY/Mid, 42B1
Methven, Cal, 33E4
Methven Jc, Cal, 33E4
Metropolitan Jc, SEC, 40C5
Mexborough, GC(Mid), 21F4
Micheldever, LSW, 4C3
Micklam, CWJ, 26E3
Mickle Trafford, BJ & CLC, 15B1; 20D3
Micklefield, NE, 21D4; 42A1
Micklehurst (Goods), LNW, 21F1
Mickleover, GN, 16D5; 41G1
Mickleton, NE, 27E4
Mid Clyth, HR, 38E2
Mid Suffolk Light Railway, MSL, 12B3; 12C3
Midcalder, Cal, 30C3
Midcalder Jc, Cal, 30B3
Middle Drove, GE, 17F4
Middle Stoke Halt, SEC, 6B5
Middlemuir Jc, NB, 44C5
Middlesbrough, NE, 28E4
Middlestown, Mid, 42C3
Middlestown Jc, Mid, 42C3
Middleton (Lancs), LY, 20B1; 24F1; 45A2
Middleton (Norfolk), GE, 17E5
Middleton (Northumb), NE, 27A4
Middleton (Salop), S&H, 9A1
Middleton (Westmorland), LNW, 24A2; 27G1
Middleton-in-Teesdale, NE, 27E3
Middleton Junc, LY, 20B1; 45A2
Middleton-on-the-Wolds, NE, 22C4
Middleton Road Goods (Heysham), Mid, 24C3
Middletown, SWP, 14A2
Middlewich, LNW, 20D2
Middlewood, LNW & GC&NSJt, 15A4
Midford, SD, 3B3; 8D1
Midford Halt, GW, 3B3; 8D1
Midge Hall, LY, 20A3; 24E3
Midgham, GW, 4A3
Midhurst, LBSC, 5E1
Midhurst, LSW, 4D1; 5E1
Midsomer Norton & Welton, GW & SD, 3B3; 8E1
Midville, GN, 17C3
Milborne Port, LSW, 3D3; 8G1
Milcote, GW, 9B5
Mildenhall, GE, 11B5
Mildmay Park, NL, 40B4
Mile End, WB, 40C3
Miles Platting, LY, 20B1; 24F1; 45A3
Milford (Surrey), LSW, 5D1
Milford & Brocton, LNW, 15E4
Milford Haven, GW, 7D1
Milford Jc (Wilts), LSW, 4D5
Milford Jc (Yorks), NE, 21D4
Milkwall for Clearwell, SVW, 8A2; 9E1
Mill Hill (IoW), IWC, 4F3
Mill Hill (Lancs), LY(LNW), 20A2; 24E2
Mill Hill (Middx), Mid & GN, 5A3
Mill Houses, Mid, 16A5
Mill Road Halt, GE, 11E4

Mill Street Goods (Aberdare), GW, 8A5; 43D2
Millbay (Plymouth), GW, 1D5 and inset
Millbrook (Beds), LNW, 10C1; 11D1
Millbrook (Hants), LSW(MSW), 4E4
Millerhill, NB, 30B2
Miller's Dale, Mid, 15A5
Millers Dale Jc, Mid, 15A5
Millfield, NE, 28C5
Millhouses & Ecclesall, Mid, 16A5; 41A2
Milliken Park, G&SW, 29C4
Millisle, P&W, 25D4
Millom, Fur, 24A5
Milltimber, GNS, 37G3
Millwall Docks, GE, 40D3
Millwall Junc, GE, 40C3 and inset D1
Millwood Jc, Fur, 24B5
Milnathort, NB, 33G5
Milner Royd Jc, LY, 21E1; 42C5
Milner Wood Jc, Mid/O&I, 21C2
Milngavie, NB 29B4; 44E5
Milngavie Jc, NB, 29C4; 44E5
Milnrow, LY, 20B1; 45A1
Milnthorpe, LNW, 24A3
Milton (Staffs), NS, 15C3; 20E1
Milton Halt, GW, 10C4
Milton Jc (Glasgow), Cal, 44D4
Milton of Campsie, NB, 29B5
Milton Road, WCP, 3A1; 8D3
Milverton (Som), GW, 8F4
Milverton (Warwick), LNW, 10B5
Mindrum, NE, 31E3
Minehead, GW, 8E5
Minety & Ashton Keynes, GW, 9F4
Minffordd, Cam & Fest, 19F2
Minions, LC, 1C4
Minories Jc, Met/Dist, 40C4
Minshull Vernon, LNW, 15B2; 20E2
Minster (Thanet), SEC, 6C2
Minster 'B' Jc, SEC, 6C2
Minster East Jc, SEC, 6C2
Minster West Jc, SEC, 6C2
Minster-On-Sea (Sheppey), SEC, 6B4
Minsterley, SWP, 14B1
Mint Street Goods, GN & Mid, 40C4
Mintlaw, GNS, 37D4
Mirehouse Jc, Fur, 26F3
Mirfield, LY(LNW), 21E2; 42C4
Mislingford (Goods), LSW, 4E3
Misson (Goods), GN, 21G5
Misterton, GN&GEJt, 22G5
Mistley, GE, 12E4
Mitcham, LBSC, 5B3; 39G5
Mitcham Junc, LBSC, 5B3; 39G5
Mitcheldean Road, GW, 9D2
Mitchell & Newlyn Halt, GW, 1D1
Mithian Halt, GW, 1D1
Mitre Bridge Goods, LNW, 39C4
Mitre Bridge Jc, LNW, 39C3
Moat Lane Junc, Cam, 14C3
Mobberley, CLC, 20C1; 15A3; 45B5
Mochdre & Pabo, LNW, 19D4
Moffat, Cal, 30G3
Moira, Mid, 16E5
Mold, LNW, 20E5
Mold Jc, LNW, 20D4
Mollington, BJ, 20D4
Molyneux Brow, LY, 45B2
Molyneux Jc, LY/LNW, 45B2
Moniaive, G&SW, 26A5
Monifieth, D&A, 34E4
Monikie, Cal, 34D4
Monk Bretton, Mid, 21F3; 42E2
Monk Bretton Jc, Mid/HB, 42E2
Monk Fryston, NE(LY/GN), 21D4
Monkhill (Pontefract), LY(NE), 21E4; 42C1
Monkland Jc, NB, 44C5
Monks Lane Halt, LBSC, 5C4
Monkseaton, NE, 28B5
Monkton, G&SW, 29E3
Monkton & Came Halt, GW, 3F3
Monkton Combe, GW, 3B3; 8D1
Monkwearmouth, NE, 28C5
Monmore Green, LNW, 15F3
Monmouth, GW, 8A2; 9E1
Monsal Dale, Mid, 15B5
Montacute, GW, 3D2; 8G2
Montgomerie Pier (Ardrossan), Cal, 29D3
Montgomery, Cam, 14B2
Montgreenan, G&SW, 29D3
Monton Green, LNW, 45B3
Montpelier, CE, 3 (inset)
Montrave (Goods), NB, 34G4
Montrose, NB & Cal, 34C2
Monument, Dist&MetJt, 40C4
Monument Lane, LNW, 13C3
Monymusk, GNS, 37F2
Moor End (Goods), GC, 21F3; 42E3
Moor Row, WCE, 26F3
Moor Street Wharf (Burton-on-Trent), LNW, 15D5 (inset)
Moorbridge Jc, GN/GC, 16C4; 41F4
Moore, LNW, 15A1; 20C3; 45D4
Moorfields Goods (Hereford), Mid, 9C1
Moorgate, LNW, 21F1
Moorgate Street, Met(Dist/GN/GW/H&C/Mid), 40C4
Moorhampton, Mid, 14E1
Moorhouse & South Elmsall, HB, 21F4; 42 D1
Moorside & Wardley, LY, 45B2
Moorswater Jc, LL/LC, 1D4
Moorthorpe & South Elmsall, SK(GC), 21F4; 42D1
Moorthorpe South Jc, SK(GC), 42D1
Moortown, GC, 22F3
Morar, NB, 32B5
Morchard Road, LSW, 2A4
Morcott, LNW, 16F1
Morden Halt (Surrey), LBSC, 39F5
Morebath, GW, 8F5
Morecambe, Mid & LNW, 24B3
Moresby Parks, CWJ, 26E3
Moreton (Ches), Wir, 20C5; 24G4
Moreton (Dorset), LSW, 3F3
Moreton-in-Marsh, GW, 9D5
Moreton-on-Lugg, S&H, 9C1
Moretonhampstead, GW, 2B4
Morlais Jc, BM/LNW, 8A5; 43C1
Morley, LNW & GN, 21E3; 42B3
Mormond, GNS, 37C4
Morningside Road, NB, 30 (inset)
Morningside, Cal & NB, 30C5
Morpeth, NE(NB), 27A5
Morriston, GW & Mid, 7B4; 43G2
Mortehoe, LSW(GW), 7E3
Mortimer, GW, 4A2
Mortlake, LSW, 5B2; 39E3
Morton Pinkney, SMJ, 10C4
Morton Road, GN, 17E1
Moseley, Mid, 15G4
Moses Gate, LY, 45B2
Moss (Denbigh) & Pentre, GC, 20E4
Moss (Yorks), NE, 21E5
Moss Bank, LNW, 20B3; 24F3; 45D3
Moss Halt (Denbigh), GW, 20E4
Moss Road Halt, CM, 29 (inset)
Moss Side, PWY, 24D4
Mossblown Jc, G&SW, 29E4
Mossbridge, CLC, 20B4; 24F4; 45F2
Mossend, Cal, 30C5; 44B3
Mossley Halt, NS, 15B3; 20E1
Mossley, LNW, 21F1
Mossley Hill for Aigburth, LNW, 20C4; 24G4; 45F4
Mosstowie, HR, 36C2
Moston, LY, 20B1; 24F1; 45A2
Mostyn, LNW, 20C5
Motherwell, Cal, 30C5; 44B2
Mottisfont, LSW(MSW), 4D4
Mottram & Broadbottom, GC, 21G1
Mouldsworth, CLC, 15B2; 20D3; 45D5
Moulinearn Crossing, HR, 33D4
Moulton (Lincs), MGN, 17E3
Moulton (Yorks), NE, 27F5
Mount Florida, Cal, 44E3
Mount Gould & Tothill Halt, GW, 1A2
Mount Gould Jc, GW, 1 (inset)
Mount Hawke Halt, GW, 1E1
Mount Melville, NB, 34F4
Mount Pleasant, NE, 28B5
Mount Pleasant Road Halt, LSW, 2C3
Mount Vernon, Cal & NB, 29C5; 44C3
Mountain Ash, GW & TV, 8B5; 43C2
Mow Cop & Scholar Green, NS, 15B3; 20E1
Moy, HR, 36E4
Much Wenlock, GW, 15F2
Muchalls, Cal, 34A1
Muir of Ord, HR, 35D5
Muirend, Cal, 29C5; 44E2
Muirhouse South Jc, Cal, 44F1 (inset)
Muirkirk, G&SW(Cal), 29E5
Mulben, HR, 36D1
Mumbles Pier, Mum, 7B3; 43G3
Mumbles Road, LNW & Mum, 7B3; 43G3
Mumby Road, GN, 17A4
Mumps (Oldham) LY, 21D1 (inset)
Muncaster, RE, 26G3
Mundesley-on-Sea, NSJ, 18D2
Munlochy, HR, 36D5
Murrayfield, Cal, 30 (inset)

Murrow, GN&GEJt & MGN, 17F3
Murthly, HR, 33E5
Murtle, GNS, 37G4
Murton, NE, 28C5
Murton Lane, DVL, 21C5
Musgrave, NE, 27F2
Musselburgh, NB, 30B2
Muthill, Cal, 33F4
Mutley, GW(LSW), 1A2 (inset)
Mwyndy Jc, GW, 43C4
Mynydd-y-Garreg (Goods), GV, 7A2
Myrtle Hill Jc, GW, 13G4
Mytholmroyd, LY, 21E1

Naburn, NE, 21C5
Nafferton, NE, 22C3
Nailsea & Backwell, GW, 3A2; 8D2
Nailsworth, Mid, 9F3
Nairn, HR, 36D4
Nancegollan, GW, 1F5 (inset)
Nannerch, LNW, 20D5
Nanstallon Halt, LSW, 1D3
Nantclwyd, LNW, 19E5
Nantgaredig, LNW, 13G4
Nantgarw Halt, AD & Car, 43C3
Nantlle, LNW, 19E2
Nantmawr, Cam, 20G5
Nantwich, LNW(GW), 15C2; 20E2
Nantybwch, LNW, 8A4; 43C1
Nantybwch, Rhy, 9A5; 43C1
Nantyderry, GW, 8A3; 43A2
Nantyffyllon, GW, 7B5; 43E3
Nantyglo, GW, 8A4; 43B1
Nantymoel, GW, 7B5; 43D3
Nantyronen, VR, 14C5
Napsbury, Mid, 11G1
Napton & Stockton, LNW, 10B4
Narberth, GW, 7C3
Narborough (Leics), LNW, 16F4
Narborough (Norfolk), GE, 17E5
Nassington, LNW, 11A1; 16F1; 17F1
Nast Hyde Halt, GN, 11F2
Nateby, KE, 24D3
Navenby, GN, 16B1; 17C1
Naworth, NE, 27C1
Nawton, NE, 21A5
Neasden & Kingsbury, Met, 5A2; 39B4
Neasden Jc, GC/Mid, 39B3
Neasden Railway Works, LNW, 39B3; 36E5
Neath, GW, GW(N&B), RSB & N&B, 7B4; 43F2
Neath Abbey, GW, 7B4; 43F2
Neath Jc, RSB, 43F3
Neath Low Level, RSB, 43F2
Needham, GE, 12C4
Needingworth Jc, GN&GEJt/GE, 11B3
Neen Sollars, GW, 9A2
Neepsend, GC, 21G3; 42G2
Neilston, GBK & Cal, 29C4; 44G2
Nelson (Glam), TV, 8B4; 43C3
Nelson (Lancs), LY, 21B1 (inset); 24D1
Neptune Street (Goods) (Hull), HB, 22 (inset)
Nesscliff & Pentre, S&M, 14A1
Neston & Parkgate, GC, 20D4; 45F5
Neston, BJ, 20D4; 45F5
Netherburn, Cal, 30D5
Nethercleugh, Cal, 26A3
Netherfield, GN(LNW), 16C3; 41F5 *see also* Carlton, Mid
Netherton Goods (Fife), NB, 30A3
Netherton Goods (Renfrew), Cal, 29C4; 44F2
Netherton (Staffs), GW, 13B1; 15G4
Netherton (Yorks), LY, 21E2; 42D5
Nethertown, Fur, 26F3
Nethy Bridge, GNS, 36F3
Netley, LSW, 4E3
New Barnet, GN(NL), 5A3; 11G2
New Basford, GC, 41F4
New Beckenham, SEC, 40F3
New Beckenham Jc, SEC, 40F3
New Biggin, Mid, 27E1
New Bolingbroke, GN, 17C3
New Brighton, Wir, 20C4; 24G4; 45F3
New Clee, GC, 22F2
New Cross (Goods), GE, 40D3
New Cross (Pass), LBSC(EL) & SEC(EL), 40D3
New Cumnock, G&SW, 29F5
New Cut Lane Halt, LY, 20B4; 24F4; 45F1
New Eltham & Pope Street, SEC, 5B4; 40E1
New England Sidings, GN, 11A2; 17F2
New Galloway, P&W, 26B5
New Hailes, NB, 30B2
New Hall Bridge Halt, LY, 24D1
New Hey, LY, 21F1
New Holland, GC, 22E3
New Inn Yard Jc, NL/LNW, 40C4
New Lane, LY, 20A4; 24F3; 45E1
New Luce, G&SW, 25B2
New Machar, GNS, 37F4
New Mills (Derbys), LNW, Mid & GC&MidJt, 15A4; 21G1
New Milton, LSW, 4F5
New Monkton Main Colliery, WRG, 42D1
New Radnor, GW, 14E2
New Road (Ynysybwl), TV, 43C3
New Romney & Littlestone-on-Sea, SEC, 6E3
New Southgate, GN, 5A3
New Street (Birmingham), LNW&MidJt, 13C3; 15G4
New Tredegar & Tir Phil, BM, 8A4; 43B2 *see also* Tir Phil
New Wandsworth, LBSC, 39F2 (inset)
Newark, GN & Mid, 16C2
Newarthill (Goods), Cal, 44A2
Newbiggin-by-the-Sea, NE, 28A5
Newbigging, Cal, 30D4
Newbridge (Mon), GW, 43B2
Newbridge-on-Wye, Cam, 14E3
Newburgh, NB, 34F5
Newburn, NE, 27B5; 28 (inset)
Newbury, GW, 4A3
Newbury (West Fields) Halt, GW, 4A3
Newbury Park, GE, 40A1
Newbury Racecourse, GW, 4A3
Newby Wiske, NE, 21A3; 28G5
Newcastle Emlyn, GW, 13F3
Newcastle-on-Tyne, NE(NB) & NE, 27B5/C5; 28 (inset)
Newcastle-under-Lyme, NS, 15C3; 20F1
Newcastleton, NB, 27A1
Newchapel & Goldenhill, NS, 15C3; 20E1
Newchurch, IWC, 4F3
Newent, GW, 9D2
Newham (Northumb), NE, 31E5
Newham Goods (Truro), GW, 1E1
Newhaven (Leith), Cal, 30 (inset)
Newhaven Harbour (Sussex), LBSC, 5F4
Newhaven Town (Sussex), LBSC, 5F4
Newhouse, Cal, 30C5; 44A3
Newick & Chailey, LBSC, 5F4
Newington (Edinburgh), NB, 30 (inset)
Newington (Kent), SEC, 6B4
Newland, GW, 8A2; 9E1
Newlay & Horsforth, Mid, 21D3; 42A3
Newmains, Cal, 30C5
Newmarket Warren Hill, GE, 11C4
Newmilns, G&SW, 29E4
Newnham, GW, 8A1; 9E2
Newnham Bridge, GW, 9A2
Newpark, Cal, 30C3
Newport (East Riding), HB, 22D5
Newport (Essex), GE, 11E4
Newport (IoW), IWC(FYN) & FYN, 4F3
Newport (Mon) (Alexandra Dock), AD, 8C3; 43A4
Newport (Mon), GW(LNW/BM) & GW, 8B3; 43A3
Newport (North Riding), NE, 28E4
Newport (Salop), LNW, 15E2
Newport Pagnell, LNW, 10C2
Newquay, GW, 1D1
Newseat, GNS, 37D5
Newsham, NE, 28A5
Newsholme, LY, 24C1
Newstead, Mid & GN, 16C4; 41E4
Newstead Lane Jc, MGN/NSJ, 18D3
Newthorpe, GN, 41F3
Newton (Ches), GC, 21G1
Newton (Lanarks), Cal, 29C5; 44C3
Newton Abbot, GW, 2C3
Newton Heath, LY, 20B1; 24F1; 45A2
Newton Jc, NB, 44C3
Newton Kyme, NE, 21D4
Newton-le-Willows, LNW(BJ), 20C3; 24G2; 45D3
Newton-on-Ayr, G&SW, 29F3
Newton Poppleford, LSW, 2B2
Newton Road, LNW, 13B3; 15F4
Newton St Cyres, LSW, 2B3
Newton Stewart, P&W, 25B4
Newton Tony, LSW, 4C5
Newtonairds, G&SW, 26A4
Newtongrange, NB, 30C2
Newtonhill, Cal, 34A1
Newtonmore, HR, 33A2
Newtown (Mon), Cam, 14C3
Newtyle, Cal, 34D5
Neyland, GW, 7D2
Nidd Bridge, NE, 21C3
Niddrie, NB, 30B2
Nigg, HR, 36B4

Nine Elms Goods, LSW, 40D5
Nine Mile Point, LNW, 8B4; 43B3
Nine Wells Jc, Cal, 34E4 and inset G2
Ningwood, FYN, 4F4
Nisbet, NB, 31E1
Nitshill, GBK, 29C4; 44F3
No 5 Pet Sidings, M&C, 26D3
Nocton & Dunston, GN&GEJt, 16B1; 17B1
Noel Park & Wood Green, GE, 40A5
Norbiton for Kingston Hill, LSW, 5B2; 39F3
Norbury (Surrey), LBSC, 40F5
Norbury & Ellaston, NS, 15C5
Norham, NE, 31D3
Normacot, NS, 15C3
Norman's Bay Halt, LBSC, 5F5
Normanby Park (Goods), GC, 22E4
Normanton (Yorks), Mid(LY/NE), 21E4; 42C2
North Berwick, NB, 31B1
North Blyth (Goods), NE, 28A5
North Bridge (Halifax), H&O, 21E2; 42B5
North Cave, HB, 22D4
North Connel, Cal, 32E4
North Docks (Liverpool), LY, 45F3 and inset
North Drove, MGN, 17E2
North Dulwich, LBSC, 40E4
North Ealing, Dist, 39C3
North Eastrington, HB, 22D5
North Elmham, GE, 18E4
North Greenwich, GE, 40D3
North Grimston, NE, 22B5
North Harrow, Met&GCJt, 5A2; 39A1
North Hayling, LBSC, 4E2
North Howden, NE, 22D5
North Jc (Derby), Mid, 16D5
North Kelsey, GC, 22F3
North Kent Jc, SEC, 40D3
North Kent West Jc, SEC, 40D4
North Leith, NB, 30 (inset)
North Maindee Jc, GW, 8B3; 43A3
North Mersey (Goods), LY, 45F3 and inset
North Pole Jc, GW/LNW/WL, 39C4
North Quay Jc (Yarmouth), MGN, 18F1
North Queensferry, FB, 30B3
North Road (Darlington), NE, 28E5
North Road (Plymouth), GW&LSWJt, 1D5 and inset
North Rode, NS, 15B3; 20D1
North Seaton, NE, 27A5
North Shields, NE, 28B5
North Skelton, NE, 28E3
North Staff Jc, Mid/NS, 15D5 (inset)
North Sunderland, NSL, 31E5
North Tawton, LSW, 2B5
North Thoresby, GN, 22F2
North Wales Narrow Gauge Railway, NWNG, 19E2
North Walsham, GE & MGN, 18D2
North Water Bridge, NB, 34C2
North Weald, GE, 11G4
North Wembley, LNW(LE), 39B2
North Woolwich, GE, 5B4; 40D1
North Wootton, GE, 17E5
North Wylam, NE, 27B5
Northallerton, NE, 21A3; 28G5
Northallerton Low Jc, NE, 28G5
Northallerton South Jc, NE, 21A3; 28G5
Northam (Devon), BWHA, 7F2
Northam (Hants), LSW(GW), 4E4
Northampton, LNW & Mid, 10B2
Northenden, CLC(LNW), 20C1; 24G1; 45A4
Northern Jc, GC&MidJt/GC&Mid&HBJt, 21G4
Northfield, Mid, 9A4
Northfield & Little Ealing, Met & Dist, 39D2
Northfleet, SEC, 5B5
Northgate (Chester), CLC, 20D4
Northiam, KES, 6E5
Northolt Halt for West End, GW, 39B1
Northolt Junc, GW&GCJt, 5A2; 39B1
Northorpe (Lincs), GC, 22G4
Northorpe (Yorks), LNW & LY, 42C4
Northumberland Park, GE, 40A4
Northwich, CLC(LNW), 15A2; 20D2; 45C5
Northwood (Middx), Met&GCJt, 5A2
Norton (Ches), BJ, 15A1; 20C3; 45D4
Norton (Yorks), LY(GN), 21E5
Norton Bridge, LNW(NS) & NS, 15D3; 20G1
Norton Fitzwarren, GW, 8F4
Norton-in-Hales, NS, 15D2; 20F2
Norton Junc, GW, 9B3
Norton-on-Tees, NE, 28E5
Norwich, GE & MGN, 18F3
Norwood Jc (Newcastle-on-Tyne), NE, 28B2 (inset)
Norwood Junc (Surrey), LBSC(SEC & LNW), 5B3; 40G4
Nostell, WRG, 21E4; 42C1
Nostell N, S, E & W Jcs, GC & GC/WRG, 21E4
Notgrove, GW, 9D4
Notting Hill Gate, Met(Dist), 39C4
Nottingham (Goods), Mid, GC, GN & LNW, 16C/D; 41G4/5
Nottingham (Pass), Mid, GC&GNJt & GN(LNW), 16C/D; 41G4/5
Nottingham Road, (Derby), Mid, 16D5; 41G2
Notton & Royston, GC, 21F3; 42D2 *see also* Royston, Mid
Novar, HR, 36C5
Nunburnholme, NE, 22C5
Nuneaton (Abbey Street), Mid, 16F5
Nuneaton (Trent Valley), LNW, 16F5
Nunhead, SEC, 40D4
Nunnery (Goods) (Sheffield), LNW, 41A2; 42G2
Nunnington, NE, 21A5
Nunthorpe, NE, 28E4
Nursling, LSW(MSW), 4D4
Nutbourne Halt, LBSC, 4E1
Nutfield, SEC, 5D3
Nysddu, LNW, 8B4; 43B3

Oakamoor, NS, 15C4
Oakengates, GW & LNW, 15E2
Oakenshaw (Goods), Mid, 21E4; 42C2
Oakenshaw Jc, LY/Mid, 42C2
Oakham, Mid, 16E2
Oakington, GE(Mid), 11C3
Oakle Street, GW, 8A1; 9E2
Oaklea Jc, Fur, 24B5
Oakleigh Park, GN(NL), 5A3; 11G2
Oakley (Beds), Mid, 10B1; 11C1
Oakley (Fife), NB, 30A4
Oakley (Hants), LSW, 4B3
Oakley Jc, Mid, 10C1; 11D1
Oakworth, Mid, 21D1
Oatlands, WCE, 26E3
Oban, Cal, 32F4
Occumster, HR, 38E2
Ochiltree, G&SW, 29F4
Ockendon, LTS, 5A5
Ockley for Capel, LBSC, 5D2
Oddington Halt, LNW, 10E4
Offord & Buckden, GN, 11C2
Ogbourne, MSW, 4A5
Ogmore Vale, GW, 7B5; 43D3
Okehampton, LSW, 2B5
Old Colwyn, LNW, 19D4
Old Cumnock, G&SW, 29F5
Old Dalby, Mid, 16E3
Old Ford, NL, 40B3
Old Hill (High Street) Halt, GW, 13C1; 15G4
Old Kent Rd Jc, LBSC, 40D4
Old Kilpatrick, Cal, 29B4; 44G5
Old Leake, GN, 17C3
Old Main Line Jc, BJ/LNW, 15A1; 20C3; 24G2
Old Meldrum, GNS, 37E3
Old Mill Lane Halt, LNW, 45E3
Old North Road, LNW, 11C2
Old Oak Common West Jc, GW, 39C3
Old Oak Jc, LNW/NSW, 39C3
Old Oak Lane Halt, GW, 39C3
Old Roan Halt, LY, 20B4; 24F4; 45F3
Old Street, GN, 40C5
Old Trafford, MSJA(CLC), 45B3
Old Woods (Goods), 15E1; 20G3
Old Ynysybwl Halt, TV, 43C3
Oldbury (Goods & Pass), GW, 13B2; 15G4
Oldbury & Bromford Lane, LNW, 13B2
Oldham, OAGB, LY, LNW, & GC, 21F1 and inset D1; 45A2
Oldham Clegg Street, OAGB, 21D1
Oldham Road (Ashton) (Goods), LNW, 21A2 (inset)
Oldham Road (Ashton) (Pass), OAGB(LY), 21A2 (inset)
Oldham Road (Manor) (Goods), LY, 45A3
Oldham Werneth, LY, 21D1
Ollerton, GC, 16B3
Olney, Mid, 10B2
Olton, GW, 9A5; 15G5
Omoa, Cal, 30C5; 44A2
Omoa Jc, Cal, 44A2
Ongar, GE, 11G4
Onibury, S&H, 9A1; 14C1
Onllwyn, N&B, 7A5; 43E1
Orbliston Junc, HR, 36D1
Ordens Platform, GNS, 37C2
Ordsall Lane, LNW(BJ), 45B3
Ore, SEC, 6F5
Oreston, LSW, 1 (inset)
Ormesby, NE, 28E4

Ormiston, NB, 30B1
Ormsgill Jc, Fur, 24B5
Ormside, Mid, 27E2
Ormskirk, LY(LNW), 20B4; 24F3; 45E2
Orpington, SEC, 5B4; 40G1
Orpington Jc, SEC, 40G1
Orrell, LY, 20B3; 24F3; 45D2
Orrell Park, LY, 45F3
Orton, HR, 36D1
Orton Waterville, LNW, 11A1; 17F2
Orwell, GE, 12D3
Ossett, GN, 21F3; 42C3 *see also* Horbury
Osterley & Spring Grove, Dist, 5B2; 39D2
Oswestry, GW & Cam, 20G4
Otford, SEC, 5C5
Otley, O&I, 21D2
Otley & Ilkley Jc (Mid/NE(O&I), 21C2
Otley & Ilkley (Mid & NE) Jc, Mid/Mid & NE, 21C2
Otterham, LSW, 1B3
Otterington, NE, 21A3; 28G5
Otterspool, CLC, 45F4
Ottery St Mary, LSW, 2B2
Ottringham, NE, 22E2
Oughterside Colliery Platform, M&C, 26D3
Oughty Bridge, GC, 21G3; 42F3
Oulton Broad, GE, 12A1; 18G1
Oundle, LNW, 11A1; 16G1
Outwell Village, WUT, 17F4
Ovenden, H&O, 21E2; 42B5
Over & Wharton, LNW, 15B2; 20D2 *see also* Winsford & Over
Over Jc, GW, 9D3
Overstrand, NSJ, 18D3
Overton (Hants), LSW, 4B3
Overton (Renfrew), Cal, 29B3
Overton-on-Dee, Cam, 20F4
Overtown, Cal, 30D5
Oxenholme, LNW(Fur), 24A3; 27G1
Oxenhope, Mid, 21D1
Oxford, GW, 10E4
Oxford (Rewley Road), LNW, 10E4
Oxford Road, (Oxon), LNW, 10E4
Oxford Road Halt (Oxon), LNW, 10E4
Oxheys (Goods), LNW, 24D3
Oxshott & Fair Mile, LSW, 5C2
Oxted & Limpsfield, CO, 5C4
Oxton, NB, 30C1
Oyne, GNS, 37E2
Oystermouth, Mum, 43G3

Padbury, LNW, 10D3
Paddington, GW, 5B3; 39C5 and inset C3 *see also* Bishops Road *and* Praed Street
Paddock Wood, SEC, 5D5
Padeswood & Buckley, LNW, 20E4 *see also* Buckley
Padgate, CLC, 20C2; 24G2; 45C4
Padgate Jc, CLC, 45C4
Padiham, LY, 24D1
Padstow, LSW, 1C2
Paignton, GW, 2D3
Paisley, G&P, Cal & G&SW, 29C4; 44F3
Palace Gates (Wood Green), GE, 5A3; 40A5
Pallion, NE, 28C5
Palmers Green, GN(NL), 5A3
Palnure, P&W, 25B4
Palterton & Sutton, Mid, 16B4; 41C3
Pampisford, GE, 11D4
Pandy, GW, 14G1
Pangbourne, GW, 4A2; 10G3
Pannal, NE, 21C3
Pannal Jc, NE, 21C3
Pant (Glam), BM, 8A5; 43C1
Pant (Salop), Cam, 14A2; 20G4
Pant Glas, LNW, 19E1
Panteg & Griffithstown, GW, 8B3; 43A2
Panteg Jc, GW, 8B3; 43A2
Pantydwr, Cam, 14D4
Pantyffynnon, GW(LNW), 7A3; 43G1
Pantysgallog, BM, 43C1
Papcastle, M&C, 26D3
Par, GW, 1D3
Paragon (Hull), NE(GC/LNW/LY), 22E3
Parbold, LY, 20B3; 24F3; 45E1
Parham, GE, 12C2
Park (Aberdeen), GNS, 34A2; 37G3
Park (Barrow) (Goods), Fur, 24B5
Park (Birkenhead), Wir&MerJt, 45F4
Park (Kincard), GNS, 37G3
Park (Manchester), LY, 45A3
Park (Sheffield) (Goods), GC, 41A2; 42G2
Park Bridge, OAGB, 21F1
Park Drain, GN&GEJt, 22F5
Park Jcs (Newport, Mon), GW, 43A3
Park Lane Goods (Liverpool), LNW, 45F4 and inset
Park Lane Jc (Lancs), LNW, 45D3
Park Lane Jc (Gateshead), NE, 28 (inset)
Park Parade (Ashton), GC, 21A2 (inset)
Park Royal, GW, 39C3
Park Royal & Twyford Abbey, Dist, 39C3
Park Street & Frogmore, LNW, 11G1
Parkend, SVW, 8A1; 9F2
Parkeston Quay, GE, 12E3
Parkgate (Ches), BJ, 20D4; 45F5 *see also* Neston
Parkgate & Aldwarke (Yorks), GC, 21G4; 42F1
Parkgate & Rawmarsh (Yorks), Mid, 21G4; 42F1
Parkhead for Celtic Park (Glasgow), Cal & NB, 44D3
Parkhead (Goods), NE, 27D4
Parkhill, GNS, 37F4
Parks Bridge Jc, SEC, 40E3
Parkside Jcs, LNW, 45D3
Parkstone, LSW(SD), 3F5
Parracombe, LB, 7E4
Parsley Hay, LNW, 15B5
Parsons Green, Dist, 39D4
Partick, Cal & NB, 29C4; 44E4
Partick Central, NB, 44E4
Partick West, Cal, 44E4
Partington, CLC, 20C2; 24G1; 45B3
Parton (Cumb), LNW, 26E4
Parton (Kirkcud), G&SW, 26B5
Partridge Green, LBSC, 5E2
Paston & Knapton, NSJ, 18D2
Patchway, GW, 8C1; 9G1
Pateley Bridge, NE & NV, 21B2
Patna, G&SW, 29F4
Patney & Chirton, GW, 3B5
Patricroft, LNW(BJ), 20B2; 24F1; 45B3
Patrington, NE, 22E2
Patterton, Cal, 29C4; 44E2
Paulton Halt, GW, 3B3; 8D1
Peacock Cross, NB, 44B2
Peak Forest for Peak Dale, Mid, 15A5
Peakirk GN, 17F2
Pear Tree & Normanton, Mid, 16D5: 41G2
Peasley Cross, LNW, 45D3
Peasley Jc, LNW, 45D3
Peasmarsh Jc, LSW/LBSC, 5D1
Peckham Rye, LBSC(SEC), 40D4
Peckham Rye Coal Depot, LNW&MidJt, 40D4
Pedair Ffordd, Tan, 14A3; 19G5
Peebles, NB & Cal, 30D2
Peel, IMR, 23B2
Peel Road, IMR, 23B2
Pegswood, NE, 27A5
Pelaw, NE, 28C5 and inset
Pellon, HHL, 21E2; 42B5
Pelsall, LNW, 15F4
Pelton, NE, 27C5
Pemberton, LY, 20B3; 24F3; 45D2
Pembrey, BPGV, 7B2
Pembrey & Burry Port, GW, 7B2
Pembridge, GW, 14E1
Pembroke, GW, 7D2
Pen Mill (Yeovil), GW, 3D2; 8G2
Pen-y-ffordd, GC, 20E4
Pen-y-graig, GW, 8B5; 43D3
Penallta Branch Jc, Rhy, 43B3
Penallta Jc, GW/Rhy, 43V3
Penally, GW, 7D3
Penar Jc, GW, 43B3
Penarth, TV, 8D4; 43B5
Penarth Branch Jc, TV, 43C4
Penarth Curve Jc, GW/TV, 8C4
Penarth Dock TV, 8C4; 43B5
Pencader, GW, 13F4
Pencaitland, NB, 30C1
Penclawdd, LNW, 7B3
Pencoed, GW, 8C5; 43D4
Pendlebury, LY, 45B2
Pendleton, LY, 45B3
Pendleton (Broad Street), LY, 45B3
Pendre, Tal, 13B5
Pengam & Fleur-de-lis (Mon), BM, 8B4; 43B2
Penge, LBSC & SEC, 40F4
Penge Jc, SEC, 40F3
Penicuik, NB, 30C2
Penistone, GC&LYJt, 21F3; 42E3
Penkridge, LNW, 15E3
Penmaenmawr, LNW, 19D3
Penmaenpool, Cam, 14A5
Pennington, LNW, 45C3
Penns, Mid, 15F5
Penpergwm, GW, 8A3; 43A1
Penrhiwceiber, GW & TV, 8B5; 43C2
Penrhiwfelin Goods, Rhy, 43B3

Penrhos Jc, Rhy/BRY/AD, 43B3
Penrhyndeudraeth, Cam & Fest, 19F2
Penrith, LNW(CKP/NE), 27E1
Penruddock, CKP, 26E1
Penryn, GW, 1F1
Pensford, GW, 3A2; 8D1
Penshaw, NE, 28C5
Penshurst, SEC, 5D4
Pentir Rhiw, BM, 8A5; 14G3; 43C1
Penton, NB, 26B1
Pentraeth, LNW, 19D2
Pentre Broughton Halt, GW, 20E4
Pentre Halt, TV, 43D2
Pentrebach, TV, 8A5; 43C2
Pentrecourt Platform, GW, 13F4
Pentrefelin, Tan, 14A2; 20G5
Pentrepiod Halt, GW, 43A2
Pentresaeson Halt, GW, 20E4
Pentwyn Halt, GW, 43A2
Penwithers Jc, GW, 1E1
Penwortham Jc, LY, 20A3; 24E3
Penybont, LNW, 14D3
Penybontfawr, Tan, 14A3; 19G5
Penychain, Cam, 19F1
Penygroes, LNW, 19E1
Penyrheol, Rhy, 8B4; 43B3
Penzance, GW, 1F4 (inset)
Peplow, GW, 15E2; 20G2
Percy Main, NE, 28B5
Perivale Halt, GW, 39C2
Perranporth, GW, 1D1
Perranwell, GW, 1E1
Perry Barr, LNW, 13B3; 15G4
Pershore, GW, 9C4
Persley, GNS, 37F4
Perth (General) (Pass), Cal(NB/HR), 33F5
Perth (Goods), Cal & NB, 33F5
Perth (Princes Street), Cal, 33F5
Peterborough, GE(LNW/Mid) & GN(Mid/MGN/GE), 11A2; 17F2
Peterborough Jc, LNW&GEJt, 11A2
Peterchurch, GW, 14F1
Peterhead, GNS, 37D5
Petersfield, LSW, 4D2
Peterston, GW 8C5; 43C4
Petteril Jc (Carlisle), NE/Mid, 26 (inset)
Petworth, LBSC, 5E1
Pevensey & Westham, LBSC, 5F5
Pevensey Bay Halt, LBSC, 5F5
Pewsey, GW, 4B5
Philorth (private), GNS, 37C4
Philorth Bridge Halt, GNS, 37C4
Philpstoun, NB, 30B3
Pickburn, HB, 21F4
Pickering, NE, 22A5
Pickhill, NE, 21A3
Picton, NE, 28F5
Piddington, Mid, 10B2
Piel, Fur, 24B4
Pier Head (Ryde, IoW), LBSC&LSWJt(IW/IWC), 4F3
Piercebridge, NE, 27E5
Piershill, NB, 30 (inset)
Pill, GW, 3A2; 8C2; 9G1
Pillbank Jc, GW, 43A3
Pilling, KE, 24C3
Pilmoor, NE, 21B4
Pilning, GW, 8C2; 9G1
Pilsley, GC, 16B4; 41D3
Pilton Jcs, Cal, 30 (inset)
Pinchbeck, GN&GEJt, 17E2
Pinchinthorpe, NE, 28E4
Pinged, BPGV, 7A2
Pinhoe, LSW, 2B3
Pinmore, G&SW, 25A3
Pinner, Met&GCJt, 5A2; 39A1
Pinwherry, G&SW, 25A3
Pinxton & Selston, Mid, 16C4; 41E3
Pinxton, GN, 16C4; 41E3 ***see also*** Kirkby, GC
Pipe Gate, NS, 15C2; 20F2
Pirbright Jc, LSW, 4B1; 5C1
Pitcaple, GNS, 37E3
Pitcrocknie Platform, CR, 34D5
Pitfodels, GNS, 37G4
Pitlochry, HR, 33C4
Pitlurg, GNS, 37E4
Pitmedden, GNS, 37F4
Pitsea, LTS, 6A5
Pitsford & Brampton, LNW, 10B2
Pittenweem, NB, 34G3
Pittington, NE, 28D5
Pitts Hill, NS, 15C3; 20E1
Plaidy, GNS, 37D3
Plains Jc, NB, 44A4
Plains, NB, 30C5; 44A4
Plaistow, LTS(Dist), 40C2
Plank Lane, LNW, 45C3
Plantation Halt, CM, 29 (inset)
Plas Marl, GW, 7B4; 43G2
Plas Power, GW & GC, 20E4
Plashetts, NB, 27A2
Platt Bridge, LNW, 45D2 ***see also*** Hindley
Plawsworth, NE, 27C5
Plealey Road, SWP, 14B1
Plean Branch Jc, Cal, 30A5
Plean for Cowie, Cal, 30A5
Pleasington, LY, 20A2; 24E2
Pleasley, Mid & GN, 16B4; 41D4
Plenmeller Halt, NE, 27C2
Plessey, NE, 27B5
Plex Moss Lane Halt, LY, 20B4; 24F4; 45F2
Plockton, HR, 35E1
Plodder Lane, LNW, 20B2; 24F2; 45C2
Plowden, BC, 14C1
Pluckley, SEC, 6D4
Plumley CLC, 15A2; 20D2; 45B5
Plumpton (Cumb), LNW, 27D1
Plumpton (Sussex), LBSC, 5F3
Plumpton Jc, Fur, 24A4
Plumstead, SEC, 40D1
Plumtree, Mid, 16D3
Plym Bridge Platform, GW, 2D5
Plymouth, GW(LSW), GW & LSW, 1D5 and inset
Plymouth North Road, GW, 1 (inset)
Plympton, GW, 2D5
Plymstock, LSW(GW), 1 (inset)
Pochin Pits, LNW, 43B2
Pocket Nook Jc, LNW, 45D3
Pocklington, NE, 22C5
Point Pleasant Jc, LSW, 39E5
Pokesdown, LSW, 4F5
Polegate, LBSC, 5F5
Polesworth, LNW, 16F5
Pollok Jc, G&SW/G&P, 44F1 (inset)
Pollokshaws, GBK, 44E3
Pollokshaws East, Cal, 44E3 and inset F1
Pollokshields East, Cal, 44E3 and inset F1
Pollokshields West, Cal, 44E3 and inset F1
Polmont, NB, 30B4
Polsham, SD, 3C2; 8E2
Polsloe Bridge Halt, LSW, 2B3
Polton, NB, 30C2
Pomathorn, NB, 30C2
Pond Street (Sheffield) (Goods), Mid, 16A5; 21G3
Pond Street (Sheffield) (Pass), Mid(HB/NE/LY), 16A5; 21G3
Ponder's End, GE, 5A3; 11G3
Poneil Jc, Cal, 30E5
Ponfeigh, Cal, 30E4
Pont Lawrence, LNW, 8B4; 43B3
Pont Llanio, GW, 13E5
Pont Rug, LNW, 19D2
Pont Yates, BPGV, 7A3
Pontardawe, Mid, 7A4; 43F2
Pontardulais, GW&LNWJt, 7A3
Pontcynon Bridge Halt, TV, 43C3
Pontdolgoch, Cam, 14B3
Pontefract (Baghill), SK(GC/GN), 21E4; 42C1
Pontefract (Monkhill), LY(NE), 21E4; 42C1
Ponteland, NE, 27B5
Pontesbury, SWP, 14B1
Pontfadog, GVT, 20F5
Pontfaen, GVT, 20F5
Ponthenry, BPGV, 7A3
Ponthir, GW, 8B3; 43A3
Pontllanfraith, GW & LNW, 8B4; 43B3
Pontlliw (Goods), GW, 7B3; 43G2
Pontlottyn, Rhy, 43C2 ***see also*** Rhymney, BM
Pontnewydd, GW, 8B3; 43A3
Pontnewynydd, GW, 43A2
Pontrhyddfen, RSB, 43E3
Pontrhythallt, LNW, 19D2
Pontrilas, GW, 14G1
Pontsarn for Vaynor, BM&LNWJt, 8A5; 43C1
Pontsticill Junc, BM, 8A5; 43C1
Pontwalby Halt, GW, 43E2
Pontyberem, BPGV, 7A3
Pontycymmer, GW(PT), 7B5; 43D3
Pont-y-Pant, LNW, 19E3
Pontypool, GW, 8B3; 43A2
Pontypool East Jc, GW, 43A2
Pontypool Middle Jc, GW, 43A2
Pontypool North Jc, GW, 43A2
Pontypool Road, GW, 8B3; 43A2
Pontypool South Jc, GW, 43A2
Pontypridd, TV(AD) & BRY, 8B5; 43C3
Pontyrhyll, GW(PT), 7B5; 43D3
Pool-in-Wharfedale, NE, 21C3
Pool Quay, Cam, 14A2

Poole, LSW(SD), 3F5
Poplar (East India Road) Tidal Basin, GE, 40C2
Poplar (Goods), GN, GW, LNW, Mid & NL, 40C3/D3 and inset D1/E1
Poplar (Pass), GE & NL, 40C3 and inset D1
Poppleton, NE, 21C4
Poppleton Jc, NE, 21C5 and inset A4
Port Carlisle, NB, 26C2
Port Carlisle Branch Jc, Cal, 26C1 and inset
Port Clarence, NE, 28E4
Port Dinorwic, LNW, 19D2
Port Dundas (Goods) (Glasgow), Cal & NB, 44E4
Port Eglington Depot, G&SW, 44F1 (inset)
Port Elphinstone (Goods), GNS, 37F3
Port Erin, IMR, 23C1
Port Glasgow, Cal, 29B3
Port Gordon, GNS, 37C1
Port Isaac Road, LSW, 1C3
Port Meadow Halt, LNW, 10E4
Port of Menteith, NB, 29A5
Port St Mary, IMR, 23C1
Port Soderick, IMR, 23C2
Port Sunlight (Goods), BJ, 45F4
Port Talbot (Aberavon), RSB, 7B4; 43F3
Port Talbot (Central), PT, 7B4; 43F3
Port Talbot & Aberavon, GW(PT), 7B4; 43F3
Port Victoria, SEC, 6B4
Portbury, GW, 3A2; 8C2; 9G1
Portchester, LSW, 4E2
Portcreek Jc, LSW/LBSC, 4E2
Porterfield (Renfrew), G&P, 44F4
Portesham, GW, 3F2
Portessie, GNS, 37C1
Porth, TV(BRY), 8B5; 43C3
Porthcawl, GW, 7C5; 43E4
Porthcawl Golfers Platform, GW, 43E4
Porthywaen, Tan, 14A2; 20G5
Portishead, GW & WCP, 3A2; 8C2; 9G1
Portishead South Portbury Road, WCP, 3A2; 8C2
Portknockie, GNS, 37C1
Portland, WP, 3G3
Portlethen, Cal, 34A1; 37G4
Portmadoc, Cam, Fest & PCB, 19F2
Portobello, NB, 30 (inset)
Portobello Jc, GW, 39C5 and inset C1
Porton, LSW, 4C5
Portpatrick, P&W, 25C1
Portreath, GW, 1E5 (inset)
Portskewett, GW, 8B2; 9F1
Portslade, LBSC, 5F3
Portsmouth (Yorks), LY, 20A1; 21E1
Portsmouth Arms, LSW, 7G3
Portsmouth Harbour, LSW&LBSCJt, 4E2
Portsmouth Town (Hants), LSW&LBSCJt, 4E2
Portsoy, GNS, 37C2
Possil Goods, Cal, 44E4
Possilpark, NB, 44E4
Postland, GN&GEJt, 17E2
Potter Hanworth, GN&GEJt, 16B1; 17B1
Potter Heigham, MGN, 18E2
Potterhill (Paisley), G&SW, 29C4; 44 G3
Potters Bar, GN(NL), 11G2
Potto, NE, 28F4
Potton, LNW, 11D2
Poulton (Lancs), PWY, 24D4
Poulton Curve Halt, PWY, 24D4
Pouparts Jc, LBSC, 39E3 (inset)
Powderhall, NB, 30 (inset)
Powerstock, GW, 3F2
Poynton, GC&NSJt, 15A4
Poynton, LNW(NS), 15A3; 20C1; 45A4
Praed Street, Met(Dist), 39C5 *see also* Paddington
Praze, GW, 1E5 (inset)
Prees, LNW, 15D1; 20F3
Preesall, KE, 24C4
Preesgweene, GW, 20F4
Prescot, LNW, 20C3; 24G3; 45E3
Prescott Siding, CMDP, 9A2; 15G2
Prestatyn, LNW, 19C5
Prestbury, LNW(NS), 15A3; 20D1; 45A5
Presteign, GW, 14D2
Presthope, GW, 15F1
Preston (Goods), LNW, LY, PL & PWY, 24E3
Preston (Pass), NU & LY, 24D3
Preston Brook, LNW, 15A1; 20C3; 45D5
Preston Junc, LY, 20A3; 24E3
Preston Park, LBSC, 5F3
Preston Platform, GW, 2D3
Preston Road (Middx), Met, 39A3
Preston Road (Lancs), LY, 20C4; 24G4; 45F3
Preston Street Goods (Whitehaven), Fur, 26E4
Prestonpans for Tranent, NB, 30B1
Prestwich LY, 20B1; 24F1; 45B2
Prestwick, G&SW, 29E3
Priestfield, GW, 13A1
Primrose Hill Jc, LNW, 40A2 (inset)
Princes Dock (Glasgow), PDJ, 44E3
Princes End, GW, 13A1; 15F4
Princes Pier (Greenock), G&SW, 29B3
Princes Risborough, GW&GCJt, 10F2
Princes Street (Edinburgh), Cal, 30B2 and inset
Princes Street (Perth), Cal, 33F5
Princetown, GW, 2C5
Priory (Dover), SEC, 6D2
Priory Road, Wells (Som), SD, 3C2; 8E2
Prittlewell, GE, 6A4
Privett, LSW, 4D2
Probus & Ladock Platform, GW, 1E2
Proof House Jc, LNW/Mid, 13C4
Prudhoe, NE(NB), 27B4
Pudsey Greenside, GN, 21D2; 42A4
Pudsey Lowtown, GN, 21D2; 42A4
Pulborough, LBSC, 5E1
Pulford (Goods), GW, 20E4
Pulham Market, GE, 12B3; 18G3
Pulham St Mary, GE, 12B3; 18G3
Puncheston, GW, 13F1
Purfleet, LTS, 5B5
Purfleet Rifle Range, LTS, 5B5
Purley, LBSC(SEC), 5C3
Purley Oaks, LBSC, 5C3
Purton, GW, 9F4
Putney, LSW, 5B3; 39E4
Putney Bridge, Dist, 39E4
Puxton & Worle, GW, 3B1; 8D3
Pwllheli, Cam, 19F1
Pye Bridge, Mid, 16C4; 41E3
Pye Hill & Somercotes, GN, 16C4; 41E3
Pye Wipe Jc (Lincoln), GC/GN/GN&GEJt, 16B1 and inset
Pyle, GW, 7C5; 43E4
Pylle, SD, 3C2; 8E1
Pylle Hill Goods (Bristol), GW, 3 (inset)
Quainton & Aylesbury Tramroad, OAT, 10E3
Quainton Road, Met&GCJt & OAT, 10E3
Quainton Road Jc, GC/Met&GCJt, 10E3
Quaker's Drove (Goods), GE, 11A3; 17F3
Quaker's Yard (High Level), GW(Rhy), 8B5; 43C2
Quaker's Yard (Low Level), GW&TVJt, 8B5; 43C2
Quarter, Cal, 29D5; 44B1
Queen Street (Cardiff), TV, 8C4; 43B4
Queen Street (Exeter), LSW, 2B3
Queen Street (Glasgow), NB, 29C5; 44E4
Queen's Park (Glasgow), Cal, 44E3 and inset F1
Queen's Park, West Kilburn, LNW(NL/LE), 39B5
Queen's Road (Battersea), LSW, 39D5 and inset E4
Queen's Road (Peckham), LBSC, 40D4
Queens Road Goods (Sheffield), Mid, 16A5; 21G3; 41A2; 42G2
Queenborough, SEC, 6B4
Queenborough Pier, SEC, 6B4
Queensbury, GN, 21D2; 42B5
Queensferry, LNW, 20D4
Quellyn Lake, NWNG, 19E2
Quintrel Downs Platform, GW, 1D1
Quorn & Woodhouse, GC, 16E4 *see also* Barrow-on-Soar
Quy, GE, 11C4

Racks, G&SW, 26B3
Radcliffe, LY, 20B1; 24F1; 45B2 *see also* Black Lane
Radcliffe Bridge, LY, 45B2
Radcliffe-on-Trent, GN(LNW), 16D3
Radford & Timsbury Halt, GW, 3B3; 8D1
Radford, Mid, 16D4; 41G4
Radipole Halt, GW, 3G3
Radlett, Mid, 11G1
Radley, GW, 10F4
Radstock, GW & SD, 3B3; 8E1
Radway Green, NS, 15C2; 20E1
Radyr, TV, 8C4; 43C4
Raglan, GW, 8A3
Rainbow Hill Jc (Worcester), GW, 9B3
Rainford Junc, LY(LNW) & LNW, 20B3; 24F3; 45E2
Rainford Village, LNW, 20B3; 24F3; 45E2
Rainham (Essex), LTS, 5A4
Rainham (Kent), SEC, 6B5
Rainhill, LNW, 20C3; 24G3; 45E3
Rampside, Fur, 24B4
Ramsbottom, LY, 20A1; 24E1; 45B1
Ramsden Dock, Fur, 24B5
Ramsey (Hunts), GN, 11A2/B2; 17G2
Ramsey (IoM), IMR & ME, 23A3; 25G4
Ramsey High Street (Hunts), GN&GEJt, 11B2
Ramsey Plaza (IoM), MER, 23A3; 25G4
Ramsgate Harbour, SEC, 6B1

Ramsgate Town, SEC, 6B1
Ramsgill, NV, 21B2
Randle Jc, LNW, 20B3; 24F3; 45E2
Rankinston, G&SW, 29F4
Rannoch, NB, 32C1; 33D1
Ranskill, GN, 16A3; 21G5
Raskelf, NE, 21B4
Ratby, Mid, 16F4
Ratgoed Quarry, Cor, 14A5
Rathen, GNS, 37C4
Ratho, NB, 30B3
Rathven, GNS, 37C1
Rauceby, GN, 16C1; 17C1
Raunds, Mid, 10A1; 11B1
Ravelrig Halt, Cal, 30C3
Raven Square, W&L, 14B2
Ravenglass, Fur & RE, 26G3
Ravensbourne, SEC, 40F3
Ravenscar, NE, 28F1
Ravenscourt Park, LSW(Dist), 39D4
Ravenscraig, Cal, 29B3
Ravensthorpe, LY, 42C4
Ravensthorpe & Thornhill, LNW, 42C3 ***see also*** Thornhill
Ravenstonedale, NE, 27F2 ***see also*** Kirkby Stephen
Ravenstone Wood Jc, Mid/SMJ, 10B2
Ravenswood Jc, NB, 31E1
Rawcliffe, LY, 21E5 ***see also*** Airmyn
Rawtenstall, LY, 20A1; 24E1
Rawyards, NB, 44A4
Raydon Wood, GE, 12D4
Rayleigh, GE, 6A5
Rayne, GE, 11E5
Rayner's Lane, Met(Dist), 39B1
Raynes Park, LSW, 5B3; 39F4
Raynham Park, MGN, 18D5
Reading, GW & SEC(LSW), 4A2
Reading West, GW, 4A2
Rearsby, Mid, 16E3
Rectory Jc, GN, 16D3; 41F5
Rectory Road, GE, 40B4
Red Hill Jc (Hereford), GW/LNW, 9C1; 14F1
Red Hills Jc, (Penrith), CKP/NE, 27E1
Red House, Van, 14C4
Red Lion Crossing Halt, GW, 43F1
Red Posts Jc, LSW/MSW, 4C4
Red Rock, LU, 20B3; 24F2; 45D2
Red Wharf Bay & Benllech, LNW, 19C2
Redbourn, Mid, 11F1
Redbridge, LSW(MSW), 4E4
Redbrook, GW, 8A2; 9E1
Redcar, NE, 28E4
Redcastle, HR, 36D5
Redding (Goods), NB, 30B4
Reddish, LNW(LY) & GC&MidJt, 21G1; 45A3
Reddish Jc, GC&MidJt, 45A3
Redditch, Mid, 9B4
Redheugh (Goods), NE, 28 (inset)
Redhill (Surrey), SEC(LBSC), 5C3
Redland, CE, 3 (inset)
Redmile, GN&LNWJt, 16D2
Redmire, NE, 21A1; 27G4
Rednal & West Felton, GW, 20G4
Redruth, GW, 1E5 (inset)
Redruth Jc, GW, 1E5 (inset)
Reedham (Norfolk), GE, 18F2
Reedley Hallows Halt, LY, 24D1
Reedness, AJ, 22E5
Reedsmouth, NB, 27A3
Reepham (Lincs), GC, 16A1; 17B1
Reepham (Norfolk), GE, 18E4 ***see also*** Whitwell
Reigate, SEC, 5C3
Relly Mill Jc, NE, 27D5
Renfrew, G&P & G&SW, 29C4; 44F4
Renfrew Porterfield, GSW, 44F4
Renton, D&B, 29B3
Repton & Willington, Mid(LNW), 16D5
Resolven, GW, 7A5; 43E2
Restalrig (Goods), Cal, 30 (inset)
Reston, NB, 31C3
Retford (Goods), GN & GC, 16A3
Retford (Pass), GN(GC), 16A3
Retford N & S Jcs, GC/GN, 16A3
Rhayader, Cam, 14D4
Rheidol Falls, VR, 14C5
Rhewl, LNW, 19E5
Rhigos, Halt, GW, 43D1
Rhiwbina Halt, Car, 43B4
Rhiwderin, BM, 8B4; 43A3
Rhiwfron, VR, 14C5
Rhondda Branch Jc, TV, 43C3
Rhoose, BRY, 8D5; 43C5
Rhos (Denbigh), GW, 20F4
Rhos Tryfan, NWNG, 19E2
Rhosgoch, LNW, 19C1; 23G1
Rhosneigr, LNW, 19D1
Rhostyllen, GW, 20E4
Rhosymedre Halt, GW, 20F4
Rhuddlan, LNW, 19D5
Rhuddlan Road, LNW, 19C5
Rhydowen, GW, 13F3
Rhydyfelin Halt, AD & Car, 43C3
Rhydymwyn, LNW, 20D5
Rhydyronen, Tal, 13B5
Rhyd-y-Saint, LNW, 19D2
Rhyl, LNW, 19C5
Rhymney, Rhy, 8A5; 43B4; 43C2
Rhymney & Pontlottyn, BM, 8A4; 43C1
Rhymney Bridge, LNW&RhyJt & LNW, 8A5; 43C1
Ribble Jc, LY, 24E3
Ribblehead, Mid, 24A1
Ribbleton, PL, 24D2
Riccall, NE, 21D5
Riccarton & Craigie, G&SW, 29E4
Riccarton Junc, NB, 27A1; 31G1
Richborough Port (Goods), EK, 6C1
Richmond (Surrey), LSW(Dist/NL), 5B2; 39E3
Richmond (Yorks), NE, 27F5
Rickmansworth, Met&GCJt & LNW, 5A2; 10F1
Riddings, NB, 26B1
Riddings Jc, Mid, 41E3
Ridgmont, LNW, 10C1
Riding Mill, NE(NB), 27C4
Rifle Range Halt, GW, 9A3
Rifle Range Platform, LSW, 1C2
Rigg, G&SW, 26B2
Rillington, NE, 22B5
Rimington, LY, 24C1
Ringley Road, LY, 20B1; 24F1; 45B2
Ringstead & Addington, LNW, 10A1
Ringwood, LSW, 4E5
Ripley, Mid, 16C5; 41E2
Ripley Valley, NE, 21C3
Ripon, NE, 21B3
Rippingale, GN, 17D1
Ripple, Mid, 9C3
Ripponden & Barkisland, LY, 21E1
Risca, GW(LNW), 8B4; 43B3
Risca Jc, GW, 43B3
Rishton, LY, 24D1
Rishworth, LY, 21E1
Riverside (Cardiff), GW(BRY/TV), 43B4
Riverside (Liverpool), MDHB(LNW), 45 (inset)
Riverside Jc, NE, 28A1
Roade, LNW, 10C2
Roade Jc, LNW/SMJ, 10C2
Roath (Goods), GW & TV, 8C4; 43B4
Roath (Pass), GW, 8C4; 43B4
Roath Branch Jc, TV, 43B4
Roath Dock Jc, TV/Car, 8C4
Robertsbridge, SEC(KES), 6E5
Robertstown Halt, TV, 43C3
Robin Hood, EWY, 21E3; 42B2
Robin Hood's Bay, NE, 28F1
Robroyston, Cal, 29C5; 44D4
Roby, LNW, 20C4; 24G3; 45E4
Rocester, NS, 15D5
Rochdale, LY, 20A1; 45A1
Rochdale East Jc, LY, 21E1
Rochdale Road Halt, LY, 42C5
Roche, GW, 1D2
Rochester, SEC, 6B5
Rochester Bridge Jc, SEC, 6B5
Rochester Bridge, SEC, 6B5
Rochford, GE, 6A4
Rock Ferry, BJ(Mer), 20C4; 24G4
Rockcliffe, Cal, 26C1
Rockingham, LNW, 16F2
Rodmarton Platform, GW, 9F3
Rodwell, WP, 3G3
Roe Lane Jc, LY, 20A4; 24E4; 45F1
Roffey Road Halt, LBSC, 5E2
Rogart, HR, 36A5
Rogate for Harting, LSW, 4D1
Rogerstone, GW, 8B4; 43A3
Rolleston Junc, Mid, 16C2
Rolleston-on-Dove, NS(GN), 15D5
Rollright Halt, GW, 10D5
Rolvenden, KES, 6E4
Romaldkirk, NE, 27E4
Roman Bridge, LNW, 19E3
Roman Road (Woodnesborough), EK, 6C2
Rome Street Jc (Carlisle), M&C/NE, 26C1 and inset
Romford, GE & LTS, 5A4
Romiley, GC&MidJt, 21G1
Romsey, LSW(MSW), 4D4
Rookery Bridge (Goods), LNW, 15B2; 20E2

Rookery, LNW, 20B3; 24F3; 45E3
Roose, Fur, 24B5
Ropley, LSW, 4C2
Rose Grove, LY, 24D1
Rose Hill, GC&NSJt, 21G1 *see also* Marple
Rosebush, GW, 13F2
Rosedale (Goods), NE, 28F3
Rosemill (Goods), Cal, 34E4
Rosemount, Cal, 33D5
Rosherville, SEC, 5B5
Roskear, GW, 1E5 (inset)
Roslin, NB, 30C2
Ross Jc (Lanarks), Cal, 44B2
Ross-on-Wye, GW, 9D1
Rossett, GW, 20E4
Rossington, GN, 21F5
Rosslyn Castle, NB, 30C2
Rosslynlee, NB, 30C2
Rosyth Halt, NB, 30B3
Rothbury, NB, 31G4
Rotherfeld & Mark Cross, LBSC, 5E5
Rotherham & Masborough, GC, 21G4; 42F1
Rotherham (Masborough), Mid(NE/LY), 21G4; 42F1
Rotherham Road, GC, 21G4; 42F1
Rotherham Westgate, Mid, 21G4; 42F1
Rotherhithe, EL, 40D4
Rotherwas Jc (Hereford), GW/LNW, 9C1
Rothes, GNS, 36D1
Rothie Norman, GNS, 37E3
Rothiemay, GNS, 37D1
Rothley, GC, 16E4
Rothwell (Yorks), EWY, 21D3; 42B2
Rotton Park Road, LNW, 13C3
Roudham Junc, GE, 12A5; 18G5
Roughton Road Jc, GE/NSJ, 18D3
Round Oak, GW, 15G3
Roundwood Jc, Mid/GC&MidJt, 42F1
Row, NB, 29B3
Rowden Mill, GW, 9B2
Rowfant, LBSC, 5D3
Rowland's Castle, LSW, 4E2
Rowlands Gill, NE, 27C5
Rowley, NE, 27C4
Rowley Regis & Blackheath, GW, 13C2; 15G4
Rowrah, WCE, 26E3
Rowsley, Mid, 16B5; 41C1
Rowthorn & Hardwick, Mid, 16B4; 41C3
Roxburgh, NB, 31E2
Roy Bridge, NB, 32B2
Royal Oak, GW(H&C), 39C5 and inset C1
Roydon, GE, 11F3
Royston (Herts), GN, 11D3
Royston & Notton, Mid, 21F3; 42D2 *see also* Notton, GC
Royston Jc, Mid, 21E3; 42D2
Royton, LY, 21F1; 45A2
Royton Junc, LY, 21F1
Ruabon, GW, 20F4
Rubery, HJ, 9A4
Ruddington, GC, 16D4; 41G4
Rudgwick, LBSC, 5E2
Rudyard (Horton), NS, 15B4
Rudyard Lake, NS, 15B4
Rufford, LY, 20A3; 24E3; 45E1
Rugby, LNW(Mid) & GC, 10A4
Rugeley (Trent Valley), LNW, 15E4
Rugeley Town, LNW, 15E4
Ruislip & Ickenham, GW&GCJt, 10G1
Ruislip, Met(Dist), 5A2
Rumbling Bridge, NB, 30A4; 33G4
Rumworth & Daubhill, LNW, 45C2
Runcorn, LNW, 15A1; 20C3; 45D4
Runcorn Dock, LNW, 45E4
Runnymede (Goods), GW, 5B1
Runnymede Range, GW, 5B1
Runton E & W Jcs, MGN/NSJ, 18D3
Rushbury, GW, 15G1
Rushcliffe Halt, GC, 16D4
Rushden, Mid, 10B1
Rushey Platt (Goods), MSW, 9G5
Rushton (Staffs), NS, 15B4
Ruskington, GN&GEJt, 17C1
Ruspidge, GW, 8A1; 9E2
Ruswarp, NE, 28F2
Rutherford, NB, 31E1
Rutherglen, Cal, 29C5; 44D3
Rutherglen Jc, Cal, 44D3
Ruthern Bridge, LSW, ID2
Ruthin, LNW, 19E5; 20E5
Ruthrieston, GNS, 37G4
Ruthven Road Crossing, Cal, 33E5
Ruthwell, G&SW, 26B3
Rutland Street (Swansea), Mum, 7B4; 43G3
Ryburgh, GE, 18D5
Ryde (Esplanade), LBSC&LSWJt(IW/IWC), 4F3
Ryde (Pier Head), LBSC&LSWJt(IW/IWC), 4F3
Ryde (St John's Road), IW & LBSC&LSWJt(IWC), 4F3
Ryde Locomotive Works, IW, 4F3
Rye, SEC & RCT, 6E4
Rye & Camber Tramway, RCT, 6C3
Rye Harbour, SEC, 6E4
Rye Hill, NE, 22E2
Rye House, GE, 11F3
Ryecroft Jc, LNWR/Mid, 15F4
Ryeford, Mid, 9E3
Ryeland, Cal, 29 D5
Ryhall, GN, 16E1; 17F1
Ryhill, GC, 21E3; 42D2
Ryhill Halt, LY, 42D1
Ryhope, NE, 28C5
Ryhope East, NE, 28C5
Ryhope Grange Jc, NE, 28C5
Rylstone, Mid, 21C1
Ryston, GE, 11A4; 17F4
Ryton, NE(NB), 27B5

Saddleworth, LNW, 21F1
Saffron Walden, GE, 11D4
St Agnes, GW, 1E1
St Albans, Mid, LNW(GN) & GN, 11F1
St Albans London Road, LNW, 11F1
St Andrew's Dock (Goods) (Hull), NE, 22 (inset)
St Andrews, NB, 34F4
St Andrew's Jc, Mid, 13C4
St Ann's Road, THJ(LTS), 40A4
St Ann's Well, GN, 16C3; 41F5
St Anne's Park, GW, 8C1
St Annes Park Jc, GW, 3A3 and inset G1
St Annes-on-the-Sea, PWY, 24E4
St Anthonys, NE(NB), 28 (inset)
St Asaph, LNW, 19D5
St Athan Road, TV, 8D5; 43C5
St Austell, GW, 1D2
St Bees, Fur, 26F4
St Blazey, GW, 1D3
St Boswells, NB, 31E1
St Botolph's, GE, 12E4
St Briavels & Llandogo, GW, 8A2; 9E1
St Bride's Crossing, Cal, 33G2
St Budeaux Platform, GW, 1D5
St Budeaux, LSW, 1D5
St Catherine's Jcs, SYJ/LY/GN&LYJt, 21F5
St Clears, GW, 7A1; 13G3
St Columb Road, GW, 1D2
St Combs, GNS, 37C5
St Cyrus, NB, 34C2
St David's (Exeter), GW(LSW), 2B3
St Dennis Jc, GW, 1D2
St Denys, LSW(GW), 4D4
St Devereux, GW, 14F1
St Dunstans, GN, 42B4
St Enoch (Glasgow), G&SW, 29C5; 44E4 and inset E2
St Erth, GW, 1F4 (inset)
St Fagans, GW(BRY) & BRY, 8C4; 43C4
St Fillans, Cal, 33F2
St Fort, NB, 34E4
St Germains, IMR, 23B2
St Germans, GW, 1D5
St Harmons, Cam, 14D4
St Helens (Glam), Mum, 43G3
St Helens (IoW), IW, 4F2
St Helens (Lancs), LNW & GC, 20C3; 24G3; 43D3
St Helens Junc, LNW, 20C3; 24G3; 45D3
St Ives (Cornwall), GW, 1E4 (inset)
St Ives (Hunts), GN&GEJt(Mid), 11B2
St James (Cheltenham), GW, 9D4
St James (Liverpool), CLC, 45F4
St James (Paisley), Cal, 44G3
St James's Bridge Jc, NE, 28 (inset)
St James's Park, Dist(Met), 40D5
St John's (IoM), IMR, 22B2
St John's (London), SEC, 40E3
St John's Chapel, NE, 27D3
St John's Road (Ryde, IoW), IW & LBSC&LSWJt(IWC), 4F3
St John's Wood Road, Met, 39C5
St Kew Highway, LSW, 1C2
St Keyne, LL, 1D4
St Lawrence, IWC, 4G3
St Leonards (Edinburgh) (Goods), NB, 30 (inset)
St Leonards (Sussex), SEC, LBSC & SEC(LBSC), 6F5
St Leonards (Warrior Square), SEC(LBSC), 6F5
St Leonards (West Marina), LBSC, 6F5
St Luke's (Southport), LY, 20A4; 24E4; 45F1
St Luke's Jc (Barrow), Fur, 24B5

St Margaret's (Herts), GE, 11F3
St Margaret's (Middx), LSW, 39E2
St Margarets Jc, LBSC, 5D4
St Marnocks (Goods), G&SW, 29E4
St Mary Church Road, TV, 8C5; 43C5
St Mary Cray, SEC, 5B4; 40G1
St Mary Cray Jc, SEC, 40F1
St Mary's (Hunts), GN, 11A2; 17G2
St Mary's (London), Dist&MetJt(H&C), 40C4
St Mary's Bridge Goods (Derby), Mid, 41G2
St Mary's Crossing Halt, GW, 9F3
St Marys Jc, Mid, 41G2
St Michael's, CLC, 20C4; 24G4; 45F4
St Monan's, NB, 34G3
St Neots, GN, 11C2
St Olaves, GE, 18F1
St Olaves Jc, GE, 18F1
St Olaves Swing Bridge, GE, 12A2; 18F1
St Pancras (Goods), Mid, 40B5
St Pancras (Pass), Mid(LTS/GE), 5A3; 40C5
St Pancras Jcs, NL/Mid & NL/GN, 40B5
St Paul's (Halifax), HHL, 21E2; 42B5
St Paul's (London), SEC, 40C5
St Paul's Road Jc, Mid, 40B5
St Peter's, NE, 28 (inset)
St Philip's (Bristol), Mid, 3 (inset)
St Philip's Marsh (Bristol)(Goods), GW, 3 (inset)
St Quintin Park & Wormwood Scrubbs, WL, 39C4
St Rollox, Cal, 29C5; 44D4
St Thomas (Exeter), GW, 2B3
St Thomas (Swansea), Mid, 43G3
St Vigean's Jc, D&A/Cal/NB, 34D3
St Winifrides, LNW, 20D5
Sale & Ashton-on-Mersey, MSJA(CLC), 20C1; 24G1; 45B3
Salehurst Halt, EK, 6E5
Salford Priors, Mid, 9B4
Salford, LY(Mid), 20B1; 24F1; 45A3
Salfords Goods, LBSC, 5D3
Salhouse, GE, 18E2
Salisbury, LSW(GW), LSW & GW, 4C5
Salt, GN, 15D4
Saltaire, Mid, 21D2; 42A5
Saltash, GW, 1D5
Saltburn, NE, 28E3
Saltcoats, G&SW & Cal, 29D3
Saltfleetby, GN, 17A3; 22G1
Saltford, GW, 3A3; 8D1 ***see also*** Kelston
Salthouse Jc, Fur, 24B5
Saltley, Mid, 13B4; 15G5
Saltley Jc, Mid, 13C3
Saltmarket Jc, G&SW, 44E2 (inset)
Saltmarshe, NE(GC), 22E5
Saltney, GW, 20D4
Saltney Ferry, LNW, 20D4
Saltoun, NB, 30C1
Salwick, PWY, 24D3
Salzcraggie Plat, HR, 38F4
Sampford Courtenay, LSW, 2B5
Sandal & Walton, Mid, 21E3; 42C2
Sandal, WRG, 21E3; 42C2
Sandbach, LNW & NS, 15B2; 20E2
Sandbach (Wheelock), NS, 15B2; 20E2
Sanderstead, CO, 5C3
Sandford & Banwell, GW, 3B1; 8D3
Sandgate, SEC, 6D2
Sandhills, LY, 45 (inset)
Sandholme, HB, 22D5
Sandhurst Halt, SEC, 4B1
Sandilands, Cal, 30E4
Sandling Junc, SEC, 6D3
Sandon, NS, 15D4
Sandon Dock (Goods), Mid, 45G4 (inset)
Sandown, IW, 4F3
Sandplace, LL, 1D4
Sandsend, NE, 28F2
Sandside, Fur, 24A3
Sandtoft (Goods), AJ, 22F5
Sandwich, SEC, 6C2
Sandwich Road, EK, 6C2
Sandy, GN & LNW, 11D2
Sandy Lodge, Met&GCJt, 5A2
Sandycroft, LNW, 20D4
Sankey Bridges, LNW, 45D4
Sankey for Penketh, CLC, 20C3; 24G3; 45D4
Sanquhar, G&SW, 30F5
Santon, IMR, 23C2
Sarnau, GW, 7A2; 13G3
Sarsden Halt, GW, 10D5
Sauchie, NB, 30A4
Saughall, GC, 20D4
Saughton, NB, 30B3
Saughtree, NB, 27A1; 31G1
Saundersfoot, GW, 7D3
Saunderton, GW&GCJt, 10F2
Savernake, GW, 4A5
Sawbridgeworth, GE, 11F3
Sawdon, NE, 22A4
Sawley, Mid, 16D4
Sawley Junc, Mid, 16D4
Saxby, Mid(MGN), 16E2
Saxham & Risby, GE, 11C5
Saxilby, GN, 16A1
Saxmundham, GE, 12C2
Saxondale Jc, GN/LNW, 16C3
Scafell Halt, Cam, 14C3
Scalby, NE, 22A4; 28G1
Scalford, GN&LNWJt, 16E2
Scarborough, NE, 22A3; 28G1
Scarborough Excursion, NE, 22A3; 28G1
Scarcliffe, GC, 16B4; 41C4
Scawby & Hibaldstow, GC, 22F4
Scholes, NE, 21D3; 42A2
Schoolhill, GNS, 37G4
Scopwick & Timberland, GN & GE, 17C1
Scorrier, GW, 1E1 and inset E5
Scorton (Lancs), LNW, 24C3
Scorton (Yorks), NE, 27F5
Scotby, Mid & NE, 26C1
Scotch Dyke, NB, 26B1
Scotland Street (Goods), NB, 30 (inset)
Scotland Street Jc, G&SW/Cal, 44F2 (inset)
Scotscalder, HR, 38D3
Scotsgap, NB, 27A4
Scotstoun, Cal, 29C4; 44F4
Scotstoun West, Cal, 29C4; 44F4
Scotstounhill, NB, 29C4; 44F4
Scotswood, NE(NB), 27B5
Scotswood Works Halt, NE(NB), 27B5; 28 (inset)
Scremerston, NE, 31D4
Scrooby, GN, 21G5
Scruton, NE, 21A3; 28G5
Sculcoates, NE & HB, 22 (inset)
Scunthorpe, GC, 22F4 ***see also*** Frodingham
Sea Mills, CE, 3A2; 8C2; 9G1
Seacombe & Egremont, Wir(GC), 45F3
Seacroft, GN, 17B4
Seaford, LBSC, 5G4
Seaforth & Litherland, LY(LNW/LOR), 20B4; 24G4; 45F3
Seaham Colliery, NE, 28C5
Seaham, NE, 28C5
Seahouses, NSL, 31E5
Seamer, NE, 22A3
Seamer Jc, NE, 22A3
Seascale, Fur, 26F3
Seaton (Cumb), CWJ, 26D3
Seaton (Devon), LSW, 2B1
Seaton (Durham), NE, 28C5
Seaton (Rutland), LNW, 16F1
Seaton Carew, NE, 28E4
Seaton Delaval, NE, 28B5
Seaton Junc (Devon), LSW 2B1
Seaton Snook, NE, 28E4
Sedbergh, LNW, 24A2; 27G2
Sedgebrook, GN, 16D2
Sedgefield, NE, 28E5
Sedgeford, GE, 17D5
Sedgley Jc, LNW, 13B1
Seedley, LNW(BJ), 45B3
Seend, GW, 3B4
Seer Green Halt for Beaconsfield Golf Club, GW&GCJt, 5A1; 10F1
Sefton & Maghull, CLC, 20B4; 24F4; 45F2 ***see also*** Maghull
Sefton Park, LNW, 20C4; 24G4, 45F4
Seghill, NE, 28B5
Selby, NE(GN/GE/LNW), 21D5
Selby East Jc, NE, 21D5
Selby Swing Bridge, NE, 21D5
Selham, LBSC, 5E1
Selhurst, LBSC, 5B3; 40G5
Selhurst Jc, LBSC, 40G5
Selkirk, NB, 30E1
Sellafield, Fur, 26F3
Selling, SEC, 6C3
Selly Oak, Mid, 9A4; 15G4
Selsdon Road, CO/WSC, 5C3
Selsey, SL, 4F1
Selsey Golf Links Platform, SL, 4F1
Selsey Light Railway, SL, 4E1
Semington Halt, GW, 3B4
Semley, LSW, 3D4
Senghenydd, Rhy, 8B4; 43C3
Serridge Jc, SVW, 8A1; 9E2
Sessay, NE, 21B4
Settle, Mid, 24B1
Settle Jc, Mid, 24C1
Settrington, NE, 22B5

Seven Hills Halt, GE, 12B5
Seven Kings, GE, 5A4
Seven Sisters (Glam), N&B, 7A5; 43E1
Seven Sisters (Middx), GE, 5A3; 40A4
Seven Stars, W&L, 14B2
Sevenoaks Bat & Ball, SEC, 5C4
Sevenoaks Tub's Hill, SEC, 5C4
Severn Beach, GW, 9G1
Severn Bridge, SVW, 8A1; 9E2
Severn Tunnel Junc, GW, 8B2; 9F1
Severus Jc, NE, 21A4 (inset); 21C5
Sexhow, NE, 28F4
Shackerstone, AN, 16F5
Shadwell, GE & EL, 40C4
Shaftholme Jc, GN/NE, 21F5
Shafton Jc, LY/DV, 21F4; 42D1
Shalford, SEC, 5D1
Shalford Jc, LSW/SEC, 5D1
Shandon, NB, 29A3
Shankend, NB, 31F1
Shanklin, IW, 4G3
Shap, LNW, 27F1
Shapwick, SD, 3C1; 8E3
Sharlston, LY, 21E4; 42C1
Sharnal Street, SEC, 6B5
Sharnbrook, Mid, 10B1; 11C1
Sharpness, SVW, 8B1; 9F2
Shaugh Bridge Platform, GW, 2D5
Shaw & Crompton, LY, 21F1
Shawclough & Healey, LY, 20A1; 24E1; 45A1
Shawford & Twyford, LSW(GW), 4D3
Shawforth, LY, 20A1; 24E1; 45A1
Shawhill Jc, Cal, 26B2
Shawlands, Cal, 44E3
Sheepbridge, Mid, 16A5; 41B2
Sheepbridge & Whittington Moor, GC, 16A5; 41B2
Sheerness Dockyard, SEC, 6B4
Sheerness East, SEC, 6B4
Sheerness-on-Sea, SEC, 6B4
Sheet Factory Jc, GE, 40B2
Sheet Stores Jc, Mid, 16D4
Sheffield (Goods), GC, LNW, Mid & SHD, 16A5; 21G3; 41A2; 42G2
Sheffield (Pass), GC(LY) & Mid(NE/LY), 16A5; 21G3; 41A2; 42G2
Sheffield Midland, Mid, 41A2
Sheffield Park, LBSC, 5E4
Shefford, Mid, 11D1
Shelford, GE, 11D3
Shelwick Jc, S&H/GW, 9C1
Shenfield & Hutton, GE, 5A5; 11G4
Shenstone, LNW, 15F5
Shenton, AN, 16F5
Shepherds, GW, 1D1
Shepherds Bush, H&C, 39C4
Shepherd's Well, SEC & EK, 6D2
Shepley & Shelley, LY, 21F2; 42D4
Shepperton, LSW, 5B2
Shepreth, GN, 11D3
Shepreth Branch Jc, GE, 11C3
Shepshed, LNW, 16E4
Shepton Mallet, GW, 3C2; 8E1
Shepton Mallett (Charlton Road), SD, 3C3; 8E1
Sherborne, LSW, 3D3; 8G1
Sherburn Colliery, NE, 28D5
Sherburn House, NE, 28D5
Sherburn-in-Elmet, NE(GN), 21D4
Sheringham, MGN, 18D3
Sherwood, GN, 16C3; 41F5
Shettleston, NB, 29C5; 44C3
Shide, IWC, 4F3
Shield Row, NE, 27C5
Shieldhall Goods, G&P, 44F4
Shieldhill, Cal, 26A3
Shields, G&SW, 44F1 (inset)
Shields Jc, Cal/G&P/G&SW, 44F1 (inset)
Shields Road, G&P, 44F1 (inset)
Shielmuir Jc, Cal, 44A2
Shifnal, GW, 15E2
Shildon, NE, 27E5
Shillingstone, SD, 3E4
Shilton, LNW, 10A5; 16G5
Shincliffe, NE, 28D5
Shiplake, GW, 10G2
Shipley Bridge Street, GN, 42A5
Shipley Gate, Mid, 16C4; 41F3
Shipley Station Street, Mid(NE) & GN, 21D2; 42A5
Shippea Hill, GE, 11B4
Shipston-on-Stour, GW, 9C5
Shipton, GW, 10D5
Shirdley Hill, LY, 20A4; 24F4; 45F1
Shirebrook, Mid(GC) & GN, 16B4; 41C4
Shirehampton, CE, 8A2; 9G1
Shireoaks, GC(Mid), 16A4; 41A4
Shirley, GW, 9A5
Shobhall Wharf, Mid, 15D5 (inset)
Shoeburyness, LTS, 6A4
Sholing, LSW, 4E3
Shooters Hill & Eltham Park, SEC, 40E1
Shore (Invergordon), HR, 36C5
Shore Road Goods (Stirling), NB, 30A5
Shoreditch (Goods), LNW, 40C4
Shoreditch (Pass), EL & NL, 40C4
Shoreham (Kent), SEC, 5C4
Shoreham-by-Sea (Sussex), LBSC, 5F3
Shorncliffe Camp, SEC, 6D2
Short Heath (Clark's Lane), Mid, 15F4
Shortlands, SEC, 5B4; 40F2
Shortlands Jc, SEC, 40F2
Shotley Bridge, NE, 27C4
Shottle, Mid, 16C5; 41F1
Shotton, LNW, 20D4 ***see also*** Connah's Quay
Shotton Bridge, NE, 28D5
Shotton E & W Jcs, GC, 20D4
Shotts, Cal & NB, 30C4
Shrawardine, S&M, 14A1
Shrewsbury (Goods), S&H, GW, LNW & S&M, 15E1
Shrewsbury (Pass), S&H & S&M, 15E1
Shrewsbury Line Jc, LNW, 15C2; 20E2
Shrewsbury West, S&M, 14A1; 15E1
Shrivenham, GW, 9F5
Shrub Hill (Worcester), GW&MidJt, 9B3
Shustoke, Mid, 16G5
Sible & Castle Hedingham, CVH, 11E5
Sibley's for Chickney & Broxted, GE, 11E4
Sibsey, GN, 17C3
Sidcup, SEC, 5B4; 40E1
Siddick, LNW&CWJJt, 26D3
Sideway Halt, NS, 20F1
Sidlesham, SL, 4F1
Sidley, SEC, 6F5
Sidmouth, LSW, 2B2
Sidmouth Junc, LSW, 2B2
Sigglesthorne, NE, 22D3
Sight Hill (Goods), NB, 44D4
Sileby, Mid, 16E3
Silecroft, Fur, 24A5
Silian Halt, GW, 13E5
Silkstone, GC, 21F3; 42E3
Silkstone Colliery, LY, 21F3; 42E3
Silkstone Jc, LY, 42D2
Silloth, NB, 26C3
Silverdale (Lancs), Fur, 24B3
Silverdale (Staffs) NS, 15C3; 20F1
Silvermuir Jc South, Cal, 30D4
Silver Street, GE, 5A3
Silverton, GW, 2A3
Silvertown, GE, 40C2
Simonstone, LY, 24D1
Sincil Jc, GN/GN&GEJt, 16B1; 17B1 (inset)
Sinclairtown, NB, 30A2
Sinderby, NE, 21A3
Sindlesham & Hurst Halt, SEC, 4A1
Singer, NB, 29C4; 44F4
Singleton (Lancs), PWY, 24D4
Singleton (Sussex), LBSC, 4E1
Sinnington, NE, 22A5
Sirhowy, LNW, 8A4; 43B1
Sirhowy Jc, LNW/GW, 43B3
Sittingbourne, SEC, 6C4
Six Bells Halt, GW, 43B2
Six Mile Bottom, GE, 11C4
Skares, G&SW, 29F4
Skegby, GN, 16B4; 41D4
Skegness, GN, 17B4
Skelbo, HR, 36A4
Skellingthorpe, GC, 16B1
Skellow Jc, WRG, 21F4
Skelmanthorpe, LY, 21F3; 42D3
Skelmersdale, LY(LNW), 20B3; 24F3; 45E2
Skelton Jc, CLC, 45B4
Skewen, GW, 7B4; 43F2
Skinningrove, NE, 28E3
Skipton, Mid, 21C1
Skipton North Jc, Mid, 21C1
Skipwith & North Duffield, DVL, 21D5
Skirlaugh, NE, 22D3
Slades Green, SEC, 5B4
Slaggyford, NE, 27C2
Slaithwaite, LNW, 21E2; 42D5
Slamannan, NB, 30B5
Slamannan Jc, NB, 30B5
Slateford, Cal, 30B2 and inset
Sleaford, GN(GN&GEJt), 16C1; 17C1
Sleaford East Jc (Boston), GN, 17D3
Sleaford N & S Jcs, GN&GEJt, 17C1

Sledmere & Fimber, NE, 22B4
Sleights, NE, 28F2
Slinfold, LBSC, 5E2
Sling, SVW, 8A2; 9E1
Slingsby, NE, 21B5
Sloane Square, Dist(Met), 39D5
Slochd Crossing, HR, 36F4
Slough, GW, 5B1; 10G1
Small Heath, GW, 15G5
Smallbrook Jc, IW/IWC, 4F3
Smallford, GN, 11F2
Smardale, NE, 27F2
Smeafield, NE, 31D4
Smeaton, NB, 30B2
Smeeth, SEC, 6D3
Smeeth Road, GE, 17F4
Smethwick, LNW, 13B2 *see also* Handsworth
Smethwick Junc, GW, 13B2
Smitham, SEC, 5C3
Smithfield Goods, GW, 40C5
Smithy Bridge, LY, 20A1; 45A1
Snae Fell, ME, 23B3
Snailbeach, SBH, 14B1
Snailham Halt, LBSC, 6E5
Snailwell Jc, GE, 11C4
Snainton, NE, 22A4
Snaith, LY, 21E5
Snaith & Pollington, GC&HBJt, 21E5
Snape (Goods), GE, 12C1
Snape Jc, GE, 12C2
Snapper, LB, 7F3
Snaresbrook & Wanstead, GE, 5A4; 40A2
Snarestone, AN, 16E5
Snatchwood Halt, GW, 43A2
Snell's Nook Halt, LNW, 16E4
Snettisham, GE, 17D5
Snodland, SEC, 6C5
Snowdon, NWNG & SM, 19E2
Snowdown & Nonington Halt, SEC, 6C2
Snowdon Mountain Railway, SM, 19E2
Snow Hill (Birmingham), GW, 13C3; 15G4
Snelland, GC, 17A1
Snydale Jc, Mid, 42C2
Soap Works Jc (Soho), LNW, 13C2
Soham, GE, 11B4
Soho, LNW, 13C2; 15G4
Soho & Winson Green, GW, 13C3; 15G4
Soho East Jc, LNW, 13C3
Soho Goods, LNW, 13C3
Soho Pool, LNW, 13B3
Soho Pool Jc, LNW, 13B3
Soho Road, LNW, 13B3; 15G4
Sole Street, SEC, 5B5
Solihull, GW, 9A5
Somerleyton, GE, 12A1; 18F1
Somers Town Goods, Mid, 40C5
Somerset Road, Mid, 13D3; 15G4
Somersham, GN&GEJt, 11B3
Somerton (Som), GW, 3D2; 8F2
Sorbie, P&W, 25C4
South Acton, NSW & Dist, 39C3
South Bank, NE, 28E4
South Beach (Ardrossan), G&SW, 29D3
South Bermondsey, LBSC, 40D4
South Bromley, LNW, 40C3
South Canterbury, SEC, 6C3
South Caradon, LC, 1C4
South Cave, HB, 22D4
South Dock (Millwall), GE, 40D3
South Docks Goods (Liverpool), LY, 45 (inset)
South Ealing, Dist, 39D2
South Eastrington, NE, 22D5
South Elmsall, WRG, 21F4; 42 D1 *see also* Moorhouse
South Farnborough, LSW, 5C1 *see also* Aldershot North Camp
South Gosforth, NE, 27B5
South Hampstead, LNW, 39B5
South Harrow, Dist, 5A2; 39B1
South Harrow, GC, 39B2
South Hetton, NE, 28D5
South Howden, HB, 22E5
South Kensington, Dist & Met(Dist), 39D5
South Lambeth Goods, GW, 39E4 (inset); 40D5
South Leicester Jc, LNW/Mid, 16F5
South Leigh, GW, 10E5
South Leith, NB, 30 (inset)
South Leith (Goods), NB, 30 (inset)
South Leith Docks, Cal, 30 (inset)
South Lynn, MGN, 17E4
South Milford, NE, 21D4; 42B1
South Molton, GW, 7F4
South Molton Road, LSW, 7G4
South Queensferry (Goods), NB, 30B3
South Renfrew, G&SW, 44F4
South Rhondda (Goods), GW, 8C5; 43D4
South Shields, NE & SSM, 28B5
South Shore Goods (Blackpool), PWY, 24D4
South Side Goods (Glasgow), Cal & GBK, 44, Inset E1
South Street Halt, SEC, 6B3
South Tottenham, THJ(LTS), 40A4
South Tottenham Jc, GE, 40A4
South Town (Yarmouth), GE, 18F1
South Willingham & Hainton, GN, 17A2
South Witham, Mid(MGN), 16E1
Southall, GW, 5B2; 39C1
Southam & Long Itchington, LNW, 10B4
Southam Road & Harbury, GW, 10B5
Southampton (Town), LSW(GW/MSW), 4E4
Southampton (West), LSW(MSW), 4E4
Southborough, SEC, 5D5
Southbourne Halt, LBSC, 4E1
Southburn, NE, 22C4
Southcoates, NE, 22 (inset)
Southcote Jc, GW, 4A2
Southease & Rodmell Halt, LBSC, 5F4
Southend (Glam), Mum, 43G3
Southend-on-Sea, LTS & GE, 6A4
Southend-on-Sea for Westcliff & Thorpe Bay, GE, 6A4
Southerham Jc, LBSC, 5F4
Southern Jc, SYJ, 16A4; 21G4; 41A4
Southerndown Road, BRY, 7C5; 43D4
Southfield Jc, Cal, 30D5
Southfields, LSW(Dist), 39E4
Southfleet, SEC, 5B5
Southill, Mid, 11D1
Southminster, GE, 12G5
Southport, LY(LNW), LY & CLC, 20A4; 24E4; 45F1
Southrey, GN, 17B1
Southwaite, LNW, 26D1
Southwark Park, SEC, 40D4
Southwater, LBSC, 5E2
Southwell, Mid, 16C3
Southwick (Durham) Goods, NE, 28C5
Southwick (Kircud), G&SW, 26C4
Southwick (Sussex), LBSC, 5F3
Southwold, SWD, 12B1
Southwold Railway, SWD, 12B1
Sowerby Bridge, LY, 21E1; 42C5
Spa Road Bermondsey, SEC, 40D4
Spalding, GN(GE/MGN) & Mid, 17E2
Spalding North Jc, GN/GN&GEJt, 17E3
Spalding South Jc, GN/MGN, 17E3
Sparkford, GW, 3D2; 8F1
Sparrowlee, NS, 15C5
Spean Bridge, NB, 32B2
Speech House Road, SVW, 8A1; 9E1
Speen, GW, 4A3
Speeton, NE, 22B3
Speke, LNW, 20C4; 45E4
Speke Jc, LNW, 45E4
Spennithorne, NE, 21A2; 27G5
Spennymoor, NE, 27D5
Spetchley (Goods), Mid, 9B3
Spetisbury, SD, 3E4
Spey Bay, GNS, 36C1
Spiersbridge (Goods), GBK, 44E2
Spilsby, GN, 17B3
Spink Hill for Mount St Mary, GC, 16A4; 41B3
Spital, BJ, 20C4; 45F4
Spitalfields Goods, GE, 40C4
Splott Jc, TV, 43B4
Spofforth, NE, 21C3
Spon Lane, LNW, 13B2; 15G4
Spondon, Mid, 16D5; 41G2
Spondon Jc, Mid, 16D5, 41G2
Spooner Row, GE, 12A4; 18F4
Spratton, LNW, 10A3
Spring Vale, LY, 20A2; 24E2
Springbank Jcs (Hull), HB, 22 (inset)
Springburn Park (Goods), Cal, 29C5; 44D4
Springburn, NB, 44D4
Springfield, NB, 34F5
Springside, G&SW, 29E3
Springwood Jc, LNW&LYJt/LNW/LY, 21E2; 42D5
Sprotborough, HB, 21F4
Sprouston, NE, 31E2
Sprouston Jc, NB/NE, 31E2
Stacksteads, LY, 20A1; 24E1
Staddlethorpe, NE(GC/LNW), 22E5
Stafford, LNW(NS/GN), 15E3; 20G1
Stafford Common, GN, 15D3; 20G1
Stafford Jc, LNW/SWN, 15E2
Staincliffe & Batley Carr, LNW, 42C3 *see also* Batley Carr

Staincross for Mapplewell, GC, 21F3; 42D2
Staines, LSW & GW, 5B1
Staines Jc, LSW, 5B1
Stainforth & Hatfield, GC(NE), 21F5
Stainland & Holywell Green, LY, 21E2; 42C5
Staintondale, NE, 28G1
Stairfoot, GC, 42E2
Staithes, NE, 28E2
Stalbridge, SD, 3D3; 8G1
Staley & Millbrook (Goods), LNW, 21F1
Stalham, MGN, 18E2
Stallingborough, GC, 22F2
Stalybridge, GC&LNWJt & LY, 21F1 and inset A2
Stamford, Mid(LNW) & GN, 16F1; 17F1
Stamford Bridge (Yorks), NE, 22C5
Stamford Brook, (LSW(Dist), 39D4
Stamford Hill, GE, 40A4
Stammerham Jc, LBSC, 5E2
Stanbridgeford, LNW, 10D1
Standish (Lancs), LNW, 20B3; 24F2; 45D1
Standish Jc (Glos), GW/Mid, 9E3
Standish Jc (Lancs), LNW, 20B3; 24F3; 45D2
Standon, GE, 11E3
Standon Bridge, LNW, 15D3; 20F1
Stane Street Halt, GE, 11E4
Stanford-le-Hope, LTS, 5A5
Stanhoe, GE, 18D5
Stanhope, NE, 27D4
Stanley (Lancs), LNW, 45F3 *see also* Knotty Ash
Stanley (Yorks), MJ, 21E3; 42B2
Stanley Bridge Halt, GW, 3A4
Stanley Junc (Perth), Cal(HR), 33E5
Stanmore, LNW, 5A2
Stanner, GW, 14E2
Stannergate (Goods), D&A, 34E1 (inset)
Stanningley, GN(LY), 21D2; 42A4
Stannington, NE, 27A5
Stansfield Hall, LY, 21E1
Stansted, GE, 11E4
Stanton, GW, 9F5
Stanton Gate, Mid, 16D4; 41G3
Staple, EK, 6C2
Staple Hill, Mid, 3A3; 8C1; 9G2
Stapleford & Sandiacre (Notts), Mid, 16D4; 41G3
Staplehurst, SEC, 6D5
Stapleton Road, GW, 3 (inset); 8C1
Starbeck, NE, 21C3
Starcross, GW, 2C3
Staveley (Westmorland), LNW, 27G1
Staveley Town (Derbys), GC & Mid, 16A4; 41B3
Staveley Works, GC, 16A4; 41B3 *see also* Barrow Hill
Staverton (Devon), GW, 2D4
Staverton Halt (Wilts), GW, 3B4
Staward, NE, 27C3
Stechford, LNW, 15G5
Steele Road, NB, 27A1; 31G1
Steelend (Goods), NB, 30A3
Steens Bridge, GW, 9B1
Steeplehouse (Goods), LNW, 16C5; 41E1
Steer Point, GW, 2E5
Steeton & Silsden, Mid, 21C1
Stenson Jc, Mid, 16D5
Stepford, G&SW, 26A4
Stepney (Hull), NE, 22 (inset)
Stepney (London), GE(LTS), 40C3
Stepney Green, WB, 40C3
Stepps Road, Cal, 29C5; 44C4
Stevenage, GN, 11E2
Stevenston, G&SW & Cal, 29D3
Steventon, GW, 10F4
Stewarton, GBK, 29 D4
Stewarts Lane Goods, SEC, 39E4 (inset)
Stewarts Lane Jc, SEC, 39E4 (inset)
Steyning, LBSC, 5F2
Stickney, GN, 17C3
Stillington, NE, 28E5
Stirchley, GW, 15F2
Stirling, Cal & NB, 30A5
Stixwould, GN, 17B2
Stobcross, Cal & Cal&NBJt, 44E4
Stobo, Cal, 30E3
Stobs, NB, 31F1
Stobs Camp, NB, 31F1
Stockbridge, LSW(MSW), 4C4
Stockcross & Bagnor, GW, 4A4
Stockingford, Mid, 16F5
Stockport, LNW(NS/LY) & CLC, 20C1; 21G1; 45A4
Stocksfield, NE(NB), 27C4
Stocksmoor, LY, 21F2; 42D4
Stockton (Durham), NE, 28E5
Stockton Brook, NS, 15C3; 20E1
Stockwith (Goods), GN&GEJt, 22G5
Stogumber, GW, 8F5
Stoke (Suffolk), GE, 11D5
Stoke Bruern (Goods), SMJ, 10C3
Stoke Canon, GW, 2B3
Stoke Edith, GW, 9C2
Stoke Ferry, GE, 11A4; 17F5
Stoke Golding, AN, 16F5
Stoke Mandeville, Met&GCJt, 10E2
Stoke Newington, GE, 40B4
Stoke-on-Trent, NS(LNW), 15C3; 20F1
Stoke Works (Goods), Mid, 9B4
Stoke Works (Pass), GW(Mid), 9B4
Stokesley, NE, 28F4
Stone, NS, 15D3; 20F1
Stone Cross Halt, LBSC, 5F5
Stone Cross Jc, LBSC, 5F5
Stone Crossing Halt, SEC, 5B5
Stonea, GE, 11A3; 17G3
Stonebridge Park, LNW(LE), 39B3
Stoneferry (Goods), NE, 22D3
Stonehall & Lydden Halt, SEC, 6D2
Stonehaven, Cal(NB), 34A2
Stonehouse (Glos), GW & Mid, 9E3
Stonehouse (Lanarks), Cal, 30D5
Stonehouse Jcs, Cal, 44A1
Stonehouse Pool, LSW, 1 (inset)
Stoneywood (Aberdeen), GNS, 37F4
Storeton for Barnston, GC, 20C4; 24G4; 45F4
Stottesdon, CMDP, 9A2; 15G2
Stoulton, GW, 9C3
Stourbridge, GW, 9A3; 15G3
Stourbridge Junc, GW, 9A3; 15G3
Stourport, GW, 9A3
Stourton Jc, Mid/EWY, 21D3; 42B2
Stow (Midlothian), NB, 30D1
Stow (Norfolk), GE, 17F4
Stow Bedon, GE, 12A5; 18F5
Stow-on-the-Wold, GW, 9D5
Stow Park, GN&GEJt, 16A2
Stowmarket, GE, 12C4
Stracathro, Cal, 34C3
Stradbroke, MSL, 12B3
Stranraer, P&W, 25C2
Strata Florida, GW, 14D5
Stratford, GE, 5A4; 40B3
Stratford Market, GE, 40B2
Stratford-on-Avon, GW & SMJ, 9B5
Strathaven (Central and North), Cal, 29D5
Strathaven Jc, Cal, 44C2
Strathblane, NB, 29B5
Strathbungo, GBK, 44E3 and inset F1
Strathcarron, HR, 35E2
Strathmiglo, NB, 34F5
Strathord, Cal(HR), 33E5
Strathpeffer, HR, 35D5
Strathyre, Cal, 33F2
Stratton, GW, 9F5
Stravithie, NB, 34F3
Strawberry Hill, LSW, 5B2; 39E2
Strawfrank Jc, Cal, 30D4
Streatham, LBSC, 5B3; 40F5
Streatham Common, LBSC, 40F5
Streatham Hill, LBSC(LNW), 40E5
Streatham Jc, LBSC, 40F5
Streatham North Jc, LBSC, 40F5
Streatham South Jc, LBSC, 40F5
Streetly, Mid, 15F5
Strensall, NE, 21B5
Stretford, MSJA(CLC), 45B3
Stretford Bridge, BC, 14C1
Stretford Bridge Jc, BC/GW&LNWJt, 14C1
Stretham, GE, 11B4
Stretton (Derbys), Mid, 16B5; 41D2
Stretton & Clay Mills (Staffs), NS(GN), 15C5 (inset)
Stretton Jc, LNW/NS, 15C5 (inset)
Stretton-on-Fosse, GW, 9C5
Strichen, GNS, 37C4
Strines, GC&MidJt, 15A4; 21G1
Strome Ferry, HR, 35E1
Strood, SEC, 6B5
Stroud, GW & Mid, 9E3
Stroud Green, GN(NL), 40A5
Struan, HR, 33C3
Stubbins, LY, 20A1; 24E1; 45B1
Stubbins Jc, LY, 45B1
Studland Road Jc, LSW/Dist, 39D4
Studley & Astwood Bank, Mid, 9B4
Sturmer, GE, 11D5
Sturminster Newton, SD, 3E3
Sturry, SEC, 6C2
Sturton, GC, 16A2
Stutton (Goods), NE, 21D4
Styal, LNW, 15A3; 20C1; 45A4
Suckley, GW, 9B2

Sudbrook (Goods), GW, 8B2; 9F1
Sudbury (Staffs), NS(GN), 15D5
Sudbury (Suffolk), GE, 12D5
Sudbury & Harrow Road, GC, 39B2
Sudbury Hill, Dist, 39B2
Sudbury Town, Dist, 39B2
Sugar Loaf, LNW, 14E4
Sulby Bridge, IMR, 23A3; 25G4
Sulby Glen, IMR, 23A3; 25G4
Sully, TV, 8D4; 43B5
Summer Lane, GC, 21F3; 42E2
Summerseat, LY, 20A1; 24E1; 45B1
Summerston, NB, 29B5; 44E5
Sunbank Halt, GW, 20F5
Sunbury, LSW, 5B2
Sunderland, NE, 28C5
Sundridge Park, SEC, 40F2
Sunilaws, NE, 31D2
Sunningdale, LSW, 5B1
Sunnywood Halt, LY, 45B1
Surbiton, LSW, 5B2; 39G2
Surfleet, GN, 17D2
Surrey Canal Jc, SEC, 40D3
Surrey Docks, EL, 40D4
Sutton (Cambs), GE, 11B3
Sutton (Surrey), LBSC, 5C3
Sutton Bingham, LSW, 3E2
Sutton Bridge, MGN, 17E4
Sutton Bridge Jc, MGN, 17E3
Sutton Coldfield, LNW, 15F5
Sutton-in-Ashfield, Mid, GC& GN, 16B4; 41D4
Sutton Junc, Mid, 16B4; 41D4
Sutton Oak, LNW, 45D3
Sutton-on-Hull, NE, 22D3
Sutton-on-Sea, GN, 17A4
Sutton Park, Mid, 15F5
Sutton Scotney, GW, 4C3
Sutton Weaver, LNW, 15A1; 20D3; 45D5
Swadlincote, Mid, 16E5
Swaffham, GE, 18F5
Swaffhamprior, GE, 11C4
Swainsthorpe, GE, 18F3
Swalwell, NE, 27C5; 28 (inset)
Swalwell Branch Jc, 28 (inset)
Swan Village, GW, 13B2; 15F4
Swanage, LSW, 3G5
Swanbourne, LNW, 10D2
Swanbridge Halt, TV, 43B5
Swanley, SEC, 5B4
Swannington, Mid, 16E4
Swanscombe Halt, SEC, 5B5
Swansea, GW, LNW, Mid, RSB & Mum, 7B4; 43G3
Swansea Bay, LNW, 7B4; 43G3
Swanwick, LSW, 4E3
Swavesey, GE(Mid), 11B3
Sway, LSW, 4E5
Swaythling, LSW(GW), 4D4
Swimbridge, GW, 7F4
Swinderby, Mid, 16B2
Swindon, GW, 9G5
Swindon Town, MSW, 9G5
Swindon Works, GW, 9G5
Swine, NE, 22D3
Swineshead, GN, 17D2
Swing Bridge Jc (St Olaves), GE, 18F1
Swing Bridge Jc (Trowse), GE, 18F3
Swinton (Lancs), LY, 20B2; 24F1; 45B2
Swinton (Yorks), Mid(NE) & GC, 21F4; 42F1
Swiss Cottage, Met, 39B5
Sydenham, LBSC, 40F4
Sydenham Hill, SEC, 40F4
Sykehouse, GC&HBJt, 21E5
Sykes Jc, GC/GN&GEJt, 16A2
Sylfaen, W&L, 14B2
Symington, Cal, 30E4
Symonds Yat, GW, 8A2; 9E1
Syston, Mid(MGN), 16E3
Syston N, S & E Jcs, Mid, 16E3

Tadcaster, NE, 21D4
Tadworth & Walton-on-Hill, SEC, 5C3
Taff Bargoed Jc, GW/TBJ, 43C3
Taffs Well, TV(Rhy), 8C4; 43C4
Tain, HR, 36B4
Takeley, GE, 11F4
Talacre, LNW, 20C5
Talbot Road (Blackpool), PWY, 24D4
Talerddig, Cam, 14B4
Talgarth, Cam(Mid), 14F3
Talley Road, VT, 13G5
Tallington, GN, 17F1
Talsarn Halt, GW, 13E5
Talsarnau, Cam, 19F2
Talybont Halt, Cam, 13A5; 19G2
Talybont-on-Usk, BM, 14G3
Tal-y-Cafn & Eglwysbach, LNW, 19D4
Talyllyn Junc, BM(Mid/Cam), 14G3
Tamerton Foliot, LSW, 1D5
Tamworth, LNW & Mid, 15F5
Tanat Valley Railway, Tan, 19G5; 20G5
Tanfield, NE, 21A3
Tanhouse Lane, GC&MidJt(CLC), 45D4
Tankerton Halt, SEC, 6B3
Tannadice, Cal, 34C4
Tanshelf, LY, 21E4; 42C1
Tan-y-Bwlch, Fest, 19F3
Tan-y-Grisiau, Fest, 19F3
Taplow, GW, 5B1; 10G2
Tapton Jc, Mid, 16B5; 41B2
Tarbolton, G&SW, 29E4
Tarff, G&SW, 26C5
Tarset, NB, 27A2
Tattenhall, LNW, 15B1; 20E3
Tattenhall Jc, LNW, 15B1; 20E3
Tattenhall Road, LNW, 15B1; 20E3
Tattenham Corner, SEC, 5C3
Tattershall, GN, 17C2
Taunton, GW, 8F4
Tavistock, LSW & GW, 1C5
Tavistock Jc, GW, 2D5
Tay Bridge (Dundee), NB, 34 (inset)
Taynuilt, Cal, 32E3
Tayport, NB, 34E4
Tean, NS, 15D4
Tebay, LNW&NEJt, 27F1
Teddington, LSW, 5B2; 39F2
Teigngrace, GW, 2C3
Teignmouth, GW, 2C3
Temple Hirst, NE, 21E5
Temple Meads (Bristol), GW&MidJt, 3A2 and inset; 8C2
Temple Sowerby, NE, 27E1
Temple, Dist(Met), 40C5
Templecombe, LSW&SDJt & SD, 3D3; 8G1
Templecombe Lower Platform, SD, 3D3; 8G1
Templeton, GW, 7C3
Tempsford, GN, 11C2
Tenbury Wells, S&H, 9A1
Tenby, GW, 7D3
Tennochside Jc, NB, 44C3
Tenterden St Michael's, KES, 6D4
Tenterden Town, KES, 6D4
Tern Hill, GW, 15D2; 20G2
Terrington, MGN, 17E4
Teston Crossing Halt, SEC, 6E5
Tetbury, GW, 9F3
Teversall, Mid & GN, 16B4; 41D3
Tewkesbury, Mid, 9D3
Teynham, SEC, 6C4
Thackley, GN, 21D2; 42A4
Thame, GW, 10E3
Thames Ditton, LSW, 5B2; 39G2
Thames Haven, LTS, 6A5
Thankerton, Cal, 30E4
Thatcham, GW, 4A3
Thatto Heath, LNW, 20C3; 24G3; 45E3
Thaxted, GE, 11E4
The Dyke, LBSC, 5F3
The Hale Halt, GN, 5A2
The Lodge Halt, GW, 20E4
The Mound, HR, 36A4
The Oaks, LY, 20B2; 24F2; 45B1
Theale, GW, 4A2
Theddingworth, LNW, 16G3
Theddlethorpe, GN, 17A3; 22G1
Thelwall, LNW, 15A2; 20C2; 24G2; 45C4
Theobalds Grove, GE, 11G3
Thetford, GE, 12B5; 18G5
Thetford Bridge, GE, 12B5
Theydon Bois, GE, 11G3
Thingley Jc, GW, 3A4
Thirsk, NE, 21A4
Thongs Bridge, LY, 21F2; 42D5
Thorganby, DVL, 21D5
Thorington, GE, 12E4
Thornaby, NE, 28E4
Thornbury, Mid, 8B1; 9F2
Thorne, GC & NE(GC), 21E5
Thorne Jc, GC, 21F5
Thorner, NE, 21D3
Thorney, MGN, 17F2
Thorneyburn, NB, 27A2
Thorneywood, GN, 41F5
Thornfalcon, GW, 8F4
Thornhill (Dumfries), G&SW, 26A4; 30G4
Thornhill (Yorks), LY, 21E3; 42C3 *see also* Ravensthorpe
Thornielee, NB, 30E1
Thornley, NE, 28D5

Thornliebank (Goods), GBK, 29C5; 44F2
Thornliebank (Pass), Cal, 29C5; 44E2
Thornly Park Jc, G&SW, 44G3
Thornton (Lancs), PWY, 24D4; and inset
Thornton (Yorks), GN, 21D2; 42A5
Thornton (Yorks), Mid, 21C1
Thornton Abbey, GC, 22E3
Thornton Dale, NE, 22A5
Thornton Heath, LBSC, 5B3; 40G5
Thornton-in-Craven, Mid, 21C1
Thornton Junc, NB, 30A2; 34G5
Thorntonhall, Cal, 29D5; 44E2
Thorp Arch, NE, 21C4
Thorp Gates (Goods), NE, 21D5
Thorpe (Northants), LNW, 10A1; 11B1
Thorpe (Norwich), GE, 18F3
Thorpe Bay, LTS, 6A4
Thorpe Cloud, LNW, 15C5
Thorpe Culvert, GN, 17B4
Thorpe-in-Balne, GC&HBJt, 21F5
Thorpe Jc, GE, 18F3
Thorpe-le-Soken, GE, 12E3
Thorpe-on-the-Hill, Mid, 16B1
Thorpe Thewles, NE, 28E5
Thorpness Halt, GE, 12C2
Thor's Cave, NS, 15B5
Thorverton, GW, 2A3
Thrapston, LNW & Mid, 10A1, 11B1
Three Bridges, LBSC, 5D3
Three Cocks Junc, Cam(Mid), 14F2
Three Counties, GN, 11E2
Three Oaks & Guestling Halt, LBCS, 6F5
Threlkeld, CKP, 26E1
Thringstone Halt, LNW, 16E4
Throsk Platform, Cal, 30A5
Throstle Nest Jc, CLC, 45B3
Thrumster, HR, 38D2
Thrybergh Jc, GC/GC&MidJt, 42F1
Thurcroft (Goods), GC/Mid&HBJt, 16A4; 21G4; 41A4
Thurgarton, Mid, 16C3
Thurgoland (Goods), GC, 42E3
Thurlby, GN, 17E1
Thurnby & Scraptoft, GN, 16F3
Thursford, MGN, 18D4
Thurso, HR, 38C3
Thurstaston, BJ, 20C5
Thurston, GE, 12C5
Thuxton, GE, 18F4
Thwaite Flat Jc, Fur, 24B5
Tibbermuir Crossing, Cal, 33E5
Tibshelf & Newton, Mid, 16B4; 41D3
Tibshelf Town, GC, 16B4; 41D3
Ticehurst Road, SEC, 5E5
Tickhill & Wadworth, SYJ, 21G5
Tidal Basin, GE, 40C2
Tiddington, GW, 10E3
Tidenham, GW, 8B2; 9F1
Tidworth, MSW, 4B5
Tilbury, LTS, 5B5
Tilbury Docks, LTS, 5B5
Tile Hill, LNW, 10A5
Tilehurst, GW, 4A2; 10G3
Tillicoultry, NB, 30A4
Tillietudlem, Cal, 30D5
Tillyfourie, GNS, 37F2
Tillynaught, GNS, 37C2
Tilton, GN&LNWJt, 16F2
Timperley, MSJA(CLC), 20C1; 24G1; 45B3
Tingley, GN, 21E3; 42B3
Tinsley, GC, 21G4; 42G2
Tintern for Brockweir, GW, 8B2; 9F1
Tipton, GW & LNW, 13B1; 15F4
Tipton St John's, LSW, 2B2
Tiptree, GE, 12F5
Tir Phil & New Tredegar, Rhy, 8A4; 43B2 *see also* New Tredegar
Tirydail, GW(LNW), 7A3; 43G1
Tisbury, LSW, 3D4
Tissington, LNW, 15C5
Tisted, LSW, 4C2
Titley, GW, 14E1
Tiverton, GW, 2A3; 7G5
Tiverton Junc, GW, 2A2
Tivetshall, GE, 12A3; 18G3
Tiviot Dale (Stockport), CLC, 45A3
Tochineal, GNS, 37C1
Toddington, GW, 9D4
Todmorden, LY, 20A1; 21E1
Toft & Kingston (Goods), LNW, 11C3
Tolcarn Jc, GW, 1D1
Tollcross, Cal, 44D3
Toller, GW, 3F2
Tollerton, NE, 21B4
Tollesbury, GE, 12F5
Tollesbury Knights Halt, GE, 12F5
Tolleshunt D'Arcy, GE, 12F5
Tomatin, HR, 36E4
Tonbridge, SEC, 5D5
Tondu, GW, 7C5; 43D4
Tonfanau, Cam, 13B5
Tonge & Bredon, Mid, 16D4
Tongham, LSW, 4B1; 5D1
Tongwynlais, Car, 43C4
Tonteg Halt, TV, 43C3
Ton-y-Groes Jc, PT, 43F3
Tonypandy, TV, 43D3
Tonyrefail, GW, 43D3
Tooting Junc, LBSC&LSWJt, 39F5
Topcliffe, NE, 21A3
Topsham, LSW, 2B3
Torksey, GC, 16A2
Torpantau, BM, 8A5; 14G3, 43C1
Torphins, GNS, 34A3; 37G2
Torquay, GW, 2D3
Torrance, NB, 29B5; 44D5
Torre, GW, 2D3
Torrington, LSW, 7G3
Torrisholme Jcs, Mid, 24B3
Torryburn, NB, 30A4
Torver, Fur, 24A4; 26G2
Totnes, GW, 2D4
Toton Yard, Mid, 41G3
Tottenham Hale, GE, 40A4
Totteridge, GN(NL), 5A3; 11G3
Tottington, LY, 20A1; 24F1; 45B1
Totton, LSW, 4E4
Touch South Jc, NB, 30A3
Tovil, SEC, 6C5
Tow Law, NE, 27D5
Towcester, SMJ, 10C3
Tower Hill, LSW, IB5
Towiemore (Goods), GNS, 37D1
Town Green & Aughton, LY, 20B4; 24F3; 45F2
Towneley, LY, 24D1
Towyn, Cam & Tal, 13B5
Trabboch, G&SW, 29F4
Trafford Park, CLC, 20C1; 24G1; 45B3
Tram Inn, GW, 9D1; 14F1
Tranent, NB, 30B1
Travellers' Rest, TV, 43C3
Trawscoed, GW, 13D5
Trawsfynydd, GW, 19F3
Treamble, GW, 1D1
Treborth, LNW, 19D2
Trecynon Halt, GW, 43D2
Tredegar, LNW, 8A4; 43B1
Treeton, Mid, 16A4; 21G4; 41A3; 42G1
Treeton Jc, GC/Mid/SHD, 42G1
Trefeglwys, Van, 14C4
Trefeinon, Cam(Mid), 14F3
Treferig, TV, 8B5; 43C3
Treferig Railway Jc, TV, 43C3
Trefnant, LNW, 19D5
Treforest, TV & BRY, 8B5; 43C3
Treforest Halt, AD, 43C3
Tregaron, GW, 14D5
Tregarth, LNW, 19D2
Trehafod, TV(BRY), 8B5; 43C3
Treharris, GW(Rhy), 43C3
Treherbert, TV(RSB), 7B5; 43D2
Trelewis Halt, TBJ, 43C2
Trench Crossing, LNW, 15E2
Trench Halt, Cam, 20F4
Trenholme Bar, NE, 28F5
Trent, Mid, 16D4
Trent Jc, Mid, 16D4
Trent Valley Jc, LNW, 15E3
Trentham, NS, 15C3; 20F1
Trentham Park, NS, 15D3; 20F1
Treorchy, TV, 8B5; 43D2
Tresavean, GW, 1E5 (inset)
Tresmeer, LSW, 1B4
Trethomas, GW, 8B4; 43B3
Trevil, LNW, 8A4; 43B1
Trevor, GW, 20F5
Trewerry & Trerice Halt, GW, 1D1
Trewythan, Van, 14C4
Triangle, LY, 21E1
Trimdon, NE, 28D5
Trimingham, NSJ, 18D2
Trimley, GE, 12E3
Trimsaran (Goods), BPGV, 7A3
Trimsaran Road, BPGV, 7A2
Tring, LNW, 10E1
Trinity & Newhaven, NB, 30 (inset)
Trodigal Halt, CM, 29 (inset)
Troedyrhiew Garth, GW, 7B5; 43E3
Troedyrhiw, QYM & TV, 43C2

Troedyrhiw Platform, QYM, 43C2
Troon, G&SW, 29E3
Troutbeck, CKP, 26E1
Trowbridge, GW, 3B4
Trowell, Mid, 16C4; 41F3
Trowse (Norwich), GE, 18F3
Trowse Upper Jc, GE, 18F3
Troy (Monmouth), GW, 8A2; 9E1
Trumper's Crossing (for South Hanwell & Osterley Park) Halt, GW, 39D2
Truro, GW, 1E1
Trusham, GW, 2C3
Truthall Platform, GW, 1F5 (inset)
Tryfan Junc, NWNG, 19E2
Tucker Street (Wells, Som), GW, 3C2; 8E2
Tue Brook, LNW, 20C4; 24G4; 45F3
Tuffley Jc, Mid, 9E3
Tufnell Park (Goods), GE, 40B5
Tufts Jcs, SVW, 8A1; 9E2
Tullibardine, Cal, 33F4
Tullock, NB, 32B1
Tulse Hill, LBSC, 5B3; 40E5
Tumble, LM, 7A3
Tumby Woodside, GN, 17C2
Tunbridge Wells, SEC & LBSC(SEC), 5D5
Tunbridge Wells West, LBSC, 5D5
Tunnel Jc (Neepsend), GC, 22G4
Tunnel Jc (Salisbury), LSW, 4C5
Tunnel Jc (Worcester), GW, 9B3
Tunstall, NS, 15C3; 20E1
Turnberry, G&SW, 29G2
Turnchapel, LSW 1D5 and inset
Turnham Green, LSW(Dist), 39D3
Turnhouse, NB, 30B3
Turriff, GNS, 37D1
Turton & Edgworth, LY, 20A2; 24E1; 45B1
Turvey, Mid, 10B1
Tutbury, NS(GN), 15D5
Tuxford, GN & GC, 16B2
Tweedmouth, NE, 31C3
Twenty, MGN, 17E2
Twerton-on-Avon, GW, 3A3
Twickenham, LSW, 5B2; 39E2
Twizell, NE, 31D3
Twyford (Berks), GW, 4A1
Twywell, Mid, 10A1
Ty Croes, LNW, 19D1
Tycoch Jc, GW/BPGV, 7A2
Tydd, MGN, 17E3
Tyldesley, LNW, 20B2; 24F2; 45C2
Tylorstown, TV, 8B5; 43D2
Tylwch, Cam, 14C4
Tyndrum, NB & Cal, 32E1
Tyne Dock, NE, 28B5
Tynehead, NB, 30C1
Tynemouth, NE, 28B5
Tyseley, GW, 15G5
Tytherington, Mid, 8B1; 9F2

Uckfield, LBSC, 5E4
Uddingston, Cal & NB, 44C3
Uddingston Jc, Cal, 44C3
Uddingston West, NB, 44C3
Udny, GNS, 37E4
Uffculme, GW, 2A2; 8G5
Uffington (Berks), GW, 10F5
Uffington & Barnack, Mid, 17F1
Ufford Bridge, GN, 16F1; 17F1
Ulbster, HR, 38E2
Ulceby, GC, 22E3
Ulleskelf, NE, 21D4
Ullesthorpe & Lutterworth, Mid, 16G4
Ullock, WCE, 26E3
Ullock Jc, WCE, 26E3
Ulverston, Fur, 24A4
Umberleigh, LSW, 7F3
Underwood Goods (Paisley), Cal, 44G3
Union Bank Farm Halt, LNW, 45D4
Union Mills, IMR, 23B2
Unstone, Mid, 16A5; 41B2
Up Exe, GW, 2A3
Uphill, NB, 30C3
Uphill Jc, GW, 3B1; 8D3
Upholland, LY, 20B3; 24F3; 45D2
Uplawmoor, Cal, 29D4; 44G2
Uplawmoor East Jc, Cal, 29D4
Upminster, LTS, 5A5
Upper Bank, Mid, 7B4; 43G3
Upper Batley, ON, 42B3
Upper Boat, AD & Car, 43C3
Upper Broughton, Mid, 16D3
Upper Holloway, THJ(LTS), 40B5
Upper Lydbrook, SVW, 8A1; 9E1
Upper Pontnewydd, GW, 8B3; 43A3
Upper Port Glasgow (Goods), G&SW, 29B3
Upper Sydenham, SEC, 40F4
Upper Warlingham, CO, 5C3
Upperby New Jc, LNW, 26 (inset)
Uppermill, LNW, 21F1
Upperthorpe & Killamarsh, GC, 16A4; 41B3 *see also* Killamarsh
Uppingham, LNW, 16F2
Upton (Ches), GC, 20C4; 24G4; 45F4
Upton & Blewbury, GW, 10F4
Upton & North Elmsall, HB, 21E4; 42D1
Upton Magna, SWN, 15E1
Upton-on-Severn, Mid, 9C3
Upton Park, LTS(Dist) & LNW, 40C2
Upwell, WUT, 17F4
Upwey, GW, 3F3
Upwey Jc, GW(LSW), 3G3
Upwey Wishing Well Halt, GW, 3F3
Uralite Halt, SEC, 6B5
Urmston, CLC, 20C1; 45B3
Urquhart, GNS, 36C1
Ushaw Moor, NE, 27D5
Usk, GW, 8B3
Usworth, NE, 28C5
Utterby Halt, GN, 22G2
Uttoxeter, NS(GN), 15D5
Uxbridge, GW & Met(Dist), 5A2; 10G1
Uxbridge, Met, 5A3
Uxbridge High Street, GW, 5A2; 10G1
Uxbridge Road (Goods), GW & LNW, 39D4
Uxbridge Road Jc, GW & Met(Dist), 39C4
Uxbridge Road (Pass), WL(H&C), 39D4
Uxbridge Vine Street, GW, 5A2; 10G1

Vale of Rheidol Light Railway, VR(Cam), 14C5
Vallance Road Jc, Dist/WB, 40C4
Valley, LNW, 19B2
Van, Van, 14C4
Varteg, LNW(GW), 7A4; 8A4; 43A2
Vauxhall, GE, 18F1
Vauxhall (London), LSW, 40D5
Vauxhall (Yarmouth), GE, 18F1
Vauxhall & Duddeston, LNW, 13C4
Vauxhall Fishmarket (Yarmouth), GE, 18F1
Velvet Hall, NE, 31D3
Venn Cross, GW, 8F5
Ventnor, IW, 4G3
Ventnor Town, IWC, 4G3
Verney Junc, LNW & Met&GCJt, 10D3
Verwood, LSW, 3E5
Vicarage Crossing Halt, GW, 20E5
Victoria (London), LBSC(LNW), SEC&GWJt & Dist(Met), 5B3; 39D5
Victoria (Manchester), LY(LNW/Mid), 20B1; 24F1; 45A3
Victoria (Mon), GW, 8A4; 43B2
Victoria (Norwich), GE, 18F3
Victoria (Nottingham), GC&GNJt, 16C4; 41F4
Victoria (Sheffield), GC(LY), 16A5; 21G3; 41A2; 42G2
Victoria (Swansea), LNW, 7B4; 43G3
Victoria Basin Goods (Wolverhampton), GW, 15E3 (inset)
Victoria Park (London), NL & GE, 40B3
Victoria Park (Whiteinch), NB, 44F4
Vine Street (Uxbridge), GW, 5A2; 10G1
Virginia Water, LSW, 5B1
Vobster (Goods), GW, 3B3; 8E1
Vobster Colliery (Goods), SD, 8E1
Vowchurch, GW, 14F1

Wadborough, Mid, 9C3
Waddesdon, OAT, 10E3
Waddesdon Manor, Met&GCJt, 10E2
Waddesdon Road, GW, 10E3
Waddington, GN, 16B1; 17B1
Waddon, LBSC, 5C3
Wadebridge, LSW(GW), 1C2
Wadhurst, SEC, 5E5
Wadsley Bridge, GC, 21G3; 42G2
Waenavon, LNW(GW), 8A4; 43B1
Waenfawr, NWNG, 19E2
Wainfleet, GN, 17C4
Wakefield (Kirkgate), LY&GNJt, 21E3; 42C2
Wakefield (Westgate) (Goods), GC&MidJt, 21E3; 42C2
Wakefield (Westgate) (Pass), GN&GCJt, 21E3; 42C2
Wakerley & Barrowden, LNW, 16F1
Walberswick, SWD, 12B1
Walcot, SWN, 15E1
Waldron & Horeham Road, LBSC, 5F5
Waleswood, GC, 16A4; 41A3
Walham Green, Dist, 39D4
Walkden, LY & LNW, 20B2; 24F1; 45B2

Walker, NE, 28B5
Walkerburn, NB, 30D1
Walkergate, NE, 28B5
Walkeringham, GN&GEJt, 22G5
Walkinshaw Branch Jc, Cal, 44G3
Wall, NB, 27B3
Wall Grange, NS, 15C4
Wallasey, Wir, 20C4; 24G4; 45G3
Wallasey Village, Wir, 20C4; 24G4; 45G3
Wallingford, GW, 10F3
Wallneuk Jc, G&SW/G&P, 44F3
Wallsend, NE, 28B5
Walmer, SEC, 6C1
Walpole, MGN, 17E4
Walsall (Goods), LNW & Mid, 13A2; 15F4
Walsall (Pass), LNW(Mid), 13A2; 15F4
Walsall Street Goods (Wolverhampton), GW, 15E3 (inset)
Walsall Wood, Mid, 15F4
Walsden, LY, 20A1; 21E1
Walsingham, GE, 18D5
Waltham, GN, 22F2
Waltham Cross & Abbey, GE, 11G3
Waltham-on-the-Wold, GN, 16D2
Walthamstow, GE & TFG, 40A3
Walthamstow St James Street, GE, 40A3
Walthamstow Wood Street, GE, 40A3
Walton (Northants), Mid, 17F2
Walton & Anfield, LNW, 45F3
Walton for Hersham, LSW, 5C2
Walton-in-Gordano, WCP, 3A1; 8C3
Walton New Jc, LNW/BJ, 45D4
Walton-on-the-Hill (Lancs), CLC, 20C4; 24G4; 45F3
Walton-on-the-Naze, GE, 12E3
Walton Park, WCP, 3A1; 8C3
Walworth Road, SEC, 40D5
Wamphray, Cal, 26A3; 30G3
Wanborough, LSW(SEC), 5C1
Wandsworth Common, LBSC(LNW), 39E5
Wandsworth Road, SEC(LBSC), 40E5
Wandsworth Town, LSW, 39E5
Wanlockhead, Cal, 30F4
Wansford, LNW(GN), 11F1; 17F1
Wansford Road, GN, 11A1; 17F1
Wanstead Park, TFG, 40B2
Wanstrow, GW, 3C3; 8E1
Wantage, WT, 10F5
Wantage Road, GW, 10F5
Wantage Tramway, WT, 10F5
Wappenham, SMJ, 10C3
Wapping, GE, 40C4
Wapping & Salthouse (Liverpool) Goods, LY, 45 (inset)
Warblington Halt, LBSC, 4E2
Warboys, GN&GEJt, 11B2
Warcop, NE, 27E2
Wardhouse, GNS, 37E2
Wardleworth, LY, 20A1; 21E1; 45A1
Ware, GE, 11F3
Wareham, LSW, 3F4
Wargrave, GW, 4A1; 10G2
Wark, NB, 27B3
Warkworth, NE, 31F5
Warlingham, SEC, 5C3
Warminster, GW, 3C4
Warmley, Mid, 3A3; 8C1
Warmsworth, GC, 21F4
Warnham, LBSC, 5D2
Warren Hill Jc, GE, 11C4
Warrington, LNW(BJ), LNW & CLC, 15A1; 20C2; 24G2; 45D4
Warrior Square (St Leonards), SEC(LBSC), 6F5
Warriston Jc, NB, 30 (inset)
Warsop, GC, 16B4; 41C4
Warthill, NE, 21C5
Wartle, GNS, 37E3
Warwick, GW & LNW, 10B5
Warwick Road Goods, GW & LNW, 39D4
Warwick Road Jc, Dist, 39D5
Washford, GW, 8E5
Washingboro', GN, 16B1; 17B1
Washington, NE, 28C5
Waskerley Goods, NE, 27D4
Wassand, NE, 22D3
Watchet, GW, 8E5
Watchingwell, FYN, 4F4
Water Orton, Mid, 15F5
Waterbeach, GE, 11C4
Waterfall, IMR, 23B2
Waterfoot, LY, 20A1; 24E1
Watergate, SR, 7G3
Waterhall Jc (Cardiff), TV, 43B4
Waterhall Jc (Pyle), PT, 43E4
Waterhouses (Durham), NE, 27D5
Waterhouses (Staffs), NS, 15C5
Wateringbury, SEC, 6C5
Waterloo (Aberdeen), GNS, 37G4
Waterloo (Lancs), LY(LNW), 20B4; 24F4; 45F3
Waterloo (Liverpool) Goods, LNW, 45F3/G5
Waterloo (London), LSW, 5B3; 40D5
Waterloo Halt (Glam), BM(Rhy), 43B3
Waterloo Junc (London), SEC, 40D5
Waterloo Road (Blackpool), PWY, 24D4
Waterloo Road (Staffs), NS, 15C3; 20E1
Waterside, G&SW, 29F4
Waterside Jc, NB, 29B5; 44C5
Watford High Street, LNW(LE), 5A2; 11G1
Watford Junc, LNW(LE), 5A2; 11G1
Wath, Mid & HB, 21F4; 42E1
Wath-in-Nidderdale, NV, 21B2
Wath-on-Dearne, GC, 21F4; 42E1
Wath Road Jc, Mid/SK, 21F4; 42E1
Watlington, GW, 10F3
Watnall, Mid, 16C4; 41F4
Watsons Crossing Halt, LY, 21E2
Watten, HR, 38D2
Watton, GE, 12A5; 18F5
Wattsville, LNW, 43B3
Waverley (Edinburgh), NB(NE), 30B2 and inset
Waverton, LNW, 15B1; 20E3
Wavertree, LNW & CLC, 45F4
Wear Valley Junc, NE, 27E5
Wearhead, NE, 27D3
Weaste, LNW, 45B3
Weaver Jc, LNW, 15A1; 20D3; 45D5
Weaverthorpe, NE, 22A4
Weddington Jc, AN, 16F5
Wednesbury, GW & LNW, 13A2; 15F4
Wednesfield, Mid, 15F4
Wednesfield Heath, LNW, 15F4
Weedon, LNW, 10B3
Weekday Cross Jc, GC/GN, 16 C4; 41F4
Weeley, GE, 12E3
Weelsby Road, GN, 22F2
Weeton, NE, 21C3
Welbury, NE, 28F5
Weldon & Corby, Mid, 16G1
Welford & Kilworth, LNW, 10A3; 16G3
Welford Park, GW, 4A4
Welham Jc, LNW/GN&LNWJt, 16G2
Well Hall for North Eltham, SEC, 5B4; 40E2
Welland Bank Jc, MGN, 17E2
Wellfield, NE, 28D5
Welling, SEC, 5B4; 40E1
Wellingborough, LNW & Mid, 10B1
Wellington (Leeds) (Pass), Mid(LY), 42A2
Wellington (Salop), SWN, 15E2
Wellington (Som), GW, 8G4
Wellington College, SEC, 4B1
Wellington Street (Leeds) (Goods), GN, LNW&LYJt & NE, 21B2 (inset); 42A3
Wellow, SD, 3B3; 8D1
Wells (Norfolk), GE, 18C5
Wells Priory Road (Som), SD, 3C2; 8E2
Wells Tucker Street (Som), GW, 3C2; 8E2
Welnetham, GE, 12C5
Welshampton, Cam, 20F4
Welshpool, Cam(SWP) & W&L, 14B2
Welshpool & Llanfair Light Railway, W&L(Cam), 14B2
Welton (Northants), LNW, 10B3
Welwyn, GN, 11F2
Welwyn Garden City Halt, GN, 11F2
Wem, LNW, 15D1; 20G3
Wembley Hill, GC, 39B3
Wembley, LNW(LE), 5A2; 39B2
Wembley Park, Met, 5A2; 39B3
Wemyss Bay, Cal, 29C2
Wemyss Castle, NB, 30A2; 34G5
Wendlebury Halt, LNW, 10D4
Wendling, GE, 18E5
Wendover, Met&GCJt, 10E2
Wenford, LSW, 1C3
Wenhaston, SWD, 12B2
Wennington (Lancs), Mid, 24B2
Wensley, NE, 21A2; 27G4
Wensum Jc, GE, 18F3
Wentworth & Hoyland Common, Mid, 21F3; 42F2
Wenvoe, BRY, 8C4; 43C5
Wern (Goods), Cam, 19F2
Wern Las, S&M, 14A1; 20G4
Werneth (Oldham), LY, 20B1; 21D1; 45A2
Werrington Jc, GN, 17F2
West Auckland, NE, 27E5
West Bay (Bridport), GW, 3F1
Weat Bexhill Halt, LBSC, 6G5
West Bridge (Leicester), Mid, 16F4
West Brompton, Dist & WLE, 39D5

West Bromwich, GW, 13B2; 15G4
West Calder, Cal, 30C4
West Cornforth, NE, 28D5
West Cross, Mum, 43G3
West Croydon, LBSC, 5C3; 40G5
West Cults, GNS, 37G4
West Derby, CLC, 45F3
West Drayton & Yiewsley, GW, 5B2; 10G1
West Ealing, GW, 39C2
West End Lane, LNW(NL), 39B5
West Fen Drove (Goods), GE, 11A3; 17G3
West Ferry, D&A, 34E1 (inset)
West Gosforth, NE, 27B5
West Green, GE, 40A4
West Grinstead, LBSC, 5E2
West Hallam, GN, 16C4; 41G3
West Halton, GC, 22E4
West Ham, LTS(Dist), 40C2
West Hampstead, Met & Mid, 39B5
West Harrow, Met, 39A1
West Hartlepool, NE, 28D4
West Hoathly, LBSC, 5E4
West Holmes Jc, GC/GN/GN&GEJt, 16B1 (inset)
West India Docks, GE, 40C3
West Jesmond, NE, 27B5
West Jc (Colwich), LNW/NS, 15E4
West Kensington (Goods), Mid, 39D4
West Kensington (Pass), Dist, 39D4
West Kilbride, G&SW, 29D2
West Kirby, BJ & Wir, 20C5; 24G5
West Leigh, LNW, 45C3
West Leigh & Bedford, GC, 45C3
West London Extension Jc, WL/WLE, 39D4
West London Jcs, GW & LNW, 39C4
West Meon, LSW, 4D2
West Moors, LSW, 3E5
West Newport, NB, 34E4
West Norwood, LBSC(LNW), 40F5
West Norwood Jc, LBSC, 40F5
West Pennard, SD, 3C2; 8E2
West Rounton Gates, NE, 28F5
West Runton, MGN, 18D3
West St Leonards, SEC, 6F5
West Stanley (Goods), NE, 27C5
West Street (Gravesend), SEC, 5B5
West Street (Glasgow) Goods, Cal, 44F1 (inset)
West Street Jc (London), Met/SEC, 40C5
West Thurrock Jc, LTS, 5B5
West Timperley, CLC, 45B4
West Tinsley, GC & SHD, 42G2
West Vale, LY, 21E2; 42C5
West Wemyss, NB, 30A2; 34G5
West Wickham, SEC, 5B4; 40G3
West Worthing, LBSC, 5F2
West Wycombe, GW&GCJt, 10F2
Westbourne Park, GW & H&C, 39C5 and inset C1
Westbrook, GW, 14F2
Westburn Jc, Cal, 44C3
Westbury (Salop), SWP, 14A1
Westbury (Wilts), GW, 3B4
Westcliff-on-Sea, LTS, 6A4
Westcombe Park, SEC, 40D2
Westcott, OAT, 10E3
Westcraigs, NB, 30C4
Westenhanger, SEC, 6D3
Westerfield, GE, 12D3
Westerham, SEC, 5C4
Westerleigh Jcs, GW & Mid, 3A3; 8C1; 9G2
Western Jetty (Immingham), GC, 22E3
Westerton, NB, 44E5
Westfield, NB, 30B4
Westgate (Rotherham), Mid, 21G4; 42F1
Westgate (Wakefield) (Goods), GC&MidJt, 21E3; 42C2
Westgate (Wakefield) (Pass), GN&GCJt, 21E3; 42C2
Westgate-in-Weardale, NE, 27D3
Westgate-on-Sea, SEC, 6B2
Westham Halt, WP, 3G3
Westhead Halt, LY(LNW), 20B3; 24F3; 45E2
Westhoughton, LY, 45C2
Westhouses & Blackwell, Mid, 16B4; 41D3
Westmill, GE, 11E3
Westminster, Dist(Met), 40D5
Westmoor, Mid, 14F1
Westoe Lane, SSM, 28B5
Weston (Bath), Mid, 3A3; 8D1
Weston (Lincs), MGN, 17E2
Weston & Ingestre (Staffs), NS, 15D4 ***see also*** Ingestre
Weston-on-Trent, Mid, 16D5
Weston-sub-Edge, GW, 9C5
Weston-super-Mare, GW & WCP, 3B1; 8D3
Westward Ho!, BWHA, 7F2
Westwood, GC, 21F3; 42F2
Wetheral, NE, 27C1
Wetherby, NE, 21C4
Wetherby E & W Jcs, NE, 21C4
Wetmore Jc, Mid, 15C5 (inset)
Wetton Mill, NS, 15B5
Wetwang, NE, 22C4
Weybourne, MGN, 18D4
Weybridge, LSW, 5C2
Weyhill, MSW, 4B4
Weymouth, GW(LSW), 3G3
Weymouth Harbour, GW, 3G3
Weymouth Jc, GW, 3G3
Weymouth Town, GW, 3G3
Whaley Bridge, LNW, 15A4
Whalley, LY, 24D1
Whaplode, MGN, 17E3
Wharf Station (Towyn), Tal, 13B5
Wharram, NE, 22B5
Whatstandwell, Mid, 16C5; 41E2
Whauphill, P&W, 25C4
Wheathampstead, GN, 11F2
Wheatley (Oxon), GW, 10E3
Wheatley (Yorks), HHL, 21E2; 42B5
Wheelock, NS, 15B2; 20E2 ***see also*** Sandbach
Wheldrake, DVL, 21C5
Whelley (Goods), LNW, 45D2
Whelley Jc, LNW, 20B3; 24F2
Wherwell, LSW, 4C4
Whetstone (Leics), GC, 16F4
Whickham Jc, NE, 28 (inset)
Whifflet, Cal & NB, 30C5; 44B3
Whifflet Low Level, Cal, 44B3
Whimple, LSW, 2B2
Whimsey Halt, SVW, 8A1; 9E2
Whippingham, IWC, 4F3
Whiskerhill Jc, GC, 16A3
Whissendine, Mid, 16E2
Whistlefield, NB, 29A3
Whitacre, Mid, 15F5
Whitburn, NB, 30C4
Whitby Town, NE, 28F2
Whitby West Cliff, NE, 28F2
Whitchurch (Glam), Car, 43B4
Whitchurch (Hants), GW & LSW, 4B3
Whitchurch (Salop), LNW(Cam), 15C1; 20F3
Whitchurch Down Platform, GW, 1C5
White Bear, LU, 20A2; 24F2; 45D1
White Colne, CVH, 12E5
White Fen (Goods), GE, 11A3; 17G3
White Hart Lane, GE, 5A3
White Moss Crossing Halt, LY(LNW), 20B3; 24F3; 45E2
White Notley, GE, 11F5
Whiteboro', Mid, 16B4; 41D3
Whitechapel, EL & WB(H&C), 40C4
Whitecraigs, Cal, 29C5; 44E2
Whitecroft, SVW, 8A1; 9E2
Whitedale, NE, 22D3
Whitefield, LY, 20B1; 24F1; 45B2
Whitegate, CLC, 15B2; 20D2
Whitehall Road (Leeds) (Goods), LNW&LYJt, 21C2 (inset)
Whitehaven (Bransty), LNW&FurJt, 26E4
Whitehaven (Corkickle), Fur, 26E4
Whitehaven (Goods), Fur & LNW, 26E4
Whitehouse, GNS, 37F2
Whitehouse Jc, LY, 24E3
Whitehurst Halt, GW, 20F4
Whiteinch, Cal, 44F4 ***see also*** Victoria Park, NB
Whitemoor (Goods), GE, 11A3; 17F3
Whiterigg, NB, 30C5; 44A4
Whithorn, P&W, 25D4
Whitland, GW, 7A1; 13G2
Whitley Bay, NE, 28B5
Whitley Bridge, LY, 21E5
Whitlingham, GE, 18F3
Whitmore, LNW, 15C3; 20F1
Whitney-on-Wye, Mid, 14E2
Whitrigg, Cal, 26C2
Whitstable Harbour, SEC, 6B3
Whitstable Town & Tankerton, SEC, 6B3
Whitstone & Bridgerule, LSW, 1A4
Whittingham, NE, 31F4
Whittington (Derbys), Mid, 16A5; 41B2
Whittington (Salop), GW & Cam, 20G4
Whittlesea, GE, 11A2; 17F2
Whittlesford, GE, 11D3
Whitton (Lincs), GC, 22E4
Whitton Jc, LSW, 39E1
Whitwell (Derbys), Mid, 16A4; 41B4
Whitwell (IoW), IWC, 4G3
Whitwell & Reepham, MGN, 18E4
Whitwick, LNW, 16E4
Whitwood Jc, Mid/NE, 42B1

Whitworth, LY, 20A1; 24E1; 45A1
Whyteleafe, SEC, 5C3
Wichnor (Goods), Mid, 15E5
Wichnor Jc, Mid/LNW, 15E5
Wick, HR, 38D2
Wick St Lawrence, WCP, 3A1; 8D3
Wickenby, GC, 17A1
Wicker (Goods), Mid, 42G2
Wickford, GE, 6A5
Wickham (Hants), LSW, 4E3
Wickham Bishops, GE, 12F5
Wickham Market, GE, 12C2
Wickwar, Mid, 8B1; 9F2
Widdrington, NE, 27A5; 31G5
Widford, GE, 11F3
Widmerpool, Mid, 16D3
Widnes, LNW & GC&MidJt(CLC), 15A1; 20C3; 24G3; 45D4
Widnes Jc, GN, 15A1; 20C3; 45D4
Widney Manor, GW, 9A5
Wigan, LNW, LY & GC, 20B3; 24F2; 45D2
Wigston Central Jc, Mid, 16F3
Wigston Glen Parva, Mid, 16F3
Wigston Magna, Mid, 16F3
Wigston North Jc, LNW/Mid, 16F3
Wigston South, Mid, 16F3
Wigston South Jc, Mid, 16F3
Wigton, M&C, 26C2
Wigtown, P&W, 25C4
Wilburton, GE, 11B3
Wilby, MSL, 12B3
Willaston, LNW, 15C2; 20E2
Willenhall, LNW & Mid, 15F4
Willerby & Kirk Ella, HB, 22D4
Willersley Halt, GW, 9C5
Willesden Green, Met, 39B4
Willesden Junc, LNW(NL/LE), 5A3; 39C4
Willingdon Jc, LBSC, 5F5
Willington (Beds), LNW, 11D1
Willington (Durham), NE, 27D5
Willington Jc, Mid/NS, 16D5
Willington Quay, NE, 28B5
Williton, GW, 8E5
Willoughby (Lincs), GN, 17B4
Willow Walk Goods, LBSC, 40D4
Wilmcote, GW, 9B5
Wilmington, NE, 22 (inset)
Wilmslow, LNW, 15A3; 20C1; 45A5
Wilnecote, Mid, 15F5
Wilpshire, LY, 24D2
Wilsden, GN, 21D2; 42A5
Wilsontown, Cal, 30C4
Wilsontown Jcs, Cal, 30D4
Wilstrop (Siding), NE, 21C4
Wilton, GW & LSW, 3C5
Wimbledon, LSW(Dist) & LBSC&LSWJt, 5B3; 39F4
Wimbledon Park, LSW(Dist), 39E4
Wimblington, GN&GEJt, 11A3; 17G3
Wimborne, LSW, 3E5
Wincanton, SD, 3D3; 8F1
Winchburgh, NB, 30B3
Winchcombe, GW, 9D4
Winchelsea, SEC, 6E4
Winchelsea Harbour, SEC, 6E4
Winchester, LSW & GW, 4D3
Winchester Cheesehill, GW, 4D3
Winchester Jc, LSW, 4B3
Winchfield, LSW, 4B1
Winchmore Hill, GE 5A3
Wincobank & Meadow Hall, Mid, 21G3; 42G2 *see also* Meadow Hall
Winder, WCE, 26E3
Windermere, LNW, 26D1
Windermere Lake Side, Fur, 24A4; 26G1
Windmill Bridge Jc, LBSC, 40G4
Windmill End, GW, 13C1; 15G4
Windsor & Eton, GW & LSW, 5B1; 10G1
Windsor Street Wharf, LNW, 13B4
Winestead (Goods), NE, 22E2
Wingate, NE, 28D5
Wingfield, Mid, 16C5; 41E2
Wingham Colliery, EK, 6C2
Wingham Town, EK, 6C2
Winkhill Halt, NS, 15C4
Winnington & Anderton, CLC, 45C5
Winscombe, GW, 3B1; 8D3
Winsford, LNW, 15B2; 20D2
Winsford & Over, CLC, 15B2; 20D2 *see also* Over & Wharton
Winsford Jc, LNW, 15B2; 20D2
Winslow, LNW, 10D2
Winslow Road, Met&GCJt, 10D3
Winson Green, LNW, 13C3; 15G4 *see also* Soho
Winston, NE, 27E5
Winterbourne, GW, 8C1; 9G2
Winteringham, GC, 22E4
Wintersett Jc, GC, 42C2
Winterton & Thealby, GC, 22E4
Winton, NB, 30B1
Winton Pier, G&SW, 29D3
Winwick Jc, LNW, 20C2; 24G2; 45D3
Wirksworth, Mid, 16C5; 41E2
Wisbech, GE(WUT) & MGN, 17F3
Wisbech St Mary, MGN, 17F3
Wishaw, Cal, 30C5; 44A2
Wishford, GW, 3C5
Wistow, NE, 21D5
Witham (Essex), GE, 12F5
Witham (Som), GW, 3C3
Withcall, GN, 17A2
Withernsea, NE, 22E2
Withington (Glos), SW, 9E4
Withington (Hereford), GW, 9C1
Withington (Lancs), Mid, 20C1; 24G1; 45A3
Withnell, LU, 20A2; 24E2
Withyham, LBSC, 5D4
Withymoor Basin (Goods), GW, 13C1
Witley & Chiddingfold, GW, 5D1
Witney, GW, 10E5
Witney Jc, GW, 10E4
Wittersham Road, KES, 6E4
Witton, LNW, 13B4
Witton Gilbert, NE, 27D5
Witton-le-Wear, NE, 27D5
Wiveliscombe, GW, 8F5
Wivelsfield, LBSC, 5E3
Wivenhoe, GE, 12E4
Wixford, Mid, 9B4
Woburn Sands, LNW, 10C1
Wofferton, S&H, 9A1
Woking, LSW, 5C1
Wokingham, SEC(LSW), 4A1
Woldingham, CO, 5C3
Wolferton, GE, 17D5
Wolfhall Jc, GW/MSW, 4A5
Wolfs Castle Halt, GW, 13G1
Wolsingham, NE, 27D4
Wolvercot Platform, GW, 10E4
Wolvercote Halt, LNW, 10E4
Wolvercote Jc, GW/LNW, 10E4
Wolverhampton, GW & LNW(Mid), 15F3
Wolverton, LNW, 10C2
Wolverton Carriage Works, LNW, 10C2
Wombridge (Goods), LNW, 15E2
Wombwell, GC & Mid, 21F3/4; 42E1/2
Womersley, LY(GN), 21E4
Wooburn Green, GW, 5A1; 10F1
Wood End Platform, GW, 9A3
Wood Green (Middlesex), GN(NL), 5A3; 40A5
Wood Green (Staffs), LNW, 13A2
Wood Lane (White City), H&C, 39C4
Woodborough, GW, 3B5
Woodbridge, GE, 12D3
Woodburn, NB, 27A3
Woodburn Jc (Sheffield), GC, 41A2
Woodbury Road, LSW, 2B3
Woodchester, Mid, 9F3
Woodend, WCE, 26F3
Woodford (Essex), GE, 5A4
Woodford & Hinton (Northants), GC(SMJ), 10B4
Woodford Jc, GC/SMJ, 10B4
Woodgrange Park, LTS, 40B2
Woodhall Junc, GN, 17B2
Woodhall Spa, GN, 17B2
Woodham Ferrers, GE, 6A5; 11G5
Woodhay, GW, 4A3
Woodhead, GC, 21F2; 42F5
Woodhouse (Yorks), GC, 16A4; 21G4; 41A3; 42G2
Woodhouse Mill, Mid, 16A4; 21G4; 41A3; 42G1
Woodkirk, GN, 21E3; 42B3
Woodland, Fur, 24A4; 26G2
Woodlands Road Halt, LY, 45A2
Woodlesford, Mid(LY), 21D3; 42B2
Woodley, GC&MidJt(CLC), 21G1
Woodley Jc, NB, 44C5
Woodnesborough, EK, 6C2
Woodside (Aberdeen), GNS, 37F4
Woodside (Birkenhead), BJ, 15A1; 20C4; 24G4; 45F4
Woodside (Halebank) Goods, LNW, 15A1; 20C3; 45E4
Woodside & Burrelton, Cal, 33E5
Woodside & South Norwood, SEC, 5B3; 40G4
Woodside Jc, SEC/WSC, 40G4
Woodside Park, GN(NL), 5A3
Woodvale, CLC, 20B4; 24F4; 45F1
Woodville, Mid, 16E5
Woody Bay, LB, 7E4

Wookey, GW, 3C2; 8E2
Wool, LSW, 3F4
Woolaston, GW, 8B1; 9F1
Wooler, NE, 31E3
Woolfold, LY, 20B1; 24F1; 45B1
Woolston, LSW, 4E3
Woolwich Arsenal, SEC, 40D1
Woolwich Dockyard, SEC, 5B4; 40D2
Wooperton, NE, 31E4
Wootton, IWC, 4F3
Wootton Bassett, GW, 9G4
Wootton Broadmead Halt, LNW, 10C1; 11D1
Wootton Pillinge Halt, LNW, 10C1; 11D1
Wootton Wawen Platform, GW, 9B5
Worcester (Goods), GW & Mid, 9B3
Worcester (Pass), GW & GW&MidJt, 9B3
Worcester Park, LSW, 5B3; 39G4
Worgret Jc, LSW, 3F4
Workington, LNW, 26E3
Workington Bridge, LNW, 26E3
Workington Central, CWJ, 26E3
Worksop, GC(Mid), 16A3; 41B5
Worle, GW, 3B1; 8D3
Worle Jc, GW, 3A1; 8D3
Worle Town, WCP, 3A1; 8D3
Worleston, LNW, 15B2; 20E2
Worlington Golf Links Halt, GE, 11B5
Worlingworth, MSL, 12B3
Wormald Green, NE, 21B3
Wormit, NB, 34E4
Worplesdon, LSW, 5C1
Worsborough (Goods), GC, 42E2
Worship Street Goods, LNW, 40C4
Worsley, LNW, 45B3
Worsley Jc, LNW, 45B2
Worstead, GE, 18E2
Worth Valley Branch Jc, Mid, 21D1
Worthing, LBSC, 5F2
Worthington, Mid, 16E4
Worthy Down Platform, GW, 4C3
Wortley (Sheffield), GC, 21F3; 42F3
Wortley Jcs, GN, 21 (inset C1)
Wotton, GC & OAT, 10E3
Wrabness, GE, 12E3
Wrafton, LSW(GW), 7F3
Wragby, GN, 17A1
Wrangaton, GW, 2D5
Wrangbrook Jc, HB, 21E4
Wrawby Jc, GC, 22F3
Wraysbury, LSW, 5B1
Wrea Green, PWY, 24D4
Wreay, LNW, 26C1
Wrenbury, LNW, 15C1; 20E2
Wrenthorpe Jc, GN, 42C2
Wressle, NE, 21D5
Wretham & Hockham, GE, 12A5; 18G5
Wrexham, GW, 20E4
Wrexham (Central), GC(Cam), 20E4
Wrexham (Exchange), GC, 20E4
Wrington, GW, 3B1; 8D2
Wrotham for Borough Green, SEC, 5C5
Wroxall, IW, 4G3
Wroxham, GE, 18E2
Wryde, MGN, 17F3
Wycombe Jc, Mid/GN, 16D2
Wye, SEC, 6D3
Wye Valley Jc, GW, 8B2; 9F1
Wyke & Norwood Green, LY, 21E2; 42B4
Wyke Jc, LY, 21E2
Wyke Regis Halt, WP, 3G3
Wykeham, NE, 22A4
Wylam, NE(NB), 27B5
Wylde Green, LNW, 15F5
Wylye, GW, 3C5
Wymondham (Norfolk), GE, 18F4
Wymondham Jc, Mid, 16E2
Wynn Hall, GW, 20F4
Wynyard, NE, 28E5
Wyre Dock, LY, 24C4
Wyre Dock Jc, LY/PWY, 24C4
Wyre Forest, GW, 9A2
Wyrley & Cheslyn Hay, LNW, 15F4

Yalding, SEC, 5C5
Yarde (workmen), SR, 1A5
Yardley Wood Platform, GW, 9A5
Yarm, NE, 28F5
Yarmouth Beach (Norfolk), MGN, 18F1
Yarmouth South Town (Norfolk), GE, 18F1
Yarmouth (IoW), FYN, 4F4
Yarnton, GW, 10E4
Yarwell Jc, LNW, 11A1; 17F1
Yate, Mid, 8C1; 9G2
Yatton, GW, 3A1; 8D3
Yaxham, GE, 18E4
Yaxley & Farcet, GN, 11A2; 17G2
Yaxley Halt, GE, 12B4
Yeadon, Mid, 21D2
Yealmpton, GW, 2E5
Yeathouse, WCE, 26E3
Yeldham, CVH, 11D5
Yelvertoft & Stanford Park, LNW, 10A3
Yelverton, GW, 2D5
Yeoford Junc, LSW, 2B4
Yeovil Junc, LSW, 3E2; 8G2
Yeovil Pen Mill, GW, 3D2; 8G2
Yeovil Town, GW&LSWJt, 3D2; 8G2
Yetminster, GW, 3E2
Ynys-y-Geinon Jc, Mid/N&B, 7A4; 43F2
Ynys, LNW, 19F1
Ynysddu, LNW, 8B4; 43B3
Ynyshir, TV, 8B5; 43D3
Ynyslas, Cam, 13B5
Ynysybwl, TV, 8B5; 43C3
Yockleton, SWP, 14A1
Yoker, Cal & NB, 29C4; 44F4
York, NE(GC/GE/GN/LY/Mid) & DVL, 21C5 and inset A4
York North Jc, NE, 21A4 (inset)
York Road (London), GN, 40C5
Yorkhill, NB, 44E4
Yorton, LNW, 15E1; 20G3
Ystalyfera, Mid, 7A4; 43F1
Ystrad (Rhondda), TV, 8B5; 43D2
Ystrad Mynach, Rhy, 8B4; 43B3
Ystradgynlais, N&B(Mid), 7A4; 43E1
Ystradowen, TV, 8C5; 43D4

Zig Zag Lines Jc, Rhy(BM), 43C2